Heads Down Tails Up

First published in October 2013

Editors: Rosie Barham and Terry Doe

ISBN number: 978-0-9926062-1-3

Unit Four, Ashton Gate, Harold Hill, Romford, RM3 8UF

Designed and published by mpress (Media) LTD.

I'd like to dedicate this book to those,
sadly no longer with us,
who influenced our lives.

Acknowledgments

I'd like to thank all my friends for their practical advice and comments while in the process of writing and compiling 'Heads Down Tails Up' and especially to those who have contributed in some way to this book.

To Lee Jackson for his kind foreword.

To Rosie Barham and Terry Doe for their valued time editing and proof reading.

To everyone at Mpress and Calm Productions, Cliff and Tony Moulder for their faith and professionalism, and especially Paul Moulder for all the design and layout work.

To the guest writers and interviewees for their superb contributions, Tim Paisley, Lewis Read, Nick Helleur, Viv Shears, Barry and Ben O'Connor, Tim Childs, Angie Lawley and Chris Lowe, and Ashley Larman.

To Neil 'MAC' McRobert for all his drawings, paying homage to the style of Glynn Gommersall.

To Martin Ford, Simon Scott of VS Fisheries Ltd, and Mark Ayliffe for supplying some additional top-quality images.

To the following companies that have supplied the quality products that makes it all possible, to me and many others. In no particular order: Rod Hutchinson, Solar Tackle,

Richworth, Korda, ESP, Gardner, Delkim, Dymag, Free Spirit, Precision Angling, Diawa, Shimano, Leslies of Luton, and Tackle Box in Kent.

To my family, especially my wife, Louise, and daughter, Kirsty, who over the years have put up with me, and all the odd smells from my fishing tackle and bait-making.

To Canon for their quality cameras.

To all the carp anglers I have met and shared tea and time with.

Last, but not least, to the many memorable carp, past, present and future. Without them, where would we all be?

Foreword

Firstly, I've got to state that when Martin asked me to write the foreword to this book I felt quite honoured, because I'm sure that he has a lot of carp angling friends and acquaintances who know him a lot better than I do. I suppose, in reality, being asked to write it shows a little bit of respect, although I can assure everyone out there that the respect is mutual, because not only is he a nice bloke and a highly successful carp angler, but he has also given a lot back to the sport with his writing, a few DVD appearances, and slide shows over the years, plus a complete willingness to give up his precious time to support and help out at charity events.

You might have noticed that I purposely used the word 'angler' as opposed to 'fisherman'. Well, you see, in my opinion there is a very big difference. Basically, anyone can equip themselves with all the latest gear, and top quality baits that enable them to fish for carp, but only a fortunate few can manage to work out how to angle for them, especially on difficult waters or when the going gets tough. Undoubtedly, Martin falls into the 'angler' category, because as his past and present track record proves, he manages to work out for himself how to angle for them and then catch them with frightening regularity, including some real big ones along the way. In a roundabout way, although I'm not sure it was intentional, he also cleverly worked out how to make a living that enabled him to angle for them regularly; after all, how many bricklayers do you see working in inclement weather, compared to carp fishermen angling in it?

Then there's experience; Martin is no flash in the pan, as this and his previous book, Strictly Carp, proves. His carp angling career/obsession started way back in the late 1970s, a time when carp fishing was still very much in its infancy compared to modern times. There were no ready-made baits or rigs that I can recall, big carp waters were few and far between

or yet to be discovered, there were no 'how to do it' DVDs. In comparison to today, there was very little in the way of carp fishing literature or books; no Facebook or mobile phones … In other words, it was quite difficult. You had to make things, experiment, learn, and try to find out for yourself. It was all good though, because if you stuck at it you became skilled at catching carp in many different situations and with many different methods. There aren't many carp anglers about who adapted to it all as well as Martin Clarke.

If you were to slice carp anglers such as Martin Clarke through the middle, then you'd find 'carp angler' written all the way through, like a stick of Blackpool rock. It's in their blood, running through their veins, plus there's a deep, spiritual awareness of how to angle for the carp and put them on the bank. So, head down, feet up, and enjoy and learn from the words of wisdom that Martin and guests have to say throughout the following pages.

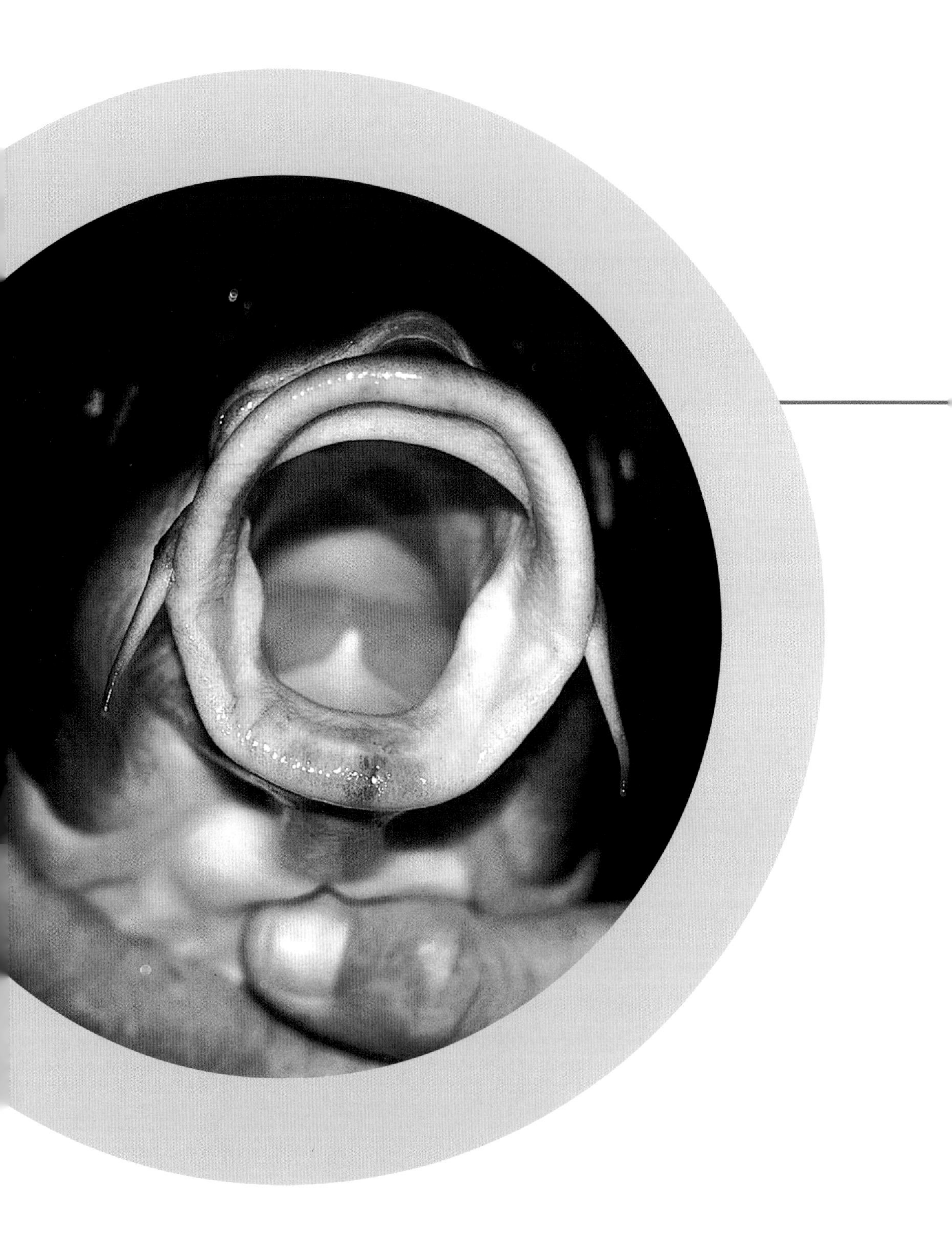

Contents

Introduction

For a number of years I've had a burning ambition to write another book about some of my carp fishing exploits, but I didn't want to write 'just another book'. It had to have the technical substance along with all the elements and features to fulfil my required objective. There are many autobiographical angling books out now, which I enjoy reading, but I wanted to write and compile one that was different and far more informative than any previous instructional books.

After a few months stewing over the format, it was plain to see that there are many ways to catch carp and sometimes it can seem easy and at other times it can be hard going. Many times we hear that effort equals reward, but there's more to carp fishing than that; there is some element of effort involved if you want to achieve your goals. Yes, we all want to admire the scenery, savour the atmosphere of the dawn breaking, the mist rising and carp rolling, but we are there for a reason and it's not camping!

We all want to get a bend in our rods and catch carp so if we can improve our awareness, gain some knowledge, and increase our chances then anything is possible. What would you rather catch next time out with your tackle, one carp or no carp, two carp or six carp? Is it possible to increase our current catch rate? I've gained more knowledge while compiling this book so I hope that within these covers you, too, will learn something from me and my friends that will benefit your fishing in some way.

There are four interviews which are topically related, and four guest chapters, one of which was also an interview. Tim Paisley's interview revolves around bait; Lewis Read was grilled on rigs, Nick Helleur's recording was on zigging and last but not least, Viv Shears' interview tells of his life and passion toward fishery management and breeding carp.

The four guest chapters begin with father and son, Barry and Ben O'Connor, who are mad-keen carp anglers who not only fish for pleasure but also have made a name for themselves in the British carp match scene, so Barry kindly wrote about some of their match fishing exploits.

Tim Childs, from the Midlands, has written a chapter and reveals some of his secret hookbaits, along with his thoughts and findings. Then there's Angie Lawley and Chris Lowe who fish many venues, both with many captures from different waters, and this was an interview on Manor Lake on the Richworth Linear fisheries complex.

The last guest chapter is from someone who I have known for a long time and have massive respect for - Ashley Larman. Drawings are from another local friend and fellow carp angler, Neil McRobert, AKA Mac, combining both our imaginations and paying homage to the style of Glynn Gomersall, who drew some excellent drawings for my first book.

I'm hoping that most will find the tactical and technical chapters helpful; the interviewees' practical advice combined with their knowledge and experiences, revealing; the guest chapters educational, thought provoking, interesting and inspiring; and my trials and tribulations, informative and enlightening.

Carp fishing is constantly evolving and there aren't any bang-up-to-date, technical carp fishing books out there right now, and certainly nothing out there like this. If you enjoy reading the book as much as I have enjoyed recapturing many of the memorable moments I've had in the last decade, then I've achieved my goal.

Chapter 1

Basic application

I would think that every generation of carp anglers develops a basic approach to their angling, and as time goes by we strive to catch carp using the baits and methods we get accustomed to and know to have produced good results, if not to ourselves, then to others. No matter who we are, we will always be interested in new rigs, baits and methods because it's in our nature to be inquisitive. Whether or not we employ this rig or that bait will be up to the individual and our results, or lack of, will come down to the decisions we make before we wet a line. Learning something from others around us should help us to catch a few more carp each year, so we're constantly learning and improving our skills along the way.

Back in the 1970s and 1980s, when I first started carp fishing, my perception of the dedicated specialists and leading carp anglers of the time was that they simply fired out as much bait as they could make, or muster, and sat there in one swim for as long as possible, with week-long sessions not uncommon. Sometimes it worked, sometimes it didn't. It seemed more like camping to someone new to the game, although in reality, long-stay angling was more prevalent at the start of each season. Opening week was almost a ritual session back in the days when there was a closed season from March 15th to June 16th.

Over the decades, the thinking carp anglers began to emerge and improvements have been made in all departments. Now, tackle, bait, rigs, tactics and a greater understanding of our quarry has inched us forward and so we reach the point where we are now, with mobile phones and Internet websites; technology which has its uses.

It was once said that 10% of those angling caught 90% of the notable captures. Whether or not this was true would be hard to prove, but there weren't so many big carp around 30 years ago. This 10% may well have been true in my early days, if not on a national level then perhaps on a few notable venues, but thanks to an age of information from magazines and now the Internet, there are undoubtedly many more capable carp anglers around, even though a few faces come and go each year. Perhaps it's not so easy to fish big carp venues while claiming benefits these days, or perhaps time means nothing when you're not on fish.

I do know, from my own experiences and that of those friends I have inside the carp media industry, that a large amount of captures throughout the UK are not publicised, so by studying the weekly angling papers, we are seeing just a small portion of what's actually getting caught each week. Twenty-pound-plus carp hardly get a mention these days, but this is a reflection of moving times because there are now so many carp venues dotted around the UK, and many of them hold big carp in numbers.

Success, for you or me, can only be measured by our results and the time we put in should have some relevance. Just like most sports or hobbies there will be those who do it occasionally, some on a regular basis and those who live and breathe their passion and who are willing to spend over half their life at the waterside. Now, we know we're not going to catch much sitting at home watching the TV, or bashing away at a keyboard. On paper, those who put in the necessary time and effort out on the banks and into their fishing should reap the rewards, and they often do well when their time is combined with some knowledge, but it's not just a case of racking up rod hours.

Over the last couple of decades, my time on the bank each year has fluctuated, just like my enthusiasm. In the year that my father passed away and my mother was diagnosed with cancer, fishing took a back seat and I only fished a couple of days and nights in the following 12 months. I didn't blank, which was nice, but I struggled to find the enthusiasm and started to struggle with depression and anxiety. It didn't stop me looking and learning, though, and time spent wandering around a few venues with my hands in my pockets wasn't a complete waste of time. Soon, I rekindled my enthusiasm to dust down the rods, get out there and start catching some reasonably large carp again.

It would be hard for me to recollect all the hours I've ever fished each year since I started carping, but I should think it would be somewhere between a minimum of 1000 hours to 2500 hours max, per calendar year. Managing to find the time is something we all have to deal with, and some weeks or months I won't fish due to work commitments, but when I do I'm fully focused and my fishing sessions can range from just a few hours with one or two rods, up to 72-hour sessions using three rods, occasionally four rods where it has been allowed.

Why mention time? Well, every one of us is different and just running through my friends and contacts in my mobile phone, some only do a handful of sessions each year while a similar amount have been clocking up 5000-plus hours. I should add here that those notching up some serious hours are full-time, professional anglers; household names in the British carp scene who live and breathe carp fishing. It doesn't take a rocket scientist to work it out. If you fish 500 hours a year and someone does 5000 hours then that's ten years' fishing compressed into one year.

The majority of my friends normally get out most weeks and fish 48-hour or 72-hour sessions, which seems to be what most of we carp anglers try to do, if not at weekends then midweek if possible, plus holiday times. Okay, there will be a few who manage to be there more often, perhaps at certain times of the year, and good luck to them. I can put myself in that boat at times, having been a self-employed bricklayer for the last 30-plus years.

Home for 48 hours, old ultra-cult, original Aqua bivvy still in use.

29lb March mirror falling for surface tactics.

Location, application, and a 34lbs 12oz mirror.

This old 30 has probably seen every rig going!

Periodically, a few anglers get labelled as 'Time Bandits', simply because of the number of nights they live under the stars. Personally, I couldn't give two hoots, so long as they look after what they catch, then everyone has a right to fish for those we all desire. I've been self-employed since I was 21 so if I don't work, I don't earn any money - no sick pay no holiday pay - but if others want to claim sick pay fraudulently from their employers, or claim other benefits and go fishing, that's their decision. The facts are there, though. We can all learn from each other, whoever we are, and how you or I apply ourselves is there to analyse.

For most, carp fishing is a pleasurable escape and for every professional carp angler there's probably a thousand for whom it's an absorbing hobby. I've seen, met, and fished alongside a lot of very capable anglers on many fisheries over the years, while at the same time seen and met a few strugglers. The old adage of there being a fine line between success and failure often rings true, but it must be said that with some it can be a big fat line. Mistakes are easily made; believe me I've made a few, though at times you're seldom aware.

On venues that receive angling pressure, application and tactics are just as important as bait and rigs. Even with a good bait or rig, we can struggle to generate action if we're not applying ourselves in a positive manner and employing effective tactics. When we're in tune with the venue and its residents, using baits, rigs and tactics which work, and getting action, it's only then we can say that we're making hay while the sun shines, and travelling in the right direction.

To reach a level of any consistency, every influencing factor will have some importance and so without some basic application skills, progress could well be a painfully slow process.

Now, some anglers who have read my articles in the past, without actually meeting me face to face, have come to the conclusion that I'm a full-time angler with a jumped up opinion of myself. Far from it; ask anyone who does actually know me! I'm not arrogant in any way - simply confident with a dash of capability - but I didn't start off like that, I made common mistakes along the way. Just like everyone else, I don't always come away with a result, but I never come home without learning something, and I'm always pleased to say that I was there come what may.

Application, for those not familiar with the term, is simply how we apply ourselves to the venues we fish, and/or the situations we're faced with. Failure to respect your quarry can hamper your fishing and that of others on some venues. Perhaps it's not so much of an issue on the more heavily-stocked venues, but it's a highly influencing factor when there are fewer carp to fish for.

If we go along with the thinking that a carp is a carp, with some a bit wiser than others, and all anglers fishing for them employing similar tactics, which we know is not the case, then what can you or I do to improve our results? Whilst I'd like to think all the answers are somewhere within this book, the truth is that our personal results depend on our application, which requires a lot of decision making while at the venue. What we do, when we do it, which rigs and baits we use, time, weather conditions, all will have their part to play and the decisions we make along the way, whether we catch or not, should help us to learn, adapt, and finally succeed.

What works well on one venue doesn't automatically work on all because this will depend on the size and stock of each one, although it does give us a good starting point. The fact that something works can give us some confidence and no doubt those of you reading this with a few years' carping under your belts will testify to that. Each venue is different, and they will fall into certain categories. Our only starting point is to make decisions on the day, based on what we see or expect to happen in the time we have at the waterside, using the baits, rigs or tactics we have some confidence in, or are willing to experiment with.

I've no doubt that we'll all have our hopes about what we expect over the next few sessions based on our ability to generate action on previous ones. If I were on an easy venue, then I would be looking for a multiple catch; on a moderate venue, perhaps a few bites, and on a hard venue I'd be happy to get one bite each session, whether it was just a day session or over three days and nights. None of us like blanking, but unfortunately, some things are out of our control, so it can take time, and/or adjustments in our approach, to build up the confidence and get the results.

We can always make excuses for blanking if we want, but how many times has it come down to poor angling on our part? Yep, been there and done that. I can hold my hand up and say that there have been times when I've fished well, and times I've fished poorly. Just how many get a prime swim in perfect conditions, though, and fail to bag up, or even blank, or worse still lose every carp they get a run from?

The carp have got to feed to survive, so it makes sense to use something they want!

Having caught so many mirrors over the years, I'm looking forward to fishing venues with a lot more commons!

Observations and instinct told me that one rod was all I needed!

We can be our own worst enemies at times and it's only once you fish moderate to hard venues, among quality anglers, that you can see all the different approaches in action. Some anglers will shine, some will suffer, but so long as we enjoy ourselves then we all end up with some memorable moments. I've had my times of despair and success and damaged a few egos, which just proves to me that we can all learn valuable information from friends and learn nothing by being anti-social or strutting round like you own the venue.

Please don't assume that carp fishing to me is a competition or it's all pounds and ounces, because if it were then I'm sure I'd not have enjoyed my journeys thus far, though I'll not deny I'd rather my next carp was over 30lbs than under 10lbs, but then who wouldn't?

The most influential factors regarding the outcome are location and/or swim choices and importantly, how, when and why we make these decisions. The last thing we want is to fish a barren zone with little chance of any action, simply because the carp are up at the other end or on the other bank. To avoid blank sessions then, choosing the right swims can only help. That sounds logical, and easy, but as we all know, we have ever-changing weather conditions and it's not always possible at busy times, or when we are new to the venue, with plenty to discover. Visual sightings and hours of observation can be crucial, and the more we look the more we learn.

My approach is based around location and observation, so if the carp are in the edge, simply fish the margins; if they're further out, then fish further out; if they're cruising around close to the surface then floater fish for them or have a go at zigging. It might take me five minutes to decide where to fish, or it might take a few hours, but visual sightings, cloudy or coloured water, bubbling, and weather conditions point me in the right direction.

This 32lb 8oz mirror came along at the expected feeding time.

33lb Oxford day-ticket chunk.

Whether we catch or not in the time we have is almost irrelevant because we're learning as we go. If we blank, session after session, then something is wrong and if we believe it isn't the swim choice, then bait or rig choices are perhaps the answer, or other factors such as fishing the wrong spots, or activities on our part were at the wrong times. When we get into the right groove, we can then understand the reasons for success and failure and then capitalise on what we learned.

Now, at the age of 52, I would like to think that I've seen most things. I accept that we're all individuals and so may make decisions differently, but it still surprises me how many anglers make up their minds about where they are going to fish before they have arrived at the venue, and don't even consider walking around it.

Another new phenomenon which makes me chuckle at times is the 'phone a friend for advice on where to cast', and that's all very well if it proves to be fruitful information, but when it doesn't then perhaps one has to accept they are one step behind! What do you do if none of your friends can help you?

Prior knowledge of the carps' movements in the 24 or 48 hours before your intended session is always useful, so if you're on the ball and have a few helpful members, or bailiffs, willing to share information, then it's better to know something rather than nothing. Of course we can make things as challenging as we want to, that decision is in our hands, but progress may be a slower process. My approach has always been that if I do the right things at the right time and place, then time will tell if I get it right or not.

The mistakes most often made can be when simply casting out, often repeatedly, at the wrong time of day. Pressured carp on venues with no close season seem to know they are being fished for, and by not being in tune with the venue we can easily get things wrong, or make mistakes. Fishing then becomes similar to tossing a coin, because every decision we make is a gamble.

How often we disturb the water in front of us depends on the action we receive, and while patience will prove valuable on the harder venues, on easier venues where there is more competition for food, simply spodding out bait draws their attention and gets our bobbins moving.

As we move through the calendar year, the carp will visit and feed in many areas of the venue and hot feeding times will change, just like the weather. When air temperatures go below 5°C in the winter months, then feeding times can be a lot shorter than normal so it becomes even more important to be in tune. The concrete proof of these feeding times will be when we start getting the runs during times of increased carp activity.

We, as anglers, have to accept that carp do not feed 24 hours a day and there will be times when it all happens at night, and times when it's only during daylight hours, just as there will be occasions when it can happen at any time, perhaps a prominent two- or three-hour window, perhaps longer or shorter depending on stock and time of year.

We have all blanked at some point, although for some it's all too frequent, and if we stick to one bait, one rig, one method, or swim, every time we fish the chosen venue we could be missing out unnecessarily. When it all clicks into place, though, and the results start, it becomes easy and our confidence is at its highest point. Then it's just down to catching those you desire before moving on to the next challenge.

Chapter 2

Carp, venues and topography

The carp

Catching a carp is one thing and not beyond anyone's capabilities, but catching larger carp with some form of consistency is something else. I would take a random guess that we're all pretty much the same and we'd rather be successful more often than not, so how is this achieved when most carp anglers these days are up to speed with the latest methods, top-quality baits and a wealth of information at their fingertips?

Luck will catch most of us a carp or two if we keep plugging away, but often the reality is, and perhaps will always be, that at any given time period only one angler and sometimes a few, will be successful while the rest are spectators, or not fishing the venue but doing something else. Yes, I've done my share of being a spectator in the past and, no doubt, I'll have some lean times in the future, but I can't escape the fact that I seem to have caught many large carp fairly consistently over the last few decades, and large to me these days means over 30lbs.

Now, I know I'm not the best carp angler in the world or even in England, but I do know that I'm capable of anything when my mind is fully focused. Generally, I don't set myself unrealistic targets other than to enjoy myself and to try to catch a few nice carp each year, and as a consequence of using years of angling knowledge, my photo album is bulging with memories. There will be target carp on my mind from time to time when I'm more focused on one particular venue, or one specific carp, and this helps with fishing more effectively. Looking back, I've probably made every mistake possible along the way, some of which I'm aware of and some perhaps were avoidable. Thankfully, I make a lot fewer mistakes now than when I first started carping.

31lb 8oz mirror, but was it luck or simply good angling?

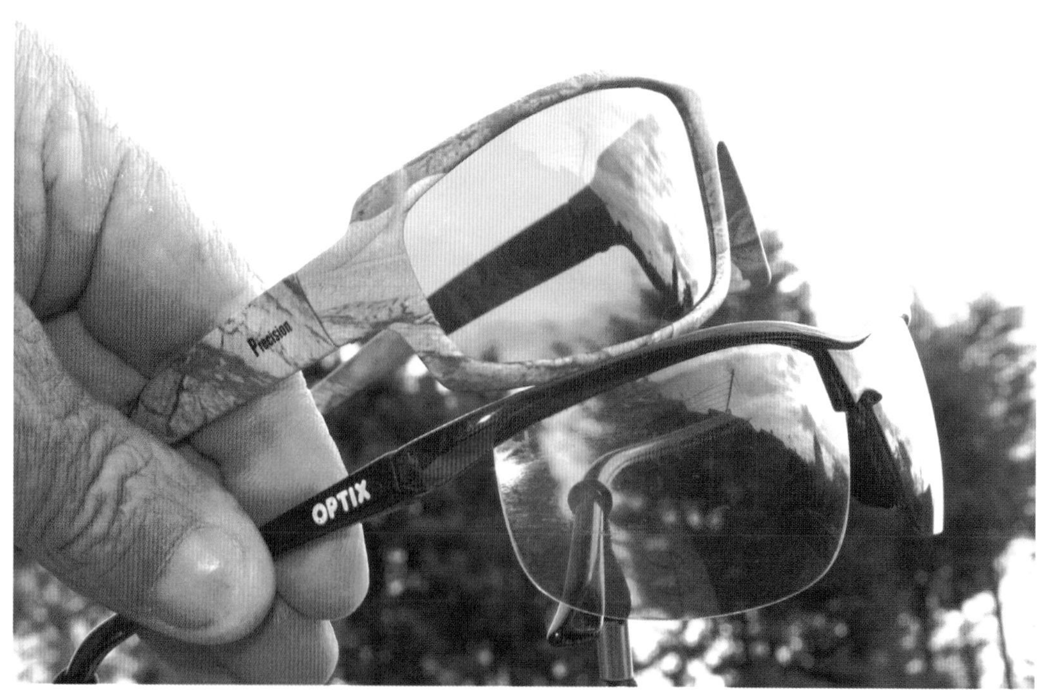

I wouldn't go fishing without polarised eyewear.

With so many factors to consider while pursuing carp, it is hard to say which is the most important factor when it comes down to fishing for them, because all will come into play each and every day of the year. Locating carp is fairly easy during the warmer months; catching them though isn't simply a case of chucking out the best bait and rig because if it were then why do most have to wait considerable lengths of time between captures? At times, when the lakes are often busy, you have to accept you're not always going to be able to fish your first choice swim, but this doesn't mean it's not impossible to come away without a result in the time you have available.

Positive thinking or a change in strategy can help but if the carp decide to shut up shop at the weekends when things are busy, then they are usually on the move most of the time and settle in areas that are either not getting any attention or being whipped to a foam. The bait buffs at this point might argue that the carp could be swimming around looking for the most appealing meal or baited spots, and it's hard to ignore this because there are plenty of observations I've witnessed happening on various venues to back up this theory.

There are a whole host of tips, tricks, and tactics that have undoubtedly helped my fishing. So, please excuse me if you think you know all there is to know, while my friends and I endeavour to pass on some wisdom throughout this book to those interested to learn, and perhaps put into practice at some point in time on their own venues.

I always seem to fish more than one venue each year, although for how long, or what times of the year is normally dependent on work and what I hope to catch in the time I have available. Looking back and having fished for carp on many fisheries in the last three decades, some for a number of years and some just a few sessions, you could say I've made a few mistakes and learned a few things along the way. Undoubtedly, I have fished a few venues where I wish I'd put in a bit more time and effort, but such is life. None of us can look into the future, or fish everywhere we'd like to. We can't turn the clock back, even though we wish we could, so it must come down to simply fishing the venues which appeal to you, regardless of how hard or easy they may be, and learn.

Like most of you reading this, my fishing really began when I passed my driving test and got myself a car. Not restricted to where my father or elder brother took me, I soon found myself fishing for carp on the local club waters. Instead of days only and the odd night I could now go anywhere, anytime for few nights. Getting married, having a mortgage and a baby girl has meant that there have been many times when I wished I was fishing, but then there's a lot more to life than fishing. Thankfully, successful carp angling is not simply a case of fishing as many days and nights as you can, clocking up hours and hours of time.

The two big misconceptions within carp fishing are that some big carp venues are so easy that all you have to do is get a ticket and they jump in your net; and the second is that cheaper club-ticket venues or day-ticket venues should be easy. Anyone can call them easy once they can back up the words with results, but are they easy for everyone? Obviously, those venues with more carp per acre of water should be an easier prospect if you are simply thinking in numbers, but catching the bigger carp will come down to either fate or good angling, or a bit of both because some residents may only visit the bank a couple of times each year. On some of the tougher venues it's not uncommon for some carp to evade capture for a few years!

The more effort we put in then the more we should expect to get out, but if one link in the chain is missing, our progress will be limited. Sure, a good bait and rig will help but we have still got to pick the right swims, and be doing the right things at the right time and place on the venue to get our bobbins moving.

For most of us, choosing which venues to fish will revolve around where we live in the UK, along with information from friends, which venues appeal to us and to some extent, what we can afford. The distance we travel can sometimes appear irrelevant, but the reality is that it will cost us more to fish further from home if we include fuel in our overall carping budget, and money doesn't grow on trees, well not in my back garden.

We can only look so far into the future and there's a limit to what we can each achieve in the time we have at our disposal, and this would be where age, energy and enthusiasm come into play. Carp Talk, carp magazines, the Internet, the friends and acquaintances we meet along the way will all give us the best sources of information of prospective big carp venues if we're looking for a change, or to keep abreast of what's out there.

Whilst some seem to do little other than slag off certain publications, or anglers who publicise a few captures, I'm the reverse. The way I see it, any information is better than none and it's only while any of us fish the venues that we really begin to build up the full picture.

There are undoubtedly a few fishery owners in England and across Europe who may not quite tell us the truth, but thankfully, these are a small minority. I mention this here because we have to accept that some carp die each year and this may include lake record fish, and some carp on the Continent get sold on each year to supplement the fishery owner's earnings. The good thing about British venues is, it's hard to keep secrets and usually you can dig up fairly reliable information with a few questions in the right ears.

Unfortunately, some carp die somewhere every year. Thankfully, it's only a small number if we take into account how many are swimming around throughout the UK. It's not nice fishing a venue and the big, old characters fade into memories, and we can only hope that new ones emerge or that a carefully considered stocking programme will bring new life, and hope of a bright future for us and the next generation of carp anglers.

Knowing what stock the venue contains will always be helpful because without this knowledge then we are simply taking a wild guess. I like to have some idea, not just how many carp and their sizes, but also the nuisance fish. It doesn't bother me whether I'm fishing for just a handful of carp or hundreds, this info will have a bearing on how I'd approach the venue, how much bait I'd expect to use each session and what the chances are of multiple catches.

Theoretically, the more carp per acre of water then the greater our chances of getting amongst them. For me, it doesn't matter how many carp I catch each year, or every time I go fishing, the most important thing is catching a few I desire at some point in the future, and enjoying myself at the waterside even though I'll be putting in some effort. If it means setting up in the swims that are producing, then so be it, but I will endeavour to pick a swim or area that I think has some potential in the time ahead, rather than the time that has passed.

Once I have some knowledge of the stock I can work on application and the potential outcome of each session. The results or lack of them will have a bearing on how I approach the venue on future sessions. Having fished venues with only 0.3 to 0.4 carp per acre and some with 80-plus carp per acre, you would be right to assume that there's a world of difference between a lightly-stocked, 50-acre venue and a heavily-stocked, 25-acre water. On some venues we would be happy just to catch one, while on another we'd be miffed if multiple runs were not forthcoming. Generating that next run, or first run, or catching that first carp from a different venue is what carp angling is all about, for each and every one of us wherever we have our rods out.

I've said it before and no doubt will again, even though I hate repeating myself; successful angling has a lot to do with the thoughts which revolve around in our heads. Decision making during the sessions and throughout the year is inevitable and thus in the passing of time our knowledge and experience grows, and our results improve. It's a process that can't be bottled and sold in a tackle shop. Those with their finger on the pulse, and catching as a consequence, are those who are usually labelled as one step ahead and not one step behind, something which some find hard to accept.

As regards big carp venues in England, then 'wow!' haven't things changed massively in the last three decades? Back when I first started fishing exclusively for carp there was a handful of venues in the UK containing carp over 40lbs, and now there are a lot more that contain carp over 50lbs, with a few that can boast lake records of over 60lbs. Now, there are many venues with more than one resident over 40lbs, and let's not forget about all those carp over 30lbs. Even 20 years ago, catching three carp over 30lbs in a season was considered a good year, and now catching that amount in one session is not uncommon.

How well do you know the stock in your venue?

Those of us who have fished for carp over a number of decades will be very aware of the larger, well-known carp that are no longer with us, and even though some of us may have buried some of these carp, it's refreshing to see certain fisheries stocking young carp from time to time, which then begs the question; when has a carp or fishery reached its full potential?

After many years of rearing and growing carp in tanks and ponds and looking into the history of certain carp and fisheries, it's become clear to me that some carp reach their peak in less than 20 years from birth, some as little as 12 years. Many others have been known to live much longer and attain their top weights with the carp over 30 years old. The odd few carp have been known to live beyond 50 years, although as far as my research goes, it has shown that most of these have not been the venue's largest residents, so one could assume that the slower growers live longer.

It was once thought that carp only grow for the first 15 to 17 years of their life, after which they decline. This may well be the case for carp of a certain heritage but certainly not all of them. I've known some to reach their peak between 12 and 25-plus years old, with some maintaining that weight for a number of years and others reaching top weight and then dying within a few years. Given the facts that some fisheries have only been stocked once, then on average, any given venue's stock will be at its peak for a decade or more. As mentioned, some will live longer, reach their peak at different times, and some venues have had more than one stocking so it may

I like scaly carp; I also like leathers.

prove useful to look into the history of fisheries where we fish for carp. It's all useful information for now and into the future.

Personally, I don't think scale readings give a clear indication of the age of a carp because the clearly-defined rings showing yearly growth have a limit. Until someone shows proof with a scale from a 30-year-old carp with 30 rings on the scale, then I'm inclined to conclude that carp scales are similar to our fingernails, in that if you lost one or pulled one off another will regrow, yet similar to trees because yearly ring marks show growth in those years. Carp scales, and other fish scales, on the other hand, differ because the outer edge of the scales perish each year once the scale has grown to the size it was always destined to be.

Having seen scales from four different, 25-year-old-plus carp under a magnifying glass, and counted the rings once dried out, not one has shown more than 16 rings. Perhaps the rings only show the growth over the last 15 or 17 years, so perhaps the number and the measurement between the rings may indicate a growth in certain years, but not show if the carp is yet to reach its peak, or one that is going backwards. I'm no biology professor, but there is some importance in actually knowing the age of the carp we are looking to catch, both in the short term and long term. I'm simply pointing out that it takes time for carp to reach their peak and if we have some idea of their ages and weights then perhaps we can see the potential of venues that have been stocked in recent years.

Knowing the depths is better than guessing.

On weedy waters, a long link on your plumbing rod will help.

Venues

Despite carp deaths and the carp that certain UK venues lose, for various reasons, there is still an abundance of venues out there to suit everyone's requirements, whether you're new to the game or a seasoned veteran.

Depending on the venues we fish, if you find yourself blanking week after week on a moderately-stocked water with little to show for the time you have put in at the end of each year, then if you want to improve your results you'd be wise to put the brakes on and have a serious rethink. It may be worth changing your bait or rig, or the way you approach each session; just a few things, or in the worst case scenario, your whole attitude to the venue and the situations you're faced with.

A little tip to start with came from a good friend of mine, 'Desperate Dan'. After each session we would analyse where we went right or wrong and learn from any mistakes, to improve our chances the next time we returned to the venue. At the time, we were fishing a few local waters and the infamous Harefield syndicate in the heart of the Colne Valley, fishing among some of the top names within the British carp scene. Of course, with a few years' experience behind us we had a reasonable starting point which at times proved valuable, and so with 100 members plus bailiffs, it would seem those carp anglers with fewer hours under their belts were usually one or two steps behind those with a bit more knowledge. Don't assume that older anglers have more knowledge, some have and some haven't, it's time spent on the venue's banks fishing and observing where knowledge is gained.

Sometimes, we can gain some knowledge about venues from friends, books, magazines or on various websites, and sometimes on our own through simple observations. Every year, crafty carpers up and down the country will be out there angling on a vast array of different venues, and while some of us may choose to settle on one water for some length of time, others will fish three, four or even more in any given year.

I'll talk more about knowledge a little further on at various points within this book, benefits and drawbacks, but for now I'd like focus on venues because before any of us even get our fishing rods out, how you or I approach any given venue will have an outcome regarding our results.

One of my favourite websites is Google Earth because we can slowly scan everywhere of interest and even find venues we never knew existed. If the images are taken on a good day, we can even see features such as bars and plateaux on venues with good water clarity, and probably of equal worth, we can even measure distances to within inches by clicking the ruler on the toolbar and with a few clicks of a mouse we have an accurate measurement. Copy the map of the venue and use this for future reference, writing down distances, depths, bottom make-up or any features you feel to be relevant.

In some parts of the UK there are not so many possible carp venues with a few miles between them, and there are parts of the country with an abundance of possibilities. Now, Luton may not be the place to live in terms of surroundings and amenities, but it's not too badly situated with many pukka fisheries within a 50-mile radius, even more if you push that radius to 100 miles. I could set my course north, east, south or west, and within 45 minutes could be fishing a venue with carp in excess of 30lbs, so even though there's nothing at the bottom of my garden, apart from one of my garden ponds, it doesn't take me long to travel to the venues I've fished in the past, although I do seem to be looking further away at present.

The vast majority of carp anglers, like me, will do their apprenticeships, excuse my terminology, on venues not too far from where they live and explore waters further away once they feel they know what they're doing. Some of us, in various towns, have a multitude of venues within 20 miles of our homes, enough to keep most of us occupied for a great number of years, so we may not feel the need to travel so far.

If I assume that the majority of you reading this have had access to the Internet for a few years now, then you have seen that there are a shed load of lakes, rivers, and canals across the UK with a lot of viable fisheries, many with restricted fishing, not forgetting those that we can't fish legally. There is free fishing out there, and there are many good, cheap club venues so please don't think you have to spend a fortune to catch big carp, because that's not quite how I see it. You can spend as much as you like on tickets, but that doesn't guarantee you are going to get your money's-worth.

Without all the facts and figures though, there is still a healthy percentage of venues that we can fish and if we dig in the right areas, opportunities and new venues will come to our attention. Every venue is different in some way although we can pigeonhole the types there are; day-ticket, angling-club controlled, syndicates with limited tickets, and those which are free or require guesting. Some will be easy, some moderate, some hard and some rock hard, all dependent on stocking density and perhaps access or restrictions.

Most of my carp fishing has been on club venues, syndicates and day-ticket waters. Virtually every year I have more venues to choose from, simply because they appealed to me and I could afford the total cost even though realistically, I knew I'd not get to fish all of them in any given year. Not a bad thing to hold on to tickets and not use them; I know plenty of other anglers who do the same; with some syndicates you have to take into account the fact that if you drop out, it might take time to rejoin. We may have to spend time on a waiting list to join some venues so, at times, we have to think ahead, unless you're happy to spend the rest of your days on the same venue.

It could be argued that there are always a few members you don't see from one year to the next on some syndicates, and that these anglers are denying others the opportunity to fish the venue. I've never seen a problem with this. I'm sure most of us don't want the venue to be rammed every time we decide to go fishing. The truth of the matter is, we are all individuals and there could be many reasons why some are seldom seen, not forgetting they probably have other waters at their disposal and simply dropping out could mean that getting back on would take a long time.

I've dropped out of some pukka venues over the last decade, or so, which I'd wished I'd spent more time on, for various reasons - in the last few years, it's because of the fickle building industry, a drop in wages and the recession. With the rising prices I simply can't afford to have more tickets and fully justify the expense. It seems everything has gone up so I have to be frugal with my carp fishing funds.

Fishing day-ticket venues on a regular basis can work out expensive and many of the top syndicates are now in excess of £500 a season, but you normally get what you pay for so perhaps it's not so bad if you're happy to stick with one venue. There are a few syndicates that I know of that are in excess of £1000 a year, and although I'd never knock them or say they are not worth it, I just can't imagine myself fishing them unless I win the Lottery. For one, my wife would probably divorce me if she found out I'd forked out £1500 to fish one lake. Over the years, I've spent thousands of pounds on tickets, but such is life, and we will all spend our money in different ways.

Realistically, we can only focus on one or two venues each year, and perhaps the only way I can justify having half a dozen tickets or venues to choose from, and sometimes more, has been a combination of thinking ahead and indecision. We can all be accused of having eyes bigger than our bellies, or having ambitions beyond our capabilities, but if any of you are like me, you like to learn a little about the venues before you go out all guns blazing, and abandon others too soon. I don't consider it crucial to learn all there is to know before you start to fish any new venue, but it certainly helps to begin the learning process by having a good look first.

Before I begin to use any valuable fishing time and bait, I will purposely have a few walks around any new venue, sometimes with a marker rod but not always, just to get a feel for the place. It doesn't really matter what time of year or the weather conditions because all I want to do is learn by observation, simply looking into the water and climbing the odd tree, if it helps. I wouldn't consider casting out with a marker rod without first walking round the lake looking and learning, and not just because I don't want to disturb the water and unknowingly spook carp.

I don't want to cast out a lead near anyone who may be fishing but not visible; if it were me tucked away and a marker float came flying into my water I'd not be best pleased. Consciously, I will be looking for fish, but primarily, looking in the marginal areas for spots which are clean, what sort of weed growth is around, and which areas look neglected.

Another reason for simply looking and learning, other than to test my location skills, is to kick-start the process of formulating a strategy in my head. By using stealth every time I approach the water's edge and not charging around like a bull in a china shop, quite often I will see a few carp. The bonus is that location is half the battle, in my eyes, and it's not very often that I fail to locate carp during the warmer months, even on rock-hard venues, but then as we all learn, seeing them is one thing; catching them can be something else.

Topography

When I do get my marker rod out to investigate the open water I will try to do this without upsetting anyone who may be fishing - common courtesy and to avoid tongues wagging. I much prefer to do any major plumbing in the winter on days, or half days, when I have no intention of actually fishing. I cast out numerous times, in different

Try and learn something from every cast.

directions in a few of the swims, checking out depths and generally getting a feel for what's out there. The beauty of doing plumbing work in the winter is that usually, many venues are deserted or just a few anglers may be fishing and the weed is less of a problem which makes learning the venue's topography easier.

After a few casts, I find areas or features which may have some potential; silty areas, gravel or hard clay, bars, plateaux, mounds, craters, weed of varying thicknesses and types, at what depths, range and direction; all little pieces of information which may prove useful. We can probably learn more about the carp and venue by fishing or taking advice from a friend with some knowledge, but if we're without any assistance or personal knowledge, we can quite easily blank on our first session, with perhaps a few more blanks for those who pay little attention to location or observation of the carp activities at that particular time of year.

On some venues, a marker rod seems a way of life and, indeed, does prove a valuable tool to many of us, but it's not a tool that has to be used on every occasion to catch carp. There must be countless times that frothing up the water has proved detrimental, not just for the angler doing it, but also for those close by if done at the wrong times of day. Sure, there will be times, and venues, where those extra few casts will not prove detrimental, such as certain weather conditions, but only experience and the rest of your session will tell you the outcome. This is where marking or measuring our lines and clipping up helps us to put our rigs on the exact spot, even in darkness.

Picture the scenario; cast out the rods to a small, clean area at 6pm, don't bother marking or measuring the lines and bait up; start catching bream as the light starts to fade, continue to catch bream into darkness then, after repeated casts, action slows down. Midnight comes around and now there are carp boshing over the spot; you wake up in the morning and the carp have disappeared, Mmm, no carp that session; why? Having been there and done it I know that guessing, and not marking my lines, has on some venues and occasions cost me carp.

Not only does this make me think of how many hours may have been wasted on my part, but also how many other anglers in the past, the present, and future have had, or will have, similar sessions. When I became aware of the need to be more accurate and the benefits which came along, I began to measure and mark my lines on all future sessions whenever casting out into open water. A simple stop knot with some 0.1mm fluoro latex pole elastic is my preferred method of marking my lines on my fishing rods and marker rod.

If you're going to fish a venue for a number of years, then drawing up a little map will come in handy as you could, if you so wish, measure distances to certain features to within inches, which will help keep unnecessary casting to a minimum and improve your chances of success on future sessions.

Whenever I'm fishing on the bottom in open water beyond the margins and using my marker rod, I always like to view my popped-up marker float from different swims. Two reasons - the first being that by viewing a float from different swims the angles of view act as a cross reference for pinpoint accuracy on subsequent sessions. The second is that when carp show themselves, when looking for a swim at the start of a session or during a session, I have some references should I decide to move swim. I used to take a notepad and note down

A digital compass will enable you to pinpoint spots and features for future reference.

markers on the far bank or horizon, but these days I use the digital compass on my iPhone, which is superb because you can never rely on there being a distinct feature in a straight line beyond the float.

The braid on my marker rod is marked every yard with a permanent felt-tip pen out to 120 yards. This means that I know exactly how far out to the float once it has been pulled back down to the lead on the bottom. I marked my braid by winding it around two bank sticks in my back garden, which were measured exactly at five yards so that when using the pen, I gathered the braid every yard and marked all the strands at the same time. Personally, I prefer to fish with my rigs just past the lead on the marker rod, because this is the ground which I have just pulled the lead over so I have some idea of the bottom make-up.

To ensure accuracy in any depth of water, I will pull the float on my marker rod down to the lead and then pay off some line so I can hold it at the angle I'll be holding my fishing rod when casting out clipped-up. Then, by marking the braid on the marker rod and clipping up before reeling in, I can measure the distance before casting the marker float back out to the spot.

There's a couple of ways of then measuring, marking, and clipping up the fishing rods. The first is to trap the lead around a bank stick or bivvy peg and then walk the line out and mark the ground, perhaps with a stone or twig, so you then have a distance between two fixed points. The second is to stick two bank sticks in the ground at either a rod length between them or five yards apart, and wrap the braid on the marker rod around until you hit the clip so you'll know the distance by counting the wraps around the bank sticks. When it comes to marking the fishing rods and clipping them up, all you have to do is either walk the rod out between the two marks, or wrap your main line carefully around the bank sticks until you reach the required distance - plus one to three feet if you then want the rig to land just past the spot where the marker float was popped up.

Once the marker float is cast back out to the clip and then popped up, I can then cast my chosen rig, out to the clip either side of the float, confident in the knowledge that the rigs are where I want them. If the feature or spot is at an angle to my casting position, then I sometimes stagger the rigs; if so, then I will mark each rod accordingly. Obviously, walking up the bank and having rigs in the water could be considered going unattended and there will be places were you haven't got a straight path behind you, such as fishing on an island, so wrapping your line between two bank sticks is the best method to use on most fisheries. I'll talk more about the benefits of accuracy in Chapter Four.

Measuring and marking main lines on our fishing rods takes out some of the guesswork and very often the benefits come from when the action is happening at night, and on subsequent sessions in familiar swims. Fishing accurately in open water where we are casting really does pay dividends, especially if you go to all the trouble of baiting up a spot/area that's not that big, as once we have generated feeding and induced a take, we can then reassuringly, recast back to the exact same spot. With some spots as small as a paving slab and some the size of a tennis court, only the individuals fishing them will know what they have in front of them. There is no set size to every spot as some get bigger and some get smaller and some never seem to change.

Quite often, clean spots or clean areas become larger once a few fish have fed there on anglers' bait, and once the area receives more bait with some frequency it can at times look like a bomb has gone off. This increase in the size of some of the spots is down to the fact that the bait introduced never all lands in the exact same spots, perhaps more so if a few anglers fish the same areas, plus the carp will distribute the bait themselves, which I'll cover in the bait chapter.

Nice, clean, stalked low-30.

Chapter 3

Under the rod tips

Margin fishing is a major part of my angling and has been for many years, and for many reasons. Firstly, it's effective! I've been praising the virtues of this style of angling for as long as I can remember and it would seem that many other anglers have also come to grips with fishing at very close quarters, not just the few of us that have written about it in various magazines in the last couple of decades, but also many carp anglers who never write about any of their angling exploits.

Carp like shallow water and on most venues the margins are the biggest feature we can use to catch our quarry. The trick is knowing how, when, and where to fish under the rod tips, relatively speaking, and more to the point, how to get the best from the margins. Sometimes, a little preparation may be needed, but not always. The main criterion is, we're thinking close range regardless of the size of the venue and stock within it.

Having fished many venues, observed other anglers, talked with hundreds of carp anglers and answered many emails, it would appear that most anglers prefer to fish further out for the majority of their fishing. They fish further out for many reasons, explained in the next chapter, but they all confess that it doesn't pay off all the time. Sadly, there are some anglers who think the only way to catch carp requires overhead casting or sending out their bait boat, simply because that's all they know. I hope that this book will prove that there's more than one way to get a bend in your rod.

Now this may sound crazy, but I know one angler who stopped fishing a venue because he believed the carp only wanted to feed in the edge. Rather than fish the margins for carp, heads down tails up, under his nose, he proceeded to fish 70 yards out and blanked. True, the carp were happy to feed in a few marginal areas, but he whinged about it and went elsewhere for a few months. Dear, oh dear; clearly he's never looked a gift horse in the mouth!

Granted, we're all different; perhaps he's the type of guy to find a £50 note in the street and hand it in to the local police station. Knowing that he's fished for carp longer than me makes me wonder just how many other opportunities have been wasted.

Not only can we catch carp while fishing the margins, but we can also learn a lot more by doing so, which can only prove useful when we do fish further out. We cannot observe carp feeding on the bottom beyond our vision, and equally important, we cannot observe the efficiency of our end tackle or hookbait presentation when fishing further out.

Because of our close proximity, we can see when we're safe to get a rig in the water, when to bait up, when to reel in or alter our presentation, when to expect action, and when the moment has passed. All this information enables us to make decisions that much easier. There are so many advantages to fishing in the edge that I find it hard to believe some anglers refuse to give the margins any consideration. If you've never caught any carp close in, then you've either not been carp fishing long, are not aware of the merits, or firmly believe that you're going to catch more by fishing further out all of the time.

Like any method, when it's done at the right times in the right swims it's hard not to catch carp. No doubt some of my writings in the past and within this book will strike a nerve and for some they may see this as arrogance, but I hope more will see things for what they are – simple, honest observations whilst out and about fishing for carp. I mention this now as some anglers may feel offended by the next statement. Some carp anglers are like sheep. I can't remember who first came out with that analogy but it's not far

If you look for margin opportunities you will find them.

Pretty margin muncher from a 35-acre gravel pit.

from the truth, not that it's a bad thing as most of us have faith in what we are using or doing most of the time, and none of us blank forever, even the sheep!

Perhaps, with all the gear and capabilities we have nowadays, we have to use it all if we want multiple catches. Well, if you think it's impossible to have multiple catches fishing the margins then, sorry, I've had plenty, and so have many other anglers. So why do I fish the margins? Apart from the fact that I can see carp within 20 yards of the bank, the two biggest reasons would be that it's extremely effective and easy. Obviously, if I feel the margins are not a worthwhile prospect, having spent some time looking while walking around the venue, then I will fish further out, but there will always be an opportunity another day, so plan ahead!

At some point, rest assured, carp will visit the margins and feed so my line of attack would be, 'think margins first then adapt to what I see or feel'. What I mean by that is, I may start a 72-hour session fishing in the margins or fishing further out, and change tactics or even move swim if, after a period of time, I felt as though I am flogging a dead horse. The end game is to catch those I desire sooner rather than later.

One of my mates, Mark Ayliffe, just the other day commented that there is an art to fishing the margins and he's right. Like all methods, it has some disadvantages but once mastered, the results will prove what can be achieved. For those yet to achieve any success from the margins, the first few steps are vital so listen to Uncle Clarkey and you'll not make unnecessary mistakes - all of which I've made in the past.

It can be very easy to ruin our chances before we've even wet a line because the carp can detect our presence as we approach the margins, and once they have rumbled all is not as safe as they'd like, we arouse their suspicions and may spook them completely from the area. They have an uncanny way of detecting vibrations transmitted through ground to water. Car doors slamming or heavy footsteps in close proximity are all detected unless they are already preoccupied, feeding. The same goes with their vision. The moment they can see us watching them they realise there's an element of danger. That said, though, we can never know how hungry they are, and it can be surprisingly easy to catch a hungry carp and vice versa, it's hard to tempt a carp which isn't hungry.

Whenever you stand close to the edge, try to blend in, ideally wearing green or khaki coloured clothing, and keep movements to an absolute minimum. If someone can detect you're smoking a fag or scratching your head from 100 yards away, then a carp can if we're less than 10 yards away and in full view. All this stealth may seem unnecessary in choppy, windy conditions but as we know, it's not always windy and any little edges we can gain over our quarry raise our chances of success.

To get the maximum benefit from the margins, I find it best to commit myself fully, by that I mean to put all my eggs in one basket and not have any visible lines going through the swim or marginal area I'm concentrating on. If I can fish another spot perhaps further out without a line interfering, then sometimes I'll do this but generally it'll be all rods in the edge, or all further out.

From simple observations, we can get away with a lot of things on venues which have poor water clarity but when the water is crystal clear, lines going over marginal areas usually have an adverse effect on margin feeding possibilities.

There is more than one way to use a bobbin.

If you pre-bait marginal spots, remember, that spot hasn't got your name on it.

As there is no casting involved other than swinging the rig into position on a tight line, the next few things can be ditched to improve our chances; anti-tangle tubing and hanging a bobbin on our line in a conventional manner. For one, anti-tangle tubing is not necessary when fishing within a couple of rod lengths, and one fewer item of tackle to arouse any suspicions can only help. Secondly, if we're fishing a semi-fixed lead under our rod tips, then there's absolutely no need to hang a bobbin on our line. We are highly unlikely to get a drop back unless they jump on to dry land, and with ultra-slack lines we increase our chances considerably by not having any visible lines going through the water, perhaps more critical when the water is crystal clear.

My preference is to use a flat, inline pear lead coupled with the right size swivel, thus making it semi-fixed, or with a smaller swivel or ring with a sliding backstop which will allow the lead to move, albeit against a rubber float stop or rubber bead, and a Korda Sinker. A 3oz lead if there are nuisance fish present, and 4oz when I only expect carp. Once the rig is swung into position I then slacken off sufficient line so that it's really slack from the rod tip, perhaps four feet of slack line when fishing shallow water, or double that when fishing deep water marginal spots. The main objective is for the carp to cruise through the swim, visit the baited spot and not detect the fact they are being fished for. Less cautious carp are more inclined to feed, believe me.

Once the rod is in position, I will bait up over the rig and then settle back well away from the edge and patiently wait for a positive situation to develop. If I feel the need to bait up super-accurately then I'll attach a small Funnelweb bag of stick mix with an old pop-up inside so that when it pops to the surface I can throw bait directly at it, ensuring that the freebies land close to the hookbait. Some swims may offer bankside cover to hide behind, enabling us to view the situation, but if there is little cover then stay away from the water's edge if possible. If and when I do decide to have a look I will approach the margins very cautiously, and at the very instant I see a carp I will freeze like a statue and only move when it's safe to do so.

The next step is not to put any bobbins on your lines, unless you're fishing close to snags. There is little point in creating any tension from rod tip to rig or having bobbins lying on the ground, because mice, rats or even hedgehogs can walk through them giving us false bleeps. I could tell you a funny story about a mate who had his new bobbins chewed to bits by rats one night, but I'll save that one for my memoirs if ever I get down to it; laugh? I nearly peed my pants! I prefer to clip my bobbins onto my line behind the buzzer, creating a tight line from buzzer to reel and thus avoiding any false bleeps even in windy conditions. True, the rig could get picked up and dumped a few feet away without a proper run, although this is rare, and the same can happen when fishing further out.

Old school camouflage; coat your lead in mud and let it dry out before swinging your rig into place.

34lb mirror from a raked marginal spot.

Pukka low-30 from the far margin of a bay.

Mid-30 and part of a mutiple margin catch.

38lbs, the biggest of three 30s on the same day.

Carp have excellent vision and if they are not heads down tails up, they will cruise around observing their surroundings and anything that moves is either danger, food or another resident of the venue: i.e. anglers, other fish or birdlife. There's probably no way of distinguishing whether we have better eyesight than carp, or vice versa, but when fishing the margins if we can see them, then they can see us. If we don't move and we're not too blatant, we can get away with watching them. Once we move, though, it's as if they have a movement detection system built into their nervous systems. As a fair amount of their natural food moves, it's little surprise that carp can detect us anglers, their only real danger - not forgetting the merciless otters.

The biggest beauty of margin fishing is that nine times out of ten you know when they're on your bait, and equally, when they are not. When fishing at range, then half the time we're guessing or hoping our assumptions are correct.

I'll hold my hands up and say that margin fishing is my preferred style of carp fishing and even though some may say it's not as productive as fishing further out, all I know is I seem to catch my fair share most years from the margins and let my results dictate how I approach certain venues and their productive marginal spots.

Sometimes a little preparation is needed to get the best results, all this depends on the individual, but don't be afraid to pre-bait or even rake a spot with a weed rake to clear weed, disrupt the spot or clear debris.

Like all methods, there's a right time and place. The art is choosing the right method, at the right time and place, in the time you have available. I do believe that on most venues in any 24-hour period there is a high probability that there will be some carp feeding somewhere in the margins. Whether or not anyone capitalises on this opportunity though, is another thing to consider.

I've spoken to many anglers over the years on the bank, and over the Internet, and it seems that there is some reluctance to fish the margins because others could capitalise on fishing the same spots when you're not there. It's true, but it's also laughable really because that's a misguided perception. This can happen at all ranges and would you not be considered selfish if you begrudge others catching from a spot or situation you had created? Simply, judging by the numbers of carp I've caught from the margins, it doesn't worry me if someone jumps in my grave. Far better to throw your remaining bait in the margins to feed fish at the end of a session than to throw it in the bushes and feed the rats!

The other major misconception within our world of carp angling is that once you've hooked, played and landed a carp caught from your margin, then it ruins any chances of further action. Granted, if fishing further out you're not playing the carp directly over your baited spot, but chances are, there will be other opportunities, always dependent on numbers of carp present, weather conditions and the situation you have created. The facts though do prove that margin fishing will produce multiple catches and that moderate-to-hard venues respond well to the strategy. I've had many occasions when I've had multiple takes within an hour, summer, winter, day and night, although, that said, I believe the capture, or loss, of certain carp can be the end of further action as the others realise they are not as safe as they thought, when one of the key characters has either bolted off or is being pulled into a waiting net.

My philosophy with margins in mind is, if I can get them feeding and catch them in the edge then I should be capable of catching them further out; they obviously like the bait and the rigs are working. As a field tester/consultant, observations and results are very useful, but as anglers we can all learn and gain confidence with our bait from observing the carp actually feeding at close quarters.

Going back in time a bit, to the days when I made and rolled boilies for myself, I would purposely visit a couple of venues which had some pukka areas to feed and observe, and to be fair, all the recipes I've ever rolled seemed fine on paper, but in reality 25% were crap, 50% okay, and 25% clearly taken with real gusto. Using the same baits again while fishing the margins showed the same results; flavour levels or base mixes were then either adjusted or ditched in favour of what worked best. It's far easier to catch carp with a bait they want than one which they avoid, ignore or pick away at.

In the summer, I have caught carp just a foot out from the bank in two feet of water, while during the winter most would come from a couple of rod lengths out in depths of usually three-feet-plus, although deeper spots between eight and 12 feet prove to be favourites of mine. On virtually every venue I've fished, carp have succumbed to margin-fishing tactics, but not all swims are the same and some produce carp consistently while some are a waste of time.

It's almost impossible to give guidance on a venue I've never clapped eyes on, as most margins have the potential naturally without any preparation. It then comes down to us anglers to introduce bait and rigs in a fishing situation to realise the potential of that spot.

The other beauty of margin fishing though, is that everything is much easier and quicker. Where it might take an hour to spod out a bucket of bait, we could put the same amount out in seconds in the margins, under the cover of darkness if necessary. We could also walk round the whole venue, sticking in a handful of bait here and there, priming spots for observation, for fishing during our time on that particular session, or for the future.

The whole process of pre-baiting is to establish your bait on productive spots, the end game being getting the results. Doing it in the margins gives you all the confidence you need wherever you find yourself fishing, and to repeat the process on other venues. Over a period of years/seasons on the same venue, a pattern will begin to emerge and there will be certain residents which we'll become very familiar with, and some not so familiar. The only conclusion I've come to is, it's either the bait used or that some only feed in specific places in certain conditions.

Given that a fair portion of my fishing in these last few years has been done at Elstow Pit 1, it's been all too often that I've had repeat captures, yet weirdly, the repeats of certain carp have happened in the same year while margin fishing. Obviously, those repeated carp liked the bait I used, and the different spots fished produced a number of repeats of some of the residents, which makes you think that a proportion of them are margin munchers.

Having used the same bait for the last few years, Richworth's XLR-8, I can easily think of half a dozen Elstow residents all over 30lbs which have visited my net three, or more, times within a six-month period. Similar has occurred elsewhere, which makes you think that certain carp are addicted to that bait; worth bearing in mind if you're after those particular carp or perhaps looking to avoid repeats.

Twin Scale, one of the larger Elstow Pit 1 residents, had never graced my net before 2010, and since switching to XLR-8 I caught her three times in three different swims, but each time while fishing the margins. I used the same slip-D rig, with double bottom baits on two occasions and pop-ups on another. The first time, I caught her at 40lbs 2oz fishing the far margin in the Reeds while using my pipe trick. Then I had her at 40lbs10oz under the rod tips in White Stick, and at 43lb fishing the Monks in the edge, and at 43lbs in November.

My only consolation was that each time I caught her she was getting bigger, not that any of us have the right to grumble when we have a repeat capture, only perhaps those chasing that particular carp. Clearly, a fair percentage of carp feel safe to feed on bait within close proximity to the edge, and all we then have to do is concentrate on presentation and have the faith to fish under the rod tips!

Chapter 4

Beyond the margins

Once we venture out into open water beyond the margins and start fishing areas or spots we may not have much knowledge of, then unless we've been out in a boat and viewed the terrain from above, we're are all technically, using calculated guesswork, our brains and imagination, to form an image of what's out there. Only by using a marker rod with braided line on the reel, so we can determine the depth and feel of the bottom make-up, can we begin to take the speculation out of our fishing.

I'll be the first to agree that we don't always need to use a marker rod to catch carp, but there will be times and places where accuracy and information makes our lives a darned sight easier, and allows us to fish more effectively; at least, that's the theory. The facts are there, though. Use a marker rod to build a picture of topography and for getting your rods out, but they should all carry a warning label, 'frothing the water to foam can be detrimental!'

On venues with little, if any, variation in depth from swim to swim, and no weed to contend with, then a marker rod is less essential, and perhaps the same could be said of the times when we're fishing single hookbaits, stringers or PVA bagging. When we decide to fish and put bait out, however, a marker rod is a handy piece of kit. At least, with the float up, we have a visible target on the surface to use as a point of reference.

On some venues, angling is often a repetitive cycle, inasmuch as most anglers will fish beyond the margins virtually all the time, and so bait is introduced at different ranges. As a consequence, with bait and rigs out there, then carp will get caught and only time will tell if your assumptions with accuracy, baiting strategy and rig choice works. Not wishing to make matters worse or complicate the issue, whether we like it or not we have to think of the whole water, because we can fish at any depth, depending on our method, rig, and the underwater topography.

Frothing the water to a foam can be detrimental.

Some carp are hard to catch, others are easy, but is it the carp or is it us that creates the problem? When everything clicks into place and the bobbins are moving, the bites start coming; get it wrong, though, and the bobbins may move but we're blanking. Blanking is part of carp fishing; we've all done it, but it is part of our learning curve and a process we all go through at some time. The trick is to learn from mistakes made and to capitalise on the knowledge.

Of course, it's easy to say this or that based on many hours pursuing carp, but some anglers stand out because they catch more carp than others, and there may be many reasons for this, accuracy being just one of them. It's probably fair to say that they know what they are doing, and confidence for them is very high most of the time. It could be their bait or rigs that are more effective; it could be location, method, knowledge or ability, or it could be all of these factors which make the difference. Once we start catching our fair share beyond the margins, though, we then understand the reasons for success and failure on that particular venue.

The more we go fishing, the more we learn, but for some it's a painful process, perhaps due to a blinkered approach or simply because there'll always be some anglers who do well, and some who will do the complete opposite. Ask any bookie and he'll tell you that for every winner there are plenty who keep trying. We're all different and we can all learn something from each other.

There are probably many reasons for us to fish beyond the margins, but once we commit ourselves to fishing further out, then distance, direction and accuracy will be the deciding factor. In an ideal world, we would turn up at the fishery and find carp showing themselves at 50 yards straight out in front of a vacant swim.

Most of us, I would hope, get some tackle in the swim and fish the area in which the carp are showing. Our only problem is that it's not always an ideal world, and we're not alone chasing our dreams on busy venues, so choosing the right swim every time will come down to many other factors. Hours of observation or fishing should tell us were to fish, or where fish feed, and hopefully we get our chances and get some action on the rods.

It's not simply a case of casting straight out a comfortable distance in every swim, expecting to get action every five minutes; if that were the case we'd all be doing it. On an easy venue with little in the way of features or no weed we can get away with a lot of things, but as easy venues are only a small percentage of those in the UK the rest require a bit more than the 'chuck it and chance it' approach.

If we look at all the water we can cast to, or even fish with the aid of a boat if allowed, then it's a lot of water. If we then think of the fish, then the greater number of residents means that more water could be productive at any point in time. Even in heavily-stocked venues, if every inch of water was productive each and every day then no one would blank, so based on the fact that there's plenty of blanking going on, what does this mean? Could it be that there are fewer productive spots than we think, poor angling, the carp have the upper hand? Or all of these reasons plus a few more like luck or fate? Looking at the facts then, it's of no great surprise that everyone doesn't get action all the time and the harder the venue, the tougher it gets.

Carp do not feed 24/7 and they have the ability to feed on the surface, on the bottom, and anywhere in between. They will swim around their residence as and when it suits them, therefore specific carp can only be in one place at one time, numbers or groups of carp may be in different parts of the venue at times, not forgetting there will be times when it seems that every carp in the lake wants to be in the same place. Not only will our own individual fishing sessions have an influence on some of the carp and their feeding patterns, but other anglers, the sun, the moon, wind, temperature and time of year could also have an effect.

With so many factors to consider while fishing for carp, we can see why low-stocked fisheries are more challenging; fewer carp equals lower chances, no carp - no chance! Even when you're in the right place at the right time, it's just as easy to get things wrong than right so if you're losing fish or not getting much action, you have to look at where you're fishing, what you're using, and when you do things like recasts or baiting up.

Having spent time on a wide variety of venues, I accept that I've learned a lot of things, but even with a good bait and rig it's not always going to go my way. I always look at my fishing objectively, try not to make the mistakes I've made in the past and accept that whenever fishing venues for the first time, I'm starting from the bottom rung of the ladder. We all have the attributes necessary to find success; add a little more fishing time and a sprinkling of good luck, and don't forget to turn your buzzers on!

It's fair to say that I've done my share of writing in various carp magazines over the years, along with many other successful anglers, and it's hard not to repeat ourselves when it comes down to writing instructional material. Carp fishing is what it is, you or I can't make out it's any more or less than that, fishing!

Whilst it might be hard for the older anglers to stomach the younger generation of writers coming through, the magazines around these days mostly cater for those with a thirst for knowledge and there's never any harm in passing on information. Most things aren't new but, slowly and surely, all the little edges and developments reveal themselves in the end and what might seem old hat to me and many friends, is a revelation to the newbies to the carp scene who join our ranks each and every year.

Now, having met so many other carp anglers, I know I'm not as competitive as some, or as exploratory with different baits, rigs and alternative methods. I'm not far behind because 90% of the time I'm there to fish and not to admire the scenery, but admit that I have wasted many hours reluctant to try different baits, rigs or methods. We all like to think we make the right decisions most of the time, but have to accept that there will be times when guesswork seems the only way. I should imagine there have been many captures each year which have come to 'chuck it and chance it' tactics, very much like the 'nothing ventured, nothing gained' scenario, but as with any method, it cannot be relied upon each and every time, when it proves to be far more productive fishing beyond the margins. Once we have gained some knowledge of the venue's stock and topography we're then one step closer.

Unlike floater fishing and, to some degree, stalking when there's less chance of the attentions of nuisance fish, by the very nature of fishing further out we could be recasting our rigs more often than we'd prefer, during daylight or in darkness. Recasting is where I, and many others, make mistakes which prove detrimental, although at times we're not aware of the facts until the end of the session or season where we can be more critical with ourselves and draw some conclusions.

33lb mirror from the back of a bar.

36-pounder from the top of a bar on a spot the size of a pool table at 78 yards.

True, we have to get a hookbait back in the water if there are many hours remaining to our session, but the very fact of recasting without some considerations can result in failure, or make the difference between a single capture and a multiple catch. Many of us make common mistakes and we should learn from these moments and move forward. So just what mistakes have I made which once corrected have had a major influence in improving my results?

I can recall many frustrating hours fishing a couple of very challenging gravel pits, many moons ago, and all sessions encountering either a problem with nuisance fish, or not, taking into account the weather conditions, the carp, or other winning methods.

One of the gravel pits of around 20 acres was used daily by water-skiers or yachts, another lake and a classic mistake! Picture the scene; at the time, only 24 mirrors from doubles up to 40lbs, and approximately 75 commons up to 20lbs, and shed loads of bream and tench. Six weeks into the season, and seven times a mirror had graced the banks. I'd been fortunate enough to have had six of those captures from the margins, including a repeat capture of the lake record carp, so I couldn't grumble. All of my captures that season up to this point had come from fishing the margins, either stalking with one rod or using two rods, which was the rod limit at the time. My confidence was sky-high, while a few members were literally pulling their hair out.

Over the next two weeks, for some reason, the carp fishing became rock hard, with just nuisance fish and the odd common gracing anyone's net, perhaps due to them waiting for the moment to spawn. The fact was that no one was having any joy.

On my next visit to the fishery, I spent hours walking around, climbing trees, looking, searching for inspiration … and the only mirrors I found during the day were in a massive weeded area that had grown up in front of one particular swim. I'm not sure how many mirrors were present, but I could count six from a few feet up a nearby tree.

The weed was so thick in the swim that it would have been impossible to land anything, so it seemed impractical even to try. They didn't appear to be feeding in the weed bed, but resting, because they hardly moved for hours and hours. I was convinced that they must be feeding at night, but where and at what time I had no idea, so I decided not to fish and stay awake all night, if need be, in an attempt to find out if and where they were feeding during the hours of darkness. A few carp showed during the daylight hours, these being small commons out in the middle of the main part of the lake.

It wasn't until just after midnight that I became aware of any sights and sounds of the possibly big, elusive mirrors and I'd found them showing about 50 yards out from the Clubhouse swim. No one was fishing the swim so I sat there for almost two hours and counted 20 carp shows, all pretty much in the same area, toward a distant street light. Convinced that I'd found the answers, I slept in the van for the rest of darkness and then set up my gear in the swim at sunrise. I should have taken a chance and cast hookbaits out, but I didn't.

In the morning, there seemed to be little point rushing to get the rods out and a bait in the water because the moment had passed, and I only had a vague idea about where to cast so I casually got everything sorted. With everything ready, I then investigated the area with a marker rod. After probably 20 casts, I eventually came to the conclusion that the spot where the carp had shown was around a clean, sandy spot in ten feet of water, surrounded by Canadian weed, which I assumed, was about three-feet thick. A few casts with a rigged-up rod, each side of the float confirmed that there was indeed a clean spot, albeit not that big. This must be it, or so I thought.

The Clubhouse must be the worst swim you'd ever likely want to fish. It's virtually a waste of time during most of the daylight hours because of its close proximity to the clubhouse and launch pad for the water activities; yachts one day, skiers the next. I'd never fished the swim before so I was going in green, my only hope being the return of the carp during darkness.

My next move seemed a good one, although a few hours later I regretted it so I'll give you all the details. At the time, we could only fish 48 hours, so pitching up for a week was out of the question, with no return for 24 hours. My float was popped-up when the ski-boat arrived and as the driver wasn't in any rush to do anything, I asked him if he'd take me out to the float so I could tip in a bucket of hemp. He agreed, and after doing a circuit of the lake in his V8-powered speedboat, he pulled alongside the float, allowing me to tip the gallon of hemp directly on top of it. The float was only roughly 50 yards out and I could have spodded bait out, but thought I could take advantage of the situation.

I didn't see any reason to cast out hookbaits or put boilies out because the mirrors were once again happy to sit among the same weedbed during the day, this being perhaps 60 to 70 yards away from the spot I'd baited. I sunk the float to the bottom, positioned my marker rod in the margins, and then all I had to do was wait for the end of the boating activities. I did try having a kip, but it was impossible.

As I sat there for most of the day, I soon began to think that I should have baited up at the end of the boating activities because the spot took a real pounding throughout the day. It was virtually beneath the path of the speedboat each time he took out a skier from the floating pontoon they used. Had the force of the currents caused by the speedboat caused the hemp to move? I had no idea. Thankfully, I'd decided to spod the boilies out when they dragged the boat up the slipway at the end of the day.

The moment had come, so I popped up the float and two pop-up rigs were cast each side of it, followed by a kilo of 14mm fishmeal boilies. As the sun went down, my confidence level rose; surely I was in with a shout? An hour or so into darkness and a few bream began to roll over the spot, and shortly after, I began getting a few bleeps, and now and then a bobbin would rise and fall. Over the next few hours I caught half a dozen big, slimy slabs and in the process lost both the markers on my main line. At the time, these were little tabs of electrical tape because I'd forgotten to replace the pole elastic used up while fishing a local venue a few weeks before.

As midnight approached the bream therapy stopped, and as I sat there staring into the darkness, a carp boshed pretty much bang on the spot. It seemed as if one would show or roll every ten or 15 minutes, and with each sign I sat there in pole position thinking it was just going to be a matter of time before one of the Delkims would light up. I managed to stay awake until 1.30am when I put my head on the pillow and went to sleep, still hearing the odd splosh as I drifted off.

I woke up at dawn and as the mist lifted I sat there drinking tea and dunking biscuits for the next few hours, hoping there was still a chance that a rod would burst into life, yet feeling that the moment had passed and wondering why no carp came my way. All the doubts started to creep in and as I slowly started packing up, I just wondered what had gone wrong when all had seemed so positive. Before I reeled the rods in, I had an inkling about what I'd done wrong because the last two casts were without any markers on my line. I had no worries with the bait and had confidence in the hookbait presentation, and if the bream fed on the spot, then the carp must have muscled in and polished off the lot.

When I reeled in, both rigs were covered in weed. Neither came back clean as they had when originally cast out each side of the marker rod. Either the carp had done me by dumping the rigs in the weed and those last few liners were in fact pick-ups, or those last two casts after the bream weren't as accurate as I'd hoped. I returned home scratching my head; I hadn't placed enough importance on accuracy and it had cost me a blank. I made a quick call into Leslies of Luton on my way home to get some pole elastic, and after a shave and shower I was already thinking of the next session.

I returned a couple of days later. As before, there were a number of mirrors visible in the big weedbed, and with no one fishing the Clubhouse swim it seemed a logical choice. This time, though, I decided to spod all the bait out and once the rods were cast, I marked both lines using pole elastic. A couple of members watched from the other side of the bay to my right, as you do, while they pondered where to fish. As darkness fell, not long after the last few yachts were winched up the slipway, the bream began to feed and roll in my baited area.

Over the next few hours, I suffered more bream therapy; I must have had ten runs and then the bream activity stopped and the carp began to make their presence known. Once again, a few carp crashed right over my baited spot and, once again, I fell asleep to the sound of carp and a couple of fierce liners, half-expecting a run at any moment.

When I woke up in the morning having had no further action on my rods, I sat there dejected, scratching my head, and after a few more hours I decided to reel my rods in. When I picked up the first rod I was a little shocked to find it stuck fast in the weed and after some severe rod bending with nothing moving, I had to resort to straight-rod tactics. Slowly, I walked back and as the line was reaching breaking point I began to gain a little. It must have taken me nearly five minutes to drag a massive clump of weed 50 yards back to the margin - it was ridiculous.

Sure enough, after peeling off the entire mountain of weed it revealed a 6lb-plus male tench with my rig firmly planted in its bottom lip. This was turning into a fun session, not! When I reeled in the other rod, the rig was tangled, hooklink wrapped around the anti-tangle tubing. Another blank, I just wasn't having any luck, but neither was anyone else so I wasn't suffering alone. Time to reflect and rack my brains as to what had or hadn't occurred, while considering the lessons learned for the future.

I came to the conclusion that the tench on the right-hand rod had probably been on all night, probably bolted straight into the weed and stayed there; sod's law. The left-hand rod which came back tangled must have happened when I cast out because I could remember hitting the clip a bit hard after a recast from the last bream. I felt a right Muppet – I'd slept all night hoping, and thinking I was going to catch a carp, when in reality I didn't stand a cat in hell's chance.

Perhaps foolishly, I told a couple of anglers of my experiences and that the carp were having it at night in front of the Clubhouse swim. I'd used up all my available time for any mid-week sessions because I was committed to building a block of flats back in Bedfordshire, so all I had to look forward to was weekends here and there.

The next time I returned to the venue, the Clubhouse swim was occupied, and unsurprisingly, it had produced a couple of big mirrors to local carp anglers. Over the next few weeks, the spot was fished by a number of anglers and produced a total of six mirrors before it faded. The spot had grown from the size of a pool table to the dimensions of a tennis court. In the same period, only one other mirror was caught from the rest of the lake.

Funnily enough, no other spot in the entire venue produced as much action from the mirror carp, and perhaps this was due to me sparking off the spot and then it getting baited fairly regularly with quality bait. I added another three mirrors to my year's tally, during December, fishing a silty area near the middle of the lake, on single hookbaits. I never did get around to fishing that spot in front of the clubhouse again.

Looking back, there were a lot of lessons to be learned from those few blank sessions; lessons which, after rectifying, helped to pave the way on other venues and in more recent fishing sessions.

Lesson one: If you expect multiple runs from any fish while fishing over bait on a small clean area, then accurate casting is a necessity. Five feet too short, or too long, or to the side, simply isn't good enough. If you're marking your lines and the cast is bang on then the next carp is going to come your way sooner rather than later, provided, of course, you're using a good bait and rig.

A 32lb 4oz mirror from a spot 22 feet deep and at 45 yards range.

A 32lb 8oz mirror from a clean spot among weed at 60 yards.

More lessons on fishing beyond the margins came from another gravel pit, with a lot fewer carp and a lot more water along with its share of nuisance fish. With only one bream, the problem was the tench, and to some degree the pike. I wasn't complaining about the lack of carp because that's what made the venue so special. It was never going to be easy, but it wasn't until after one particular session that the penny dropped and from that moment onward my fortunes changed immensely on that very difficult venue.

Being a bit of a pop-up fan I was using them on all three or four rods and although having caught two carp plus a number of tench and pike, I didn't see much of a problem. There was a problem, though. I got lucky with an early brace, with the biggest at 40lbs 2oz, and then couldn't buy a bite from any carp, except one which I lost over the next 18 months involving around a dozen 48-hour sessions. Admittedly, I gave up when the blue-green algae got really bad, because it was like fishing in pea soup and the one I lost was possibly the biggest resident, which was a bitter pill to swallow.

On my third year as a member, I started by baiting one particular spot on the far bank of a bay, which could be viewed quite nicely by climbing a nearby tree into which I'd discreetly screwed some BT steps, salvaged from some telegraph poles that happened to be lying around on another venue. This was the spot I'd lost a big'un from so I had every reason to believe it could prove productive. All I needed was the carp to venture into this corner of the venue. I had fished and viewed the spot on the last 48-hour session and had seen two of the carp feeding on the spot so not only was I keen to get back in the swim, but I was also feeling confident that I'd have another chance. I'd caught three tench so I was thinking there wasn't much wrong with my bait or rigs.

On the second day of a three-day session, a mate came over to see me and while we drank tea, one of my rods rattled off and the culprit was another tench. A carp had showed itself only half an hour before so when the buzzer went I thought my time had come.

Wisely, I thought it best not to recast the rig before checking out the spot, so while my mate stood by the rods I quickly walked round and climbed the tree to have a look. I could clearly see one carp and half a dozen tench feeding on the bottom in six feet of water. I didn't stay long and went back to my swim to tell my mate to go and have a look, as I'd done, while I put the kettle on, and to give me the thumbs-up if and when the carp was feeding. Imagine my excitement when seconds after he'd climbed into position he gave me the thumbs up. About five minutes later there were a few bleeps on the buzzer and then the spool started spinning. No sooner had I got the rod in my hands and a curve on the rod than my mate shouted out, "Tench!" – and as he walked back I reeled in yet another red-eyed demon of around 5lbs.

My mate said that as the tench bolted so did the carp, only to stop and settle within a weed bed on the other side of the bar which is so prominent in this swim. My other two rods were fishing on the bar, though some 20 yards away from the weedbed, and without this information I'd have been none the wiser. Still, all was not lost so I put fresh hookbaits back on the rigs and made ready for re-casting.

I had already placed markers in the grassy field behind my bivvy, so I walked each rod out and clipped the main line up on the spool clip, confident that at least I'd get two rigs back on the spot with minimum fuss. My mate went back round to the climbing tree to relay the situation and to give me the all-clear to cast out. I soon got the thumbs-up so I cast both rods toward a marker I'd positioned in the margins, hit the clip and dropped sweetly on the spot. When my mate returned he said the carp was still in the weedbed and there were two tench feeding on the bottom. Not a lot happened when the first rig went in, but on the second cast the carp reacted almost immediately and slowly swam off from the area, heading toward a big snag tree 100 yards or so away.

I was gutted to hear it had swum off but with time remaining, I thought my only option was to hope it returned, possibly with a few mates. For the rest of the session, no carp came my way although I did hear one crash out close by when I got up for a pee in the middle of the night. However, I did catch another tench from the far bank spot and a pike from the bar. That was the last time I used a pop-up rig on that venue.

The answer to my problem was to avoid catching any tench, and the occasional pike; I just had to find a rig and bait combination that only caught carp. I racked my brains, searching for something that would fit the bill and came up with the double-baited, bottom bait rig that I christened, 'The Eliminator', after I'd put it through some trials. I was a little unsure of its effectiveness at first, but it worked admirably and was instrumental in all my carp captures from that venue, from the first time I tried it to the last time I fished there. Not one tench or pike was caught on that rig.

Accuracy

Having done my apprenticeship on deeper venues, I had to adjust to fishing shallower water, or shallow features. As accuracy at different depths became paramount so I began to play around with a few methods, looking to learn something in the process.

I can remember having a discussion with an angler at Harefield Lake who seemed to be casting a fair way past his marker float. As I was fishing the south bank, and he was on the west bank, I was almost at a right angle to his float and when he cast out his rigs, they appeared to be at least a couple of rod lengths past it; most of the boilies he put out landed around it, with a fair few landing short.

At first, I thought he had some little strategy going. The following day when I packed up I had to walk past him and we got chatting, like you do, and when I questioned him about where his rigs landed he was adamant that they were either side of his float, which was popped-up in ten-foot of water. When I told him how far I thought they had landed past his float, he then said they may have been a rod length past but that he'd trapped the line with his finger when the lead hit the surface so the rigs had swung back in a rod length toward him, either side of his float. Anyway, we seemed to get off the topic and started talking about something else for 15 minutes before we said farewell and I carted my gear back to my van to return home.

At work the following week, I got chatting with a plumber who was also into carp fishing and told him about how I'd been getting along on Harefield, after he gave me the details on his last few sessions on a venue near Northampton. When I told him that in some swims on Harefield, if you couldn't cast 100-plus yards you'd be wasting your time, we got chatting about distances. I told him that on my last session I was fishing 75 yards out and he seemed quite surprised that I had measurement marks on the braided main line on a marker rod, which was in the back of my van. Tea breaks are never long enough, so we arranged to have another chinwag when we finished work at 4.30pm.

While everyone vacated the site we had a brew and started chatting about distances and, once again, the question of distance and accuracy came up.

"How far is that wooden post?" he said, pointing toward a few markers set out in the open field beside us soon to be built on.

"I don't know - at a guess, 50 yards. How far do you think it is?" I replied.

He guessed and estimated it at something between 60 to 65 yards away. Out came my marker rod, there was only one way to satisfy our curiosity. As it turned out it was 54 yards, perhaps mine was a lucky guess, being closer, but we were both wrong with our guesses.

As we both had the 5m tape measures, I suggested another experiment. I told him to turn his back and walk back to my van while I placed two empty Coke cans behind the post; one 12 feet, the other 24 feet. He guessed one was six feet past the post, and the other 15 feet, and found it hard to believe his estimations were so far off so he walked out to the post to have a look. My turn now, so while I walked back to the van he placed the two cans, one at five feet past the post the other at 15 feet. I guessed the closest was four feet and the other about 12 feet, so once again we were both out with our estimations. Clearly, there's a difference between reality and making assumptions, and judging the distance between objects from afar depends on an ability to gauge it by eye. Another ten minutes of chin-wagging and my belly was rumbling so we ended our chat and made our way home.

This lovely 20 liked its boilies!

A few days later and once again my mind drifted back to fishing, and accuracy. It seemed obvious that a lead would swing back in if cast out to a hit the line clipped up, and then holding the rod at an angle as the lead drops through the water on a tight line, which enables us to feel the lead touch down on the bottom. The question is how far, at a certain distance, at a certain depth?

On my next session to Harefield, conditions looked favourable to return to the same swim as the previous week, although I did get decoyed into fishing another swim for the first 24 hours as it also looked promising. When I returned to the swim on the south bank, I cast out my marker rod to land just behind the gravel bar and then pulled back gently until I felt the first few taps on the gravel. I loosened off the spool cap, paid off a little line, and held the rod at an angle of about 60 degrees before clipping the line behind the clip on the spool. I reeled the float back and cast it down to my left to land a couple of rod lengths out from the bank, then popped the float up, which just happened to be the same depth as I knew it was at the back of the bar, ten-feet deep.

I then took a rig off one of my fishing rods and set it up with another marker float. First cast to the popped-up float and I feathered it down to what looked like a rod length past it and held the rod at an angle so as to feel the lead down on a tight line. So, after popping up the second float, I went for a walk up the path to see what the actual distance was between the two floats when standing at right angles to the first float. Well, I must have got my estimations wrong, or so I thought, because the second float looked more than a rod length, perhaps a 15-foot difference.

As I walked back, I began to wonder if the lead had swung back much; it felt as if it should have done, but perhaps my eyes were deceiving me. I reeled in some line and

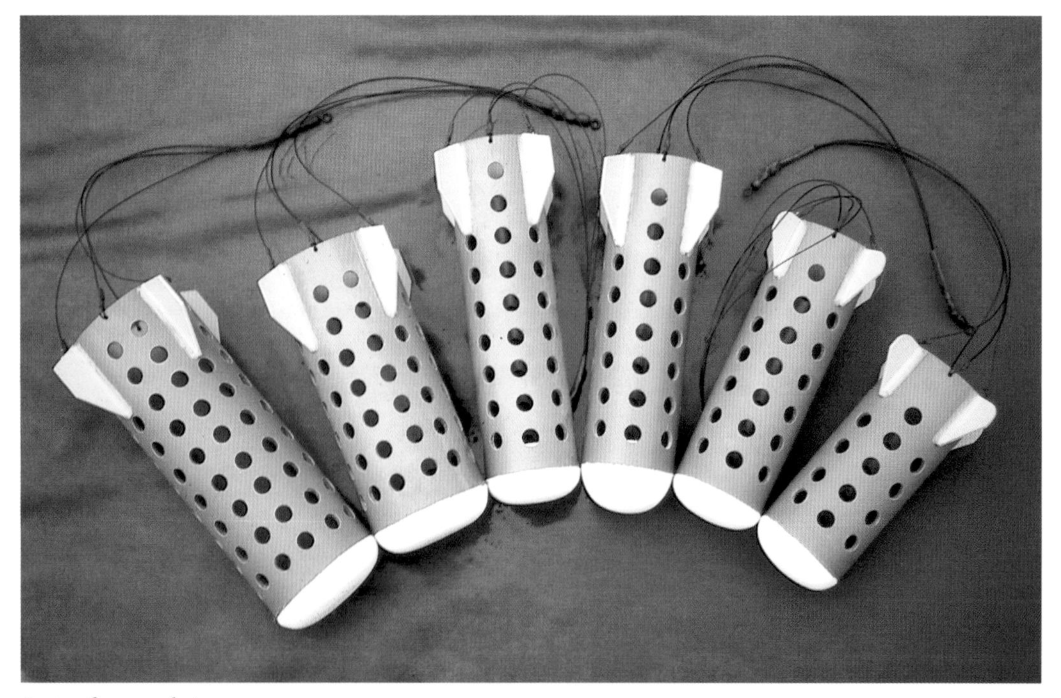

Just a few spods in my armoury.

trapped it in the clip, then reeled the float back for another cast. The next cast hit the clip nicely and looked to have landed about a rod length past the first float. I popped the float up once again and walked up the path to see if it was any closer. This time it looked to be an eight or nine feet difference.

Once again, I walked back to my swim, somewhat bemused. I unclipped the line and wound half a dozen turns of line onto the spool by hand before re-clipping the line for another cast. Next cast, and on this occasion when it hit the clip I held the rod almost vertically while the lead descended to the bottom. It looked to have landed about half a rod length behind the float. This time, however, after walking up the bank yet again, there was only about four feet difference, perhaps I should add that the distance casting was just shy of 70 yards, so back once again for another go.

I unclipped the line, pulled the float down and pulled the lead back to what I thought would be four feet, held the rod at about 60 degrees and then re-clipped the line. Next cast, and this time it looked to have landed just beyond the popped-up float on my marker rod, not by much though, so I popped the float up and went trundling off down the path for another look. This time the two floats were almost parallel with each other. Blimey! The lead hadn't swung back as much as I'd imagined; ten feet of water and less than a couple of feet. The idea that a cast lead weight swings back anything close to the depth of the water is a massive misconception.

As I walked back to my swim, I realised that I hadn't wasted my time. I'd learned something and the notion that a lead swings back feet rather than inches is more like self-deception. Perhaps it was the bloke who'd seen carp sucking up baits from six inches who came up with that idea. The consequence of this may mean that a fair few anglers are fishing a bit further out than they think when fishing beyond 50 yards, or perhaps closer in than they presumed at short distances in deep water.

Back in the swim, I reeled the rods back, re-tackled the fishing rod and then walked two rigs up the bank until one of the reels stopped spinning as the line was in a clip, lay the rigs on the ground and stuck a bivvy peg in the ground in case a re-measure was called for. After reeling these back onto the reels, I then cast the marker float back out to the base of the bar, and cast two rigs either side of the float before peppering the surface around the float with a kilo of 18mm fishmeal boilies intermittently, between attacks from the ever-hungry seagulls. Thankfully, I was rewarded with a 30lb-plus mirror shortly after losing one the next morning, so the return journey back to Luton and getting stuck in a traffic jam on the M25 seemed worth it.

When I began fishing the Linear Fisheries venues near Bedford, and a few of their venues on the Oxford complex in the mid-90s, I began to realise that accuracy didn't just mean direction and distance to within a few feet, but to within a few inches by viewing your marker float from different swims.

I suppose when we use a marker rod for baiting up and positioning rods, we each develop our own methods depending on the venues we fish and how tight or spread out we fish multiple rods. Those that use a marker rod on a regular basis seem to get better at it and as a consequence are fishing more accurately, some more than others, and their results are a possible reflection of them getting things right more than those getting it wrong.

If your swim is a bit tight for space then you can always make use of a path to measure lines.

Now, I know there may be a few reading this book who have never used markers on their main line, or used the clip on the side of the spool of their fishing reels when casting out, and may be wondering how to go about it. So for the benefit of those starting from scratch, and for those interested to hear about other anglers' methods, I will relay my guide to accuracy, which I teach the youngsters whenever fishing the charity fundraising events on the Oxford Linear complex.

Clarkey's guide to accuracy

Technically, if we cast out with the line trapped in the line clip at a certain distance, then each time we cast out it should land near enough on the same spot, providing each cast is in the same direction. If we assume the spot we're casting to is, for argument's sake, one metre in diameter, then we are all capable of recasting our rigs back to the same spot again and again, providing we maintain our style of casting and angle of rod while the lead hits the clip and descends to the bottom.

Now, we all have our own style or stance when we cast out at different ranges, but the aim of the game is consistency because we want each cast to have sufficient force for the distance required, so the lead hits the clip moments before it hits the surface. We don't really want to be casting with enough force to cast 100 yards if we're only casting 70 yards, otherwise the snatch on the rod when the lead hits the clip is fierce, and mono main lines stretch which can result in the line acting like elastic and the rig travelling backwards, which can result in tangles. Personally, I like to hit the clip between one and four metres above the water surface.

In most situations, when the lead hits the clip, I will allow the rod tip to be pulled which softens the impact of hitting the clip and slows down the impact of the lead hitting the water surface. I often allow the tip to be pulled between one and two metres and then raise the rod back to the angle it was at the moment the lead hit the clip.

Not quite ABS, but a good comparison is putting the brakes on when driving a car. Use enough brake pressure to stop safely, and without all your passengers, or fishing tackle, flying forward.

If you're happy with the spot, then the next step is to mark your line and I prefer to mark my lines six inches from my line clip, just in front of my reels. You can tie your markers anywhere. Some anglers prefer the marker near the tip ring; some halfway down the rod blank. So long as the rod is clipped up with the marker in your desired position each time you recast, it's all the same. Remember to unclip the rod if you have hookbaits on, soon after casting, otherwise you may have it pulled in!

When you get a run and land your fish, the next step is to cast the rig back to the productive spot. Now, you could cast out away from your spot a similar range until the marker comes off the spool, and then re-clip with your marker in its desired position before reeling back in, or you could peel off line by hand until your marker comes off the spool. Other alternatives would be to walk the rod and reel down the path, after fixing the end tackle so you don't drag it along the ground, until the marker comes off the spool to the required position, or wrapping the line around two fixed points, such as two bank sticks placed a few metres apart.

All fine if there's enough space to do this so what I do, and many friends, is place two bank sticks a rod length apart using the fishing rod to measure and then use these to wrap the line around. If you take a note of the exact distances for various features in various swims this will enable you to reposition a rig accurately should you lose any tackle, or re-cast to that spot at night or in the fog.

Now, to some, being analytical or using markers may seem unnecessary. In a flat-bottomed swimming pool with no weed perhaps it's not so crucial, but when fishing a fair-sized venue with more features than an egg box and/or small holes among weed, it can make all the difference. Having markers on your line doesn't guarantee action, but it does enable us either to get more action after the first run, or reposition the rods slightly further or shorter in darkness or even in foggy conditions.

Generally, I like to land my rigs just behind the lead which is on the bottom beneath the marker float, depending on how clean the spot is, but normally between one and three feet behind the lead, because this is what I've just gently dragged the lead across. So if the marker rod was cast out using a clip and measured, then the fishing rod would measure the same plus two feet, therefore two feet longer. There may be times I'll want the rigs to land the exact same distance as the lead on the marker rod, i.e. bang on top of a feature, or right on the edge of a feature, or perhaps I'm trying to squeeze two or three rigs on to a small area. There also may be times when I want to stagger the rigs, perhaps when a feature or clean area isn't parallel from the swim, i.e. the left-hand rod or right-hand rod is fished further out to compensate for the angle or shape of the feature.

Hi-viz pole elastic markers enable accurate re-casts.

Back to angling

A couple of years ago, while fishing Elstow Pit, a fellow Elstownian, Mark Ayliffe 'The Bailiff', was with me one day while I was getting my rods out and we were discussing the virtues of accuracy. I was in a swim called the White Stick and was fishing an area to the left, aiming almost at 9 o'clock, if you imagine 12 o'clock to be straight out, which enabled Mark to view my casts standing further along the bank, parallel with my popped-up marker float.

I'd told Mark I wanted my rigs to land a few feet behind the float, which was on a clean clay patch in 21 feet of water, 19 feet deep, five feet to the left of the float and 23 feet deep, five feet to the right of the float. Rather than measure the rods out accurately by walking them out in the car park behind me, I cast one rod toward the float, feathered the cast to land behind the float and held the tip high as the lead dropped to the bottom.

I'd attached a bright yellow pop-up with some PVA so we could see it pop to the surface and judge how far past the float the rig had actually landed. As it turned out, the pop-up popped to the surface about eight feet past the float, not as close as I wanted it so I unclipped the line and wound half a dozen turns of line back on to the spool and then re-clipped the line into the line clip. One turn of line on my Diawa 5000TS roughly equates to eight inches of line, three turns roughly two feet. Another PVA pop-up was attached and duly cast out to the spot while Mark stood watching further up the bank, parallel with the float. Mark reckoned the lead landed about a rod length, 10 to 12 feet past the float. It looked a bit further from my casting position, and the pop-up came up about five feet past the float. I should add that this was cast into the deeper side of the float.

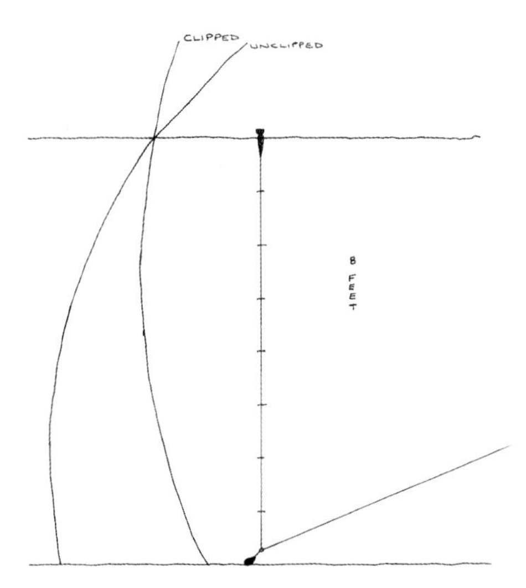

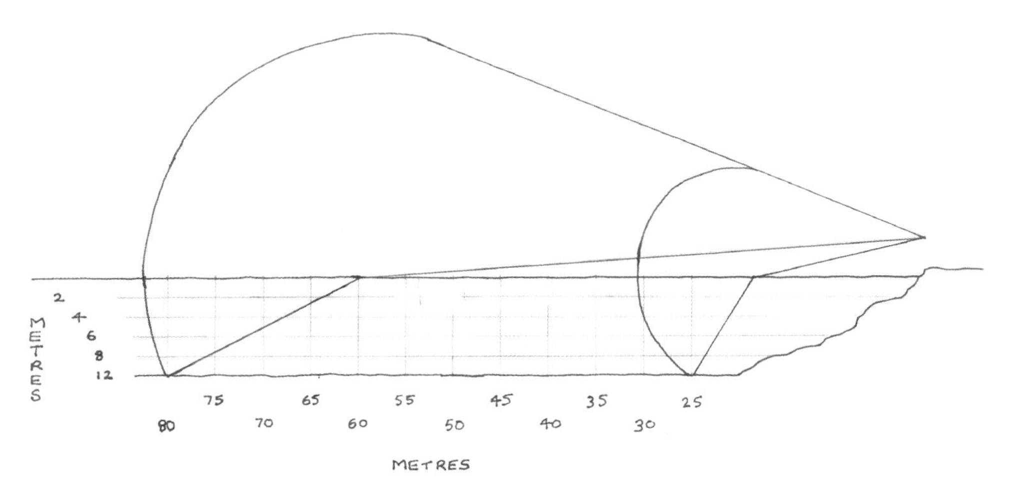

I wanted to be a little closer so I repeated the process, this time winding on another four turns of line before re-clipping. Another pop-up attached and another cast, and this time Mark reckoned the lead landed six or seven feet behind the float. While we stood there waiting for the pop-up to surface, another mate of mine, Gazza, strolled into the swim inquisitive as to what we were up to. This time the pop-up came up between two to three feet behind the float, pretty much where I wanted it, so that was my middle rod sorted; time to put the kettle on!

As the kettle was on, I measured out the rod I'd just cast out, after reeling it in, by walking the rod out behind the swim and placing a stick in the grass at the point the line hit the clip, for future reference. I then measured out my left-hand rod and right-hand rod, one two feet shorter and the other two feet longer, and marked my lines with pole elastic.

As the tea was brewing and we began chatting, as you do, our mate, Gazza, strolled into the swim and remarked that a certain angler had recently written that the lead swings in at a ratio of 1:3, one foot for every three feet in depth. Mark and I looked at each other and both said at the same time, 'What a load of bollocks'. The conversation continued while I cast my three rods out before the topic changed to the venue's residents, so I spodded out some bait just past the float, full of anticipation as to what may come my way during the predictable evening feeding spell.

Gazza went off on a walk around the lake and Mark and I chatted away for the next hour before the 1:3 ratio recommendation cropped up, and possible consequences of teaching youngsters, or the next generation, misleading information. The 1:3 ratio is flawed because it

Low-30 from range on a single hookbait.

Nice-looking 20 from a gravelly spot.

could only be this at a set distance, at a set depth, so therefore shouldn't be applied for all distances at every depth possible. The further out we fish, the less the lead swings back in; and the deeper the water and shorter range we fish, the more a lead swings. Not so much of an issue if the venue is shallow, for example three feet deep all over, because you'll never be more than a few feet out, but do it in deep water at range and you'll be fishing a couple of yards further out than you think, and at short range, possibly a couple of yards closer in than you think.

In six feet of water and casting out to the clip, if the lead hits the clip perfectly and not too aggressively, then the lead lands virtually directly beneath the splash, if the rod tip is held pointing slightly upwards, let's say roughly between 60 and 70 degrees to the surface.

In water less than five feet deep, there is every chance the lead or rig will travel slightly further than the impact point on the surface, if you allow the lead to pull the tip down. If the rod tip is not pointing upwards then there is every chance the lead will actually travel further because there is still enough forward momentum; in shallow water the lead doesn't swing back at all.

If you allow me to be even more analytical, once again it should be remembered that a short angler standing up to his knees in the water, and a tall angler standing on the ground five feet above water level, will have slightly different results because the height of the tip ring above the water surface has to be taken into account. If you do measure out your lines, remember that if your measurements were taken in windless conditions and the next time you fish that spot you have strong crosswinds, you may find you have to make allowances for the bow in your line, when casting out to a clipped-up distance, by fishing with the marker further up the rod.

I've drawn a few diagrams showing how much a lead or rig travels when casting out using a clipped-up line at various distances and depths. I hope everyone reading this finds it more useful than assuming a1:3 ratio.

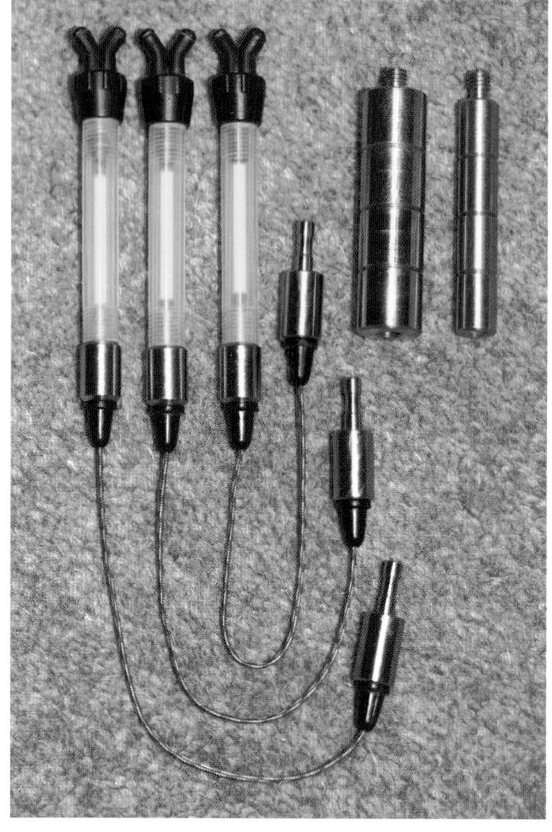

My Elstow bobbins.

Extreme range

Depending on where you fish, or where you're likely to fish in the future, there may come a time when distance becomes paramount and those extra few yards can make the difference between catching something or blanking. Now, there are a few ways of fishing at extreme range; casting out from the bank, or wading out to gain a few yards, or using a boat. I'll talk about boats in Chapter 10, so from here on I'm talking about extreme-range casting.

I've said it before in print, so just to confirm my idea of extreme range, I'm talking about casting and fishing beyond that which we can comfortably achieve with a marker rod or spod, basically fishing single hookbaits at the extremes of your ability. As we are all different, the distances we can each achieve could range from 100 yards up to 200 yards, that's with bait attached, not just a lead, and these parameters are determined by the conditions, i.e. wind speed and direction. No matter how far we can each cast, we'll all have a maximum distance and the outer limits of what we can each achieve is our extreme.

Now, in order to achieve greater casting distances, which again push our boundaries, we may have to gear ourselves up with the tools to do it safely. Failure to take into account the force which can be applied with a rod and 4oz lead will only result in frequent crack-offs, not what any of us want to be doing, especially the bloke on the opposite bank!

It should be said that location and accuracy, along with a good bait and presentation, is vital when fishing single hookbaits. Being able to cast further than everyone doesn't make you the best angler if you're launching out too far or in the wrong direction with a rig or bait that doesn't work.

For my extreme-range fishing I have 12-foot Free Spirit XSivs which feel more like 3.75lb test, about as stiff as you'd want and still remain a fishing rod. Reels, old collector's items, Diawa GS9000s loaded with either 6 or 8lb GR60 mono main line, with a Diawa 30lb tapered leader. Leads would range from 4oz to 5oz, pear and long-distance varieties from the Korda range. I've no doubt that there are some of us who can cast lighter leads a very long way but to have the lead and rig stay in position beyond 100 yards in windy conditions when our main line will be subjected to wind and undertow pressures, then heavier leads are required.

Just like most things, the more you do it the more proficient you become, and although it may seem impossible to catch carp on single baits at extreme range, if you've never done it before, believe me it's not.

I wrote an article in Carpworld back in 2007, issue 197, extolling the virtues, along with the pros and cons, of fishing at extreme range with single baits. Although I haven't done a lot of extreme-range fishing since that article, nothing has changed my opinion so let's look at my views for the benefit of those who never read the article, or those interested in another angler's views. If you want to increase the distance you can cast then it will come down to selecting the tools to achieve this, then keeping your rod rings and main line clean. Lubricants, such as Kryston Greased Lighting, will help, but then so will doing a few press-ups or going to the gym to improve your upper body strength!

Advantages

We could catch carp which we wouldn't have caught had we not gone for the long chuck, so if carp show themselves and you can reach them, you can catch them. Chances are we will not be fishing over any bait so with only hookbaits out there, all we need is a carp to pick one up and this is where enhanced hookbaits work best.

If any carp are spooking from beds of baits, if there is no bait other than a hookbait there's little reason for anything to spook. Some members of the club or syndicate could lack the confidence, tackle, or technique to fish at extreme range so perhaps only a minority of members may exploit the tactic. Areas which require extreme-range tactics are subjected to less pressure than areas which can be fished comfortably.

Disadvantages

Chances are there will be no angler's baits out there, so we cannot rely on bait to create a feeding situation. The further out we fish the further it means we have to play them back and on some waters we may encounter gravel bars, weed beds or even unseen obstacles such as snapped-off tree branches. On some venues, or spots which have a smooth bottom, the further out we fish the more we'll encounter undertow problems which will cause the rig to slide or roll. We are relying entirely on our hookbait to induce a carp to sample it and make a mistake.

Reaching greater distances can only be achieved by using thinner lines, which usually means lower breaking strains, which are more susceptible to abrasion. At times, some wind can be helpful and sometimes it can be a hindrance. Casting into a headwind will knock yards off a cast and casting with the wind coming over your shoulder will add yardage. The further out we fish the more tension we need on our bobbins to help indicate what's happening on the end of the line.

Chapter 5

Stalking

If you have never done any stalking for carp then believe me you are missing out on such an awesome way to catch them; but what is stalking, and are there any benefits?

Stalking is another key element to my fishing and forms a major part of my passion for carp angling. It's not just educational, but also extremely satisfying because it doesn't require camping behind a set of rods so is ideally suited to those of us with limited time at our disposal. There are a few ways to go about stalking in an effective manner but pure stalking is all about mobility and fishing with one rod. Any more than one rod and I would call it opportunist margin fishing.

I've no doubt a few reading this think that multiple rods raises their chances of catching carp. Perhaps for some of us, yes, but if you're blanking more often than you'd like while others are getting among them, then you'd be wise to be self-critical and ask yourself what could be the possible reasons and what other methods could be worthwhile? Perhaps you should start looking at other alternatives. That old adage of 'Catch them on your own terms' will always be true, and stalking is my forte. My reputation follows me wherever I roam.

I've caught plenty of carp while fishing with multiple rods, but in my opinion, and we're all entitled to our own opinions, one carp caught while fishing with one rod is just as satisfying as three carp using three rods. Not convinced? Then how many carp were caught last year on your venue with multiple rods, and how many with just one rod? Perhaps because it's being a little bit different from the normal approach, or perhaps it's the one hook and one chance; all I know is it can be a very quick way to catch carp and very often it'll be minutes rather than hours with a rig in the water. I take my hat off to everyone who gives it a go, at least once a year, if not once a week.

Black Spot from Twynersh at 33lbs caught three feet from the bank.

Sometimes I'll use two rods but buzzers are not mandatory.

The great beauty of stalking for those of us who fish day sessions or a few hours after work, is that we only need minimal tackle, but the best bit is that nine times out of ten you are fishing within eyeball range of the carp. In the moments before you hook a carp your adrenalin is pumping and your heart is beating a bit faster than normal, because you know you're in a good position, rather than hoping and waiting for a run. Essential kit includes a decent pair of polarised shades and a baseball cap to enhance your vision; without these it's an uphill battle.

Like a lot of things within angling, confidence has a lot to do with success and because I have got the method sussed I purposely look for these stalking opportunities. Just like floater fishing, it's not just a summer method, although it must be said, carp do frequent the margins a bit more in the warmer months. That's not to say there aren't a few spots which could be stalked even in the harshest of conditions, if there are carp in that part of the venue, although it all depends on angling pressure. The more anglers fishing that particular venue the greater the angling pressure.

Before any young pup thinks I'm not qualified to write in depth about this subject, let me just remind them that I stalked my first 20 way back in 1980, my first 40 at 44lbs 4oz in 1995, and on both occasions I fished just the one rod and never even used a buzzer. Since the publication of Strictly Carp in 2001, I've had plenty more memorable moments whilst stalking and if I manage to catch my next personal best carp using one rod I'll be over the moon and on my way to Jupiter!

Essentially, the method entails making the most from the margins and a mobile, stealthy approach so as not to let the carp know they are being fished for. From observation, you can tell if they will happily munch on your chosen bait and if they do not detect any danger, even in the most exposed swims, you're halfway to catching them. So, with this in mind, it's imperative to tiptoe at times because the merest thud on the ground close to the water's edge can be detected and put the dampers on a possible positive situation. When we get it right and have a rig in the water, the buzz while waiting for the spool on your reel to start spinning is electrifying, and the bigger the carp you're trying to catch, the bigger the buzz, well it is for me.

There are several ways that we can apply this method; during a session over a period of a few days and nights, on a day session, or short sessions of just a few hours - sometimes with some pre-baiting involved, sometimes with no pre-baiting whatsoever. To get the best out of my stalking I have to strike a happy balance of patience and impatience as mobility, time, and timing is controlled by the knowledge that I only have one rod. I'm fairly positive that on most venues there will be opportunities to stalk carp. Some will try and succeed; some will try and fail; some will be totally unaware of these moments, and some will try to ignore them as they feel they can extract more carp doing something else.

In my opinion, there are no duff swims on most British carp venues, but each swim will have its moment and it's down to the anglers either to make the moment happen or make the most of the moments you encounter. Once again, I'll run through a few scenarios so you can assess or justify the method.

Picture the scene: I pull into the car-park of the fishery, get out of the van, lock the gate and begin to walk round the venue looking for carp. Within a couple of minutes,

I find some carp feeding in the edge, clouding up the water as they sometimes do. I know the spot is clean because I can't see any weed so a standard bottom bait should suffice. Time to put the rod together and stick a bait on the chosen rig; all I've got to do now is get it in the water without spoiling the situation, which is easier said than done at times.

I creep up to the edge of the lake with my landing net, my rod and a little bucket of bait, with a handful of boilies in one of my pockets. Carefully, laying the net, bucket and rod down on the ground I then throw a few grains of hemp or pellet directly over the top of the carp, to agitate them just enough to stop feeding temporarily. I watch the carp intently as the hemp or pellet falls on and around them, a few shrugged shoulders and they lift from the bottom and swim off in a casual manner, to return a short while later.

When the carp are roughly a rod length away from the spot, within a few seconds I will swiftly but gently swing the rig into position. If I have any doubts about how clean the bottom is, then I swing the rig back to hand and if it is clean, I swing it back on the spot. If there is weed then it'll be straight on to a pop-up presentation. When there is a window of opportunity to throw some bait in I will do so and on this occasion a handful goes in, bang on the money. Within a few minutes, the carp have returned, three mirrors all over 30lbs. Now it's simply a case of sitting back from the edge and waiting for the spool to start spinning. Ten minutes later, off it goes and five minutes after that, 35lbs-plus of mean, lean, fighting machine kisses my spreader block.

It doesn't stop there; before I lift the carp out for weighing and a few snaps I throw in a couple of handfuls of bait. I've disturbed the spot so why not see if it can produce more? After the photos and safe return of the fish I look down to see just the one carp feeding. Once I've checked the rig and sharpness of the hook, I then wait for that carp to swim away from the spot. It does, so patience pays off and in a flash the rig is back in the water.

After a few minutes, the carp returns, then a minute later another carp comes along and joins in feeding. Bang, off goes the rod again, another battle commences and yours truly gets the upper hand – oops, another 30!

I've repeated this method on a number of successful day sessions, sometimes a 20 and a 30, or two 30s from the same spot, within an hour. Only when the water is really cloudy will I attempt to lower a rig among feeding fish, and I'm always reluctant to do this as half the times I've tried it I've bumped carp accidentally with the lead and ruined my chances. It makes you wonder how many times we anglers must have spooked them when casting at showing carp?

The whole process only remains positive providing you don't spook anything, and dropping a rig on a spot while carp are feeding is like walking a tightrope. If you remain still and hold the rod, your presence at the waterside may alert them or other carp which may be cruising by, and if you lay the rod down, your main line could touch a carp and cause it to bolt. True, we could free-line a rig and bait with no lead, or even use a float in some situations, but this is an ideal opportunity to use something more similar to what we'd use when fishing beyond the margins, when we can't rely on the visual information gained while stalking or fishing in the edge.

I watched this 32lb 4oz mirror pick up the hookbait ...

... followed by this familiar character at 35lbs an hour later.

Here I am passing on some tips. The following day we went stalking - happy times!

There have been times in the past when I've had carp feeding while stalking, and come away scratching my head with nothing to show for my efforts. On these occasions, I felt the rig choice was to blame and on subsequent attempts, I've made adjustments to the presentation which proved beneficial. One can only assume that if they are encountering similar rigs on a regular basis they are being sampled and ejected a lot more than we'd like to think.

I've never liked shiny lead coatings so scuff them up with some wire wool.

When you're stalking with an efficient bait and rig, it really is game-on when you have carp feeding, and a take can occur in a very short space of time, in some cases less than a minute. No two situations are ever the same though, and I've had takes almost instantly, but there have been many times when I've had to wait an hour or even longer. Observation and patience will tell you if the situation remains positive. If no takes occur within the first hour, I normally change the presentation, or perhaps move the hookbait to a more promising spot.

Five minutes in the right spot with one rod is better than three rods in the wrong spot for 24 hours. If the situation looks like the moment has gone then we can simply move on to the next promising area in which we find carp at close quarters. It may be a case of following carp around because there will be times when you can have a few spots going at the same time. It really depends on the weather, the carp and the numbers of carp within the venue, not forgetting having the freedom to roam around when there are fewer anglers fishing.

Another scenario is to stalk pre-baited spots and to do this all we have to do is walk round the venue and bait up a few marginal areas, keep checking them, and then pick our moments to fish them. If the venue is busy, there may be a few opportunities to stalk them like this but pre-baiting is best done when there are not so many anglers because it can cheese people off when they see someone baiting spots and possibly not fishing them on the day. This is not so bad if it's on the far bank, but not in the next swim!

Some of the best spots to bait can be areas where it's unlikely anyone would bivvy-up or fish comfortably, so I always look for these often overlooked areas, as well as all the other promising marginal spots in virtually every swim. After a period of a few weeks spent observing marginal areas on your chosen venue, it's very much 'the more you look, the more you learn' and it will not be uncommon to make things happen on a regular basis.

At some times of the year, and during certain weather conditions, you can predict when to fish particular spots and if you keep trickling bait in on a regular basis it can prove quite productive.

Those of us who choose to bivvy-up and sit behind multiple rods all the time can be missing out on golden opportunities simply because we are tied to the swim, and I'm not saying that any of us should leave unattended rods. Mobility and stalking gives us more freedom to take advantage of the margins, and if we accept that every place has its time, or even every method has its moment, then why not use your time as efficiently as possible and work on more than one area while you're at the venue? As you stroll around with stalking in mind, you must view every clean patch as a possible place to catch carp; it's all about being there at the right time. Some spots will be good during the day, while others can be visited during the hours of darkness.

It's very easy to walk round most venues and look at these potential productive margin areas, not see any carp feeding on them and consequently deem margin fishing a waste of time. Keep trickling in bait on some of these spots though, and it doesn't take forever to make a regularly visited feeding spot to capitalise on. They are not going to feed on a clear spot if there's no food, so it's down to us to introduce some bait to get the spot going. If there are areas with no clean spots, or times when you feel they are being cautious of feeding on a clear spot, then a pop-up rig in or on the weed is my preference.

It's possible to keep carp interested in some spots for months, although this may come down to which carp get caught, and how many have been hooked and captured from the spot. Not many spots will last all year, although they can produce carp captures year after year, and that's why the method behind the madness is to develop other spots on the venue if possible. As some of the best stalking spots are tight swims, or simply a gap in the bankside vegetation where most wouldn't bother fishing, or areas which can't be cast to from nearby swims, it will be in your interest not to open up or prune the vegetation too much because this could be detrimental to the spot. If there is weed on the bottom, then we can always rake a small spot before dropping in a few handfuls of hemp and pellet, preferably prior to you actually fishing it. You could be surprised at how quickly and how often carp respond to a freshly-raked spot, especially if it really clouds up the water.

Just the very nature of angling produces good stalking spots and moments, because a fair proportion of anglers chuck their remaining bait in the edge at the end of a session - if not boilies, then certainly particles. We've all done it, no harm in that. Some of it will be eaten by the carp or other species present, some by the birdlife; molluscs and crustaceans will join in, and some, if not eaten, will rot away, just as our bait is when catapulted or spodded out beyond the margins.

Okay, it's all very nice to develop your own spots, but if you turn up, walk round, and find carp heads down tails up, in any swim, what are we to do? Well, if you want to put your bivvy up, smash a few pegs in, get the kettle on ... then feel free, but the clever angler will try to winkle one out.

Knowing what I know and having learned from the many close encounters I've had over the years, and taking into account the successes and failures along the way, I'm absolutely convinced that wearing polarised shades has helped me immensely while stalking, so I wear them all the time, so much that I wouldn't go fishing without them.

Hemp is ideal for priming stalking spots.

A low-30 caught on a four-hour session.

A cracking double, and a good start to a day spent stalking.

Apprenticeship served on Bedfordshire clay pits.

From observations and simple tests, I have an understanding of what we can and can't get away with, and if we approach every swim with little regard for what we may stumble on, then we stand the risk of turning a positive situation into a negative one. In an ideal scenario, we want to spot them before they see us and any movements should be kept to the minimum. Failing to get over that first hurdle of not betraying our presence and then getting them to feed, usually results in failure, or at best a long wait.

Generally, it's a little bit harder to stalk carp when the water is gin clear, though not impossible, and normally easier when there is some colour in the water even though we may not be able to see the bottom in the margins. On any given day of the year, there must be thousands of us catching carp, fishing multiple rods in a more conventional style of angling and probably just as many twiddling their thumbs. I just wonder how many could say at the end of the day that they'd stalked a 30 or 40!

There is a lot to be learned from stalking, not just about baits and rigs, but the icing on the cake is the initial belting run. There will be times when it all seems so easy, and there'll be times of frustration, but once you've mastered the art of stalking you can employ similar tactics wherever you roam, until you're old and grey and your teeth start falling out. Not so sure it's good for your heart, but while mine's still beating, I'll be doing my bit somewhere.

Chapter 6
2mL
1mL

Off the top

One thing that does strike me as strange, given all the material that's ever been written about carp fishing, is that very little by comparison has been written about surface fishing in all the decades I've fished exclusively for carp, and yet it is an extremely productive method once mastered.

Perhaps the reason for the lack of written material is that only a small minority of anglers actually give it a fair go, while everyone else perhaps think their chances of catching carp are increased by simply fishing two or more rods in a more conventional manner on the bottom. Granted, it's often more relaxing fishing in a more conventional way, whereas with floater fishing, sometimes you have to work like a dog. It's all a question of making the most of the golden opportunities when the fish are visible on, or near, the surface. Whenever I hear the comment, 'Carp off the top don't count', it really does make me laugh. I think surface fishing is simply a method some of us learn, some refuse to try - oblivious to what's swimming around in front of them close to the surface – and some try but fail due to lack of experience, persistence and the healthy balance of patience and impatience that's often required.

I've caught enough carp off the top, and seen others catch off the top, to realise just how effective it can be when the angler has come to terms with the method. It sometimes makes me wonder if floater fishing is a Bedfordshire trait because there are, some very capable surface anglers from my neck of the woods and I should count myself among the bunch given what I've caught off the top from the variety of venues I've fished over the years.

It could be argued that we all find a productive method or style of fishing and stick to it through thick and thin, knowing that it's only a matter of time before an alarm heralds another run. On some venues there's an awful amount of rod hours spent fishing on the bottom simply wasted because the carp are spending most of the time in the upper layers, more than they do near the bottom, and not just in the warmer months.

Like all methods, we may start off green and make a few mistakes along the way but once we've had a few results, our confidence level rises and then we've added another method to our arsenal, which can be capitalised on at any venue when the situation arises. No doubt, some noses may be put out of joint here, but hey ho, the test of our angling ability will be to catch carp using only one rod! Easy enough for many, but especially those anglers proficient with surface fishing or stalking.

If we're all capable of catching carp on the bottom, then we're all capable of catching carp off the top. All it takes is some experience and the right mindset, because theoretically, we're not fishing blind unless we're fishing for them on the top during darkness. I'm not alone in being adept at surface fishing, and for those just starting out carp fishing and yet to catch a carp off the surface, all I can say is, once you've learned how to do it effectively and get some results under your belt, it will prove a valued tactic to use wherever you roam when the moment is right for it. It can be hard work at times and a few failures could discourage further attempts. It's only easy once you've discovered the right tactic on the day, and if you're starting at the foot of the ladder then, trust me, the best is yet to come.

Am I an authority on surface fishing for carp? I would say, no, because I don't do it all the time, but I'll leave it up to you to decide how far up the ladder I may be once

A scaly Two-tone at 40lbs 2oz, off the top during an afternoon floater session.

you've read this chapter. All I know is, just like other floater anglers, I love the method, not just for the buzz, but also the results. Now I don't really wish to bash out numbers and weights because I try not to count, and I don't believe it makes good reading. but to justify my methods I should state that I've caught over thirty, 30lb-plus carp, including a couple of 40s, while fishing on the surface with just one rod in the last decade, not forgetting all those between 20lbs and 30lbs that have graced my net.

My closest mates know me well enough to know that I could drop my pen now, while writing this chapter, and within a few hours could go floater fishing and be in with a realistic shout of banking a carp off the top. Not one would bet against me, unless it was perhaps blowing a 40mph, westerly gale with rain lashing down and everything was feeding on the bottom.

As a sponsored angler, I do like to use the baits I'm supplied with and have great faith in using boilies fished on the bottom, so often I will experiment with flavours or stimulants whilst floater fishing because with limited time and budget I will fish what methods I know will work in the time I have to play with. I know how frustrating floater fishing can be at times, but I'm fully aware just how effective the method can be so continue to catch carp off the top until I throw the towel in.

Just like fishing on the bottom with boilies or particles, once we have carp interested and feeding on the surface it can be easy. It can also be slow-going at times, and it will be up to the individual to make any decisions based on what's happening in front of them, and adjust accordingly. The question we must ask ourselves at times is, will sitting behind three rods catch us a carp today? While twiddling our thumbs and watching the bobbins, time just ticks away and it can be all too easy to sit back, relax, and play the waiting game, so time will tell if we blank or catch on the bottom. Facts are facts and carp are very susceptible to feeding on or near the surface for as much time during a 24-hour period as they are on the bottom during the summer months, and sometimes during the winter. The very fact that we can observe the situation, be it positive or negative, is always helpful.

There are various floating baits we can use to entice the carp to feed on the surface and when sourced in bulk they are relatively cheap. Cat biscuits like Go-Cat or dog biscuits such as Pedigree Chum Mixers will catch carp, but the best mixers that I've used and have great faith in are made by Skretting, one of the biggest manufacturers of trout and salmon feeds in the UK. I use their 11mm standard floaters, to be precise, and they're used primarily as a salmon feed in the salmon farming industry. They are just under £20 for a 15kg sack from wholesalers, obviously a bit dearer if bought from a fishing tackle shop due to mark-up margins and smaller quantity bags, although some shops may supply large sacks or do you a deal on bulk purchases.

Richworth, have sold them for a number of years now in handy 1kg bags, calling them 'floating trout pellets', and I think Dynamite baits also sell them so they are available to all. No secret baits required, plus they absorb colours and flavours should we wish to experiment. Having read the manufacturer's ingredients label they have everything we need for an effective floating bait; 31% protein, 8% oil and just as important, a good source of vitamins, minerals and Astaxanthin.

Big bag, little bag - don't leave home without some!

Years ago, when Pedigree Chum mixers first hit the shelves of the supermarkets, they were brilliant, but these days they don't appear as oily or as effective straight from the bag. To a carp, unflavoured they must taste like a bland Rich Tea biscuit. The 11mm standard floaters are not only slightly bigger than Chummies, but they also have more attractive ingredients to our carp, including fishmeals, and as you would expect, a food source manufactured for salmon should be better than a supplementary dog food. Granted, both food industries spend a lot of money on research and nutrition, and thankfully, we carp anglers can benefit from these products and use our own experiences to evaluate which is the best. I've included some successful flavour/attractants and dye combos in the bait chapter should you wish to try something different other than mixers straight out of the bag.

I have looked into koi pellets and while some seem okay, the better ones are normally expensive and too small for practical use in my book, though this may be because I want to use a hookbait suitable for the hook size I prefer, so I want the freebies also of a similar size. Koi pellets are fine for pond enthusiasts but not we carp anglers with deep pockets.

There are a number of ways to fish on the surface for carp and I'll now run through them outlining some of the pros and cons.

Hookbait choices

When it comes down to what we use on the hook, the choices are almost endless because the only criterion is that it floats. Bread crust will work because carp love bread, so will most mixers, and no doubt pop-up boilies, either round or shaved down to a barrel or cube shape, will work as a hookbait. Now, I've done plenty of floater fishing in my time and tried most things, but I cannot escape the fact that my cork hookbaits have accounted for a great many of my captures.

I've tried gluing mixers to the hook, and hair rigging mixers, but have found this frustrating when floater fishing for any length of time. Granted, a mixer hookbait is identical to what we're feeding them, but they have their disadvantages and limitations. This is where cork hookbaits have major advantages because there is no time wasted fiddling around with hookbaits when we've got carp avidly feeding on the surface, and more importantly, we can easily focus on our cork bait as it will sit slightly higher above the surface on the water than our freebies so will not be as noticeable to the carp and not indistinguishable to us among our free offerings.

I've tried bits of foam and standard, round cork balls but my favourite, and most productive surface hookbaits, are cork cubes, followed by cork barrels. The reason they are better is that with a side-hooked cube or barrel shape there is less material on the inside edge, which aids hooking potential, compared to round balls.

I make my cork cubes by starting off with a 16mm cork ball.

To make my cork cubes, I start off with a bag of 16mm cork balls and using a sheet of sandpaper on a flat surface I will rub them lightly across the sandpaper to flatten off either four or six sides. A 16mm cork ball is too big as a hookbait, in my opinion, and a 14mm cork ball is not as effective as a 16mm cork ball rubbed down to a cube. The only other options worthy of trying are cork barrels which can be obtained from a few sources if you're prepared to search for them, or make them yourself.

To make flip-over cork baits, which enables us to have the hook in the air as opposed to hanging underneath, then drill a little hole with the tip of a 4mm drill bit, in the opposite side to that which will have a slit in, and Superglue a no.1 or BB shot into the hole. The result when placed into water, is that the shot acts like ballast and flips the bait over. These are superb for times when carp are super-cautious, or if we're more reliant on self-hooking in choppy water, during darkness or when using multiple rods.

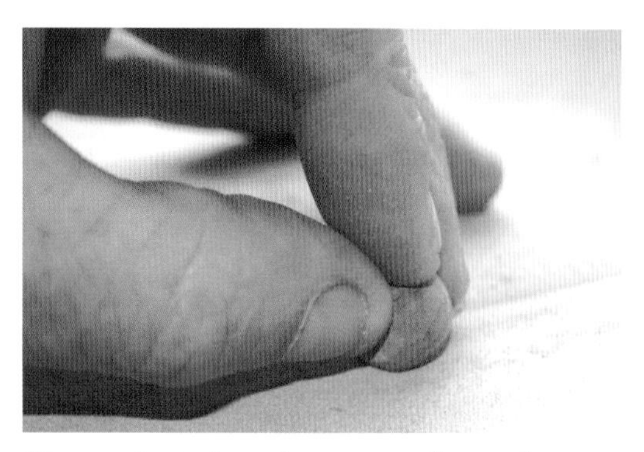

Place a sheet of sandpaper on a flat surface, then sand the six sides so it resembles a dice.

Simply push the hook shank into the cut side and butt the eye of the hook tight to the cube as shown.

Select the best-looking side and then with a sharp blade cut into the cube about 4mm.

This is what the cork cube looks like in the water.

If you find the fish are really finicky, then try a flip-over hookbait.

This is how a flip-over presents the hook.

Once I have a pot of prepared cork baits, I will then put a slit in them, using a sharp Stanley blade, about a third of the way through to mount my hooks and then add a glug of attractant or fish oil. I keep them in a pop-up tub, perhaps more for my confidence than the carp, because they never get to eat them or get much of a chance to taste them, even though a tiny amount of attractant or oil may leak on the first few casts. We can dye them quite easily, either with powdered dye and some warm water, or by adding an amino-based glug which normally darkens them slightly, matching the colour of our 11mm freebies.

When carp have been caned on normal coloured mixers, or show little interest in clean, untreated or washed-out cork hookbaits, then it's time to consider the options, colour and flavour. Solar Tackle's Salmon Trio and Squid and Octopus Pot Shots are superb attractants to use as a glug, and so are a variety of Richworth dips I've used in recent years, especially their Salmon, Ultraplex and more recent XLR-8 boilie dips, along with some Aquastim or Minamino.

Other than using those hookbaits mentioned above, we could also use other types of wood, such as balsa, or even plastic or foam imitation baits; so long as it floats there's always a chance. Personally, if I don't use cork then I will use either a shaved pop-up or Kryston's Doppelganger as a hookbait which is like a floating paste that hardens up once it has been dunked into water to cool it down. It's a very handy back-up because it can also be used for other applications such as short zigs or, with a little adjustment, a slow-sinking paste bottom bait.

Just a few liquids that carp find stimulating.

Cork hookbaits are in my floater bag at all times.

These hand-made hookbaits come in handy for when visibility becomes a problem, due to distance, wind-chop, or reflected light.

Cork barrels also work a treat.

Single rod and float

The biggest beauty of fishing a single rod and controller float is that for every capture you have full control, and virtually every capture seems to hold a higher satisfaction rating than those when using multiple rods fishing on the bottom. I'm not trying to belittle any captures, it's just that with multiple rods, theoretically we have multiple chances and more opportunities to use different rigs or baits at the same time. With one rod we only have one choice of presentation, though we can change relatively quickly and alter our presentation should we deem it necessary.

I own two rods which I use for floater fishing; both are 12 foot with one at 2.5lb tc, and the other at 2.75lb tc. Both are ideal because they can handle big carp yet are soft enough to cast a float a reasonable distance. Main line on my reel is 10lb GR60, and spare spool is 8lb GR60, both of which float for a few minutes before they slowly sink if left untreated, with the lighter line slightly less detectable and only used when I feel they're showing signs of caution, and providing there is no weed or snags to contend with. I have used other lines which required some Vaseline to help maintain surface friction and stop the line sinking but these days, sometimes I'll roll my hand in my bag of mixers so I can impart some fish oil onto the main line a few feet above my float.

I don't think it's crucial to stop your main line sinking, but some lines sink faster than others and it all depends on how long you have to wait for a bite after casting out. In an ideal scenario, you'll only have to wait a minute or two after casting, maximum half an hour, but expect the odd carp in less than a minute of the bait settling among surface-feeding fish.

My hooklink is usually six feet of 10lb or 8lb Drennan Double Strength; float choices are the superb Fox in-line bubble floats or ESP or Korum clear, weighted controllers in choppy conditions, all of which are translucent. I also have a few homemade controllers which have been made from pike floats with a 1.25oz lead glued in one end for floater fishing at range.

Hooks are preferably straight or with out-turned eyes such as Korda Wide Gapes, Gardner Tackle's Covert Chod hooks, or ESP Stiff Riggers in sizes between 6 and 4 depending on the size of hookbait and what I can get away with. If I had to stick with one size forever then it would be a size 5. I used to be a fan of the Kamasan B982 hooks, size 2 and 4, for floater fishing but since having a few open out on carp in excess of 35lbs, I'm reluctant to go back on them having now found their limitations. Whichever hook you choose, the bigger the hook the better, in my book, as it makes hooking them on the strike easier. Only scale down if you get a few aborted takes and when there is no wind rippling the surface.

Until we have been successful using one rod we may have a different opinion, but if we counted up all the hours fished with multiple rods then divided it by the number of carp caught, we will have a figure giving us carp per hour; 24 hours using three rods equates to 72 rod hours. If we then counted the hours fished with one rod and then divided the sum by the numbers of carp caught we have an answer; would we then be wrong to assume that the most productive method would be what method catches the most per rod-hour fished? Granted, using multiple rods gives us multiple opportunities, but unless we're catching in numbers then perhaps a rethink of strategy in certain weather conditions may be called for if there's a chance of extra carp to be caught each year.

I once had an argument with a fellow angler at an AGM on a venue in Berkshire, about a rule change, when I asked to raise the number of rods from two to three. He wanted to keep the rod limit to two, simply because the other venue he fished also had a two-rod limit and consequently he only had two rods, two buzzers and couldn't see the benefit of using an extra rod. I argued the point though, and said that I'd be happy to use only one rod if everyone did the same, to which he commented that I was now being stupid. No, not being stupid, because half would either give up or fish somewhere they could use three rods, and those with only one rod would use less bait and probably just as many carp would visit the bank because we'd all adapt to one-rod tactics, even though it does sound crazy at first.

As the author of this book I'm entitled to my opinions and hope I can justify them, although I would accept differing opinions from those who go in different directions with their fishing. For a number of reasons, I think a carp caught off the top with one rod is worth a little more than those caught fishing multiple rods. Number one: the thrill factor, and number two: the angler shows that he or she has the ability. The likelihood is that they had the rod in their hand the moment the carp took the bait, and bent into their prize not having to rely on buzzers and bobbins.

I'm not implying that fishing with one rod is the most effective way to fish for carp at all times, on the surface or on the bottom, but it does have massive benefits in certain situations. Thousands of carp are caught each year in the UK, but how many are caught off the top? If we studied the weekly fishing papers, only a small percentage of fish fall to surface baits, unless a few porky pies are being told to wangle some cheap bait.

Rest assured that somewhere, someone will be floater fishing; why not?

Here I am connected with a mid-30 while surface fishing.

I've caught this mid-30 twice off the top and once off the bottom; it obviously likes a floater.

This carp took a mixer without its lips breaking the surface.

Those of you who have caught carp off the top – great! You're probably much closer to my train of thought. If you haven't, then sorry, but it's possible you have at some point been missing out on perhaps one of the most exciting methods we can use to catch carp.

Fishing with just one rod and a simple float doesn't require us to take all our tackle and sundries with us, so we can be super-mobile and fully focused on the task. Minimal tackle tactics means we only take with us what's needed for a few hours fishing. Rod, landing net, unhooking mat, bait bag with bait and catapult, a few items of terminal tackle, scales and a camera, that's all we need. All we then have to do is locate carp on the venue, in the upper layers, and we're halfway there. The next step is to decide which swim to fish from and then get them feeding by introducing some freebies.

Surface fishing can be changeable due to wind fluctuations and how we conduct ourselves with accurate casting and the quantity and frequency of freebies we introduce, not to mention what happens when we hook something, so swim choice is critical because if the carp move it may help if we can move with them. As we are solely relying on our vision, high vantage points such as trees or high banks will give us a better picture, but generally, we'll be viewing the sheet of water while standing up, so our line of sight will be something between six feet and ten feet above the water surface, unless we're crouching down or standing in a ditch. The further out we look, the less depth we can see into the water, but even at reasonable casting distance with a medium-sized controller float, we should be able to see any carp, preferably in numbers, unless we're trying to target a specific carp.

Now, I prefer not to jump at the first opportunity if I have more than four or five hours' fishing in front of me, so will often look for perhaps better or bigger opportunities in the swims nearby. The difference could be fishing for a couple of 20s in one swim, and possibly dozens more a few swims away with bigger residents in attendance. If I happen to walk all the way round the venue then so be it. Hopefully, a few options may arise along the way so if action comes to an end in one area, then it's simply a case of walking to the next best option.

Often the next step, after securing the swim, will be to assess the birdlife. If I feel they could be a problem I'll either feed the swim sparingly, or feed the birds purposely, preferably a few swims away. Seagulls are often the worst problem as they have eyes like hawks and sometimes even respond to the sound of a catapult, although they are probably watching and waiting for us, knowing that someone is going to catapult out some mixers. After they have gulped down a number of mixers whole, these soon swell up inside their guts and the birds get bloated, although if they are about in numbers it may require us to give them quite a few freebies. Now, I'm sure most of us can eat three cream cracker biscuits, but could we force ourselves to eat a whole packet? The gulls, like us, will reach a point when they've had enough. When the gulls are hungry they may consume 20 or 30 mixers each in a ten-minute period, so I'll have a quick bird count-up and spray out as many pouchfuls of mixers to do the job intended.

Ducks, swans and geese can also be a problem, or should that be 'pain in the backside', so again I will treat these like the gulls and simply feed them away from where I want to fish. A cheap loaf of bread always seems a favourite with swans, so if

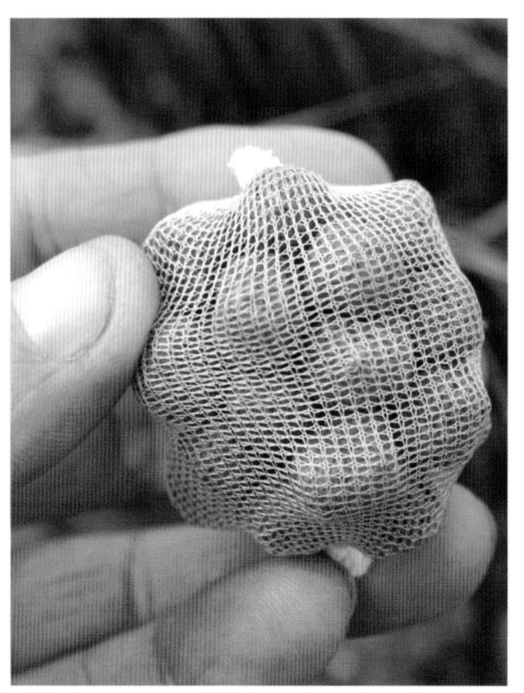

I'll always have a dozen pre-tied bags of mixers for when extra distance is required.

these are more of a problem, a few slices can keep them occupied for a while. Sometimes, it can be impossible to avoid birdlife within the area I want to fish, so you just have to put up with them because the carp are not shy of feeding even amongst a fair bit of birdlife.

Swans always seem fully aware of fish swimming beneath them and sometimes they even attempt to attack the carp. They have brains the size of a pea and we've just got to laugh, although by watching swans and other birdlife, we can use them at times to locate carp for us when we can't see them.

With the birdlife taken care of, or with no other option than to feed the swim we intend to fish with birdlife present, we can start to introduce our freebies via catapult or PVA Funnelweb meshed bags depending on the range at which we want

Nice upper-20 and part of a three-carp, surface-fishing session, in February.

to deliver them. Preferably, there will be a ripple on the water so we can drift our feed to the carp using the wind rather than catapult mixers straight on top of their heads, which can at times have an adverse effect. Usually, I will catapult the freebies a couple of rod lengths away from the prime spot, normally just two or three pouchfuls to start with, and then watch and wait until a positive situation arises. If there is a positive response, then the rod is quickly assembled along with the landing net.

Not all situations are the same, but generally the more carp there are then the greater the chances of getting a quick response to the freebies floating above them on the surface. I'll run through a few scenarios so you can quantify the effectiveness of floater fishing, having gone through the early process of locating carp, feeding off birds if any, and introducing the freebies.

Picture the scene; half a dozen carp visibly cruising around just a few feet below the surface and within minutes one or two of them begin to take freebies. While they munch on them, another one or two begin to show interest and within another couple of minutes they all begin to feed with confidence. Casting out before they have built up any confidence can often prove detrimental, so once they have taken a quantity of freebies it is now time to get a hookbait out there. Once I feel the time is right I will then overcast my float and hookbait and then retrieve some line until my hookbait is in the feeding zone, or will drift into the prime zone. I then quickly fire out another pouchful of mixers as close to my hookbait as possible, because by now they have had a few between them. While maintaining a relatively tight line to my float, I will watch my hookbait intensely and at the same time observe the carp feeding, preferably only feet away from my hookbait.

Dark Cloud at 38lbs 12oz; not a bad result on my second cast of an evening session.

When a carp comes up and takes my hookbait I waste no time and strike the moment it disappears into a mouth, hopefully connecting, which is normally 80% of the time. The other 20% of the time I will either strike too late or too early, and sometimes they will reject the hookbait within a second, or they miss it, and I'm thinking they have taken it and so strike unnecessarily, though this never seems to happen when fishing within 20 yards of the bank. When the strike is met with the satisfying feeling of a hooked carp, they can sometimes bolt off at speed so always be prepared and don't have the clutch set too tight on your reel.

If someone happens to be with me at the time I'm playing a carp, I'll often ask them to fire out some more mixers to keep the other carp interested. If I'm on my own, then once I have landed the carp I will fire out some more freebies, before I unhook the carp; weighing and photographing only if I feel I need to know, and have another photograph.

After releasing the carp, I will resume fishing if it looks good for another take. Normally, if the others haven't spooked and continue to feed then I will catch another carp, this being dependent on numbers present and favourable weather conditions. On many occasions I've caught two or three carp over 20lbs within a few hours. I've even had 30lb-plus braces a number of times, not forgetting a couple over 40lbs in very short sessions, so it's no wonder I have great faith in floater fishing!

Another scenario would be to turn up at the venue and fail to locate carp near the surface within 50 yards of the bank. Some of the time this could be because they are

37lbs 10oz on a cork barrel as the sun went down.

A 30 off the top at night; not easy but fun all the same!

simply swimming around at a lower level, or perhaps further out, or in areas where vision is hampered when viewing the water while facing the sun. Having the sun behind us is always helpful, but the carp will be where they want to be so we have to accept that there will be times when we simply can't see as well as we'd like. This is where calculated guesswork or prior knowledge can come into play when locating floater-fishing opportunities, so it may be a case of firing out mixers into open water and hoping a carp shows an interest in them. They don't often show an interest in feeding on the surface, so it's down to us to make the first move.

If I feel the carp could be further out, or I see a few, then I'll fire out a some PVA meshed bags of mixers or cast a few bags out at range, then wait and see if anything develops. Ideally, I want them to come and play within catapult territory so I'll use the wind to assist if needed. Using a spod rod to deliver freebies further out would be my last resort and I'd only do this if there were sufficient numbers of carp to warrant it.

Another scenario would be to use minimal freebies or even just a single hookbait approach. I have floater fished for the odd day with only a handful of bait used, although these seem to have been when the venue's surface was as flat as a witch's tit. I've also had days when I've not introduced any freebies, cast out a single hookbait at range and caught, and although this may seem a desperate measure, it's surprisingly effective on venues that I know to respond well to floaters.

Multiple rod alternatives

We can, if we so wish, fish multiple rods using controller float set-ups, though this can prove detrimental because we can easily be watching one float or hookbait and a carp could take and drop the other one. With little wind or a wind blowing away from us we can simply cast them out with a few yards between them and let the carp hook themselves, and the only way to find out if it works is to try it. That said, there are alternative hookbait arrangements which can help when relying on self-hookers. Personally, I find it difficult to focus on more than one rod when using floats for any length of time, but it works sometimes. We don't have to focus too much, although I'm always conscious of possibly hooking a bird if it swims through the gap between hookbait and float, while I could be playing a carp on the other rod.

Another alternative is to use an old method called 'anchored floater fishing'. This is basically using a lead and a float to hold the hookbait static. In the old days, we had to make our own floats from whole wine corks and set up the rod similar to a marker float set-up. Thankfully, Fox have made an adjustable zig float that does the job better than a wine cork, also handy because we can use them for adjustable zig fishing in deep water or for anchored floater fishing on the surface.

Time of day, time of year!

For me, floater fishing isn't something I only try in the warmer months, because every month of the year there can be possibilities. Early mornings, evenings and during darkness can be some of the better times during the warmer months, though. That said, any time can be good if you're on fish and they are up for it!

During the autumn and winter, it is very often when we are in a high pressure period that they will spend time in the upper layers; during low pressure they prefer to feed on the bottom. Even with frost on the ground it is possible to catch carp off the top. How do I know? Simples; seen it done and done it myself. My personal best floater carp was caught in February when it was below freezing the night before I fished, and believe it or not, it felt like I was destined to have that result.

I took a drive over to my local syndicate, Elstow, on the Saturday of my Pit 1 rota'd weekend, and was surprised to find only one angler fishing. He was in the furthest swim from the car park and very soon after getting out of my van, from a high vantage point overlooking the first swim from number two car park, I could clearly see quite a few carp, about six feet under the surface. The more I looked, the more I saw. Blimey! There had to be over 30 carp present, not moving around much, just maintaining their position in the water as if they had frozen there. Without sunglasses you'd struggle to see them and could easily walk past totally unaware. With so many carp present I just felt that there could be some floater fishing action to be had, but I had no fishing gear with me so planned a return trip for the following day.

Handmade controller with a 1.5oz lead glued in the bottom for extreme-range floater fishing.

During the night, the temperature dropped to minus three, and all I could do was hope that no one else had turned up and seen them and decided to pitch up in the swim. On the Sunday at 9am I was back, only this time armed with a rod and all I needed to have a go at surface fishing. Thankfully, still just the one other angler was on the venue up the other end and more importantly, the carp were in the exact same position as the previous day. There was no point wasting time so two Funnelweb meshed bags of mixers were catapulted out about 40 yards and two pouchfuls of loose feed.

As I rolled a smoke and had a cup of coffee from my flask, the first carp slurped down some mixers and as I puffed away, looking out toward the area the carp were in, others began to rise and started feeding. My floater rod was soon assembled and a cork cube pressed onto the shank of my hook; this was going to be like taking candy off a baby.

Half of the freebies had been glugged with Ultraplex additive which is similar to Minamino with a vanilla overtone, and so had my cork hookbaits, and from what I could see the carp were quite happy to feed on the freebies, so I cast out slightly beyond them confident that something would happen before I returned home. Well, to cut a

The Italian at 42lbs in February, what a result.

long story short, it only took a few minutes before I was into a fish, probably the smallest carp in the group, weighing in at 14lbs. Half an hour later after a few more casts, and a couple of near misses with one taking the float and not my hookbait, wallop! I was in again as a big pair of lips engulfed my piece of cork.

Straight away, it felt much bigger as it stripped 20 yards of line off the reel, diving deep, 28-feet deep in that particular area of the venue, and then holding its weight doggedly against my bent-over rod as it slowly kited to my left. Some ten minutes must have passed before it was anywhere near netting and after a few good looks as it swam in front of me, it certainly looked a proper chunk.

With my heart pumping and eyes bulging, I dropped the net in the water and as it came over the net cord I could clearly see that the trip had been worth it. As it kissed the spreader block I realised I'd done something special. Once on the scales, the needle confirmed my thoughts, the Italian at 42lbs exactly, a right result!

After the photos and a few smokes to calm me down, bad habit I know, I fed the swim with some more freebies and there were still a few carp interested. Blimey! Don't these carp know that it's February? Half an hour later and bang, in again; another fierce take and a spinning spool. A few tense minutes passed and before long another carp was sitting in my net, thankfully not as big as the last one because that would have been unreal.

On the scales it registered 27lbs. Blimey! Three carp off the top in a few hours from Elstow in the summer I can get my head round, but to have three carp when there is frost on the ground was a right result in anyone's book. After the photos, the other carp drifted off toward the sunken islands at range, so the moment for more had gone, and by 1pm I was on my way home, well chuffed. The 40, the Italian, was in mint condition and was my first capture of that particular character.

I've now had carp off the top in every month of the year, so like other methods don't think floater fishing is just a summer event. As we move into the colder months, it's more noticeable that carp are quite happy to spend considerable amounts of time in the upper layers during high pressure systems. Even when there is frost or snow on the ground, on a clear and sunny day it doesn't take long before the sun's rays warm things up nicely. If the venue is flat-calm in the winter the carp could be anywhere, though they tend to head for the areas on the back of the previous winds. When there is wind on the venue in the colder months some carp will prefer to follow it and feed on the bottom, while some will do the opposite.

Some venues respond well to floater fishing, while a few only now and then. If you don't try it yourself at some point in time, then that's your decision. I accept that some carp very seldom get caught on floaters, but is this down to the carp or the anglers fishing the venue in question?

Chapter 7

Food for thought

When I sat down with a blank sheet of paper with the heading 'Bait' I thought, blimey, where do I start? Having written a fair bit about bait in the past, I didn't want to repeat myself, if possible, but feel every carp book with an instructional content has to have a chapter devoted to the topic. Baits which have worked well in the past worked for a reason, and will usually continue to work. The question we must continually ask ourselves is: Are the carp showing an interest in what we offer them and what alternatives could we use to improve our results?

Bait is very important to me and to many others because it is instrumental in what we catch throughout the year; fishing with something they want makes more sense than fishing with something they don't! What's on the rig doesn't have to be edible, but the feed we introduce must be, and beneficial to the carp, supplying their nutritional needs and in no way detrimental to the health of our quarry.

What we each use next week or next time out with the rods should be based on four simple factors.

1. What we know works.

2. What we hope works.

3. What we can afford.

4. What we're asked to use depending on sponsorship/consultancy/field testing.

1. What we know works.

If we're using a particular bait that we know works we should be able to fish with 100% confidence. If we have been catching carp or our friends have, on a specific bait or combination, then it should continue catching every week, though there may come a time when action slows down and alternative baits and methods are more productive. This will probably depend on how many carp are in the venue and what percentage of the residents have been captured on any specific bait, although if there is a wide variety of foodstuffs being introduced by other anglers then this will prolong its effectiveness.

Any one of us can claim the bait as a winner from our results and observations on a good day; the test comes by using that bait over a substantial period, perhaps on a number of venues. One carp capture doesn't prove anything, but numbers of captures do, so we must judge any bait not just by what it catches but total numbers. If we then take things a stage further then we must take into account the rod hours fished with a certain bait to come to any firm conclusions.

The facts are, though, that there are now untold baits which catch carp and we can see this on a weekly basis if we subscribe to reading the angling papers such as Carp Talk. Our only real concern is what will work on the venue we're fishing, or going to fish, and what we're aiming to achieve, i.e. improved results, consistent results or even specific targets. If we're catching with some degree of consistency then there shouldn't be any great concerns about the baits' effectiveness, and if it works well on one venue then there's every chance it will work elsewhere, providing we fish effectively.

Stumpy Pec at 36lb 10oz obviously liked Richworth boilies.

The reason I feel bait is so important is that fishing for carp usually entails hundreds of hours of our valuable and irreplaceable time. It's not the cost of the bait that should be the issue, it's the fact that we want to see a fair return on our efforts.
I've done enough blanking in the past, so I know what it feels like, often while developing my angling skills and my knowledge of bait before I became a field tester. Whether we like it or not, we're all field testing baits and our results and observations determine how good the bait is.

Having caught so many carp and observed carp feeding at close quarters so many times, I am totally convinced that once a bait has been established then you will realise its full potential. With little background information on any venue you shouldn't expect immediate action on any given bait, though this sometimes happens, but rest assured that once your confidence is 100%, all you then have to think about is location and presentation.

2. What we hope will work.

This area of bait I'm quite happy to use even though 'hoping' and 'knowing' are not quite the same. A good example would be that we're using a bait which we know to have caught carp from a particular venue and now we're using it on another venue where it is untried, so until we receive action from the carp it is yet to be confirmed that it works on another venue.

Accuracy comes with practice, even when fishing a rod length out.

Time and patience is often required because with any bait, questions may not be answered immediately. Of course, getting those answers will come down to the individual and putting ourselves into those positive situations. If action is forthcoming then confidence will rise and equally importantly, if a negative response is the conclusion then confidence will go the other way. The fact that we can have blank periods using a bait we have 100% confidence with, on a venue where we know it works well, must be remembered, so chopping and changing every week may not be the best course of action unless you're totally convinced next week's bait will make the difference to your results.

One way or the other we will all learn, we have no choice, but as we are all individuals the time it takes each of us to reach any conclusions will vary. Personally, if I'm fishing a venue I'm familiar with, then it may take me two or three sessions to reach any firm conclusions. If I'm fishing a venue I am not so familiar with then it may take me half a dozen sessions. I don't like to say it, but poor angling by some, coupled with a bait which has question marks, normally equals blank after blank. Poor angling with a good bait will normally bring some success along the way; good angling coupled with a good bait equals success.

It's been a long time since I had a sustained period of blanking but I've seen many anglers go through the painful process of learning. Rest assured if you're suffering, you'll not be the only one, and your dilemma is then whether to ditch it, make a few changes, or persevere with it. If you think it's only newcomers to carp angling who make mistakes, I can assure you it isn't.

A good example of this happened the other year on one particular venue I fished, and without naming names, you'll just have to take my word for it. A few friends and acquaintances decided to use one particular bait, so between them they ordered it in bulk. They had no idea what went into the bait, they also knew no one else had used it in that venue. Therefore, they were the guinea pigs.

Without going into specific details, they blanked and blanked, and though a couple of them caught on alternative hookbaits while fishing over the bait, not one of them caught a carp with it on any rig. Two of them lost all confidence in the bait after half a dozen blank sessions, especially after some words of wisdom from me and a friend. The other anglers on the bait carried on with blind faith for another three or four sessions before they too realised that it wasn't as good as they'd hoped. I should add that none of them actually observed any carp eating the bait in areas which could be fished, the only time any of them observed any feeding was in a snaggy corner where everyone feeds them from time to time, when there are carp in that part of the venue.

It was obviously not a brilliant bait. Had it been, then among the four anglers using it a few carp would have graced their nets. Thankfully, the ducks and coots weren't so fussy! In terms of ability, and past track record, they were all capable of getting among the residents, though to be fair the best of them was a very capable angler and the last angler a moderate one. Incidentally, out of the four anglers those with the most years of carp angling under their belts caught occasionally and those with a few years less experience caught with some degree of consistency; when they changed bait they all had their string pulled.

Another nicely-scaled low- 30while field testing for Ritchworth.

3. What we can afford.

Bait costs money and one way or the other we all pay our way as we strive to catch carp. The question of cost will have a bearing on what we use, although it must be said that throwing more money into any bait or throwing more bait into the venue doesn't necessarily mean we'll catch more carp. As anglers the choices are simple. We will use what we can afford, hoping that our choices will result in the capture of some carp. Cheap baits catch carp and so do expensive baits, so where does that leave us?

My opinion is that throwing money into any bait or more bait in, is only worth it if it produces more carp, and the only way to find this out is by doing so. Fishing over more bait can be detrimental but it can also be very productive, so it will come down to the individual to adjust to the venues and its residents in the time at your disposal.

There are ways of lowering the cost of bait, though this will depend on what bait you're using. If I just talk about boilies then as you would expect the top end prices would be frozen, ready-made boilies from your local tackle shop, and the lower end would be to make them yourself or even get them free. Tackle shops, like all shops to be fair, have to have a profit margin to pay towards rent, wages and other bills, so you shouldn't expect any discounts unless you're buying in bulk. Most decent tackle shops do offer discount on bulk purchases, although they don't advertise the fact or do deals over the phone, but it doesn't cost anything to ask discreetly. Bait rolling companies, again another way to purchase bait, or get your own individual boilie recipes rolled, offer good deals. Teaming up with other anglers is another avenue worth considering.

To get the cost down even lower, then you'll have to roll your own, either buying a ready-mixed base mix or making your own base mix sourcing all the individual ingredients. You'll probably have to purchase a bait gun and rolling tables but the cost will soon be outweighed by the savings you can make, though finding the time and space has to be a consideration.

4. What we are asked to use.

You could, as I have done, become a field tester/consultant for a bait company and work your way up the ladder where you may encounter different levels of sponsorship depending on your ability and the venues you fish. Like most things in life, if you don't ask you don't get, but it's not uncommon to have some field testers on trade price, some cost price and some even free bait or have their syndicate tickets paid for. If you're prepared to write articles and contribute something to their business while fishing certain noted carp venues, then you may even get paid. The top carp anglers, with no other job outside of fishing, cannot sustain fishing virtually full time on just free bait, though some have given it a go for a year or two before either burning themselves out or running out of funds to the point where they can't afford the tickets or the petrol money to get them there.

Being sponsored may mean that you'll have to do promotional work.

Carp like sweetcorn and so do I perhaps due to its natural, sweet taste.

Finely crumbed XLR-8 boilies create an effective big carp magnet.

The fact is, carp bait is a multi-million pound industry and every bait company has a slice of the pie. If their bait is good then they survive, if their bait is not so good they fizzle away. You're probably aware that while writing this book I've been a field tester/consultant for Richworth. I was confident when I started using their baits that I'd catch my share of carp and indeed, I have had many memorable moments, so I'd like to take this opportunity of thanking Richworth for their quality baits.

Pellets, particles and alternatives.

When it comes down to feeding carp and fishing for them, then we can choose from a vast array of foodstuffs other than just boilies, as part of our feed. The choices to us are mind-boggling so it's down to the individual to find their own favourite baits and methods of enticing carp to feed and pick up our hookbaits.

The fact that there are untold baits and combinations is great, but as individuals we can't use or try them all next time we go fishing so we each do our own thing based on what we have used, previously, what we have or haven't caught on or what friends have used and the situations we find ourselves in.

I can't deny I like to use the boilie/particle approach 75% of the time when I'm fishing on the bottom. I'm not alone with this method and it accounts for a large percentage of the carp caught each year in the UK so I'll continue to employ similar tactics wherever I roam.

We could research every foodstuff until we're blue in the face studying written material, Internet websites and forums, but the reality is we don't need to know all there is to know, though it can be interesting, we just want our bobbins moving more often than not. Not only should we consider our hookbait choice but also the free offerings in terms of quality and quantity, and to some degree our baiting-up methods and timing of delivery.

We all take bait with us and when we're fishing somewhere familiar then we tend to take what we think we'll need in terms of variety and quantity to last the session, and maybe some to pre-bait with at the end of it. I'm sure many of us with our own transport take a little bit more and keep it in our vehicles to top up our spots or keep as back-up, I know I do. Because I normally fish sessions of different lengths and styles, and a few different venues each year, I like to keep my options open to cover most situations, and this is reflected in what I take with me, even though some may stay in my van and not get used for that particular session.

It doesn't take a lot of bait to catch a carp, but it does take a lot to keep 10, 20 or 50 carp feeding for a few hours, or all day every day, over a period of say 72 hours. So we must weigh up the venues we intend to fish, the situations and possibilities, and use enough bait to get some action and swing things in our favour.

Quite a few years ago, I started fishing with chopped or whizzed-up boilies in conjunction with normal ones and immediately saw the benefit as all the ingredients were exposed allowing their attractive properties to disperse and stimulate the carp I was fishing for.

Years ago, when PVA string first hit the scene, all we could do was fish stringers but now we have solid bags of different dimensions and Funnelweb tubing so we can now take things a stage further and use stick mixes or use PVA-friendly liquids to enhance our chances. It's fair to say that many of us have capitalised on the use of PVA products, and sales over the counter in tackle shops throughout the country confirms this year after year.

If you make your own stick mix, then just like boilies, the list of possible ingredients is as long as your imagination. The beauty of stick mixes is, it doesn't take much to make one kilo, and a kilo makes a hell of a lot of sticks so it goes a long way depending on where you're fishing. If you've never tried it, think of how and where you can reap the benefits, and give it a go. I normally whiz boilies or nuts in a food blender, but we can achieve similar-sized particles with a Korda Krusha while we're on the bank or at home. I've listed a few stick mixes that I've used in the last decade, all that's left to do is add some liquid food source to dampen the mix, prior to making some sticks, such as tigernut juice, Richworth Aquastim, Minamino, Krill oil or other liquid food sources. As I write this, a few friends and I are experimenting with a couple of other natural organic ingredients which could prove useful in the future; only time will tell if they are any good.

30% Powdered fishmeal pellets
30% 2.3mm fishmeal pellets
30% Groundbait
10% Green-lipped mussel powder or grated Belechan

While some favour solid bags, I prefer to use a stick mix and Funnelweb.

60% Groundbait
35% Whizzed-up prepared tigernuts
5% Cooked hemp

75% XLR-8 stick-mix
25% Whizzed XLR-8 boilies

When it comes down to pulling power and presentation, then it's hard to beat a little mountain of interesting and stimulating morsels with your hookbait in amongst it. Interestingly, on the venues where I've used the stick mix/groundbait approach and had the opportunity to view the spots either from the bank, or from a boat as on a couple of venues, the carp totally polished the spots and even created craters after a couple of sessions as they dug into the lakebed.

Not to dwell too long on the subject, or to repeat myself, pellets and particles have and always will be instrumental in the capture of many carp, for me and thousands of other carp anglers in the UK. Not only do they keep our costs down, but they are also very effective, because carp love to eat certain pellets and particles.

The list is as long as your arm but my favourites are those which have proved themselves to me in the past and present. Namely; hemp, sweetcorn, quality fishmeal pellets in various sizes and tigernuts. Most of the time I use boilies, so I have to be careful on the ratio and 50/50 seems to work just fine for me. When I use sweetcorn I will fish with either a plastic/foam imitation hookbait popped up, or a maize hookbait and/or a boilie tipped off with fake corn as a bottom bait.

This fella fancied a bit of foam and plastic corn.

Meaty alternative; Peperami chops.

When using tigernuts, I will only use them sparingly and fish tigers over hemp and pellet, with either a single nut or double nut hookbait or a combo such as boilie/nut or nut and fake corn.

Of course, there are plenty of other particles and alternatives to use which I know carp love to eat such as maples, tares, wheat or Partiblend, and perhaps when I retire I'll get around to using them just as my dad did whenever he fished, from the days he used to drag me along when I was six years old, until he passed away; bread, maggots, worms or his secret weapons, cockles and prawns. I caught my first carp of about 2lb, float fishing a cube of luncheon meat, when I was ten years of age. Meat baits are another often overlooked alternative though they still produce carp year in year out with Peperami being a firm favourite for many.

I can clearly recollect the first time I tried fishing for carp with Peperami, although the year escapes me it must have been in the early 80s. It was quite a long time ago when the vast majority of the UK had a close season from March 15th to June 16th and the only venues available to fish were so-called 'any-method' trout fisheries. Well, at least it showed some initiative to get round old-fashioned water authority rules.

A couple of friends and I went to a place called Willow Pool and on arrival we were met with a sign on the gate, 'No Boilies', so we took a quick trip to the local supermarket and back we came armed with a few sticks of Peperami.

Off we trotted halfway round the lake; we set up a couple of rods each and simply cast out two or three-bait Peperami stringers into the middle of the lake. I think we finished off with 14 carp from 5lbs to 15lbs between us that day. A couple of other carp anglers from Luton turned up to fish an overnighter, so they too rushed off to the supermarket for some spicy sausages once we'd told them what we were using.

A week later, I met them in a local tackle shop and one of them had chopped up a whole Peperami stick, then threaded the lot back onto some PVA string, butting all the pieces back together so it looked like a whole sausage, and cast it out. Three hours later he got a screaming run only to reel in the rig and stringer intact. Laugh? I nearly wet myself, still at least they returned with a few carp gracing their nets.

Boilies

As mentioned earlier, when it comes down to using boilies then we have a few options open; make them ourselves, either using our own recipe or bait company base mix, or get them made, by a friend or bait rolling company, either using our own recipe or another, or use ready-mades. There once was a day when I used to enjoy making boilies, but it seems a long while since I've rolled any large amounts. By making them yourself though, it does give you full control of the end product as you can tinker with ingredients and attractant/flavour levels. Other than common sense, there are no boundaries so you can fully customise your bait.

If you make your own base mixes then record on paper the exact weights of each ingredient for future reference, because you may find the need to adjust amounts of certain ingredients. No doubt you'll formulate the mix on paper first then hope it rolls into nice round boilies after you've mixed it with eggs and liquid additives.

Another mid-30 that liked a boilie.

If it rolls well and catches carp, then you're possibly on to a winner; time will tell. If it doesn't roll well, or doesn't catch carp, then adjust the base mix and perhaps make changes to your liquid additives.

Throughout the 80s and early 90s, my friends and I formulated some excellent base mixes which caught us plenty of carp. I've no doubt they'd all catch tomorrow. As I've said elsewhere, tried and trusted baits are winners. For some unknown reason, there were mistakes in some of the recipes published in my first book 'Strictly Carp', obvious mistakes to me which should have been questioned at the proof-reading stage. Now is my chance to make amends, so if you fancy trying these recipes as a base mix then rest assured they roll well and catch well. All you need then is a good attractant/flavour at the optimum level and you're on to a winner.

Fishmeal 1
2kg Anchovy meal
2kg Capelin meal
3kg C.L.O
2kg Semolina
1kg Full-fat soya flour

Birdie 1
5kg Red Factor
5kg Semolina
5kg Full-fat soya
1kg Robin Red
0.5kg Crushed hemp

Milk 4
5kg Rennet casein
2kg Calcium caseinate
2kg Lactalbumin
2kg Vitomealo
2kg Cow & Gate Baby Plus
10kg C.L.O
4kg Semolina
2kg Soya flour
1kg Desiccated coconut

I've no doubt many of you are aware that I've been a field tester/consultant for many years now for a few different bait and tackle companies and no doubt I have been grateful for the opportunities and money saved along the way. The cold reality is that many companies make and sell quality baits and they need anglers like us to test them, give them feedback, and promote where needed.

Now, if anyone wished to get involved with any companies, it's easy to contact them via email or meet them, because their doors are never shut. They, understandably, will be interested in what you have caught and what venues you fish, but honesty and integrity is worth a lot too. I've been with Richworth for nearly ten years now and have been pleasantly surprised not only by their baits, but also my captures. The boilies they have developed in the last decade have all proved themselves capable; KG1, Ultraplex and XLR-8 to name just a few. None of us can force carp to eat bait, they will eat it if they like it; and if they like it, we should catch carp.

HISS
KEEP OUT!
?
XXX
POP UPS
TIGER SNOT
GARLIC POWDER
MAC
CLO
ROBIN RED
FISH MEAL
GAZ
CRUSHED HEMP
SEMOLINA

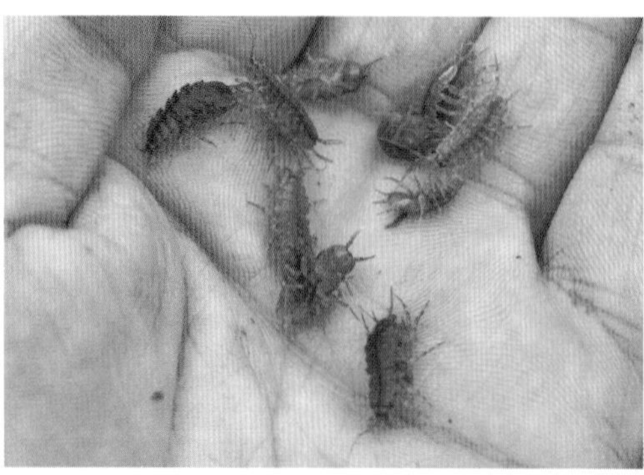

Just a few naturals that carp like to munch on!

There are advantages to getting a bait deal, although you could say that the advantage is lost because you're then tied to that company, so therefore it wouldn't be considered playing the game using any other company's products. Technically, the anglers with no loyalties can use whatever they like and jump on whichever bait is getting used a lot on their venue; they can also decide to keep their bait a secret.

Floaters

Whenever I fish for carp on the surface I like to play around by using 11mm standard floaters, some which have been flavoured or dyed. To flavour and dye them, I put a kilo of mixers into a plastic bag with no holes in, big enough to hold about 3 or 4 kilos. Then simply mix the flavour/attractant and dye in half a coffee mug of hot water, pour over the mixers and then inflate the bag with air and seal it. Give the bag a shake every ten minutes for half an hour and then keep them in the inflated bag until you're ready to use them. These floaters will soften and swell slightly as they absorb the liquid. Prior to writing this book, old favourites like Hutchie's Shellfish Sense Appeal with Protaste and Solar's Salmon Trio Pot Shot scored well for me and a few friends, who still use them to this day.

I do think there is a multitude of viable flavours and attractants we could use so the choice is yours really. Liquid Liver extracts, Minamino plus a few millilitres of flavour seem to work better than standard floaters at times, though I'll always use both to gauge their reactions. In 2007/8 I did well using Richworth's Salmon flavour along with a spoonful of Robin Red and Betaine powder, plus warm water. In 2009/10 I did well using Aquastim, Krill oil and XLR-8 flavour.

Hookbaits

Hookbaits do not have to be edible, they also do not have to look, behave or be identical to your freebies. That said, we should always be capable and confident using standard or near identical hookbaits as they obviously look the same as our freebies and the fish eat them.

Artificial hookbaits
Boilie or particle hookbaits
Enhanced hookbaits
Natural/alternative hookbaits

I would imagine that every carp angler in the UK who is reading this book, is totally aware of the vast array of artificial hookbaits available today, and most of you have used artificial baits either on their own or in combination with other hookbaits. If you haven't, then fine, but don't dismiss the idea of using a fake hookbait, because they do work.

Ever since fake sweetcorn became available, the use of sweetcorn has increased because it works. We could use bits of coloured foam as in the pre-plastic age, but the fact is, the carp see many anglers introducing sweetcorn, and as a consequence pay a visit to the bank from time to time.

Now, there are many ways of presenting boilies as hookbaits, starting with basic bottom bait to a standard pop-up, or moving on to an enhanced hookbait made to serve a specific purpose. A standard bait to me is something either exactly the same as the freebies, or using a cork-balled pop-up with the same bait encasing it, or the readily available pop-ups often supplied with most boilies sold these days. I have no qualms about using these because after all, they are virtually the same as those the fish are eating, giving us a clearer indication of the baits' effectiveness.

Although the readymade pop-ups may have different ingredients, and no doubt perform totally differently to any bottom baits, the standard again would be near-identical attractant levels. If we feel the need to source our own hookbaits, then we can either make them, or get someone to supply our needs. I must confess that as I've got older I don't roll them myself as much any more and rely on a few friends to make them. It's not so bad making fruity/creamy baits, but Mrs. Clarke understandably hits the roof if she comes home to the house smelling of Squid or Monster Crab.

When it comes down to making small batches then I have no qualms about using elevated attractant/flavour levels. They worked in the 80s; they worked in the 90s and have continued to work to the present day. How high or low we go with any attractants/flavour levels is down to the individual and what hookbaits they are using. As you would expect, during 30-plus years of fishing for carp I've tried quite a few different hookbaits. As with anything, the only way to find out if they're effective is to use them and let results tell you if you're travelling in the right direction.

My opinion may differ from yours, but I believe if the attractor/flavour level used in the freebies introduced is above its optimum tested level, or suggested inclusion rate, then yes, it may attract carp and they may eat a few, but rather than consume the lot in one continuous feeding spell they can take days to eat it. No doubt, as the baits take on water, some of the attractant/flavour has leached out so they become more acceptable and perhaps more palatable.

With hookbaits though, the carp do not get the chance to eat them, their only choice is to sample or avoid them. Logic then says, if they sample your hookbait then you have a chance of catching something and if they avoid it then that hookbait will not enter a carp's mouth and therefore you'll catch next to bugger all.

As a field tester, it's been part of my job to experiment. Every year I will have a few pots of hookbaits made with different attractant/flavour levels, so whenever I go fishing I'll have standard hookbaits and enhanced hookbaits to try out. Perhaps I should mention at this point, I have a few friends who have helped out from time to time, testing various hookbaits while fishing various other venues, and between us we have all gained some knowledge and improved our results.

Warning! Royale Horizon 23 pellets attract everything!

A friend of mine said he didn't like like the twiddly bits. Somehow, I don't think the carp care.

To give you an insight into my testing with boilies then; 80% of the time I will have slightly different baits on each rod, and swap them around. The other 20% I will have identical baits on all rods, though they may be one of a few batches.
As an example, a flavour with a suggested level of 5ml per six-egg mix equates to 0.83ml per egg. Double strength would be 1.66ml per egg and so on as shown below.

2 x 1.66ml per egg
3 x 2.49ml per egg
4 x 3.33ml per egg
5 x 4.16ml per egg
6 x 5ml per egg

If 5ml was used in a one-egg mix then the hookbaits will be six times the level of the freebies, for argument's sake six times strength, so it's possible to have the attraction or stimulus of six standard boilies.

It's very easy to simplify things by adding another liquid, such as a sweetener or liquid food source such as Minamino or liquid liver, as a buffer so that when making small batches of bait you don't have to measure out tiny amounts and you can round measurements off to within a millilitre.

To some, using a hookbait that could be between 2 or 5 x suggested level may seem ridiculous or even detrimental, to some it's logical, and to some, mild. My philosophy is simple; better results mean more memorable moments and if through chemoreception there is stimulus, then who can argue that a single hookbait can't have the attraction of a number of baits. Stimulus is the key word here because you often see the difference when fishing single hookbaits and perhaps more so on venues with coloured water or when fishing in or on silty areas.

As with any baits, with testing in mind, it can take time to evaluate results, which is why many anglers keep little edges and secrets to themselves. As a good example of how effective fishing elevated levels can be, I will go back in time to when my friends and I were fishing a few gravel pits in the winter months, all using our special microwaved pop-ups. Prior to this we used standard cork-balled pop-ups and our results were average; however, when we changed, our results were staggering. For me, it was one winter on Harefield Lake and four chances using standard baits; the following winter and fishing a similar amount of rod hours 21 chances came my way, including the biggest carp in the venue at the time at 39lbs 8oz.

I tend to experiment one year, then try to capitalise on lessons learned the following year. If something obviously effective like Richworth's XLR-8 comes along, it's time to take advantage, a few extra carp is better than a few less.

To conclude this chapter, I had the pleasure of interviewing Tim Paisley who is no stranger within the UK and global carp scene, with a few more years' carp fishing under his belt than me. Why? Well, we are two different anglers from different parts of the country who've travelled similar paths and any words of wisdom are better than none. I managed to twist his arm while we were fishing a charity event; all we had to do was find the time.

- Tim Paisley interview -

MC. Hi, Tim. Just to get the ball rolling, can you tell us a little bit about yourself? For a start when were you born, and how did you get into carp fishing?

TP. Pre-war, 1937. I'll leave you to do the sums. I didn't start carp fishing until I was well over 30 years old; before that I was just a pleasure angler catching anything that came along, and then a carp came along! I caught a carp by accident on bread flake while tench fishing, and the fight it put up, and the sight of this gorgeous mirror carp which seemingly had its own identity, made a huge impact on me, and in the direction I wanted to go in my fishing.

In the 70s there wasn't much information available dedicated to carp fishing. First book I read was 'Confessions of a Carp Fisher' from the local library, which at the time I was a little disappointed with! The first book I purchased was in 1974, Dick Walker's Stillwater Angling, Fourth Edition from Peter Mohan at the inaugural CAA meeting at Billing Aquadrome. You could say that from that point in time I was well hooked and eventually became fascinated with the bait side of carp fishing, gradually becoming aware of special paste baits, and then later, boilies. The first special I made was KiteKat and PYM, stiffened with a bit of crushed Weetabix, but at the time carp baits, or should we say commercial carp baits, were only just getting off the ground.

Over the next few years, with regards to bait developments, there were rumblings about protein and carbohydrates and my initial reactions were, 'what a load of crap', but then it started to intrigue me. I remember reading Fred Wilton's articles and was blown away! If carp needed certain nutrients in their diet, then what did we need? I started reading up on carp and human nutrition, nutrients and bait ingredients, and the more I looked into it the more I learned, and the more fascinated I became. In fact reading Fred Wilton's material had as big an impact on my own diet as it did on what I fed to the carp!

MC. So did you start thinking at that time HNV baits would be the answer; better bait equals better results?

TP. Well, not quite, and certainly not nutrition as a bait principle, no. I think the first commercial carp bait I encountered was Phillips' Hi-Pro, which was being advertised. I remember going into Bennett's of Sheffield, smelt it, and it absolutely reeked of what I later learnt was PYM. Initially, I thought 'Blimey that stinks, carp are never going to eat that!' Then over the next few years I learned what good bait ingredients PYM and other yeasts turned out to be, and still are today.

There was very little written about bait in the 70s. My first successful carp baits were bread, maggots and then luncheon meat, and it wasn't until these started to lose their effectiveness that my mind turned to alternatives and making my own baits. I caught my first double on luncheon meat, and my first 20 on Bacon Grill.

MC. Can you remember the first milk protein boilie you ever made and used?

TP. Yes, this would be late 70s. It was the E.S. Reding bait, which is probably remembered by very few people. To the best of my knowledge, Clive Diedrich, Malcolm Winkworth, and Mike Wilson, marketed that first milk protein bait, and the liquid additive was Minamino. That was my first introduction to Minamino, which is still sold today by various firms under various different names and is actually a protein health drink. Initially, I wasn't convinced about milk proteins, principally because I found them difficult to mix into a satisfactory consistency. Of course, Clive and Malcolm went on to found Richworth, but I think the Reding Mix was their first venture into bait.

MC. I can remember the first commercially available base mix I ever used, it was Rod Hutchinson's Protein Mix at the start of the 80s. Did you ever try it?

TP. I did use some of Hutchy's mixes and flavours. I caught my first 30-pounder from Waveney D Lake using a bait flavoured with Maplecreme, although I have no recollection of what the base mix was. I used Hutchy baits for two or three years after becoming friends with Rod through the CAA. He was always hugely knowledgeable and helpful on bait. We were making our own baits in those days so we were using ingredients to make up our own base mixes, and the frustrating thing was that the supply of some of the ingredients we were using was very hit and miss, especially early in the season when there was a run on baits and ingredients.

MC. Being keen to learn, like most carp anglers around the early 80s, there seemed to be a great deal of interest in high protein and HNV baits, with some milk protein mixes boasting protein levels above 80%, yet I could never find any literature that suggested a carp requires anything near this figure. What are your thoughts on protein levels?

The pantry in the late 70s. Experimental bait ingredients were far more important than food!

The way we were, and still are for some people; rolling baits ready for boiling, not one of my favourite chores of all time.

TP. I never worked on any protein percentages, even when I understood the merits of using a good bait. Coming up with a recipe that mixed well and could be converted into boilies was more important to us than the actual percentages involved. I became very friendly with Alan Smith, who I knew through fishing the Tip Lake at Darenth, and he was an influence on me – although he always held back a few secrets! Briggsy and his mates were there catching carp on Richworths, and I was there beating my brains out looking more into nutrition, and using the prototype of what became Hi-Nuval. Mark Summers, who fished it brilliantly, was the first guy to have twenty 20s in a season from the Tip Lake, all caught on Hi-Nuval. We were using an ingredient back then that was very special and because it is an ingredient used in some of Nutrabaits base mixes and boilies, I can't really be too specific, but we found a health company product with Trypsin in which was something special. Because supplies of ingredients were hit and miss and bait was at a formative stage, some of our ingredients came from health shops, which supply some excellent, highly convertible protein mixes.

MC. Before people start tapping in Trypsin into a Google search, what is Trypsin?

TP. It's an enzyme, a protein-splitting enzyme and a very efficient one. Enzymes are proteins, and they are essential in the use of the various nutrients in a diet, and they are specific in that there are different enzymes for coping with the different nutrients (fats, carbohydrate, proteins). They enable us, and all living creatures, to process food.

As I've become older my enzymes have become far less efficient. I can no longer cope with red meat, which I used to love, and I'm on lactose-free milk because I can't cope with lactose anymore. Some nights I take a couple of Gaviscon tablets before I go to bed, otherwise I'll have an uncomfortable night. If you look at chemist's shelves there are numerous digestion aids which are simply helping people to make better use of their food. It might well be that some carp's enzymes become less efficient as they get older and that their dietary requirements change. So while I was never into protein percentages per se, I was always keen on the concept of giving the carp help in using the bait I was offering them.

Carp don't have stomachs and their systems have to extract the required nutrients as their food passes though the intestines, so for me, convertibility was always a more important aspect of the bait than protein percentage. Nutrabaits' Addit-Digest dates back to our 80s thinking on bait and its convertibility, and Mainline's Activ- range suggests to me that there is a convertibility element in their baits. Bear in mind that my bait designing and bait making days were prior to the availability of the predigested ingredients that started to make an appearance in the 90s and I would think are in extensive use today.

MC. I'm glad you brought the subject of enzymes up actually, as there must be different dietary requirements with carp. A young 10lb carp must be different to a big carp which could be 30 or 40 years old!

TP. Yes, definitely. Looking back to when I took over the running of Birch Grove, many moons ago, before that it had seen a lot of particles, including three years of peanuts and the carp looked far from healthy. We started using HNV baits containing enzymes and within five years there was something like thirty 30lb-plus carp in there, and in a five-acre lake back in the early 90s this was ridiculous! There was one known 20 in the pool when I took it on, and I'm sure these weight gains were down to the quality of the baits they were consuming.

Early 80s Darenth Tip Lake 30lb-plus on the prototype HNV mix which later became Nutrabaits' HiNuVal.

An early 90s midwinter carp, 'Scaley', from the Mangrove on Mainline's Grange; along with sweetcorn, the best winter bait I've used.

When I started looking deeper into enzymes and how they work, I asked one of my sources if they are recycled, because the proteins are permanent. My source said, yes, they will keep using them and long-term the carp will benefit from that bait. That enzyme then becomes part of their system; the carp develop a more efficient protein and nutrient absorbing system. That is what I've been told, although I haven't checked out the bioscience behind the concept.

From talking to Fred Wilton, in the early days, I know he experimented with lots of ingredients, and enzymes, although he's never published all of his findings. This will make you laugh. He had a goldfish in a bowl, and it out-grew the bowl because of what he was feeding it with. In the end he couldn't get it out of the bowl without breaking it!

So, people have gone down different roads with bait. I'm sure the major bait companies are well aware of the implications of using enzymes and predigested ingredients. The problem with enzymes is triggering them, and you need the right pH, which our digestive system has. I would presume baits which are enzyme-active are dependent on the pH levels of the venue, which may be the reason they can be brilliant on some venues and not so effective on others. Enzymes can be volatile, too, when it comes to boiling. I added brown, powdered bait dye to one of my proven 80s mixes, and the dye triggered the enzymes at the boiling stage, ruining it!

MC. Instant and long term baits Tim; we both know they are effective what are your opinions?

TP. Well, long term baits are something which they will continue to eat year in, year out, as a food source. Instant baits may be more effective short term but I think the difference between instant and long term is the level of attraction, the quality of the ingredients, or both. There's a determining line: go beyond the optimum level of attraction of any flavour and the carp may not tolerate it for long, and sooner or later it will put the carp off eating the bait. If anyone puts together a bait where there is high nutrition and the level of attractors is instant and bang on the right level, and the carp eat it and benefit from it, then great. This is where some of the bait companies have come up with some real winners; the carp are on it instantly, and keep eating it.

MC. Particles, boilies or other alternatives, do you feel it's just a case of finding what works in the going conditions, or do you feel there are situations where you feel one may have the edge over the other?

TP. Now that we can get supplies of 8 and 10mm boilies, or even smaller, I don't think there is much difference when it comes down to creating a positive feeding situation. Carp do like particles but the standout favourites like tiger nuts, maples and sweetcorn seemingly contain something which they respond to, and they continue to work over the years, even in Redmire Pool. Over time they have become naturals through the carp's familiarity with them, if you like. That isn't true of all particles so I think there is something special about the three I've named. There may come a point when some carp, particularly older ones, become uncatchable on baits they aren't familiar with and simply don't recognise as food.

Ashmead proprietor, Mark Walsingham, made a comment to me about these mythical big commons which are seen from time to time on various venues but remain uncaught. He thinks that as they get older they become predators; they will mostly feast on live food and show little interest in anglers' baits as they are more familiar with all the naturals within the venue. I think these rarely caught carp can be fooled occasionally, but this will come down to the anglers to find the answer. This is where ringing the changes with attractor baits could prove fruitful in that eventually a bait may strike a chord of recognition, or even using dead baits. The odd carp gets caught each year to pike anglers using dead baits so that may be an avenue to explore.

MC. I totally agree with that Tim, red strawberry corn springs to mind as a bait to catch rarely caught carp, having watched the big, uncaught Colnemere common feed on it the year after Jason Hayward captured the big mirror.

It's been well over a decade or so that I stopped making up my own base mixes and solely used ready-made base mixes and I was playing around with products such as Belachan, Krill products, G.L.M. and Oyster powder and Astaxanthin. Do you still experiment with base mixes or are you, like me, satisfied with letting others supply you with ready-made boilies?

TP. I've not heard of Astaxanthin, but may have used it without my knowledge. No, since I started using Mainline baits many years ago I leave all the developments in their capable hands. There are a lot of products which go into the manufacturing of boilies and I no longer feel the need to know everything about the bait I'm using. I'm a big believer in yeast and Robin Red in any base mix. Common carp certainly seem to show a preference to baits with Robin Red in them. When I first went to Raduta, which was famous for its big commons, I had Kev Knight make me up some Grange baits with Robin Red in them. I mentioned this to one of the guys on the plane on the way out, and he laughed! The Big Common fell to the bait, though, and it's still my personal best at 73lbs 13oz!

Modern bait developments have now made it possible always to have a contingency supply of particles and seeds with you, 'in case'.

MC. It's probably fair to say that many carp anglers back in the 80s tried various products when producing their own boilie recipes, some of which were made public. I found it fascinating experimenting with various products while floater fishing with mixers, as the mixers never changed, only the results of my trials and I could gauge their reactions to them. Did you ever try this?

Lake Raduta's Big Common at 73lbs 13oz trapped on a Grange mix containing Robin Red. I'd noticed from my Mangrove and Birch results that Robin Red seemed to account for a higher percentage of commons.

TP. I wish I had, but not really, although I did use flavoured mixers during the first couple of years of Birch when the carp were floater orientated. I got involved with bait developments with Bill Cottam and a few of the early base mixes produced under the Nutrabaits banner were designed by me, so almost all my trials while fishing involved boilies. The Addits I designed were based on all the scientific fish nutrition papers I could find, and the carp's reaction to baits containing some of the stimulatory chemicals mentioned in the papers. They contain amino acids, enzymes and taste stimulators and have proved highly successful. Nutrabaits' Trigga, a name which might suggest it's an enzyme bait, is a big carp bait designed to catch big carp, although I have no knowledge of its contents!

MC. Let's talk a little about single hookbaits. Do you prefer to use hookbaits with their standard level of attractants, or fish with baits which have an elevated attractant level?

TP. Whatever is proving successful on the water I'm fishing is the basis for some of my thinking for single hookbaits. Most of my 'singles' are snowmen, with a pre-baited bottom bait and alternative top baits. I have an edge in that I am able to obtain alternative colours and shapes for the top bait on the snowman, and I suspect that the attractor level is elevated in these alternative baits, but ... some anglers are far more successful with singles than others, and I suspect that is because they are good thinkers. You hear talk of washed out baits being successful, which is a direct contradiction of elevated flavour levels when you think about it. Which works, elevated levels or reduced, washed out ones? When I decide to put out a single my mind goes back to the days when we used to fish anchored crust. The carp's visible reaction to that single bait was bizarre; it was as if they were annoyed by it! On a no-hoper of a day at Snowberry in the 70s, I watched a carp come back to an anchored crust 13 times, trying to break it up. In the end, and much to my complete astonishment, it took it! It was the only way it could get rid of it. I mention that because I think people tend to be impatient with singles, as I tend to be. Sooner or later it may go, but have you the patience to wait for that to happen? 'Single' doesn't mean instant, although we tend to think of them like that.

MC. So, where I've used 5ml per egg of an attractor with a recommended level of 5ml to 6 eggs, just a one-egg mix for hookbaits, you've not tried this?

TP. Not in recent years, although I've no idea of any levels that may be used in the pop-ups supplied to me which I'm using with my snowman set-ups. I'm always interested to hear other anglers' views on fishing singles. What I meant is that if there are loads of fish coming out on Mainline's Cell, or Richworth's Tuttis, then use the going bait. They are used to encountering it so it's a case of 'Oh, there's another one,' not 'What's this!' If you can come up with a different shape and colour then so much the better. If you can some up with a winning recipe of your own then better still. Keep it to yourself!

Plastic again! I'm proud of this gorgeous 28lb Redmire common, which fell to plastic corn, fished with salted corn and hemp in a PVA bag.

MC. If we look at publicity, we have gone from a couple of weekly newspapers 30 years ago, to numerous dedicated carp magazines, to a dedicated weekly carp newspaper with Carp-Talk, and now all the DVDs and various websites on the Internet. For the anglers relatively new to carp fishing, should they be influenced by what's put into print?

TP. Jack Hilton said he caught his Redmire 40 on a grey slug, when in fact it was a sultana. Chris Yates claimed he was catching Redmire carp with a cherry under a cherry tree, and there is no cherry tree at Redmire! I think those two instances were simply down to syndicate secrecy, but things can get distorted sometimes, particularly when you get sponsorship deals to be justified, or prizes and competitions to be won. At times there may well be some distortion of the truth so don't go believing every single thing you read in any publication. Most anglers will be honest so most of what's stated may well be true!

My advice would be to find out what baits are doing well on your chosen venue, or what baits have done well in the past and use these. It is a fact of life that tiger nuts have a very, very long life and account for a number of carp that are publicised as coming out on boilies. I've made the mistake of turning my back on tigers on a number of venues through thinking that they must have blown, when they've done nothing of the sort. I think the same can be said of sweetcorn and maize, too. On the other hand, the bait books and general information available now about making baits and what they contain is a different world to the one I started carp fishing in at the start of the 70s! There is almost too much information available now, to the point that it may cause confusion.

MC. Natural mineral deposits in a lake environment; do you think it's feasible that like other animals on this planet, a carp will find areas or spots which have a rich mineral source and the carp will either feed or roll on such areas because of the bottom composition?

TP. It could be something to do with minerals, I've never really given it much thought, but I agree that the carp have preferred feeding spots. Anglers fishing gravel pits learn to identify the features the carp will favour but we have to adopt a different approach on the silty meres. In the early years on the Mangrove, for instance, before the carp started to become bait orientated, seeing a fish head and shouldering in open water could be a clue to a feeding spot. It was important to get your hookbait in a spot the fish visited to feed, be it a natural food spot or one of the mineral sources you refer to. Natural feeding spots are visited regularly and the carp go there to feed, so take advantage of that.

MC. I think there is something in certain clays which carp like. I can only assume it's some form of mineral or organic compound, because I've often seen carp swim past with clay smeared along their flanks. It makes me think that the carp get some kind of benefit from it, perhaps healing properties or simply trying to rub off leeches or parasites.

TP. Terry Hearn has similar opinions to that, having observed many carp on many venues with clay streaks along their flanks.

MC. I am aware of Terry and a few other notable anglers' opinions on clay. I have used mud-coated leads to disguise my end tackle but not thinking it may attract fish in any way.

TP. It's such a massive topic, bait, but essentially the carp need to feed so they will visit these spots or areas they know has food, be it natural or introduced by anglers. If they show themselves or start bubbling in an area it's always a good sign.

MC. Now, I know you have fished many fisheries abroad, from the famous Lake Raduta in Romania to many fisheries in France, very often for a week session or even longer. What tips would you give to someone who has never visited a foreign venue before and is planning a similar trip?

TP. Never, ever underestimate the carp you are going to fish for. Treat them as hard to catch and you will make life easier for yourself. If you're going to take ready-made boilies anywhere you're not familiar with, such as a week-long session somewhere in France, then take a few alternatives rather than just the one flavour, because you never know, your first choice may not prove the best choice.

A good example of how carp can respond; we found that on the many occasions we took trips to Fishabil in France, the first two or three days we'd be catching from the off, and then as the week progressed results on the initial going bait would tail off; switch to something different and the results started coming again. Flavour levels tend to be high in shelf-life readymades and they may not be to the liking of the carp in the long-term. There is fierce price competition on shelf-lifes so the content may not be as nutritious as in higher quality freezer baits. If you can take freezer baits, great. If not then take a mix of air-dried quality baits and a couple of alternative shelf-life baits.

MC. You don't think the Fishabil results were because of angling pressure?

TP. You'll know yourself Martin that over a period of time you begin to understand the reactions of the carp in a water you become familiar with. With the Fishabil trips we were seeing this ongoing pattern around the whole lake on more than one occasion. We were seeing a familiar pattern from 28 anglers.

MC. So 28 anglers all using the same baits and then during the middle of the week the action slows right down and you all move on to another bait and the action starts to pick up again. That's interesting. Artificial baits Tim, I presume you're no different to most carp anglers and have a few in your tackle box or ready-tied on a rig for whenever. Have you got anything positive or negative to say about them?

TP. For the last decade I've fished all over the world for carp, perhaps more than in England. Some venues in France you can have problems with crayfish and poisson chat, which can be a right pain in the backside as they will nibble away your hookbaits. I've tried meshing baits but I just find it fiddly and unsatisfactory. When I fished at Kevin Nash's lake earlier this year one of the lads fishing had a big brace in the same evening, although as it's Kev's water I was using Nashbait.

Cassien's much-coveted Moonscale at 63lbs, caught in the late 90s on Nutrabaits's Trigga, a name which suggests an enzyme ingredient.

An early December 57½ from Korda's Gigantica. The fish fell to a tiger snowman, plastic tiger on top, and was the only take of the week.

The following day I asked the guy who had the brace what bait he was using. He said, 'Well I use plastic tiger nut hookbaits; I use them all the time!' Where he normally fishes on the BCSG Korda Lake the crayfish are such a nuisance that anything edible used as a hookbait simply doesn't last long and plastic hookbaits had proved to be the answer!

They were accounting for repeat captures, too. When I went to Bob Davis's lake in August I suffered 36 hours of poisson chat and crayfish wiping out my boilie hookbaits and changed my approach. Nuts are banned as freebies so I stuck a plastic tiger on one rod and cast it out, and I didn't have to wait long: 20 minutes in the water and off it went. Result, a 34lb mirror. 'Blimey,' I thought, 'This will do!' So I switched all my rods over to plastic tiger hookbaits. By the end of the week I had 28 fish, and my mate, Paul Musson, had landed a PB of 59lb on them, all on plastic tigers! This is on a water which sees no nuts of any sort because they are banned!

I've caught using plastic corn, although I tend to favour plastic corn when I'm using PVA bags. I've always felt a bit guilty using an artificial bait, but then Lee Jackson wrote a chapter for Hutchy's 2011 book 'Carp Inspirations' about there being some million-year-old recognition of an organic chemical compound used in the production of plastics, or something like that. It's in the book. There is something there which to carp suggests food in plastic hookbaits, so they'll have a go at them and sample them. So yes, Martin, I do believe plastic or artificial hookbaits have a place in the modern day carp angler's armoury, although that said I do prefer to use proper bait as a hookbait.

MC. There's only a few more months left this year, are you planning on any trips abroad before the year is finished?

TP. Yes, I'm off to Rainbow Lake next week for a two-week session. I caught the PB common I mentioned earlier from Raduta, way back in 2001, and my biggest from Rainbow thus far is 67½lbs (common and mirror), so I'm looking forward to the prospect of something over 70lbs eventually, although I know it'll not be easy.

MC. So, you're going to Rainbow Lake in France, home to many big carp. How much bait will you be taking?

TP. Well, I'm in a swim where I don't expect to bag up, although on the other hand there could be numbers of fish turn up and feed. I'll be taking 60kg of bait with me just in case, although I may well bring half that back with me. That's fishing with four rods I might add, but the quantity of bait used will be determined by how well the carp may be feeding. I'll be a little cautious about putting a lot of bait out initially, bearing in mind that it will be a late November session, and then I'll take it from there.

MC. So you'll be fishing one swim for the entire session, you'll not be piling the bait in like some faces have been known to do on some UK venues. If you haven't got carp in your swim you could be twiddling your thumbs!

TP. No, I daren't really. I'm there for two weeks and you can't move swims so I'll gauge things on how well the lake is or isn't fishing. It's 128 acres in size and the carp, like everywhere else, move around a bit so I expect to be twiddling my thumbs for a few of those days, although I'm getting good at that, ha ha!

There was a time that if I woke up in the morning and the bobbins hadn't moved I felt like a failure, but now I accept that time is a factor because of what I want to catch. When you're fishing for big carp, possibly a PB, you have to occupy your mind and simply enjoy being there and hope something turns up. The worst two days are the first two days on a long session because you know that action may be a few days away, but then you get into a rhythm of waiting and doing what's necessary.

MC. How many times have you been to Rainbow Lake?

TP. About 20 times now, over an 8-year period. Rainbow is a phenomenal venue, with an incredible number of big carp and so long as I'm fit enough to keep travelling for my fishing I'll keep returning there!

MC. Well, best of luck Tim. Give me a bell when you get back and let me know how you got on. Thanks for your time in doing this interview and I will email you the text for your approval!

After chatting away about other issues and his trip to France, I once again pointed the van towards home and off I went with my mind buzzing. Tim's library of books is massive and his enthusiasm to pursue massive carp across the globe infectious. When I got home I immediately began to put the words of the interview into print.

Once I'd typed everything up, it was clear to me that most of Tim's fishing has been on the bottom with little in the way of surface fishing, which is understandable, given his interest in the developments of commercial baits. While we had both used some products and ingredients, I'd not used anything from Nutrabaits or Mainline, but then that's not to say I wouldn't use them in the future. The fact is that there are now so many bait companies, it would be impossible for anyone to use them all in one lifetime!

I've read a few of Tim's books, and many of his past articles and editorials in Carpworld, and now having spoken to him a few times over the years I feel he has yet to exploit fully the tactics and philosophy of fishing single hookbaits with elevated attractor levels, although he'll be the first to agree that he knows plenty of anglers who do, mostly during the winter months. It was interesting Tim mentioning enzymes and then linking his age and growing intolerance to lactose. Perhaps this can be linked to the effectiveness of tiger nuts, as some carp may be intolerant to milk products, and Horchata the Spanish beverage is ideal for those with intolerance to milk.

Most of Tim's carp fishing in the last few years has been overseas and with so many large carp around the globe, who can blame him? The buzz of sitting there with the prospect of a monster carp coming along must be immense.

We are both fully aware of chemoreception and the carp's ability to recognise a food source. We also agree that as individuals, bait is just part of the jigsaw, and we have reached a point in time where we simply want to go out fishing and leave the researching and developing to others. The bait buffs among us will be trawling the Internet, perhaps on Wikipedia, while others will be watching X-Factor, and others will be out there in search of the next carp. I do feel that while some synthetic flavours and essential oils have been instrumental in the captures of carp, other attractants and other substances have proven to be more effective.

Over the last 30 years, there have been many bait companies offering anglers their products, and each year a few companies fall by the wayside and a few new companies emerge. There have been some excellent products disappear for one reason or another, which is a shame, but to be fair, part of that comes down to poor or bad management and to some extent the secrecy among those using them. One attractant that springs to mind was called 'Whotsit' from Cotswold Baits, back in the 80s. It wasn't so effective in the summer but devastatingly so in the winter and the colder it got the better it worked. I've no doubt many old-timers can think of something they can't get hold of anymore, not just sex!

I can remember back to a bait I used which was crap, but how did I know it was crap? I used it for a number of sessions and couldn't buy a bite. It was a very cheap base mix with Ylang Ylang essential oil (not Nutrabaits) and it smelt like toilet cleaner. What possessed me to try it I don't know, but it was crap, whether it was down to the wrong recommended level I have no idea, but that went out of the window and straight in the bin.

Really, it made me think; do some of these so-called bait companies actually test their products? It was no small wonder that particular company went down the pan. The base

I had a Red Letter Day at Rainbow in the session Martin refers to, including two 62lb-plus commons in a six-fish catch. A Mainline Mark One snowman fished in a gooey crumbed mix was the successful bed for this gorgeous fish.

mix may have been crap, but with other essential oils such as geranium and bergamot I did manage to catch a few, which points to the importance of a good source of attraction.

While at a show the other week, I was in a conversation with a few anglers and one of them began slagging off a particular bait. His quote of, 'the bait is crap and looks like it's been made from biscuits' did make me think, 'so what if it is? Look at all the carp getting caught on it'. That old adage, 'never judge a book by its cover' can also be applied to bait. Smell and texture may or may not appeal to us; it's the contents and the carp that will determine the results!

Today, we have the Internet and a wealth of information at our fingertips, and this simply wasn't around back in the early 80s so Tim and everyone else learned from printed material and personal experiences. Tim failed to mention during the interview that he'd won a few prestigious carp matches – including two world championships fishing with Steve Briggs – and is very well known in England and overseas, but he's a modest man, a family man, and like most of us has a passion for carp angling and an interest in bait.

Chapter 8
G.S.P
LOCTITE
SUPER GLUE
Precision
GARDNER
COVERT
HOOK TECHNOLOGY
size 6
barbed
size 4
barbed

Rig mechanics

Now just like many of you who have taken the time to read this book, I have read much material in books, magazines, DVDs, Internet websites and forums, regarding rigs and presentation. So, not forgetting the lessons we all learn along the way from our friends and acquaintances while out on the banks, you could say we're at a point in time when most of us are aware of the different rigs in use today; some anglers more than others, but then that's always been the case. Not everyone reads all there is to read on a monthly basis, and some only occasionally read the odd magazine from time to time.

There are a number of ways we can present our hookbaits and we each then test them in the water in different angling situations, hoping that a carp will come along and make a mistake, giving us a clear indication to pick the rod up and deal with it. Just like bait, our individual choices of presentation stem from our previous knowledge and results, so those anglers who catch with some consistency tend to stick to what they have confidence with most of the time, and those not so fortunate search for the answers until something positive happens. The truth is, we are all interested in what works, so all, at times, have to change our presentation to suit the different situations we may encounter.

I have a simple philosophy, which has undoubtedly helped me to catch a fair few carp in the last decade, and that is not to get stuck in the mud and use the same old rigs on every rod, week in week out, year after year, unless I have 100% confidence in the outcome. In essence, it never hurts to experiment or make subtle changes because our results, will reflect the rig's efficiency. The only way to make the most of our time is to use an effective presentation for the venue and its residents, and the question of efficiency can only be answered by using other methods or changing the dimensions or materials used to see if it

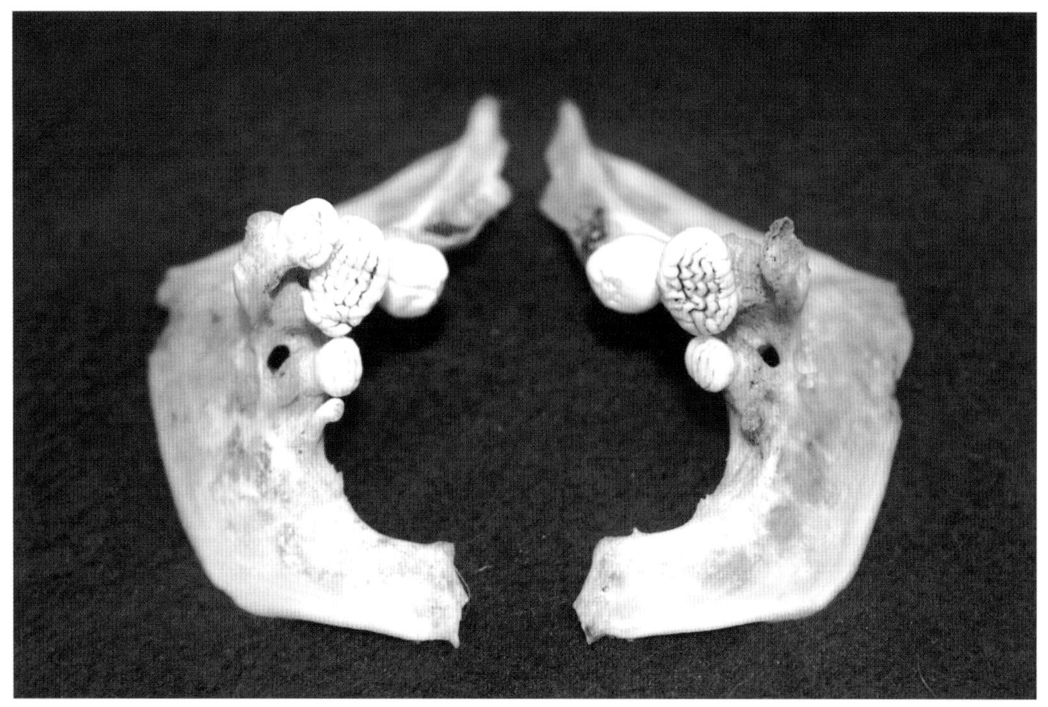

Pharyngeal teeth of deceased 30lb mirror carp.

A 33-pounder on a slip-D with the pop-up over-weighted.

has a positive impact. So, to make any firm conclusions, you have to try something before passing judgment.

Prior to the hair rig, carp fishing was sometimes frustrating because the best option seemed to be a relatively big hook, and baits such as boilies were side-hooked. However, when the original hair rig came along it kick-started a whole new way of presenting a bait, and as a consequence more carp began to visit the bank and carp fishing became a lot easier as the whole hook was exposed rather than most of the hook being hidden in the bait.

The original thinking behind the pioneers of the hair rig was that the carp would suck the bait in, and if they felt it was safe it would then be passed back to the pharyngeal teeth to be crushed, while the hook on the end of the hair would be drawn into their mouths. As the baits were on two-inch-plus hairs and totally unhindered by the rig, the hook would take hold within their mouths and the carp would bolt when they felt resistance, or simply move away from the spot unaware of what was about to happen when the angler responded. It all sounded good in theory, and no doubt it worked, but in practice the real advantage was having a fully-exposed hook.

Something which has held back some old school UK faces is the belief that the hookbait must look and behave like all the freebies. Why? The logical answer is that if the hookbait is indistinguishable among any freebies, then the carp will be tricked into thinking it is safe, and we will catch more carp. From that assumption, anglers fail to see the benefits of using pop-ups. Consequently they stick to using what are loosely termed 'confidence' rigs. Very simple rigs, 300mm to 600mm supple braided hooklinks, hair-rigged, bottom-baited hookbaits identical to the freebies on relatively small hooks, size 6 or smaller. It works for some, I'm sure, but from my observations and results on the venues I fished, once I'd switched my attentions to carp fishing at the start of the 80s, they didn't work out too efficiently for me, other than when using a nylon, multi-strand hooklink.

By the mid-80s, I found something a bit more effective and that was using shorter hooklinks and a one-inch piece of soft silicone tubing on the hook, as some of the lads fishing Savay Lake were doing, which proved extremely effective when using pop-ups. I think they called it the Looney extension rig. Around this point in time, Jim Gibbinson revealed his line-aligner rig which had the hooklink exiting from the inside edge of the tubing, which helped spin the hook over and improve the hooking efficiency. Indeed it did, and was a positive step forward in rig mechanics.

At the end of the 80s, whilst fishing Harefield Lake with a few mates, a pike angler fishing Broadwater Lake behind us, on the causeway, showed me some shrink tubing he used. Straight away, it didn't look too dissimilar to the silicone tubing I was using and I soon found a little space in my tackle box to store some.

Once again, while fishing on Harefield the following year, someone showed me the curved hook rig, which if I'm not wrong was developed by an angler who fished Longfield Lake.

Within minutes of seeing the size 1 curved hooks I'd found a piece of waste pipe to use to create a curve in the shrink tubing, without burning my fingers holding it over a steaming kettle spout. Now my curved Looney rigs looked the part and thankfully, they worked a treat.

Within a few years of fishing in the Colne Valley and having witnessed, and caught, a fair number of carp on rigs which were almost the complete opposite to confidence rigs, a few of us realised how inefficient some rigs can be. I'm not implying that inefficient rigs will not catch carp, they do, but when an improvement or different presentation receives more action, it does make you think of how many times a hookbait can enter and exit the mouth of a carp before the rig actually does what it was intended to do.

Our concern should be what we can do to improve the hooking ratio because even a small percentage of improvement could make the difference between a blank or a result. At the very least, then, a small improvement should equate to a few extra carp gracing our nets each year, and fewer blank periods. Even shortening or lengthening your hooklink an inch can have a bearing on the outcome.

As said elsewhere, we're all individuals, fishing for different carp in different venues, but the majority of us will find a rig or method of presentation that produces action and then proceed to use it everywhere, searching for spots to suit the rigs because we have gained some confidence. The typical consequence of this is, the angler either froths the water to a foam searching for the cleanest spots, or casts out hoping something will happen before it's time to wind the rods in and go home. The natural progression of most of us then leads us to modify our presentation when we feel the need, perhaps through losing fish or simply looking to improve results.

Just as with baits, the choices of materials open to us is vast if you take into account all the hooks and hooklink materials available today from companies like ESP, Fox, Gardner, Korda, Kryston or Nash, to name just a few who've accounted for the bulk of terminal tackle sales in the UK over the last decade. We can make small changes or radical changes, the end game being that more carp, or the ones at the top of our lists, come our way.

Any improvements we make should equate to more action and the only way to find out is to put them to the test, i.e. use them long enough to make any comparisons. It's probably easier to test things when using multiple rods because with one rod it can be difficult to make comparisons, though it's not impossible, because often you can be watching it work, or not.

I'm always thinking about rigs; most of us are, so don't think you're alone. When we feel confident in what we're doing and getting a fair return on the hours we fish, then we carry on catching. If, on the other hand, we feel the need to experiment or feel we're not getting enough pick-ups or perhaps the carp are getting away with it, then something needs changing to bring the 'carp to rod hours' ratio down to an acceptable level.

Hooks

Carp hooks, come in all shapes and sizes and we all tend to find a few favourites, perhaps different patterns or sizes for different applications.

If we first talk about size, which is determined on the size of the hook's gape, then the ideal is the one which works the best for you in the situations you find yourself in on that particular venue. I don't subscribe to the theory that a smaller hook will produce more takes, although I can see the logic that a smaller hook should be less detectable because it's obviously smaller and lighter than the next size up.

Whichever hook size or pattern we use it must be strong enough to handle the carp we're fishing for, wherever we may be. Every time I tie up a rig I always check the hooks for possible defects and every time it is used, I will ensure that the point is sharp; the sharper the better! If it pricks the skin on the back of a finger with the lightest of touches and looks fine under a magnifying lens, it gets used. If it doesn't, then the point will either be honed with a specialist file or consigned to the bin. It never hurts to check the eye closure from the packet to make sure it's closed fully and has no sharp edges, and although most hooks these days are normally fine, you may encounter some dodgy ones.

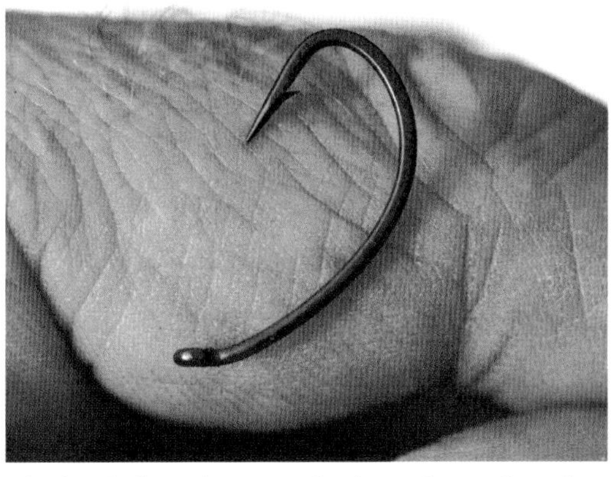

If a hook does this straight from the packet, then it's sharp enough to catch something.

The design and gape of the hook is the business end of the rig and, along with the rig's dimensions, will determine how much flesh is grabbed, which then technically determines the quality of hookhold. A good hook hold usually ensures a happy ending while a poor one normally results in them falling off.

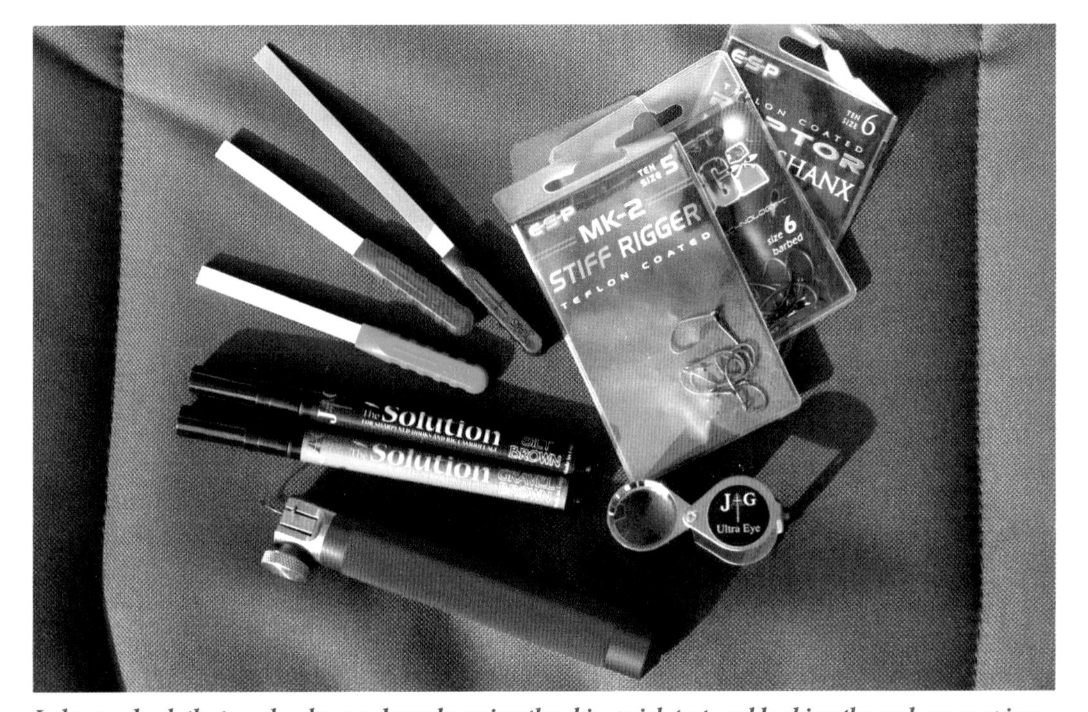

I always check that my hooks are sharp by using the skin-prick test and looking through an eyepiece.

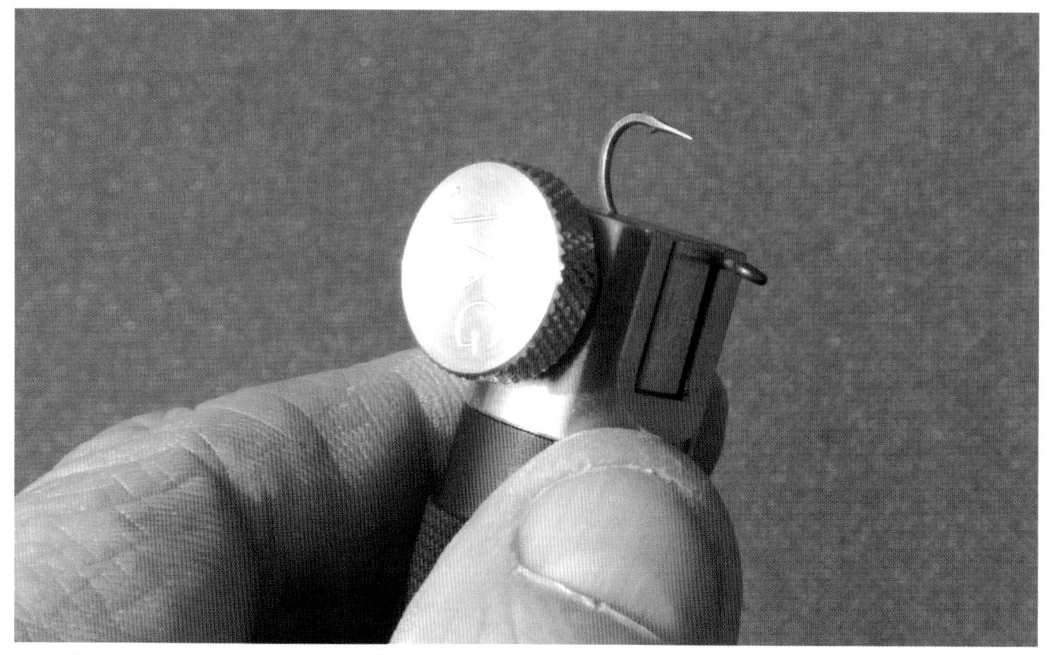

A JAG vice is a very handy piece of kit for sharpening hooks.

You know when your rigs are working; you always return home with a wet net.

There has to be a limit on what is too big or too small, but where is that limit? The answer should be determined by the size of the carp you're likely to encounter, but in reality there has to be some significance to the size of hookbait and the length and type of hooklink material. Over the years, I've used many different hooks, the biggest being size 1 Kamasans B940 and B940s with a slightly shorter shank, and the smallest size 8 ESP Big-Ts. However, I have witnessed carp captures on hooks as big as 2/0 and as small size 10.

There have been times in the past when all I'd use were 2s or 4s, with just as many times when it would be 5s or 6s. So, if you're using hooks smaller than size 6 and wondering if you'd get more bites with a bigger hook, trust me, if the rig is good and they want that bait they'll not notice the difference until it's too late. Having caught a fair number of carp on the larger hooks, or hooks with tubing, during the colder months, when others have been struggling, then I'm led to believe scaling down end tackle during the winter is a counterproductive measure.

The bigger the gape the greater opportunity for the hook point to take hold and be more effective. I would assume that most of us settle for something in the middle, or what works best, if we're totally happy with the hook. The fact that some of us use silicone or shrink tubing, or even stiff mono, to me only reinforces my belief that everything gets sampled and the tubing is technically creating a larger hook, albeit lighter due to the fact that most shrink tubing floats on its own.

One gripe I do have with some hook suppliers is the sizing. If you took the time to take a micrometer to all the hooks available and measured their gapes, there seems to be some discrepancy between suppliers. I've seen 6s the size of 4s, and 4s the size of 2s, so don't assume all size 6s have identical gapes. Why don't they print the measurements in millimetres?

This low-30 fell to a slip-D rig with two 14mm boilies and a No.1 shot hidden between the two baits.

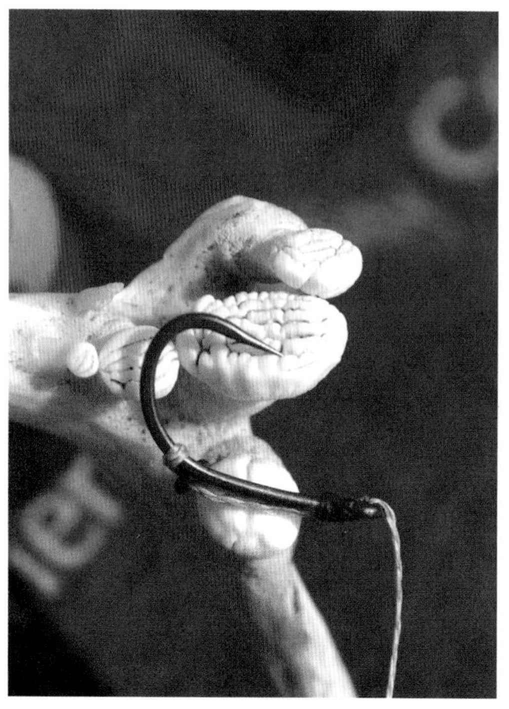

Just by looking at the main tooth you can see how hook points can get damaged.

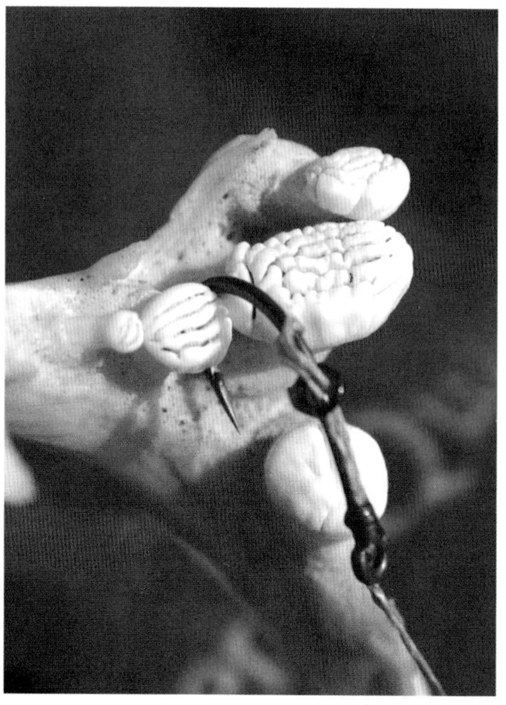

It's even feasable that a hook could temporarily lodge between teeth.

Mid-30 on an over weighted double boilie and slip-D rig.

Straight points or in-turned points? I could easily say that so long as it's sharp the difference is minimal, but in all honesty I think straight points may possibly have the edge in initial hooking potential. In-turned points have the edge in reliability, though, i.e. not so many fall off during the fight.

My preference is straight points for most of my fishing, and I only use in-turned patterns if I encounter problems, or when the situation may require a fair amount of rod pressure. I have had the occasional straight-pointed hook open out but I've never had that happen with any in-turned pointed hooks. Recollecting my thoughts over a long time span, I have encountered a problem with a packet of hooks and having two hooks snap on me in one session. Are these problems down to the odd batch being tempered differently during the manufacturing process? Your guess is as good as mine; or is this down to where the hook point takes hold within the mouth of the carp?

On the occasions when a hook has opened out, majority have been landed with not many falling off, although it must be said that on some fisheries there are a few carp with damaged mouths so these could be the ones more likely to fall off, regardless of whether the hook keeps its shape.

It was probably early 80s when I also started turning the eyes in at a slight angle, using some forceps on my hooks to see if it improved hookholds, and it did. Many manufacturers now supply hooks with straight and slightly in-turned eyes, which is great because this means all I have to do is select whichever pattern I choose to use and not have to start bending them to suit my needs. In my tackle box I have ESP, Korda and Gardner hooks, and I do like them all, but I really like the Gardner Covert range since trying them out when they first hit the tackle shop shelves.

One thing I have noted over the years is, while fishing hooklinks longer than 100mm, apart from the odd hook opening out, there has been the occasional time the hook point has shown signs of damage with the point burred over. Now, I'm sure the odd hook may have got damaged while pulling back on gravel or on retrieval, but I've had it happen in the edge while fishing without pulling back after casting out, in areas such as clay, sand and silt, with no gravel or stones present.

It could be argued that damage may occur if the carp flash their flanks on the bait, and possibly your rig, or that the carp may be munching on a snail or mussel at the same time as your hookbait, all possible theories. Personally, I think the damage is done by the carp, or more to the point, their pharyngeal teeth, which is what they use to crush all their food. It's very feasible that a carp could take a hookbait back to its teeth, crunch down on the hook then either eject the hookbait, or possibly bolt, or shake it's head, and by pure chance the hook point takes hold sufficiently to at least land the carp. With short hooklinks, and when using tubing on the hooks this doesn't seem to happen, so perhaps blunted hooks or disappearing hookbaits could simply be down to the pharyngeal teeth.

Bait attachment

As carp fishing evolved from bread, soft baits, paste baits and side hooking, on to the more commonly used methods of today, we still rely on a hook and a bait. Thankfully, we have a few options open to us on how we go about attaching baits and ultimately, this will affect the rig's efficiency.

There were great debates, soon after the hair rig became common knowledge in the British carp scene, mainly over whether the hair was best coming from the bend of the hook or from the shank adjacent to the barb, soon to be followed by the hair from near the eye of the hook. There was only one way to find out!

Even though the session I'm going to relay to you now was over 30 years ago now, I can remember it as if it were yesterday. I was fishing Vauxhall Angling Club's Woburn Sands venue, mid-June and opening week of the season, in a swim I'd nicknamed the 'Theatre' because you could view the carp feeding in the clear water in the margins from the high bank with your silhouette disguised by the trees behind. Conditions seemed perfect for the swim with a light wind gently blowing straight into that corner of the lake.

Armed with two rods and two hair-rigged, single bottom-bait boilies I swung the rigs into position just a rod length out in about eight feet of water and scattered a couple of handfuls of freebies over the top, before slackening the lines so they weren't so obvious. I had 300mm hooklinks, which were Black Spider, not the least inconspicuous hooklink for a clay bottom but there wasn't much else on offer in those days, before someone put me on to something better; one rod with a two-inch hair from the bend the other a two-inch hair from the shank.

A couple of hours after setting the trap, a couple of carp came along and after circling the swim a few times they dropped down and began to feed. Ten minutes later they were joined by another two carp, then another three, then another one, this was now looking really positive. Suddenly, one bolted and as it swam off, my spool started spinning so I quickly got hold of the rod, cupped the spool with one hand and struck lightly, expecting the rod to hoop over. Result thin air; no carp and no bait.

As I tied on another bait, the remaining rod rattled off with the same result of another fresh air strike and no carp. I couldn't fathom out what was happening and with carp still showing an interest in the bait, all I wanted to do was get my rigs back in the water as quickly as possible.

Back went the same rigs, followed by another handful of boilies, and after an hour I had at least five carp feeding before one of the Optonics signalled another run; same result as before - fresh air and no carp. Clearly, it was time for head scratching, convinced that I might have had one if I'd stuck to side-hooking boilies.

I just thought that the hairs were too long so I re-tied some fresh rigs, this time with one-inch hairs, and swung them back into position with another handful of boilies. Two or three hours passed by as I watched three to five carp feeding on my bait, then the right-hand rod rattled off, with another poxy fresh air job. This was now becoming a bad joke, and as before, while my back was turned sorting out another rig, my left-hand rod roared off. This time, however, there was a connection, but only for a second. Good job I had plenty of hair back then because I was pulling it out, literally!

I didn't fish during the night for a few reasons; one, I was mentally destroyed. Two, I didn't want to lose any more, and three, I felt confident more chances would come my way the following day. A quick trip to the fish and chip shop in the local village for some supper and over many mugs of tea back on the lake, yours truly pondered on what had happened and how I was going to rectify the situation the next day. They obviously wanted the bait!

In the morning, after having tied on some one-inch hairs again, the rigs were lowered down on the shelf a rod length out, followed by a handful of boilies, this time though with 375mm hooklinks. A couple of hours later, I looked down on the spot and three carp were showing signs of feeding. Every now and then, one would tip up and feed, head down tail up, with its pectoral fins fanning as if to keep balance. Half an hour went by and then the left-hand Optonic went into a one-toner. Paranoid about striking, I simply held the rod and cupped the spool until it stopped spinning and just when my brain thought I was connected, off it came, leaving me to reel in sweet FA yet again.

While waiting for things to develop, before I had the first take of the day, I'd tied up a couple of rigs with half-inch hairs from the shank. They looked okay, but I had no idea if they'd work so in came the other rod, and I replaced both rods back on the dinner plate, 300mm hooklinks now with a size 6 hook instead of a size 8. Two more chances came my way over the next four hours, and both mirrors of 17lbs and 19lbs were happily photographed.

Within a year, the Woburn carp were showing signs of avoiding the Black Spider hooklink material and on a trip to Stanton Harcourt in Oxfordshire, a couple of chaps showed me what they were using; three strands of 3lb mono. When this was used at Woburn Sands the following year I became a legend in my own lunchtime, which I'll touch on when I talk about hooklinks, but what was exciting was being able to watch carp feed in a few swims just a rod length out, not just in the summer but throughout the whole year. Little did I know it at the time but it would be another 20 years before I tried long hairs again, partly due to the results I was having, and those on the horizon. A couple of years watching and catching Woburn carp was a massive learning curve for me, and a few others, because on venues with poor visibility those observations weren't possible and it felt like a day spent there was comparable to a dozen days, or more simply sitting behind rods unaware of what was occurring.

After a few years, it became apparent that while slack-lining improved the situation, the materials and dimensions of the rigs were crucial. The method of bait attachment changed after one particular session while using a whipping knot normally used for spade-end hooks and mono, albeit with eyed hooks. I wanted to simplify things and use the tag end of the hooklink to form the hair for bait attachment. Sitting there on the bed chair, under my brolly and Nash overwrap, with half the contents of my tackle box spread out, I stumbled on an adaptation of the whipping knot shown to me many years ago by my dad, and a knotless knot was formed.

At the time it was called the knot with no name; it was someone else who called it the knotless knot a few years later.At that time, I didn't think for one minute that it would become such a popular knot. All I wanted was to use a small hair using the same material as the hooklink, with just a 5mm to 10mm gap between bait and hook. Having the knot on the hook shank rather than below the eye, as with the more conventional knots I was aware off, also had its benefits, from the days when my father and I used spade-end hooks.

Standard knotless knot rigs.

Ring on the shank rig.

Black Eye at 35lbs fell to a dumbell hookbait on a slip-D rig.

The next step for me was zero-length hairs. At the end of the 80s and into the start of the 90s, a few anglers, including me, began to play around with rigs, using small rings sliding along the hook shank as a method of attaching baits, simply tying the bait to the ring with dental floss, or using the actual hooklink material for bait attachment.

I also came up with another similar method but didn't fully realise its efficiency for a few years, for some reason, but this may have been down to an experimental bait I was using at the time. After a few years and some trials while fishing Harefield, I felt confident that the sliding ring method was something worth persevering with as a number of decent carp began to come my way. At the time, though, this could have been put down to good angling because I didn't think the rig was anything special. I didn't leave any hanging in the butt rings whenever I left my swim to go to the shops or pub, after being warned about the habits of some of the other anglers in the syndicate.

For a period I had a fair amount of confidence with the standard sliding ring rig until one particular frustrating session on a Berkshire venue that had seen it all, where the pressured carp were known to subject baits to individual inspection, perhaps more so with boilies. Thankfully, almost every time I used the slip-D method, something normally happened, so I kept it under wraps for the future until I could give it a proper testing, two trusted close friends were shown how to tie the rig but only one of them benefited from using it, the other got stuck in the mud, to be fair.

After the publication of Strictly Carp in 2001, I've stuck to a rig-testing attitude of having something slightly different on each rod while fishing. Now, it could have been beneficial to have identical rigs on all rods, but then I couldn't make true comparisons. A frequent example would be to have one rod with a standard knotless knot rig, a sliding ring on the shank on another rod and the slip-D rig on another. Over the course of time, testing with bottom baits and pop-ups, it has transpired from looking at my records that the slip-D was 50% more effective on two venues fished, and 100% more effective on another couple of venues. My results at Elstow, in my last few years at that venue, and at others where used, have confirmed it works, and works well with bottom baits and pop-ups!

I believe it has the edge simply because the hookbait acts more independently. The ring, which is used to attach the bait, is not connected to the shank of the hook and this allows more free movement and separation of the hook and bait. When the carp has the hookbait in its mouth, and if the carp ejects the bait, it doesn't blow the hook out along with it so easily, because the D created with the soft braid collapses and the bait and hook separation is increased.

The step-by-step images and relevant text describing various rigs will show how they are constructed, although many are now becoming viewable on websites such as YouTube. You can watch me tie the slip-D rig; simply type in Richworth100 on YouTube and you'll see. I may well do other things on YouTube in the future, or for other companies or websites. I've shown other anglers this rig over the last few years; those who have used it have had their scepticism wiped clean, with a number of fine carp gracing their nets while other rods lay idle.

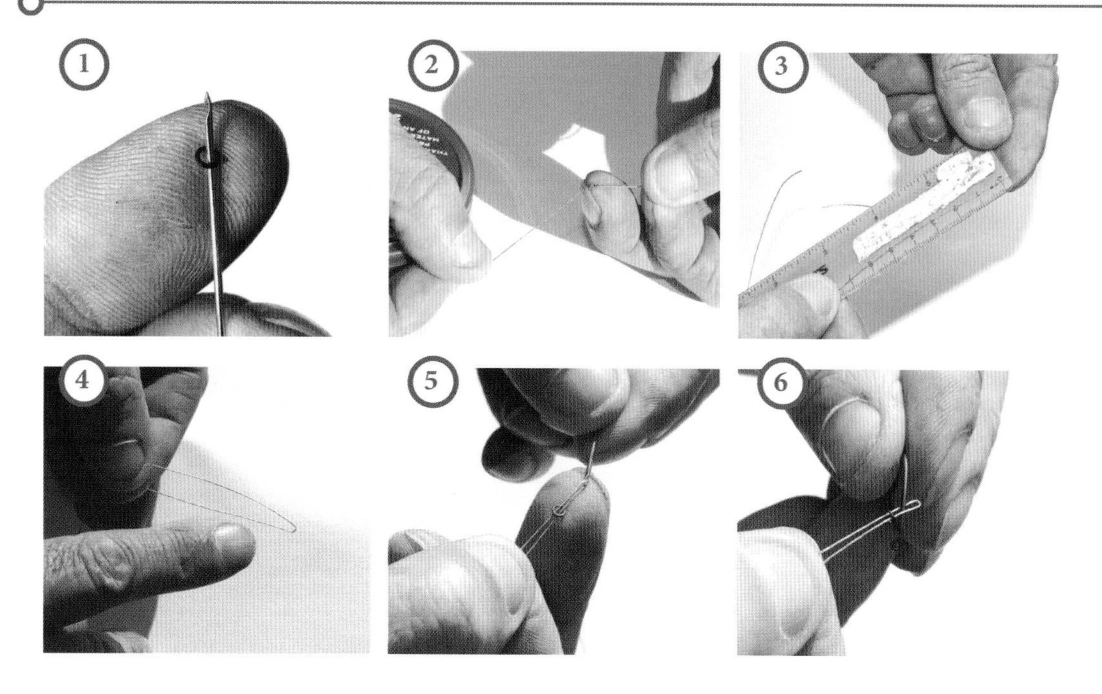

Tying slip-D rig using coated braid hooklink

1. Once you are happy with the hook you have selected, begin the rig tying process by sliding a 3mm rig ring onto a baiting needle and put to one side. You could do it further on but it makes things easier and quicker if done first.
2. Remove 150mm of the coating from your coated braid and then cut the entire hooklink allowing around 75mm for swivel attachment, and assuming you want to have about 25mm of stripped section below the hook, then take this into consideration. You could cut your hooklink longer than need be on your first attempt so you can see exactly how much wastage there is, cut it too short and you may have to scrap your first attempt at tying the slip-D rig.
3. From the point at which the hooklink coating has been stripped, hold this on a ruler at 75mm and then fold the uncoated section over the end of the ruler. Depending on what hook you use and the critical differences you want to have once the hook is tied on, then this dimension can be altered to suit.
4. By folding the uncoated braid over the edge of the ruler, you create a crease in the material which forms a loop in the braid at a measured distance from the point at which the coating has been stripped off. Failing to measure will mean you are guessing, which is fine if using a supple braid for your entire hooklink, but doesn't ensure consistent accuracy when making rigs with coated braids.
5. Hold the uncoated looped end between finger and thumb with a gap of a few millimetres and then pick up your baiting needle, hitch onto the loop at the crease, and then transfer the rig ring onto the loop.

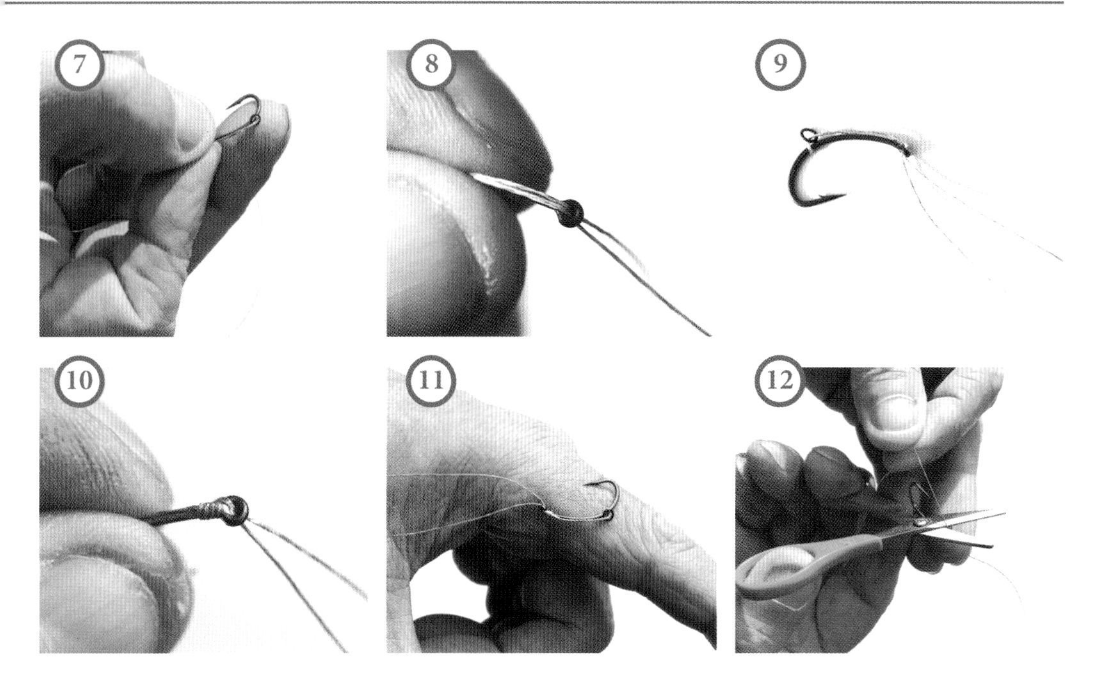

6. With the hooklink and loop in one hand and your hook in the other, place your hook into the end of loop, eye first, and then pinch your fingers together holding the hook, loop and rig ring roughly in their finished position.
7. My preferred position of the rig ring is roughly opposite the barb on the hook, or just a few millimetres higher toward the bend of the hook.
8. With the rig ring and loop trapped between finger and thumb, push the tag end through the back of the eye of the hook, and then the longer hooklink through the back of the eye. The two strands of uncoated braid between rig ring and the eye of the hook, which forms the D, should run parallel with the shank of the hook and should not be crossed over each other.
9. If you lay the materials down on a sheet of paper at this stage, then this is what it should look like. The shorter tag end should exit the eye of the hook on the same side as the hook eye closure, with the much longer hooklink exiting on the opposite side of it.
10. Whether you're left-handed or right-handed it doesn't really matter so long as when you next tie a four-turn knotless knot you start whipping the knot in a direction starting on the opposite side to the hook eye closure. After four turns pass the hooklink through the back of the eye so it exits on the inside of the hook eye and then tighten down the knot.
11. This is how it should look at this stage with the rig ring running freely on the D created with the uncoated supple braid.
12. Trim off the short tag end as tight to the eye of the hook as you possibly can, with some sharp braid scissors or a very sharp blade. Ensure that you only cut the tag end and don't damage the actual hooklink.

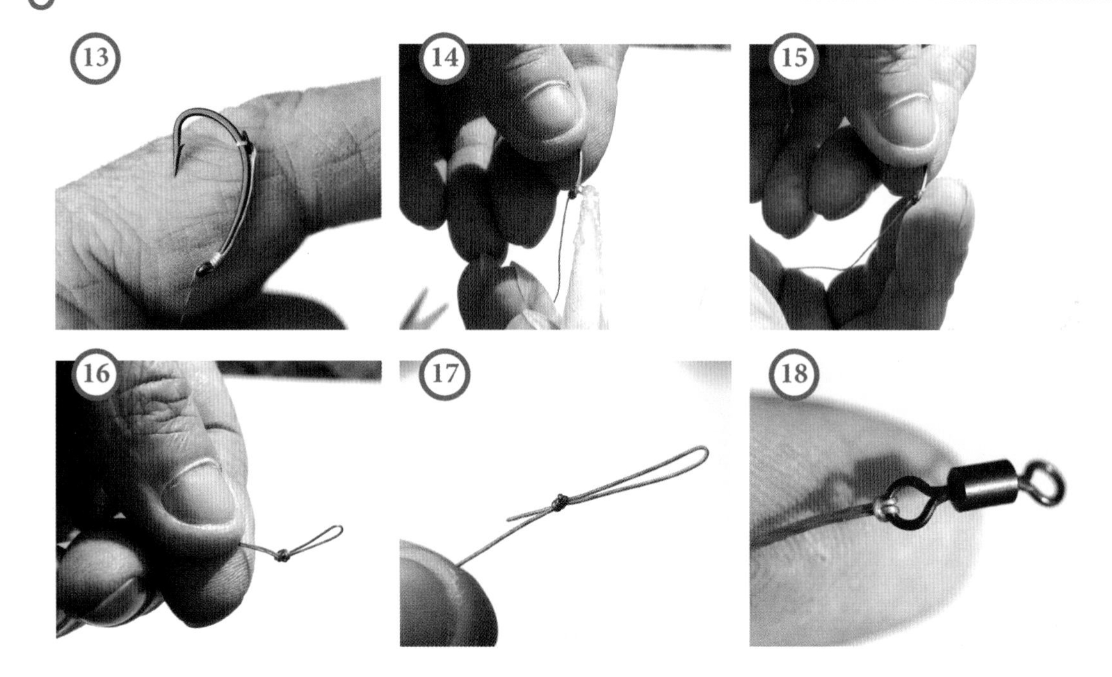

13. This is how your slip-D rig should be looking now. If you want to incorporate any shrink tubing to the rig then do so at this stage.
14. Just to ensure that the knotless knot doesn't loosen on any rigs without tubing, I like to dab the knot with a tiny amount of Superglue.
15. You only want the glue to bind the whipped knot together, nothing else, so don't let any dribble onto the slip-D or below the eye of the hook onto the hooklink. Take off any excess glue immediately after applying with a finger and wipe on a damp rag.
16. With the hook end of the rig done, now form a 20mm loop in the other end of your hooklink, at your chosen length, using a simple overhand knot. Some coated braids may require a different knot, such as a double overhand knot, or you could tie on a swivel with your own preferred method if you don't fancy my way.
17. Wet the knot with saliva and tighten down with reasonable hand pressure and then trim off the tag end 5mm from knot.
18. Push the loop through the eye on one end of a swivel and pass the loop over the swivel, then holding the swivel in one hand and the hooklink in the other, slowly tighten down so it looks like this. Very simple and quick.
19. This is then the finished end of the rig. Now store on a suitable rig board or attach straight away to one of your fishing rods ready for your next session. To attach hookbaits I recommend ESP Super floss.
20. When tying hookbaits to the rig ring, cut a 100mm to 150mm length of floss and pass it through the rig ring and double it up. Pierce your hookbait through the middle, pull the doubled-up floss back through the hookbait, and then tie on your bait stop with a few overhand knots. Trim off leaving 5mm tag ends so these can be burned down carefully using the flame on a lighter.

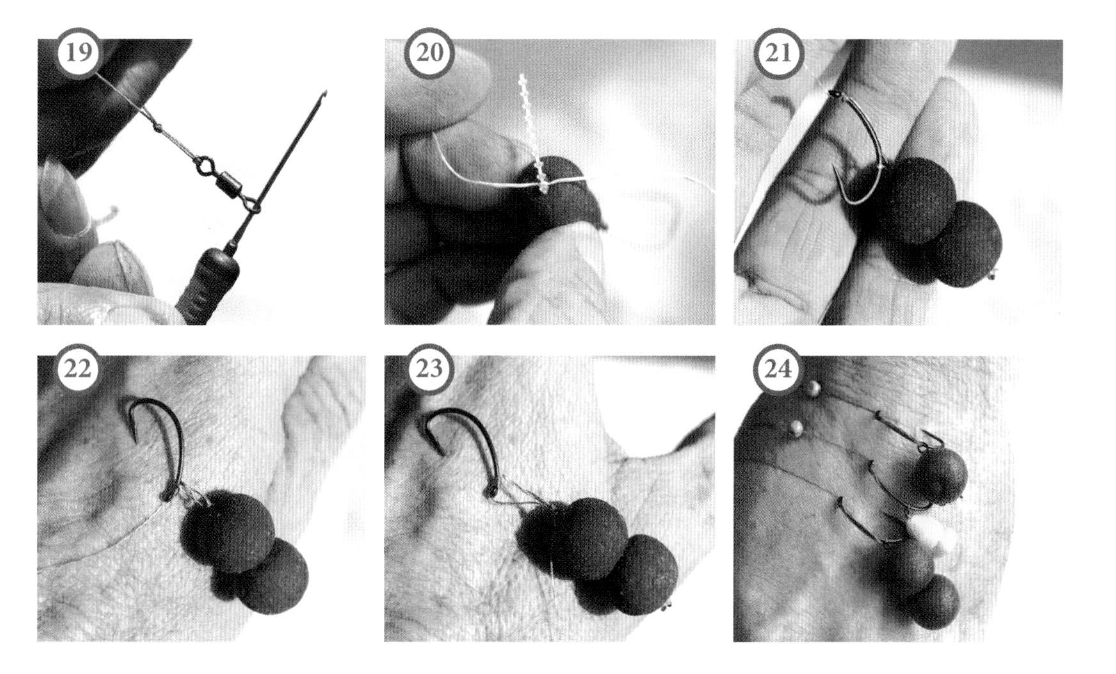

21. This is how a slip-D rig with a double boilie looks. Hookbait choices are optional; if they want your bait then this rig will work very efficiently.
22. This image shows that with supple braid the D-shape can slip and collapse easily and because the ring isn't running on the hook shank it can separate when the carp decide to give hookbaits the suck-and-blow treatment.
23. This image shows just how far the hookbait can travel away from the hook point, completely different to the 'rig ring on the shank of the hook' type rigs.
24. This image is what I had on my last session out using three rods; exactly the same rigs just with different hookbait presentations, and all having previously captured many fine carp for me and some of my friends, from different venues!

Hookbaits

Once again, we have a choice, from a standard pop-up or bottom bait to multiple baits, cocktails, and other alternatives, such as over-weighted bottom baits, over-weighted pop-ups, critically balanced baits, both bottom baits and pop-ups, snowman-style or custom-made baits such as wafters, as my mate, Tim Childs, calls them.

Which is best? Three simple words that roll off the tongue to which the simple answer would be, whatever works best! I've probably caught an equal amount of carp on bottom baits as I have with pop-ups, but I'll not use the same on all the rods until it's obvious something works better than other alternatives.

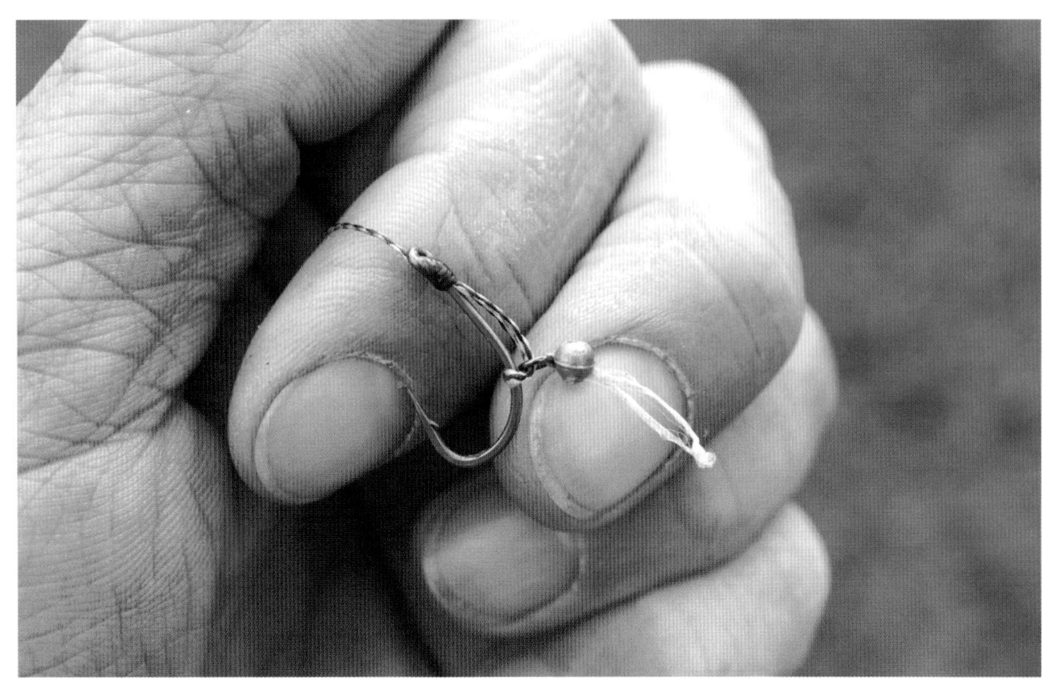

With the appropriate split shot on floss before mounting the pop-up, you can allow the weight of the hook to sink the hookbait.

Pop-ups can be fished at various heights from the bottom from just hovering above the hook on the bottom, to a more familiar couple of inches off the bottom, to straight up off the lead, or leadcore, or main line if fishing a helicopter style.

They can be critically balanced, only using sufficient counterbalance to sink them, or they can be fished over-weighted by using a counterbalance heavy enough to pin them down. A good example of overweighting would be; a No.4 shot would critically balance the pop-up, a No.4 shot plus a BB shot would pin it down harder. Why over-weight? Well, the logic is that an over-weighted pop-up is less likely to waft around when you have a few carp feeding and creating water movement with their fins. The rigs also react more efficiently because the heavier counterbalance has a greater effect due to the extra density.

On a clean lakebed, I normally fish a pop-up 30mm to 50mm off the bottom, over-weighted. On silt, normally critically balanced 40mm, or 60mm over-weighted. On weed, 40mm to 80mm critically balanced with a hooklink long enough not to drag the hookbait down into the weed.

When fishing a hookbait on the bottom, I'm a bit lazy. I'll either cadge a few wafters off a friend or use the same as the freebies, standard or over-weighted. I'll leave Tim Childs to talk about wafters because he has far more experience in this department than me. Standard bottom baits work well for me, especially double bottom baits. Over-weighting them with a split shot hidden in between the two baits is another alternative which also works; don't ask me how or why but it does well on clean spots and venues that have been flogged to death with more conventional presentations.

Hooklinks

Our choices of hooklink materials are fairly straightforward, although the variety of specific materials is growing year on year. It's probably fair to say that a few years back Kryston products were in most carp anglers' armoury of hooklink materials and still supply a range many are happy to use, but now, after a decade of many developments, we have a few companies supplying quality products which also serve our purposes admirably.

Generally, our hooklinks fit into three or four categories, soft/supple, semi-stiff/supple, stiff, or in combination. Some rigs require certain components to function as intended and if you rely on just one material, then chances are you're fishing just one venue in areas which never change, possibly with one type of rig.

The reason there are so many different materials, with their individual characteristics, is for optimum performance in different situations, with reliability as a criterion when dealing with big, powerful carp.

It's true we can only exert a certain amount of pressure on a rod while playing a carp, and therefore a limited amount of strain on the hooklink, but there is no great need to use materials which may get us more bites at the expense of unnecessary losses. Perhaps it's market forces which now dictate that the most popular brands sold have a stated breaking strain of 15lbs, which suits me and the stamp of carp I've been catching and hope to catch in the future if I ever manage to finish this book. Thinner materials should technically be less detectable to the carp, which you sometimes notice while floater fishing, but when it comes down to catching them on or near the bottom, the actual length and type of hooklink material is more important than a few thousandths of an inch in diameter.

One of my favourite hooklink materials over the last decade.

There was once a belief that carp suck baits, including boilies, into their mouths from as much as 150mm away. Now, this may be possible with baits which sink very slowly, but in the numerous situations in which I've observed carp feeding at very close quarters, from doubles to 40s, I've never seen this or anything close to it, leading me to believe it's an old wives' tale. I've also studied DVDs and video footage of decent-sized carp feeding and still not seen them sucking in baits from 150mm away.

Now, I have seen carp sucking in baits from as much as 50mm distance but the vast majority are either sucking from between zero and 25mm away from the bait, or extending their lips over the bait and sucking in, or mouthing the bottom, like pigs sniffing for truffles. Please excuse my terminology.

If my eyes are deceiving me and carp are sucking in food items from more than 50mm distance, then can someone explain how carp are caught using pop-ups straight up from the lead, as with zig rigs, chod rigs, over-weighted bottom and pop-up rigs? All of these have a limited upward movement, and all behave very differently to any unattached freebies. At the critical moment when our hook enters the mouth of a carp, the fish will do one of two things; move sufficient distance so that it either hooks itself, or the hook falls out. The latter could happen because the carp blows the hookbait out, realising it's not safe, or possibly due to a testing reflex action, which again could result in the hook point failing to find something to dig into on the way out.

Depending on the rig's efficiency or dimensions, then this moment in which they move with the hookbait within their mouths could be as little as 25mm or as much as double the

I've lost count of the numbers of carp which have fallen to the slip-D rigs.

length of the hooklink itself, however long that may be. While using bottom baits, and some pop-up rigs, then it is always possible a carp could pick up the hookbait and move back over your lead, or toward it, and we'd be none the wiser because the lead weight has not come into play.

A long hooklink gives the carp far more freedom and opportunity to eject a hookbait than a shorter one, so it's in our interest to find the optimum length to increase our chances and minimise the possibility of ejection.

Once again, I find that any major changes I make will either have an adverse or a positive effect, unless I'm already fishing with something I'm 100% confident with in familiar situations. For example, if I'm fishing a swim I haven't fished before, then I don't automatically use identical rigs on all rods.

Even though I will select a method of presenting a hookbait that I think suits the situation, in my eyes nothing is guaranteed to succeed until a carp actually goes into the landing net. Good rigs catch carp. Crap rigs occasionally work but don't catch as many carp as good rigs; simples!

What normally happens with fishing for carp is that a particular rig receives more action, and over time and analysis, I hope to arrive at something in which I have 100% confidence. Please bear in mind, I often fish just day sessions or two or three-nighters and therefore I'm not fishing full-time on one big session, only breaking away from the water to get supplies and have a shower. This learning process, depending on the venue, could take between 24 to 48 hours on an easy water, or half a dozen sessions on a harder one, and possibly longer. As we know, other factors often have a bearing on our results.

I had to chuckle one day at Harefield as I watched through binoculars a new member scrutinise my rigs. I was on the opposite bank having a brew with a friend when the angler, seeing that I wasn't there, went right up to my rigs, which were hanging in the butt rings, and eyeballed them from a foot away, bending down for a better look. If he'd touched them I would have said something to him later, but he didn't, so I let it ride.

Had he touched them, he may have learned something, not just the knotless knot under the tubing which covered the knot, but half the supple braid hooklink was, in fact, stiff with three or four applications of Superglue to stiffen it up and to help alleviate tangles. There were no coated braids around at the time.

On venues that receive a fair amount of angling pressure it can be argued that the carp, develop rig awareness after repeated captures, and as a consequence, they feed on anglers' baits and avoid capture as they feed more cautiously, or feed more positively because they feel they can eject the foreign objects they encounter on a daily basis. Now, this could happen if everyone was doing the same, all using the same bait, all fishing effectively, but does this really happen in the real world when on many venues half of the lake is devoid of carp because they're feeding on the other bank, or on the surface, or in mid-water?

On a clean, hard, weed-free bottom, the length of my hooklink could range between 100mm to 225mm depending on the material used and lead set-up. I have used shorter and I've also used longer in the past. Over these last few years, I've been using coated

An MCF spring-loaded rig board ensures that coated braid and mono hooklinks are perfectly straight when it's time to put a new rig on.

braids, such as ESP Two Tone Stripteaze or Gardner's Chod Skin, between 150mm and 200mm, to good effect. On short weed or silt, I use supple braid such as ESP's Sinklink or Gardner Sink Skin between 175mm to 275mm; longer weed between 300mm and 600mm. Zig rigs could be anything from 600mm to 3m, usually 10lb Drennan Double Strength, in deep water, then the adjustable zig rigs are the way forward. Chod rigs, which I have only used a few times, have been between 30mm and 60mm. I don't fish in thick weedbeds where it's a struggle to retrieve tackle, let alone a hooked carp.

The multi-strand mono hooklink which I was shown way back in the 80s, and still use occasionally, is really easy to tie once you've given it a go. All you need is three or four strands of 3lb or 4lb mono that the match anglers use, such as Silstar Match or Reflo Powerline from Preston Innovations. The choice is yours as to how many strands and what breaking strain you use and you should take into account the size of the carp you're fishing for, so long as they are all the same. Start off by cutting the strands about ten inches longer than your desired length of hooklink. Then hold them together at one end and tie a simple granny knot.

Next step is to run them through your mouth, to coat them with saliva so they temporarily bond together. Once wet, tie another granny knot in the other end. At this point all the strands should be exactly the same length, if they are not then start again; the trick is to make sure the strands stay wet with saliva so they act as one.

Once you're satisfied with the multi-strand, tie your hook on with whichever knot you prefer, but remember to keep the strands wet at all times. If the strands are not the same length after tying your hook on, don't worry; simply cut the knot on the free end and tie another granny knot, simply tie on your swivel and you're good to go. So long as all the strands are the same length there should be no problems. Like anything, you get better with practice so don't dismiss it if you make a cock-up on your first attempt, as I did.

The advantage of the light mono multi-strand is, it's virtually invisible in the water and unlike some braids which are quite rough when you pull some through your lips, which are very sensitive just as with the carp, the wet light mono is hardly detectable. Guaranteed to outwit even the craftiest of carp!

Leads, set-up and weights

The lead arrangement or set-up we'll use is almost the final part of rig presentation to look at and, once again, we carp anglers are faced with a few options; different weights, shapes, colours or textures, in-line or those with swivels or rings, or even drop-off leads. Now if Harry Hill from TV Burp walked into a tackle shop at this point he'd say, '...but which is best?' Followed by, 'There's only one way to find out. Fight!'

Just like hooks and hooklinks, lead choice is important because one size, shape or style of lead may not be the best option for every conceivable application we may encounter. For every angler who swears by using a light lead there'll be another who favours a heavier lead, and then there'll be those who'll be using an in-line lead and others using a lead clip set-up or a helicopter rig.

Judging by what I see others using, when casting out, I can only assume I'm not alone with favouring the lead clip system for the bulk of my fishing on the venues were I've spent many hours. Looking back through my little black books, though, it shows that my captures using lead clips would be 50%, 40% in-line leads, 5% helicopter set-ups, with the remainder either on running leads or drop-off leads. I've no doubt everyone finds something they feel does what they want, but as with everything there can be times when a different lead, weight or set-up, could prove more useful.

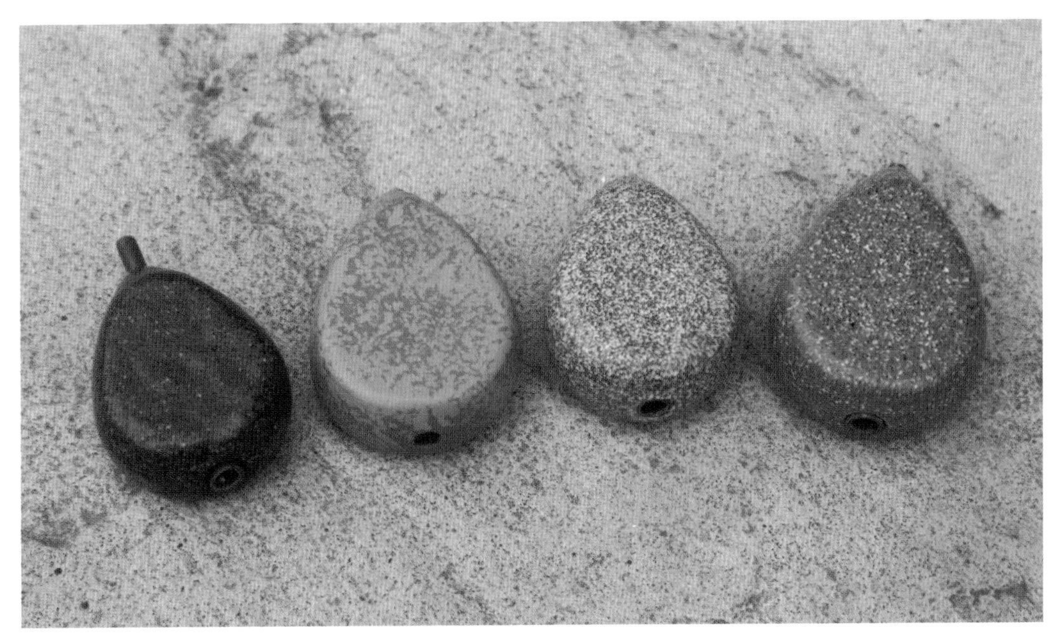

I like to have a selection of coloured in-line flat leads for marginal work.

Resting position when using a lead clip and lead weight with a swivel.

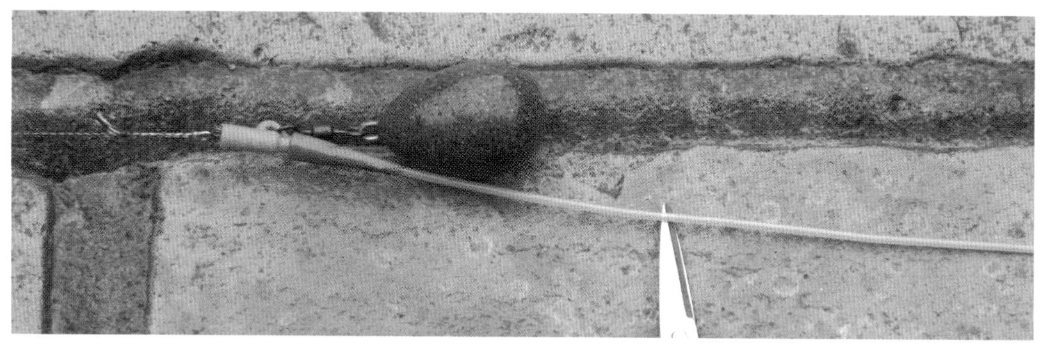

Allows the carp to move four inches before the lead weight comes into play, if fishing with slack lines.

Resting position when using a lead clip and lead weight with ring.

With a ring there is less free movement.

I can only assume, as we're all thinking about catching the venue's carp, that it's a confidence thing. We catch a few carp using a certain method so continue until we deem it's time to change, or consider the options, perhaps after losing a few carp or after several blanks. Like a lot of things regarding fishing, if it works then carry on, but if you use the same set-up week in week out, or every time you fish with poor results, then learning can be limited. Rest assured that when everything clicks into place though, the winning presentation can be extremely effective.

The answers to our problems are available in most tackle shops, to cover almost all the situations that most British carp anglers will encounter, and once we get over that hurdle of the 'what, why, where and when' then success will come with more frequency. Results should improve rather than go the other way, and our choice of presentation is just one part of the jigsaw.

If you have carp feeding on your baited patch for lengthy enough periods, where they clean you out of bait and you don't get a run, then changes need to be made so look at all the alternatives.

Which weight we use could make a difference, especially when fishing for carp that see attention from numbers of anglers all using the same leads and semi-fixed set-ups. I do believe that we need at least a couple of ounces of pressure for most rigs to work, and as a result of having watched and captured many fine carp, I'm fairly confident with the direction of my thinking. Light leads are fine if fishing in/on weed or very soft silt where a heavier lead would penetrate too much and possibly take the hookbait with it. They also seem okay when fishing firmer silt or when fishing helicopter rigs.

I once watched a hooked carp sucking and blowing, shaking its head, trying to remedy its situation, only moving the lead a few inches for a few minutes, before I decided to pick the rod up and deal with it. It had obviously pricked itself but it didn't bolt. At the time, I was margin fishing with a 2oz semi-fixed lead. When I changed to heavier leads above 3oz I started getting belting runs, the extra ounce creating the desired effect.

That was back in the early 80s and the carp was only a low double, not one that you'd have thought would have had any trouble moving a lead of that weight or being particularly cute; although it was distressed with a hook stuck in its bottom lip it didn't bolt, and bolting was what I was hoping to achieve.

When I moved up to 3oz and 4oz semi-fixed in-line leads while margin fishing, the weight began to have the desired effect. These days I tend to use leads between 3oz to 4.5oz, in-line, flat pear shape, for most of my margin fishing and they obviously work. On venues where I have observed massive head-shakers, where they have used the weight of the lead to lose the rig almost instantaneously and sometimes during the fight, I change the method slightly.

Instead of using a snug-fitting swivel, which would normally semi-fix the rig, I'll either use a ring and a pole elastic bungee system, or a smaller swivel with a couple of sliding float stops or backstop bead, both of which are safe yet allow the lead to move along the main line if they shake their heads. The sliding float stops, when used as a backstop or buffer along with an in-line lead, don't require much pressure to make them move. If they have moved then this can indicate a possible pick-up.

When it comes down to fishing beyond the margins, then I tend to stick with similar weights, from 3oz up to 6oz. Ninety per cent of the time I will use the same weight/shape lead on all rods and these would be 3.5oz to 4oz whether I'm fishing 30 yards out or 100-plus. Two reasons; firstly, they do the job required and secondly, you get the feel of the rods and leads far more easily because they're the same, which helps with accuracy when casting out multiple rods. My favourite casting lead is a homemade 3.75oz pear-shaped with a 6mm ring instead of a swivel. For extreme range casting then a 4oz or 4.5oz Korda distance lead gets me out there.

Now I've mentioned 6oz leads, I should explain because some may think 6oz is a bit extreme. I would only use these either using a lead clip or a drop-off method, such as the UFO leads, and only on venues which allow the use of a boat to position rigs, or perhaps when placing rigs in the margins, or using the pipe trick, which is discussed in Chapter 9. I have heard of anglers using bigger weights than this, even tying on half a house brick, but it's not something I feel is necessary; perhaps some anglers think they're fishing for cod. Big leads do seem to be used more on the Continent, normally on big venues in areas where undertow is an issue, I've only played at this style of angling so feel the subject of weights above 6oz is best left to someone who does it frequently.

One way of looking at it is, a 1oz lead to a 10lb carp is little different to an 80lb carp and an 8oz lead, so long as it does the job and is safe and doesn't damage the carp in any way.

The shape of the lead is perhaps of less importance when fishing on weed or silt, although a flat lead will penetrate less than a distance shape, but when fishing on a firmer bottom such as a clean sandy or gravelly spot, the shape will determine how easy it is to move. If, for example, we use a lead clip with a long lead shape and swivel, the carp have more chance of avoiding the full weight of the lead than they would have with a dumpy, pear shape lead with no swivel or an in-line lead. For this reason I use dumpy, pear-shaped leads, with rings, all the time when casting onto firm areas.

In-line leads are fine to use in open water but if there is weed around which the carp can wedge you in, then a lead clip which allows you to lose the lead does often help. Not for me to judge or criticise various manufacturers, because there are a few now and I've not used them all, but some lead clips discharge the leads easier than others and if you're losing fish in weed beds then surely it makes sense to dump the lead asap. Over this last decade, I've found three which I like: ESP's, Korda's and Gardner's, all similar though all slightly different.

The Helicopter rig, or where the lead is attached to the end of the line, is another system that many of us are familiar with and was, I think, a method which came from the northern counties, where fishing silty venues is common. I did try this method on Harefield when I first joined, but started to lose carp so I ditched it because I wasn't impressed with losing one after another. Perhaps Harefield, with its infamous, harsh gravel bars, wasn't the place to try a different method, and I've only dabbled with helicopter rigs in recent years.

Action shot taken by Adam Penning, I think; doing my bit educating the next generation.

A newPB of 25lbs for the lad. He made the most of a mad afternoon feeding spell with another five carp, my rigs doing the biz!

To complete this chapter I wanted to interview someone who's very riggy and more at home fishing helicopter rigs. In truth, my experiences are limited and I wanted someone who has fished riggy venues, and who would obligingly convey the pros and cons and developments made along the way, and with a photo album to envy. Straight away I thought of a few lads I knew from the Yateley area, who I'd spoken to, and Lewis Read, who wrote the foreword for Terry Hearn's book, 'Still Searching' immediately came to mind because we'd had a few brews on the banks of Yateley's Car Park lake some years back and got on like a house on fire. Thankfully, after tracking him down, he agreed to talk in depth about some helicopter rigs, and all we had to do was arrange a date.

We arranged to do a taped interview while Lewis was fishing on one of his current big carp venues, if the conditions looked favourable, so I wrote down a few questions, knowing full well that others would pop up, and decided to record our chat on my digital recorder.

- Lewis Read interview -

MC. Okay, Lewis, before we start talking about modern day methods, can you remember what sort of set-up you used when you first started fishing for carp?

LR. Funnily enough, I was thinking about this last night, wondering what questions you would fire at me. Back in the days when I was in my early teens, I suppose it was like everyone, pretty basic stuff. We experimented with all sorts of hooks and hooklinks. I think after we learned about the modern boilie approach, most the time the lead arrangement was just an Arlesey bomb running on the line, or with the swivel embedded in the lead with some 1.5mm soft silicone tubing, through the eye of the swivel with the main line running through the tubing not fixed in any way. That was coupled with 7 or 8lb mono hooklinks attached to a diamond swivel.

This was well after I had started carping though, when I was using Go-Cat paste or balanced bread crust and paste hookbaits on the Leg of Mutton pond, to catch the commons in there. Oh progress!

MC. So, moving on. You've been bitten by the carp bug; can you remember your set-up when you caught your first 20lb carp?

LR. Well, not a lot different, only we began fishing with the swivel jammed into the soft silicone so it was semi-fixed, quite often the lead would be sliding on the main line while playing fish so it released quite easily. My first 20 was a fish named Lucy from a lake called Whinney Hill, and to be honest I can't remember the exact rig I used. Just that I caught it over a bucketful of peanuts. She had a reputation as a 'trougher' and living near the island, so I stuck in a load of bait and along she came.

The rig most of us used for a long time, the nylon hooklink and Arlesey bomb combination, was dubbed the 'Di rig' because we were fishing the estate lakes inside Hampton Court and Bushey Park at the time. The ponds there generally have a silty bottom so most people were probably using 14-inch mono hooklinks on the Diana and Heron Pond, which was a bit of a compromise rig, really, in terms of rig mechanics, because it did the job on a firm bottom in close, or by the statue, or whenever cast into the soft stuff. The main thing was, the hookbait was presented well, and not swallowed up in the soft silt.

MC. So, you're catching carp, and they're getting bigger! Somewhere along the way you come across a different set-up commonly known as the helicopter style. Can you remember how this came about and your early recollections of fishing with a different set-up?

LR. Well, my mates and I used to share ideas and talk about stuff we'd seen in magazines so it was probably just a case that we thought 'let's try this' after reading about it somewhere or other; I think it originated from up north from anglers fishing the silty meres.

We experimented with a few components to create a secure hooklink attachment that wouldn't damage the main line and tinkered about with a fair few bits and bobs, until we got an arrangement that worked and was reliable. To be honest, it doesn't take long to piece components together when you have an idea of what you want to achieve, does it?

At the time, I think that it was Tel who found some hard, clear-plastic Drennan beads with a pre-formed plastic loop on the side which you could tie your hooklink onto. So we used these, tying our Sylcast mono hooklinks onto the bead. The set-up was just the lead weight on the end of our main line, the hooklink bead between two hard beads, and a little nylon sliding stop knot with a small piece of soft silicone tubing slid over it, which stopped the rig and beads sliding too far up the line, so it was still a fairly safe, semi-fixed arrangement.

It was really important that the mono hooklinks had to be tied on the Drennan bead with a palomar knot, because other knots would cut through the loop on the bead - and it wouldn't work with the HPPE braids that were coming to the fore at the time. Other swivel beads we tried would groove and damage your line, so when we found something which worked well, we stuck with it.

Colne Valley chunk, chodded out from a wide, silty area between steep-sided bars.

The anti-tangle effect of the helicopter set-up worked a treat and it was a very tidy, low-visibility set-up that we could adjust easily by moving the back stop up or down.

MC. Looking back, my carp fishing set-ups were similar, and like you, I thought, 'let's try this to see if there are any advantages'. Obviously, I was fishing different venues to you but I was losing more than I was catching and just couldn't pinpoint my problem. I was using braid hooklinks and when I lost something I felt perhaps the braid had twisted around my main line and once pressure was applied, this would cut through the main line so I went back to other methods. This would have been just before leadcore was available. Did you try, braided hooklinks, or other methods where you encountered any problems?

LR. Yes. We tried loads of things; different materials, different beads and swivels. It was a time when there was an explosion in material available. Of course, we even tried what some people today call the naked chod, simply having a swivel on the main line, but we suffered losses like this and the losses had to be eradicated.

Something I find very frustrating now is that we have gone through all that learning process with helicopter rigs, and know it just isn't safe to fish for big carp with a swivel on your mono main line. You can't realistically expect to land every fish, and now it's the newest, latest, greatest thing and people are fishing chod rigs with the swivel running on the mono main line and they're losing fish because their main line is breaking! Well, we learned that 25 years ago, so started to look around for ways to negate that problem; the line is shearing under pressure, it's not being cut. Thankfully, these problems can be eliminated, as you know Martin.

Mr Angry at 33lbs caught on a choddy in a clearing among weed, over a scattering of freebies.

MC. Obviously, it can be frustrating for any of us to lose fish, especially when it can take a lot of time and effort just to get the bites. After losing three on the trot, I thought, 'sod the helicopters' and went back to other methods. So moving on, where did you fish next and what developments followed?

LR. Well the next development was to use a leadcore leader. It wasn't a case of jumping from the estate lakes to Yateley. We fished a few local pits with bigger carp and we were consciously building our experience and knowledge ready for what lay ahead and upping the strength of our rigs and tackle to cope with the much greater demands they would have to cope with. We started off fishing the Copse Lake at Yateley and around this time we came across what was a good, reliable leadcore trolling line called Cortland Kerplunk. Sounds like that old game you can play with marbles. It came on 100-metre spools with a breaking strain of 45lbs.

We quickly learned how to attach the leadcore onto our main lines with a needle knot and tested it fully before we fished with it. Around the same time, we also tried other leadcore materials, but this was the best around then. To stop the top bead moving, we used a 5mm length of 0.5mm silicone tubing threaded onto the leadcore, and the appropriate bore rubber beads, so the set-up was safe right from the off. The beauty of leadcore is not only its strength, but it also acted as a buffer against snags, and most importantly, it was different at the time. You had the last five or six feet of your end tackle pinned to the lakebed and no monofilament near the rig. It was all part of the trap!

MC. When you say 'we', I assume you and your mates are bouncing ideas together. Now, if move on a few years, if I'm not mistaken the next breakthrough moment, the stiff hinge rig, originated or was developed by anglers who fished on the Yateley complex. Anglers such as you, Terry, Nigel and all the other lads pursuing their dreams, developing variations. Would you say this was a breakthrough moment in rig mechanics?

LR. Well, around that time there were anglers using stiff mono rigs. There were a few variations already in use, but when Tel and I came up with our version, with the little D on the back of the hook, I tied one up and we chucked it in my kitchen sink and thought, 'Hallelujah!'. We knew it was right and that it just had to work. We were laughing and pointing at it saying how unfair it would be and that it wasn't so much a rig as a trap. It was really exciting!

Preceding that point though, there was a whole load of steps and developments - shall we call it rig evolution? - which had to take place to arrive at what we use today. One guy who should be mentioned was Andy Kidd; his version with a ring on the hook certainly helped spark our ideas. As the rig evolved, the final pieces of the jigsaw were changing. The rig ring that we used to attach the hook section to the boom, became part of a swivel which allows the hook section to twist and turn at the hinge point on the hooklink; and of course, there was the introduction of specialist, high-memory, stiff link materials.

We did still use braided hooklinks occasionally, but tangles were always an issue. We found certain lead shapes created tangles, with the hooklink wrapping around the shoulder of the lead. Personally, I had nightmares with dumpy pear-style leads. The Roger & Kerry-style leads, with a different shape helped stop the tangling issues, and were definitely another step forward, and I still use this style a lot to this day.

MC. I can remember using a version of the stiff-hinge rig myself, using similar principles, using braid on the hook section, but this would have been using either lead clips or while using in-line flat leads when fishing the margins. When you fished the rig helicopter-style, did you prefer to have it running or trapped between beads a set distance from your lead, and did you consider other lead set-up arrangements?

LR. I did consider other set-ups, but the lakes we were fishing were relatively small with shallow water and there was no need to lose any leads, so it didn't seem necessary on the venues we fished at that time. Of course, there were exceptions and we'd often use alternative arrangements or rigs, depending upon the swim and the spots we fished. I wouldn't want anyone to think I was that much of a one-trick pony!

One of the things that is not often mentioned when we're talking about helicopter arrangements is bite indication. With the helicopter-style we'd often get one or two bleeps now and then before a proper bite developed, so we knew something was going on down there. The paternoster effect is enhanced at the buzzers by using a light bobbin on a drop, that allowed the leadcore to settle, so where we maybe sacrificed the bolt effect of the in-line lead, we'd gain something else. We always thought there was some distinct advantage in getting those early warning bleeps, so along with casting a rig out with minimal disturbance, being able adjust the beads according to the lakebed and having the indication enhanced, and allowing the leadcore to settle, the whole thing was simply working.

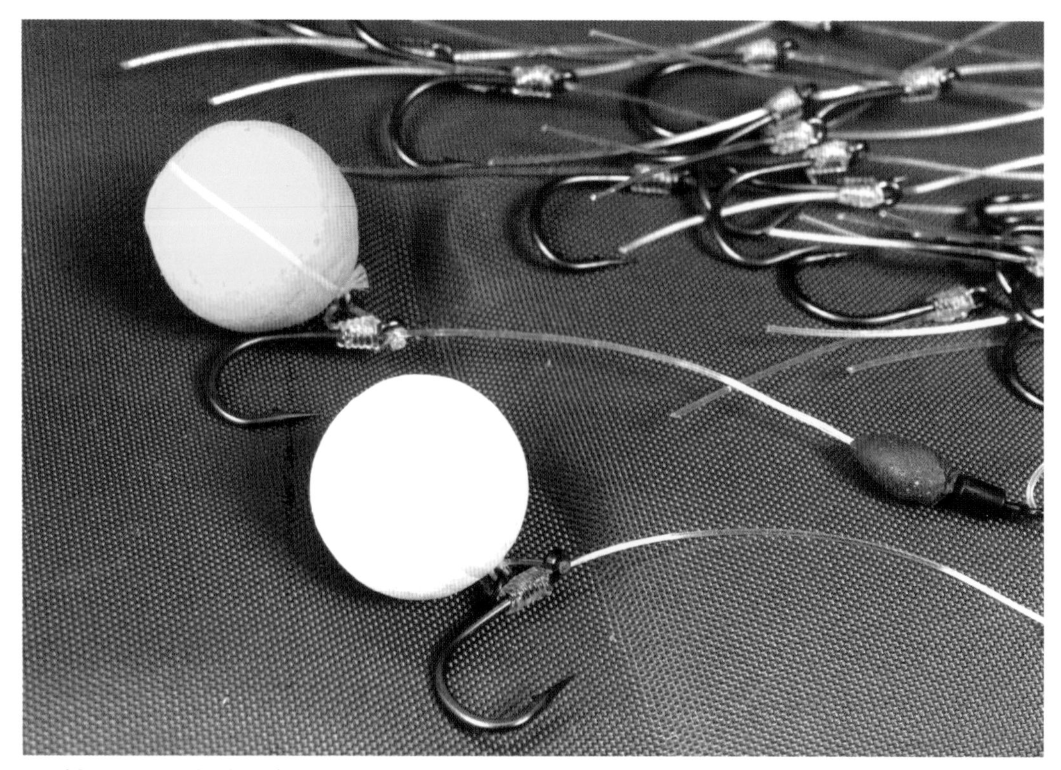

Stiff-hinge and chod rigs' end sections use the same mechanics.

MC. So do you pull the lead out of silt when you're happy where you've cast?

LR. I've never been one for pulling the leads along out of the silt because of the huge amount of variable outcomes; typically crap like leaves, twigs or weed that can cover an exposed hook point. The stiff-hinge rig was designed for relatively clean areas, or areas with a tiny bit of bottom debris, not really for fishing in/on weed, so for most of the time, the stop bead was just an inch or two above the bottom bead, down near the lead.

If the area was silty or slightly weedy, then the stop bead was moved up, away from the lead a few more inches, to ensure that the rig lay well presented. Again, this would be using leadcore leaders of four to five feet so the rig was still a long way from the mono main line that we thought the fish were most scared of.

It's not a massive conceptual leap if we look at the chod rig, which is basically just the hook section of the stiff-hinge rig. Right from the off, we fished with a top bead way up the core and found that as long as you're fishing with relatively slack lines with a light bobbin, the weight of the leadcore pins the end tackle down. The carp have only got to put their lips around the bait and then they have the weight of the leadcore and line acting in a paternoster effect, and that was another new problem for the carp to deal with.

MC. So can you remember the first time you used the chod rig, and how it got the name?

LR. Yes I can. It's funny, but even just prior to this I was experimenting with big curved Kamasan B940s and a swivel which had a similar effect, but when Tel showed us what he was using over at Oxford, after catching loads of carp, I could instantly see that this was something special.

By using the end section of the stiff-hinge rig together with the leadcore leader, the final result was technically better than Frank Warwick's early version using Amnesia. A convergence of ideas once more, and when you looked at it lying on a dark lake bed where the leadcore would simply disappear and all you could see was the pop-up, suddenly a fairly crude arrangement simply disappeared and you were left with an all-terrain rig that worked almost everywhere. It was fantastic!

MC. Whenever I'm on to something that works well, you know it works simply by an improvement in the amount of action you're getting. Once you started using the choddies did you notice an improvement to your catch rate?

LR. It's hard to say how much it improved my catch rate, because there are always other factors, as you know, Martin, but it worked well for me and many others who have tried it and we gained a lot of confidence in it. Being the working, married type of angler I just find it simple and straightforward to go for showing fish with minimum casting, and it get bites. Truthfully, the heyday of the rig has probably long gone on really busy lakes, but it's still extremely useful and catches loads of fish.

MC. As you know, Lewis, I do a lot of margin fishing using semi-fixed in-line leads and have watched many carp hook themselves over the years, and seen a few get away with it when using supple braided hooklinks. Have you witnessed carp getting hooked while you've been using helicopter presentations?

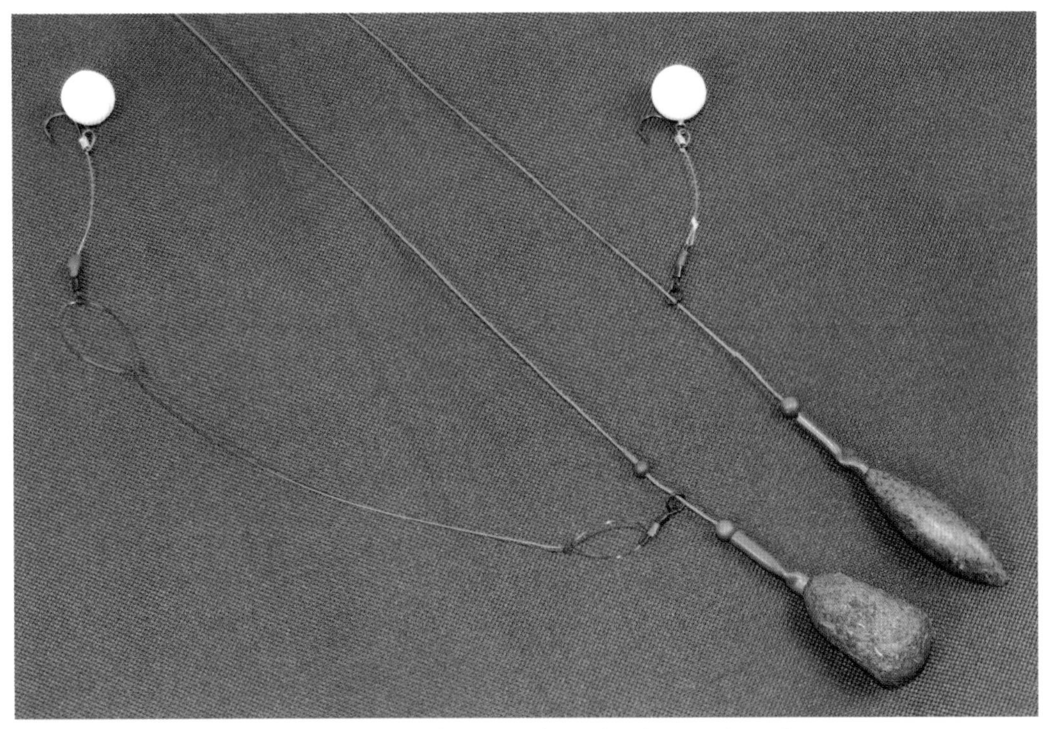

Wickedly effective rigs, but they still need to be in the right place at the right time.

Chod essentials.

LR. I'm sure a few carp are getting away with it, but I've only seen one, a fish called Scaley on the Copse lake, managing to spit the rig after it had lifted the lead and leadcore at least a couple of feet off the bottom. Who knows, possibly a heavier lead may have been more appropriate on that occasion, but I was fishing to a small hole in the weed a few rod lengths out, with fish about. A big lead going in would have probably seen the swim empty in no time. Anyway, I'm pretty convinced that an in-line lead or lead clip arrangement with the same size lead on would have resulted in the same outcome.

I'm still happiest using a light-ish lead with helicopter rigs, but that's not to say there is no reason to use heavier leads to catch carp. It just doesn't make sense to me, having a bigger lead than necessary due to the disturbance of getting it on the spot or having a lead swinging around just in front of the fish's face while playing it. Though if you want to feel the effect - which in reality is minimal - hold a lead on a bit of line the length of your hooklink and shake it around under the water. The weight is buffered so much that the chances are, it has negligible effect on the hookhold anyway.

I know other anglers like heavier leads, and I understand why, but in truth I tend to use heavier leads using the lead clips these days, though perhaps my opinions may change in the future. Looking back, the majority of fish I've caught using helicopter presentations have been using Roger & Kerry's style leads of 1.5oz and 2.25oz. I love them because they're excellent for avoiding tangles and for feeling the lead down, plus they're nice to cast. They are hard to get hold of now but luckily, Gardner does a very similar one, which is nice.

Using fairly light leads gives the angler a little bit more finesse. Although I now have every confidence with the hinge and chod rigs, I still use many others. They're still effective aren't they, but then so are other forms of presentation, as you know.

Gorgeous 33lb linear caught on a single hookbait chod rig; Carp Company Ice Red pop-up, if my memory is correct.

MC. So you wouldn't say the hinge or the choddies are a 'cast anywhere' rig?

LR. No rig is a 'cast anywhere' rig! We all have to think about whatever rig we're putting on the end of our lines, where you're fishing it and the scenario at that point in time. As you know, Martin, there can be times when they can be cautious to pop-ups and if the carp are happily feeding on baits on the bottom, then bottom baits can simply be the better option.

For fishing single hookbaits, or with just a scattering of boilies, then the hinge and choddy would probably still be my first choices. If you're sticking a bucket of pellet and particle out there, then I'd have reservations about using the rigs because I feel more confident with a bottom bait or balanced bottom bait. It's just that the fish feed differently on different types and concentrations of bait.

I can remember reading about the principles of fishing pop-ups way back in the early 80s, when the anglers were fishing among weed or on the slope of a gravel bar. On venues like the old, hand-dug pits in the Colne Valley that I've fished, the carp are naturally finding food at all levels and the bottom topography creates situations where the carp feed at all angles and levels, and pop-up rigs can work a treat.

To confuse things further, some anglers get on the pop-ups while others don't! Things change as well. For example, I've been fishing on the Dinton complex in recent times and this year there's been hardly any weed on the bottom of Black Swan, due to a massive algae bloom colouring the water, and its gone from anglers catching fish on pop-ups, to the opposite. Personally, I couldn't buy a bite on a pop-

Two on choddies with the other on a balanced bottom bait. Come on you carp!

up, and that was when bottom baits and balanced bottom baits began to work. Recognising these natural circumstances or scenarios is one of the keys to consistency, and it's the same with lead arrangements; one type may be slightly more effective than another!

MC. In the last five or six years, the choddy style has been tweaked and developed and we now have running chods and the naked chods. For the benefit of those who're not aware of these can you describe the differences?

LR. Well, the running chod is basically having the stop bead further up at the end of the leadcore, or just beyond it, allowing the rig to run freely between top bead and lead. That's pretty much how it's been used since day one, but it's just been called the running chod by someone who's simply claimed to have reinvented it!

With the naked chod, the long leadcore leader is dispensed with, so it's running on your mono main line with the back bead stopped roughly six to eight feet up the line from the lead. Instead of the leadcore balancing the pop-up, it's balanced with rig putty and it sinks gently so the hookbait settles on the main line. I still prefer to use leadcore, and using the leadcore to sink the pop-up; more often than not they are hooking themselves against the weight and resistance of the leadcore. If you want to use a naked chod, the important things to remember to ensure that your components don't fail under stress, are to fish with slack lines and light bobbins.

MC. Looking back to the early 80s, you could say I was one of the lads that used pop-ups and those first few carp that came my way gave me the confidence to use them more and more. Back in the early days, they seemed to work on silt, clay and weed provided the hookbait wasn't dragged into it rendering them useless! Two things, in my mind, made them work; one the hookbait was more visual and secondly the counterbalance weight, which helped with positioning the hook in a favourable area within the fishes' mouths. Some would say they were a novelty and perhaps they were in those early days, but they worked and 30-plus years later, pop-ups continue to catch carp on all manner of lead arrangements.

Talking about how things change, I've found specific spots can change from week to week! Years ago, when I observed carp ejecting rigs while using fairly long, supple braided hooklinks, you could see and sense the inefficiencies simply because the safe zone which the carp can move into is like an invisible dome centred around a semi-fixed lead. That's not to say the rigs didn't work, but you question how many times it had been picked up and spat out, whereas with the choddies, they haven't the freedom to do this. Now, I know there are many anglers that will be thinking of using chod rigs in the future; even I've been having the odd dabble with them in the last few years. Have you encountered much grief from nuisance fish while using choddies?

LR. No. I've not really noticed any problems from nuisance fish. I know you've encountered problems with tench and pike nailing your pop-ups on venues in the past, Martin, but I've not fished anywhere where that is an issue. I think it's something on specific venues rather than pop-ups in general.

When I've been using popped-up boilies, I've tended to catch fewer bream and tench than when I've been fishing with the same bait on a more subtle bottom bait rig. On some waters, I think it doesn't matter what rig you use, you're going to catch bream and tench if you're using bait they like. The Pads Lake at Yateley, for instance, was a nightmare when I fished there. It didn't matter what rig you used you were going to catch bream. I was reluctant to change the bait I was on as I had enormous confidence with it, and it caught shed loads of bream, but it also caught me the carp. Even if I fished it on a size 2/0 Aberdeen hook, I still caught the bream!

MC. Some venues' nuisance fish can be a right pain in the backside; introduce pellet and particle and it's like a magnet for everything. Last time out for me this year on a little estate, I caught three pike and got bitten off by four, along with three or four bream, using pop-ups, and returned home with my tail between my legs with no carp coming my way. I never realised just how many other species there were, so rigs and strategies can be venue specific. If I'd used a choddy or a bottom hookbait with just a scattering of boilies, the outcome may well have been different! How do you prefer to present bottom baits and have you ever fished the stiff-hinge rig with bottom baits?

LR. No, I've not used the hinge rig for bottom baits. After casting out, the hinge could easily fold back on itself as it settles on the lake bed leaving a really messy and ineffective pile of terminal bits. I favour using a four to six-inch stiff mono rig, with the same D as my hookbait mounting point. I often combine this with a balanced bottom bait, and a slightly bigger loop on the end that attaches to a swivel to give the rig a bit of free movement when a fish inhales the hookbait. A bit like a long version of the hook section of the stiff-hinge rig, it's a very effective and efficient hooking mechanism and is pretty much resistant to tangles.

Upper-40 mirror from an unspoilt French venue; lead tied on with 3lb mono and rig positioned on a dinner plate in five feet of water.

MC. So, if you're not using the helicopter set-up, do you prefer an in-line set-up or a lead clip set-up?

LR. Now you've mentioned in-line leads, I'll explain why I worry about them and don't use them more often. When you cast out an in-line lead with a normal rig on, that lead is going to drop nose first through the water, so the hooklink swivel impacts onto or even goes into the lake bed and that is one of the primary reasons why I can't get my head around it!

These days, when I do use an in-line lead, I ensure that it lands more softly by using a PVA bag so it lands with less impact. I have used this arrangement with drop-off in-lines a fair bit in the last couple of years, fishing in weed, and love it but I can't cast out an in-line lead. Do you use in-line leads when casting?

MC. I certainly wouldn't cast in-line leads onto gravel; this is where I'd use lead clips and a lead with a ring and no swivel!

LR. I see that. In reality, having all these options available is fantastic isn't it? Having worked in the industry a while now, and seen the range of tackle and tactics, that the guys in the GT team are successfully catching fish with, I'm using a much wider range of methods than I ever have in the past.

Despite some earlier misgivings, I now use lead clips more than I ever did in the past, because I really had a mental barrier to them. I didn't like the idea of that bulky bit of plastic and a lead attached to it, pendant-style, but with each capture I can see their merits in some situations where you'll land more if you discharge the lead. I know you have more experience using lead clips; this is why I'm keen to read this book and pick up some tips and see what rigs you've been using.

MC. So, at least that proves a point. No matter where you fish or how many you have caught, you'll all be thinking about alternatives. Even though you have a lot of faith fishing helicopter-style, you don't consider it the be-all.

LR. That's right. Most modern day carp anglers should be aware of what and how others are doing it, and looking carefully at how others are successfully approaching their angling and how they can apply it to their own fishing, if they're not already. Personally, I adopt the pretty simple approach of asking myself if I'm going to be fishing with a slack line, or a tighter line; slack lines for helicopter rigs and lead clips for tighter lines.

MC. What components do you use these days for your stiff rigs? Any final tips?

LR. I've avoided talking specific tackle because I don't want this interview to be 'pluggy', mate, but as I designed the Gardner Covert Chod hooks I feel happy to say that I use these. Normally, in the size five or six depending on hookbait, touched up to make sure they're animal sharp, with 20lb Tripwire.

I've altered a few of the components on my leadcore leaders now as well, which enables me to swap things round easier and quicker. The swivel I use to attach my hooklink is a size 12 KwikLok Flexi-ring which just means I can change rigs in seconds. I can swap between conventional helicopter rigs and chod rigs quickly without having to break everything down. I like the loop attachment of these rigs because the hook section has a little extra movement and I'm sure that helps it work better as well, so there's a double advantage.

One final important point I'd like to add; if anyone is using any helicopter rigs without leadcore and using a swivel direct on their main line, then the safest way is to use a two-inch piece of leadcore leader with the lead removed, spliced down by the lead. At least when you're playing a fish, that piece of leader material is acting as the buffer and is substantial enough to avoid breakages. I've yet to see that in any articles written on the subject in the last few years by anglers advocating naked helicopter rigs. There isn't enough emphasis on avoiding breakages to start with.

I've always said that the best way to avoid any rig safety issues with this style rig is to use good, strong main line, and to my mind that is a decent line of at least 0.35mm. In reality, that is a 17 or 18lb line and that in itself prevents a lot of potential problems. The aim of the game is to catch them, not leave a rig in a fish's mouth. None of us wants that.

MC. I think we've all lost carp at some point in time. It's down to the individual to determine what went wrong and rectify the problem, whether that's making adjustments to the presentation or changing component parts of their end tackle.

LR. Exactly. If in doubt, phone a friend!

MC. Well I think we've covered the points I had in mind, we'll call it a wrap and have another brew.

After switching off the recorder, we spoke for another hour or so, exchanging ideas, as you do, and then Lewis set off to his humble abode. Lewis had been kind enough to travel up to Luton as he'd called off the scheduled meeting on the bankside due to inclement weather.

I first met Lewis when I had a dabble on the Car Park Lake one year at Yateley, so we've known each other and chatted from time to time over the last decade. I wanted to interview Lewis because of his knowledge of rigs, especially helicopter rigs, which is undoubtedly a very effective style of presentation and warrants consideration. I hope that those who already fish helicopter-style have learned something from the interview, but as I stressed to Lewis, there are many anglers who haven't for one reason or another, so maybe everyone will learn something. I've caught hundreds of carp over the years, but I only need two hands to count those that have come my way while fishing helicopter style, which is why I wanted to interview Lewis.

For the last decade, I've been fishing venues where leadcore leaders are banned, which is perhaps one reason I've not used the helicopter set-up as much as Lewis and his friends. They are not my venues so I simple abide by whatever rules and use either in-line leads or lead clips. In most circumstances, not fishing with helicopter rigs hasn't been detrimental, but I'm positive there have been times when I should have used them, on the venues which have had no bans in place. Personally, I don't consider leadcore leaders to be unsafe, providing the whole set-up is safe should a breakage occur due to a crack off, or your line parting. The same can be said with helicopter rigs without a leadcore leader, or any other set-up.

One thing I have learned about rigs in the passing of time, bouncing ideas with your fellow anglers is the way forward. One final comment to those about to try something different; if in doubt, test your end tackle: i.e. components, materials and knots, subjecting them to stress beyond that which you're likely to use, to see what breaks. One ruined rig at home could highlight any possible problems. Just like bait and your tactics, it comes down to the individual to find which rigs and methods work best on the venues they fish.

Chapter 9
FREEZER BAITS

Tips, tricks and alternative tactics

Tips

Sometimes, it's not what we anglers are doing that brings us good fortune; it's what some of us are not doing that actually swings things in our favour. These things can often make the difference between success or failure, if compared to other anglers on the same venue using different baits, methods or tactics. That may sound strange at first, but some of us need to change our approach, if not each week, certainly throughout the year in differing weather conditions. That is, of course, if you want to improve your results and have more success and fewer failures. That's not to say we can't learn something every time we visit the venue and come away with a dry net, or a wet net. Whenever we go fishing for carp, there should come a time when lessons learned should be capitalised on if progress is to be made.

Probably the finest example of studying progress within carp angling is in the book, 'Redmire Pool', written by Kevin Clifford and Len Arbery, and first published in 1984, where the 20lb-plus captures have been logged from 1951 all the way to 1983. It's a remarkable book and well worth the read, if you haven't already, about a little pool with historic value, from its birth and original stocking by Donald Leney in 1934, right up to the book's publication. It's very plain to see that from 1951 up to the late 60s, the anglers struggled, and then a different group of anglers started using maggots and sultanas and results went up dramatically. From 1972 to the summer of 1976, sweetcorn dominated the venue, and from 1975 protein baits and other particles began to catch, then the hair rig and boilies came along and dominated captures in the early 80s. Throughout this unique book, you can get a feel for which anglers made mistakes, who shined, which swims were fished, and what baits were used on a venue that, let's not forget, produced two different British record carp.

Other carp books have followed, highlighting various venues with a wealth of information, and many more waters have featured within British carp magazines, but I doubt there will ever be a venue and a book with so much history and so many famous faces inside. The only book I can think of which comes close is, 'Carp!' published in 2002 by Tim Paisley and friends; although I must admit, I've not read every book concerning carp fishing ever published. I've built up my library of books over the years as Christmas or birthday presents and though they haven't come as surprise presents, they're all better than another pair of socks or a boxed set of shaving products. Perhaps my wife's trying to tell me something!

The last four books I've read have been Terry Hearn's 'Still Searching', Terry Dempsey's 'The Urban Myth', Lee Jackson's 'Just for the Record' and Nigel Sharp's 'Living the Dream', all very different and highly informative so thumbs-up lads. You have inspired me to get my arse in gear and finish this one. Why mention these, apart from them being a good read? Well, I've read many books and magazines ever since I switched my attention to carp fishing and we can all learn a lot from past publications and other anglers willing to share any knowledge.

How you or I measure success though, can be completely different because we each fish for the pleasure and the challenge in the time we have available, and we're not necessarily competing with the other anglers on the venue.

The facts are though, for some, carp angling is a full-time job, for others it's a hobby, and we'd all much rather the next buzzer we heard was ours, hopefully a carp, and the vast majority of us take weighing scales and a camera with us when we go fishing, so we are always hoping that something which warrants a photograph will come our way.

To me, success can be measured in numbers although personally, so long as I'm learning and enjoying the challenge, then that's the best part of the success. It's not just the result, but the journey. If you want to know where you stand on the success ladder, then you have to be aware of all the facts and figures, how many carp caught, how many hours everyone fished and number of rods used, to work out an average. If your results are above average, then you can't be doing much wrong; if below average then perhaps there is room for improvement. It's not just what we do at the start of a session but what we do throughout, and during each year.

Location, along with swim choice, on some venues is more important than others, but even on waters where location is less vital, we don't want to find ourselves in a negative situation so no matter where we fish, we want a swim that we hope will give us the opportunity to catch something. If the carp are visible or showing themselves by poking their heads out or bubbling in your swim, like me you'd be rubbing your hands. If they are not in your swim then ask yourself this; would you be better off in another swim or will it only be a matter of time before something positive happens?

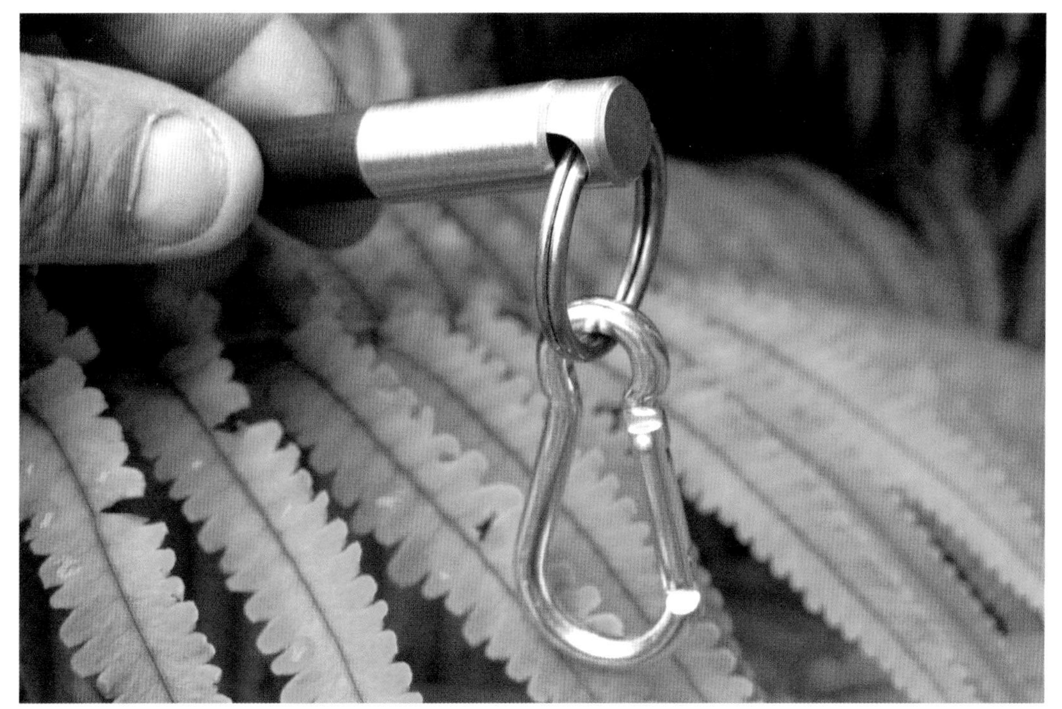

Solar goalpost adaptor, ring and clip on the end of my landing net pole, is my preferred choice of suspending scales when weighing carp.

No lead or fancy rig required to catch this 34lb mirror, just old-school freelining!

If we pick the right swims before we start fishing, then we're halfway there. If we pick the wrong swims, then results will be poor or a complete blank. Carp do not feed 24 hours a day, although it is possible to keep a feeding situation going for some considerable time. Sometimes, these positive feeding situations could be during most of the daylight hours, sometimes during darkness, but once you've caught a few, action tails off. Quite often a feeding pattern begins to emerge and productive times become apparent and it will be the carp who dictate when these times will be, giving us the window of opportunity to capitalise on their need to feed.

No two lakes ever seem the same so we must adjust to where we find ourselves fishing and then to the natural changes we discover. On some of the venues I've fished, I found it impossible to predict what the hot time was and on other waters there seemed to be one or two defined periods. These intervals only remained predictable for a few weeks, and rarely more than a few months before changing. It's only by visiting the venue on a regular basis that you become aware of any changes, provided of course you're spending a fair proportion of your time looking and learning while you're there.

Angling pressure and the weather conditions do play their parts, but I'm more inclined to think it's the natural feeding cycle that will change throughout the year, no doubting there could be some relevance with the position of the sun and moon as these change slightly each day and are nature's clock. Now, it's all too easy to follow a pattern, and if we're fishing sessions longer than 24 hours, there often comes a time when we reel in our rods, perhaps go for a walk, or to reposition with fresh hookbaits, top up the spot with more bait, or make tactical changes.

My PB zig carp, Scale on Shoulder at 37lbs 14oz.

If we religiously stick to getting the rods and bait out at the exact same time of day on every session, or throughout the year, there will undoubtedly be occasions when our timing will be wrong and we could easily be reeling in or casting out when there are carp feeding. Possibly the biggest reason behind many blank sessions up and down the country each year are down to timing issues.

Carp have a knack for knowing when they are being fished for and sometimes I've pulled the rigs in when margin fishing with no carp nearby then gone for a walk, only to return half an hour later to find carp feeding on my bait. Everything can change in an hour with no lines in the water, and if it happens in the margins you can bet your bottom dollar it happens beyond them. I wonder how many carp have been hit by a lead while they were feeding. Probably a lot more than we'd think!

We know carp travel around their venues so it stands to reason that different areas such as the surface or mid-water could have different hot times, so making correct tactical decisions will be an influencing factor on our end results.

We can't rely on carp showing themselves every time they feed or visit an area they will feed in, although they will give away these spots sometimes so it's always worth watching the water when carp are active. It's always nice to have carp showing over our baits but it's not crucial. I've had many memorable moments, with single and multiple catches, when no carp showed themselves before or during their feeding period.

Moving along with the theme of tips and the adage, 'it's not what you do but what you don't do', I'd like to talk about fads and fashions often written about and mentioned by the younger generation of magazine feature writers, who are followed by a proportion of those looking for tips and possible answers to their problems. If I told you carp don't feed on surface baits I'd be telling the truth, but the full truth is, some carp feed on the surface, some carp don't.

If an angler always fishes spots on which the lead went down with a thud or donk, and then as a consequence only caught from hard spots, does this mean carp only feed on hard surfaces? Great if the lead went down with a donk and resulted with a capture, but how many anglers are feeling the lead down with a satisfying donk and failing to generate any activity on the bobbins? Plenty! Yes carp will feed on hard, clean surfaces, if they like what they find, but they also feed in the silt and in or on weed and you'll not feel the lead down with a thud on these areas, so do you write-off these areas? Failing to fish on silt or weed could be detrimental. If you're struggling on the hard stuff, simples, fish on the soft stuff.

I could think of a few venues, mostly gravel pits, where the anglers are missing out massively by simply fishing the hard, clean areas. I've been suckered into this at times in the past, from experience though, and a number of blanks, I changed and I've caught more than my fair share fishing in silt. Bloodworms, snails, dragonfly larvae, water louse and all the other naturals which the carp love to feed on live in the silt and weed. They do not live on hard, clean features for any length of time because they are an easy meal for fish to eat. Mussels are perhaps the only aquatic organisms that can survive and establish themselves on hard surfaces, although as they breed and multiply, some find themselves getting crunched up by the carp as part of their food source.

I'm fairly convinced that certain baits we use attract the attentions of the naturals, not just crayfish, and this can create a double-whammy effect as the carp can feast on our bait along with the naturals. I'm a great believer in pre-baiting, many other anglers also, so perhaps this could be a factor which can be swinging things in our favour. All living organisms require nutrients and minerals to survive, so anglers' baits become part of that food chain.

Tricks

Now, I could write a few paragraphs highlighting tricks to play on your mates such as swapping their spools over at night, or rigging up a line to pull their lines, giving them a few bleeps while they're having 40 winks, but although we can chuckle away it isn't helpful advice. More useful advice would be to get to know your venue as well as you can and make things happen rather than hope that they do.

A small percentage are happy to make their swim choices before they have arrived at the venue; a few from looking from the car park to see who's where and what's available, and a few by walking round looking for inspiration or direction from other members, or some sightings of carp. We'll all meet a vast array of different people wherever we roam and friendships will be formed, though there are always a few anglers who simply don't want to see fresh faces on their turf.

I always take people as I find them and if they'll talk to me I'll talk to them. If they don't want to talk to me then fine, I'll walk on. Facts are though, we carp anglers are a mixed bunch; some with extreme right-wing views, others left-wing, and from all different professions. One thing I know is that you'll learn a lot from friends and nothing from enemies or the not-so-friendly anglers, and there's one of them on almost every lake, sometimes more than one, although 99% of the carp anglers I've met over all the years are sound.

That little 1% makes me laugh and really does make me wonder why they go fishing. They fall into two categories; two-faced people who talk about you but never to you, especially when other anglers are fishing the venue, and the one-way information merchants. True, a lot of us will talk about other anglers at some point in time, it seems part of our culture to talk and often, we have plenty of time to chat away. It's just a shame that there are a few sad characters amongst us who think it's amusing to blank other anglers. Perhaps they see other anglers as threats to their over-inflated egos. The trick is to not be in that 1% because it's almost guaranteed your ego will get dented, and you'll lose what friends you had. Oddly enough, it's sometimes the local top rods that slip into this 1%. Perhaps they're afraid of their status diminishing.

Nice to get the odd email from some of the young lads to whom I've taught something in the past. Jake Taylor sent me this once I'd got into Facebook, a pukka mid-30 mirror from Cotswold Water Park Lake.

33lbs 10oz; time to get the camera out again, and add this to one of many carp to fall for the pipe trick.

I've known a few very good anglers who have lost all their credibility, and their friends, and have sadly realised that without information or friends they blank a lot more than they previously did. The same goes for the one-way information merchants, because slowly they get sussed out and it comes back to bite them on the arse. I've given out loads of valuable information to my friends over the years and they too have shared knowledge, often without being asked.

The most typical one-way merchant mistake is lying. "No mate, seen diddly squat", and yet you see them watching the water like a hawk, and carp have shown themselves. If they are the type of person that blanks you when you say a simple 'hello', just give them the same treatment next time. I know one very good angler, who always relished being the centre of attention and would always blank new members, and now he's Billy No Mates! The trick is to not let it affect your demeanour; don't sink to their level. Just make sure that any further information that comes your way isn't passed on to them if you do speak to that person.

Carp magazines tend to get a bit of a slating now and then on various Interent forums, possibly because a lot of comes from anonymous sources, and it does amuse me because often, there are unseen restraints on writers and editors, which are not taken into account by the critical few. How often will you read, 'same old crap' or something similar on a forum, yet they have probably forgotten they had to read something themselves to know this.

It's pretty obvious that some editors follow a format, and why not? They're constrained by their readers and advertising and do the best they can each month with the material submitted. I think it would be easier to run this country than to be a carp magazine editor.

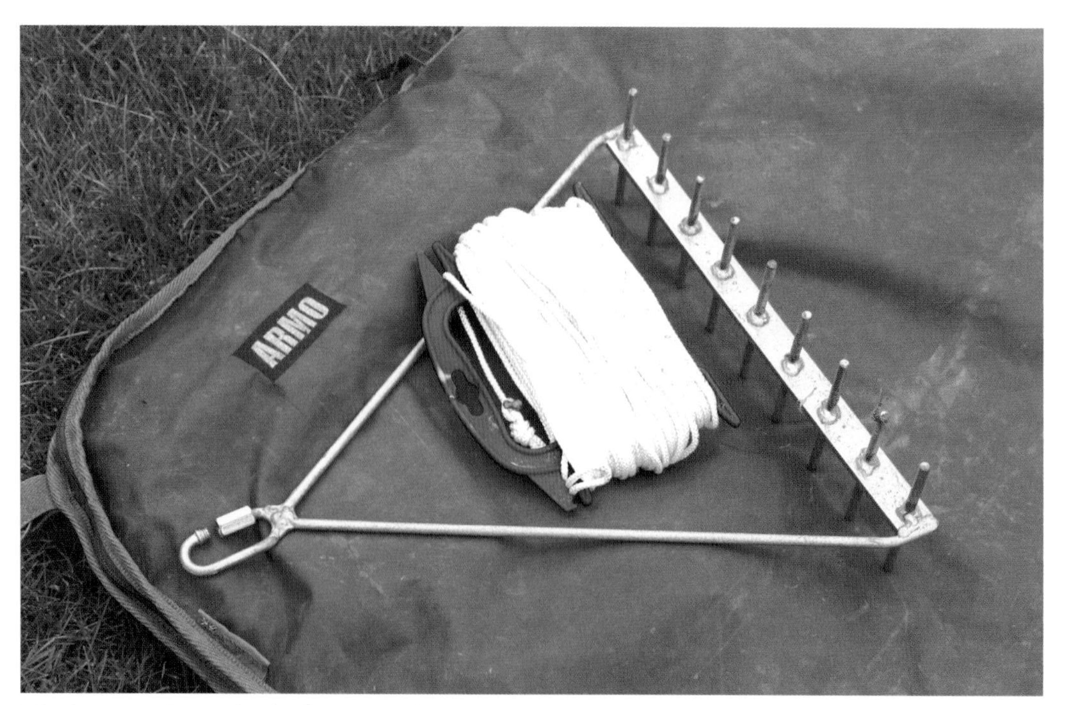

This homemade weed rake does more than clear weed. It stirs up the lakebed and clears any debris.

One of the frequent quotes 'Do something different to what everyone else is doing', also makes me laugh because you assume the writer spends more time concentrating on what the others are doing rather than what he or she is doing. There is some truth behind it though. What's new to them or us is not necessarily new to everyone, which will be the case 99.9% of the time if you've read all that's been written about carp and carp fishing in the last three or four decades.

I wonder how many of you reading this have raked a marginal area to create a feeding spot, or how many members on the venues you fish has used a rake? How many have screwed steps into trees to get an elevated view of the water to enhance your vision? How many anglers throw out a few oily floating trout pellets or mixers when viewing marginal spots on windy days, to create an oily calm window to view through?

Alternatives

I remember a few years back, when I first disclosed the snake and scorpion rigs in a Korda rig book, it was said that they were too fiddly, unnecessary, and likely to tangle. All I saw them as was another rig, an alternative pop-up rig. Yes, they may be fiddly, compared to the most basic rigs, and yes, they may be unnecessary, but writing a rig off because it looks like it might tangle is ridiculous. Anyone who uses a braided hooklink will tell you they get the odd tangle, so do we stop using braid?

What the critics failed to take into account was products such as PVA and all the methods and situations that can be fished without the need to cast any rig out, whether it's basic or radical. I hardly get any tangles gently swinging my rigs out when margin fishing, nor when using a pole and bait spoon, such as the 12M Angling Intelligence pole, or when using my pipe trick. If you think the only way to catch carp is by casting out overhead style, perhaps it may be worth considering all the alternatives.

The advantage a pole gives the angler is to position a rig, along with bait, super-accurately day or night within the length of the pole. Obviously, ideal for fishing the opposite bank on a canal or any spots on your venue you can ship the spoon out to, even simply straight out on spod spill spots, which are often overlooked. I don't think it will be long before longer pole systems will be made and used as the longer pole increases their potential. No doubt if we sourced the required components we could make one ourselves using plastic conduit pipe. The only disadvantage is that they're best suited to calm conditions, because on choppy water or during strong side-winds, the elements can make our lives difficult.

The pipe trick, or at least the one I've used to good effect, which I'd like to recommend as an alternative method of getting a rig in the water, is ideally suited to situations where we could be fishing the far margin of a bay or opposite bank and avoiding the positioning of any rigs while off the rods, thus avoiding being unattended with rigs in the water.

Imagine you want to fish the far margins of a bay. Now we could cast a rig, but is there an alternative that may have some advantages? Well, with my drainpipe trick I believe there is, so let me explain the procedure so you can perhaps see the logic behind the method.

I cast two leads across to the far bank of a one-swim bay and then used some convenient scaffold poles (used for swim building) to hold my rods in position and maintain a tight line above the surface, before going through the next phases of the trick. On both reels the clutch is set reasonably tight to allow me to pull some extra main line if needed.

I then walked round to the far margin, with all that was needed to tie on some rigs, change leads and bait up. I used old, battered or cheap leads initially, because sometimes they will plug into the ground too deeply to retrieve, or occasionally get lost in the undergrowth. No point wasting any precious coated leads at this stage.

Before attaching my preferred lead, I attached my pre-tied rig. Note the reasonably large PVA Funnelweb stick threaded onto the hooklink. Casting bags or sticks of this size normally result in the lead coming off the clip on impact, but not when using the pipe trick.

With the open-ended drainpipes in place, set at a slight upward angle to create drag and to prevent the baited rigs falling out prematurely with the slightest gust of wind. The rigs are also put to the side to avoid accidentally knocking them in while baiting up. First some hemp, fishmeal pellets and crumbed boilie ...

... followed by a nice sprinkling of boilies. By using the pipes and main lines as a guide for precision baiting up, it's hard to go wrong. Plus, with the pipes held in place with wooden rests crafted from Y-shaped willow branches, they can remain in situ for the duration of the session.

Next stage is to place the rigs onto the open end of the pipes, ensuring that the main lines are at the right pressure and not so tight that they will be catapulted out the moment I take my hands off them. The objective is to abide by rules and not have rigs in the water unattended.

The rigs should sit in position like this. The weight of the lead and PVA Funnelweb stick, plus hookbait is sufficient to avoid the rigs coming off the pipes before getting back in the swim and back on my rods. I'm using 5oz Korda flat pear leads, but have used 6oz versions when having to counteract pressure on the main lines due to strong side-winds.

Thumbs up and all set and ready to go in. Now it's time to return to the rods and to pull each rig into position, with the confidence that I couldn't have done it better by casting across!

With the rigs now in position I attached the bobbins and turned my buzzers on. I could use three rods but chose to use two instead, and my results have proved that the carp fed more confidently with one fewer line in the water.

I have two identical three-metre lengths of 75mm rainwater downpipe. They didn't cost me anything because they were retrieved from a skip, and they just happen to be brown, which is ideal. On one end I have cut through halfway to create a gutter effect for about one metre, and on the other end a 20mm hole to secure in place with a bank stick. When positioning the pipes on the far margin, they are placed directly over the water's edge at a slight upward angle over the spots I want the rigs to land on. I make two wooden rests by trimming suitable branches of a willow tree and use these to lay the pipes on, and secure them in place with a bank stick through the drilled holes at the rear of the pipes.

With the pipes in position I then go back round to my swim and cast two old leads across to the far margin, close to the pipes, and then position the rods with the tips up high, the main line kept tight and the clutch on the spool loosened slightly so that I can pull some line off from the other bank if need be. Ideally, the leads will have plugged into the soil on the far bank, or snagged up on some undergrowth, so you don't pull them into the water when you tighten up your lines as this defeats the object. The reason I use old leads is that they can plug themselves so far into the soil that it's easier to lose them than try to dig them out.

Now, with two rigs and decent leads, plus bait, I'll walk back round to the pipes and release the plugged/snagged leads; attach my chosen rigs onto my main lines, replace with suitable leads, and then position the rigs in the gutter section, making sure they stay in position and don't slide off prematurely.

PVA Funnelweb stick mixes add weight and help to alleviate this problem. I go back round to the rods and then pull the rigs off the pipes one at a time into their positions. Doing this enables the angler to do things on his own without breaking any 'unattended' rules. Now, some of you may see no advantage over casting rigs out compared to using pipes, so let me explain where I see the advantages are gained.

If you rely on casting the rigs across into the water, then you may have a few casts to get the range right, and you're then relying on your judgment. Those few casts with a lead and rig attached could be detrimental, i.e. spook carp in the near vicinity. If the rods were measured out and clipped up before any casts are made then, fine, so long as you have this information from previous experiences in the swim in order to keep casting out leads to a minimum. If you're using a braided hooklink and casting, there is always a chance of the odd tangle, although this could be only a small percentage. One fewer cast and one fewer tangle, though, could mean one more carp!

Using the pipe trick helps to eliminate those occasional tangles. It also enables the angler to make fewer disturbances as the rig is pulled off the pipe into the water, so it makes less of an impact when hitting the surface, and when it settles on the bottom. It also enables the angler to change the lead from what you and others would normally cast with, from say a 3oz or 4oz distance lead which could plug into the bottom to a 5oz or 6oz flat, pear-shaped lead. It also enables the use of large Funnelweb sticks loaded with your chosen stick mix, plus a big lead, which you wouldn't normally try to cast out. It also enables the angler to fish the exact spot with precision and relative ease, time and time again.

Another alternative method of fishing for carp is zig fishing, which is very popular on some venues and hardly used on others. Basically, it's a method of fishing a hookbait sub-surface at any depth the angler chooses. If the buoyant hookbait is on the surface, then that's called 'anchored floater fishing'.

I'll openly admit that I'm no zig expert, far from it, which is why I've chosen to interview an angler who I consider far more experienced than me in this method, to educate and I hope, inspire me and others to consider an extremely effective alternative method. There have undoubtedly been moments when I've been fishing and had to work hard to catch a carp and I've come away thinking, 'I would have been better off zig fishing'.

Now, I know I'm not alone. Many of us come away from our chosen venues thinking we should have done this or that, and perhaps there may have been a different outcome to the session had we done something different. I'm fairly convinced I've missed many opportunities in the past on some venues by not zigging, but perhaps my defence is that as a sponsored angler, I do like to catch carp on boilies, not that there should be any excuses really.

In the last decade, I've caught a fair amount of big carp off the bottom and off the top but I have only caught a handful zig fishing and have lost as many as I've caught, which says a lot about my knowledge and experience of fishing this method. I've had a couple over 30lbs and half a dozen doubles to low-20s; the biggest 37lbs 12oz from Elstow, but I always seem to use the method as a last resort which isn't how it should be because it could be the best method. Rather than have me waffle on and write about zigging, let's get the low-down on how effective it can be from my good friend, Nick Helleur.

Nick scrolls through his iPad, selecting a few images for this book.

- Nick Helleur interview -

I've known Nick for quite some time and I can recall chatting to him while on the banks of Harefield Lake at the end of the 80s, when he was a super-keen teenager and living in the heart of the Colne Valley, his playground. Nick remembers me from Stanborough Lake before this, but his memory is probably better than mine, and it must have been in the winter because I only ever fished there in January or February, so it would have been a chance encounter.

We always seem to bump into each other from time to time and have a good chat about this and that, and we're always interested to hear each other's exploits. Nick is a very good carp angler and should be thinking of writing a book himself because he has fished an incredible number of carp venues in the UK and overseas, and his photo album which I've been privileged to view, is simply awesome. I'll hold my hands up and be the first to admit that my exploits of zigging could be written on the back of a postage stamp, and my reluctance to use the method has undoubtedly meant fewer carp gracing my net. Nick has caught more carp on zigs than anyone else I know, and I'm grateful that he agreed to this interview because he's educated me and will no doubt do the same to many anglers reading this book.

MC. All right then, Nick. Now we're settled in the lodge at Horton, can you recall your early days zig fishing? What prompted you to start fishing hookbaits straight up off the lead?

NH. Blimey Martin! We're going back some time. It was well before I could drive so I would have still been in my teens. What prompted me into fishing differently from the norm was what I witnessed at Walthamstow reservoirs. Typical reservoirs really, fairly flat, almost like a bowl, fish getting chased around, and at the time a lot of carp were falling to pop-ups fished straight off the lead, especially in the colder months. I started to apply this to my own fishing and began getting action so I never got bogged down with the idea that you'll only catch carp by fishing with bait on the bottom because I knew different.

Being a mad-keen youngster, I was keen to learn and just happened to go out on to a couple of lakes in the Colne Valley with lamps at night in the winter; if we'd been caught we would have been instantly banned. It was very cold and when we got to the middle of the lake we found them, about 40 carp in one group probably covering the footprint of a house, just a couple of feet, at most, below the surface. It was mad; they were all around us at one point not even spooking from the lights! That night taught me a lot about carp behaviour during a period when carp angling 'lore' said differently. I learned quickly because I was only a nipper and beyond keen. Zig fishing as we know it today wasn't being used back then so we fished in a more conventional style and struggled, although me and my mate's hooklinks got longer and longer with each year, and more than the odd carp were coming our way to hookbaits fished well off the bottom!

MC. So if we move on in time, Nick. After fishing numerous venues you eventually found yourself fishing the Linear Fisheries complex in Oxfordshire, what next?

NH. By the time I first visited the lakes in Oxfordshire, we are talking a good decade later. Well, the complex was sponsored by Shimano back then and being part of the Shimano team meant I had the privilege of the whole complex and fell in love with the quality of the carp there; loads of scaly carp. Even back then it was very popular, with a high turnover of anglers and loads of bait going in, but in the winter, even though I frequently got on the fish, I struggled to catch them. When conditions were right, of course, I'd get one or two bites off the bottom, but for the most part I'd spend three or four days a week sitting there feeling that the carp were only a rod length away, vertically! They just seemed to be wherever they felt most comfortable, often in the areas of least disturbance, and so it seemed they'd be out in the middle or at range, no matter what the wind or weather, not really moving much or expending any energy.

I was casting into the areas the carp were holding up in and as I've always been into feeling for the drop of the leads whenever casting, I began to get funny sensations on the rod as the line cut down through the water column and touched carp, so the problem wasn't location or swim choice, they were there and I proved to myself they were there. I just had to do something to shorten the odds and as far as I could see you either had to fish for them where they were, or try to drop them to the bottom. It was this train of thought that eventually meant I ended up coming up with the dynamite stick a few years down the line.

MC. That's something I've noticed on a few occasions over the years; I've even had weird tugs and knocks fishing closer to the margins and a few while reeling in!

NH. Most of us who've been fishing for carp a number of years have probably experienced this and it's simply our lines being pulled across stationary fish sitting in mid-water as we swing the lead down to the bottom on a taut line. Sometimes, these interruptions that you feel in the descent go unnoticed, because some can just be very subtle and many anglers think they've clipped weed on the drop, or fail to notice it at all. When reeling in we also 'bump' fish causing the line to momentarily tighten up and, again, this often goes unnoticed.

I'd been fishing this lake through the winter when the carp were held up along a snaggy, sheltered margin, and had been catching consistently using maggots. After a biteless night, I crept along the margin on a freezing, high-pressure morning and, sure enough, they were there, all sitting a couple of feet off the bottom and showing no inclination to feed. Back in the swim, I set-up a couple of short zigs of 18 inches, or so, and recast the rod. Within half an hour, I had these two lovely mirrors. Would I have caught if I'd stuck to my guns? Not a chance!

MC. So you were getting in the right areas and you began to change tactics. Can you take us through this period?

NH. Well, this would be mid-winter and I was fishing an area averaging 14 feet deep, so I began by fishing various pop-ups at the depth I thought the fish were holding. To begin with I wasn't super-confident using a boilie too far off the bottom at all and quickly moved away from them. They were too obvious, too big, and I felt and they lost their buoyancy quickly which meant I was never sure what depth they were sitting.

Anyway, the first bite I got was eight feet off the bottom, in the middle of a freezing cold night, on a trimmed down cork ball, when the temperature had dropped to minus four. I thought, 'right, I've sorted it', so put two rods at eight feet the following morning, but looking back with a lot more experience under my belt, those fish dropped a few feet during the night and then rose closer to the surface during the day.

Once I sussed the fact that the hookbaits worked better closer to the surface, the action picked up immensely and my confidence rose. Once I started getting multiple catches I pretty much milked the method. I can recall a few trips that stood out for me to illustrate just how effective the method can be once you get it right. One was when it was snowing and almost blizzard conditions with a raw easterly wind, and the action was amazing fishing a foot below the surface in 14 feet of water. Another was during a bank holiday weekend, while I was doing a corporate thing on St. Johns. There were 37 anglers fishing the lake and it was rammed, every single gap taken.

After a blank 24 hours on a French lake I spent the morning drifting around looking for obvious spots, but the entire lakebed was covered with filamentous algae. I changed my presentation to fishing boilies popped-up straight from the lead and, shortly after casting out, had this common carp; the first of a dozen or so over the next couple of days!

Perfect winter zigging conditions, with the sun striking a deep, sheltered bank.

My rods produced something more than 30 bites and not one fish to any other rods anywhere else on the lake. Again, all the action coming just a foot below the surface both day and night on unflavoured tiny pieces of cork or bits of black rig foam which turned out to be more buoyant and worked better at holding up long hooklinks of over 12 feet. Zig fishing is entirely different to fishing on the bottom, because you're not trying to get them to feed and lots of people can't get their heads around that. You're simply putting your hookbait where the carp want to be. There seems to be no rhyme or reason for them to suck or mouth a piece of cork or foam, but they do! Like I've written many times, the fish don't have hands so everything to be inspected that they are not scared of is taken into the mouth.

MC. With every method, Nick, there are times and places where it works better than another. Can you highlight any circumstances such as air pressure or moon phases that can assist any of us in any way with zig fishing in mind?

NH. To some degree, the weather does play a part, but I think angling pressure plays a bigger one. As you know, Martin, I've fished many venues around Oxfordshire and most of them have a good head of carp and receive a fair amount of angling pressure, and it's this pressure that often creates these situations. Yes, carp do feed on the bottom, but not all the time. Zig fishing is all about being aware of those situations and presenting a bait where it will receive action. In the summer months, how many anglers will you see fishing on or in the weed?

I'd observed carp going in and out of a weedy bay all afternoon, showing no interest in my carefully placed rigs, and feeding on some small clear areas. I changed to fishing bits of cork suspended a foot below the surface and cast these on their patrol route. As the light faded and the carp started to exit the bay, I caught three in quick succession, including this lovely, scaly mirror, previously uncaught from this clear-water lake.

Nick, gingerly playing a very large carp on a long hooklink.

Most will look for a hard spot or chuck a solid bag out; only a few will zig fish. You know, Martin, having been around so many venues over the years, I've noticed that on some fisheries, carp fishing is so trend orientated that lots of anglers are picking up pointers from those around them.

I've recently been chatting with some of my mates, recollecting things we did for the first time, like chucking in tigernuts or using pop-ups; certain things having a large impact on the outcome. If we go right back in time, before the hair rig, before particles, what were the anglers doing? They were fishing anchored crust either on the surface or just below. What does that say, Martin? They were more right than wrong!

Here's another example. A fair while ago, a match angler was fishing one of these carp puddles, a winter match in February with ice on the surface, and fishing a little method feeder to a clipped-up spot. Throughout the match, everyone was struggling and this guy kept feeling his feeder clumping fish on the way down in his swim, which was only six-feet deep. In the last hour of the match with nothing to lose, he changed his bait to a buoyant piece of corn fished two-feet straight up off the feeder. There was obviously a group of fish in the swim and even though they were only a couple of feet at most off the bottom they just sat there and wouldn't drop to eat the bait, and remember we are talking young fish here in a hungry lake. In the last hour of the match he caught 150lb of carp, and took all the prize money by being aware of what was going on and being astute enough to act on it, rather than sit there catching nothing like everyone else. Good angling!

A lovely Oxfordshire brace from a pressured lake caught on tiny cork baits. Both in the middle of the night, out in the middle of the lake, when it was minus-four fishing zigs a foot under the surface. Understanding your quarry is paramount to success with this method.

Zigging does require thought and there are times when you can lose fish, similar to other methods, so it's a case of learning and using your common sense as to when and where it's feasible to use the method. There are many opportunities when zig fishing will get you a lot of bites, but not all the time. You have to use your judgement, and if it's too weedy or snaggy you'll struggle to land anything, and that's not what any of us want.

MC. I know you, Nick. You're always trying different things and have probably used lots of different hookbaits. What would you say are your favourite zig baits, and why?

NH. The easy answer would be whatever gets the most bites, but if I look back on the venues where the water was coloured and full of fish, then bright foam or pop-ups have worked better. When the water

I persevered with zigs at various depths while the local anglers were chucking out bottom baits and PVA bags, until I started catching. This carp was one of 30 I caught in two months after Christmas and during that time no other carp were caught!

is clear though and the carp are more wary, then brown or black hookbaits such as cork or foam have scored the best; the baits don't have to be food-based or flavoured. Having played around with all sorts, it seems the smallest possible bait to hold up whatever length of hooklink picked up more fish, so I used to trim the baits down to make them exactly how I wanted them. Cork and foam perform this task perfectly, it's as simple as that.

I've tried various small pop-ups but they can be inconsistent because some take on water, especially if you trim them down or shave bits off. They could sink a foot in an hour, or even more over a few hours, so you could be missing out, or even getting bites at a certain depth and you won't know the exact depth the bait was if you did get a take. That's not to say you won't get takes on a slow-sinking bait, and I can recall a perfect example of that happening to me not so long ago on another Oxfordshire water.

I was fishing the winter on the lake in question and using maggots as my main approach. Anyway, two young lads set up next door to me and shared an amazing catch, given the conditions and time of year, by doing something very different. They whittled down a pop-up so the weight of the hook only just sank the hookbait and then stuck some dissolving foam on the hook. Then they attached a Funnelweb bag with some stones inside for casting weight, and whacked it out as far as they could cast. They waited for the bag to melt and then reeled back in a few yards, lay the rod down after loosening the clutch and waited for the spool to start spinning. No leads required and they had 17 bites over 48 hours! I said, 'Fair play lads - that's good angling,' and it was.

First carp of 2013 taken from a small but very deep lake on a seven-foot zig in 12 feet of water. On this occasion, a piece of black foam was used as hookbait.

MC. Let's face it, Nick. Fishing would be boring if we all stuck to one method. I've tried something similar to that but while surface fishing, with a controller float and without. Do you feel zigging to be more productive in the colder months?

NH. Yes and no, Martin. It could produce action at any time throughout the year. Fishing on the bottom requires time and patience among other things, and I'm not very patient because I like to be a bit more active. You've watched carp, Martin, on many venues. They spend less time on the bottom than they do mid-water or closer to the surface; all you need is the self-belief to try it. I haven't experienced aggravation from nuisance fish or birdlife, which is another bonus many anglers don't take into consideration. It also works well on overseas venues, which as you know, Martin, is another passion of mine!

MC. Obviously, when using multiple rods you can fish hookbaits at slightly different depths to ascertain the perfect depth. This can cause a few problems. Have you encountered problems, and if so, can they be minimised?

NH. Yes, you will encounter problems with multiple zigs out, but not necessarily all the time. If a hooked carp kites left or right, depending on which rod, you may get away with it, or it will kite through other lines. If there is a little bit of weed about on the bottom this can help, as you can quickly drag the potential problem rod which can sink the zigged hookbait out of harm's way while you deal with the one you're playing, not always guaranteed though.

MC. I have to agree with you, Nick. Not only have you caught a vast amount of carp on the method, but many others have too. You know when you've got things right, when you get bites pretty quickly whatever the method. Have you had many instant bites while zigging on venues you've never fished before? If so, can you give me another example of how effective it can be?

NH. Loads of instant bites, Martin, too many to recall! There have also been times when I've had to work at it and it has taken time to suss out the right depths in certain areas, and it may have taken a number of days or sessions to build up a mental picture. When everything is right though, it's embarrassingly effective.

This is a good example: a few years ago, Rob Maylin phoned to tell me there was a free week's fishing on a French lake. It was a prize won by someone who didn't want it; not exactly sure on the details but it was a free week and the whole lake for a small party of anglers. I made a few calls and before you know it a bunch of mates and I arrived at this lake, a commercial venue which allowed bait boats. Half of us went on one bank and the other half opposite. Picture the scene, a power cable going over the lake which made casting out to the middle a tad awkward. While everyone was sorting their gear out, necking a few green bottles, a couple of carp showed in the middle so I whacked a lead out to the area, just missing the overhead lines. The lead went down with a thud and I estimated the depth to be something like nine feet.

I tied up two zig rigs, one at seven feet, the other eight feet long, with one brown hookbait, the other black. I cast the first rod out, pukka first cast exactly where the fish had showed, and put the rod on the buzzer. I walked back to pick up the second rod and the first rod was off before I'd taken four steps. 'Oi Oi!' they all shouted, seeing me bent into one, so they all wandered round to see what was on the other end. Once it was in the net, I said to one of my mates, "Hold on, let me cast the other rod out." Just as we got the carp out for weighing and photographing, bang, off went the other rod and I was in again. I can't remember which was which but one was an upper-30. the other a low-40, all the boys were calling me golden balls - plenty of good banter! After the photos I whacked the rods back out and had another one within minutes.

The lads went back to their swims and by the time they were getting out I'd had another four or five bites. The first bait boat went out at 8pm, and after that everything went quiet, almost like flicking a switch. To cut a long story short, by the end of the week I had 11 bites on zig rigs and all my mates who fished on the bottom over bait struggled to get one, not because they were poor anglers but because they were in lazy mode.

MC. I can remember fishing Horseshoe Lake back in the 80s, spodding out bait and the carp responding to the spod, like ringing a dinner bell. I've had this happen a few times at various venues, and clearly the carp were feeding on the bait as it descended through the water. Now, we have various sloppy spod mixes designed for these situations, and we even have carp matches being won with anglers spodding over zig hookbaits. Have you done this while zigging?

NH. I have played around with a few things to create a cloud or haze. On venues with a massive head of carp, which respond to spod tactics, I doubt that half the bait actually gets to the bottom and a lot of other anglers are realising this. To be honest, it's not really my style of fishing. I prefer to fish zigs as you would with single hookbaits, but that said, I do think there will be future developments in catching carp mid-water because it's still in its infancy.

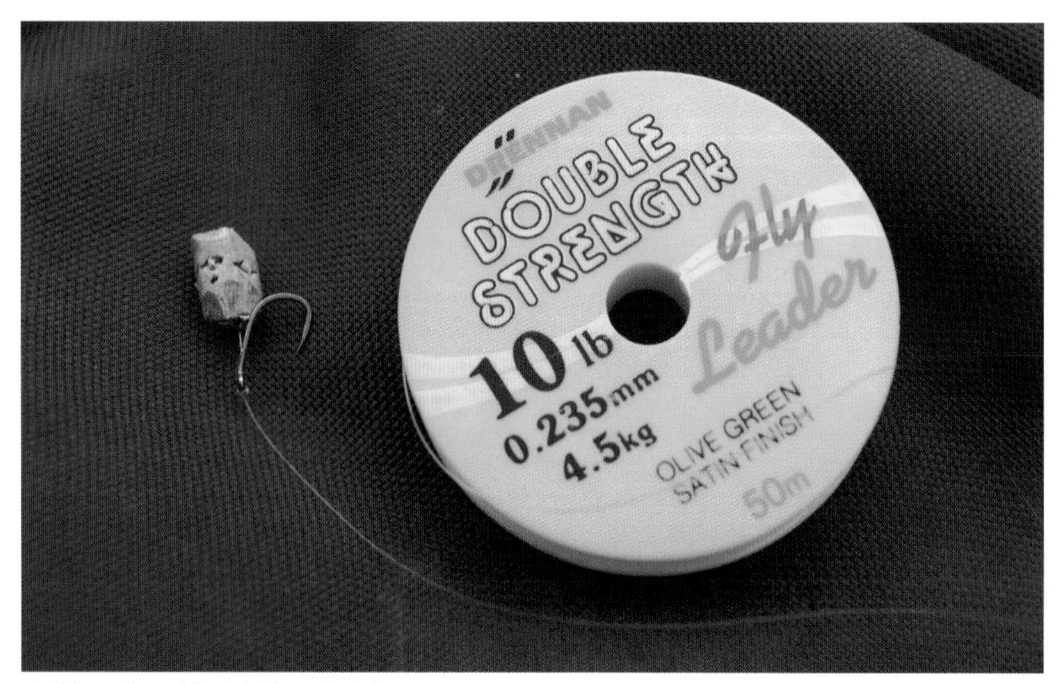

Nick's preferred hooklink material.

MC. So let's have a closer look at your zig set-up. Can you run through the components?

NH. Well, a simple helicopter set-up with a four-ounce lead; hooklink is either 8lb or 10lb Drennan Double Strength which just happens to be 12 feet in length. Hooks, usually a size 10 or 12 Korda Wide Gape, which I prefer to tie with a palomar knot and then half-hitch the hair once around the shank, small foam or cork hookbait with a small slit cut in, to sit part of the hook shank in, and that's about it, really simple. A few anglers advocate the use of lighter leads although personally, I don't feel this is essential unless fishing at very close range. If it were, then why have I caught so many using bigger leads? I have used bigger hooks but it unbalances what is a delicate set-up. I've a lot of faith in using small hooks so will continue to use these because you can use smaller hookbaits!

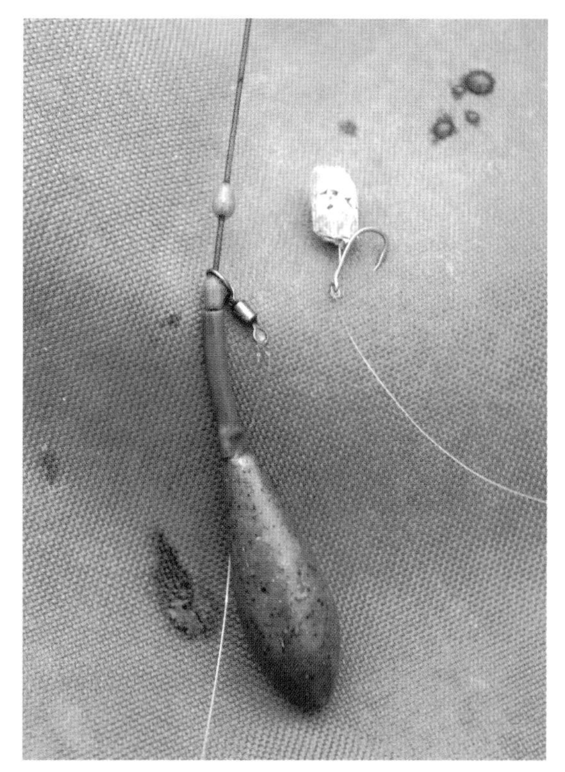

Nick's zig rig set-up.

MC. Cheers, Nick, you're a star. We'll call that a wrap.

After another cup of tea in the lodge and another look at Nick's impressive image library on his iPad, I pointed the van toward Luton. All I had to do now was type it all up!

Now I know just how good zigging can be, I hope to do much more of it in the future. Rather than zigging being a last resort, it should be considered the best option on some venues, and in some situations. From my early days fishing Woburn Sands, I've always known carp to be shoaled up during the colder months and spend the majority of their time in the upper layers rather than on the bottom. Nick has caught hundreds of carp by zigging, while I only need two hands to count how many bites I've had using the method. Quite a few of my friends have had success while zigging, but then quite a few of them haven't even tried it and haven't had any. I'm positive that many anglers are missing out, the question is how many?

Chapter 10

Using boats

For the majority of UK carp anglers, using a boat of any description isn't an option until they venture on to venues where they are allowed, and then we're faced with a choice - to use a boat or not? If you have never used one then you may not be aware of the advantages and disadvantages and if your experiences of using a boat can be written on the back of a postage stamp then you have little ammunition to criticise. Boats have had a fair amount of stick on the Internet carp fishing forums, some of it justified, some not. I can certainly see a problem with some practices, and safety and ethics are contentious issues.

In truth, we should all be capable of catching carp without the use of any boat. Even on the bigger venues it's never impossible to catch carp without using one, but use a boat properly and safely, and you'll enjoy doing something a bit different to the norm. From experiences I've had whilst fishing these venues, actually using a boat is a brilliant and exciting way to learn more about the venue and catch carp, which may or may not have come your way without the assistance of a boat. When it comes down to landing your prize, then so long as you're not trying to pull the wool over the eyes of others and you use common sense there shouldn't be a problem.

There are problems to overcome though, and if you're not aware of the possible pitfalls and don't take these into account, not only could it be detrimental to your fishing but it could also prove costly in other ways. It should always be remembered that there's more than one way to catch carp and using a boat is just another method which needs to be learned to reap any rewards. There is always the temptation to stick too much bait out, so remember, once you've put it in you can't take it out unless you can scoop it up off the bottom, which could result in a lengthy time period waiting for something to pick up a hookbait.

Rowing boats

Fellow carp anglers, please note that once you take to the water on any type of boat, you can be putting your life, and possibly others, in danger, so make sure the boat is sound with no leaks, and not a deathtrap before you push away from the bank. Whether you're on a duck pond or an inland ocean, make a mistake and you could regret it, or worse still, not be around too long. Lifejackets do not cost much and are a 'must have' piece of kit on any fishery that allows anglers to go out on the water, in my opinion. Having had friends lose some of their best mates through drowning you soon realise the danger is real, sadly. If they had been wearing lifejackets they may still be around today, R.I.P. to all those anglers no longer with us.

I was a keen swimmer in my youth and obtained lifesaving certificates. I know how to swim fully-clothed; that was all part of the training. I've also swum in a few freshwater lakes, though mostly in the warmer months. The cold water is very hard to handle if you fall in. You will go into shock mode as the cold water begins to take effect on your brain and body; add some weed to that and it's an easy assumption to make; panic sets in!

Boats which we can get into and explore the venue with, and even play fish from, come in all shapes and sizes, from little inflatable dinghies to larger, solid plastic or fibreglass models which are large enough to transport you and all your tackle with relative ease. Personally, I would avoid inflatables as they have to be treated with kid gloves to avoid punctures. Solid boats are much more stable, user-friendly, and less prone to damage on stones or rocks when pulling on to dry land, or punctures from anything sharp such as fishing tackle or anything else that could affect the buoyancy chambers of an inflatable.

As with all methods of angling, there are some advantages and disadvantages and while using a boat you soon discover a whole new way of fishing and learning. I should add that boats suitable for carp fishing, such as the Bic 252 or fibreglass rowing boats around 8 feet to 10 feet long, are best suited to the larger venues in the UK and those abroad, which gives us access to islands or swims that would be otherwise inaccessible, making our life easier because we haven't got to hump all the gear on our backs or on a barrow. Moving swims in a boat, or getting to a swim with a boat, is easy with the right gear, even in rough conditions, although it must be said, your first thought must always be your personal safety.

I haven't used a boat of any sort in the last five years, but I still have the gear and knowledge on how and when to use a boat effectively, so hope to do so in the future when I find another nice piece of water to settle on.

Basically, there are a few ways we can use a boat; with oars, with an electric outboard engine, or using a pole to punt yourself if it's shallow enough or extremely weedy. Rowing is the cheap option, and an electric engine is the sensible one. The difference is immense because with oars you cannot get the full benefit of a boat, single-handed, and with an engine you have an edge as you can use the boat without any assistance. Obviously, the biggest edge a boat gives the angler is the ability to learn about the venue's topography much quicker, and possibly fish further out than one could cast, if allowed to position rigs using the boat.

Viewing spots through a glass-bottomed bucket is addictive on venues with good water clarity.

On large venues an echo sounder can prove useful. A lifejacket is essential on any venue!

You simply can't beat the speed and handling you get with an electric engine.

When you use oars as your method of propulsion, you will lose some of the advantages a boat can give you. With an engine you can remain standing, observing at all times, even when you are out on the water on your own. True, you can look and learn using oars, but not half as much as with an engine, and as conditions go from flat calm to choppy, you will be spending more time controlling the boat with the oars than looking into the water.

Believe me, I've done it with oars, and even though I'm fairly adept at using them, they are nowhere as good as an electric engine. I've seen and heard of so many nightmares when oars have been used, and in my opinion, they should only be used as a two-man operation. Not only have I rescued anglers struggling to play carp on their own and at the mercy of the wind, but also every year someone, somewhere, puts their desire to catch above fish safety, and simply winches their way out to weeded carp. I do think it is unethical for an angler to jump into a boat, with or without oars, to then winch themselves toward the fish using their reel and rod pressure. Then they'll spin round or get towed around in an uncontrolled fashion, eventually land the fish, and then row back with the landing net hanging off the back of the boat. I've even heard of tales where the angler went out on a boat with no oars or engine, managed to land a 50lb-plus carp, and then had to be rescued.

I'd rather use an engine, be in total control, and not have to rely on other people to row the boat or land the fish, and then get back to dry land within a few minutes. Without an engine it takes four times longer to land the fish, on the calm days, and rowing back to the bank with a carp in a net and in the water is like riding a bike with a parachute on. Why not have an unhooking mat in the boat, place the fish on the mat and either unhook it and let it go, or whizz back to shore if it warrants getting the scales or camera out?

I brought my Minn Kota engine mail-order straight from America and have every faith in giving it a glowing review because it has never let me down and has done everything expected of it. It has a 55lb thrust engine, which is a Maxim motor and slightly more energy-efficient than the slightly cheaper versions. It also doesn't have gears, with set speeds like on cheaper engines, which makes using it such a pleasure because you simply wind the throttle on the handle to go faster or slower and it really does come into its own league when playing fish, and when holding position against almost any wind.

Although having a variable throttle on an electric engine is not essential, you soon notice the benefits, so they're worth that little bit more if you're considering forking out hard-earned money for an electric engine. I've used both types of engine while out on the water looking and learning, and while playing carp, on my own and with friends, and the engines with gears can at times be frustrating because the ride and speed changes aren't smooth with quite sharp differences between gear changes. Very often you feel you're going too slowly or too quickly and when you make a gear change or cut the power when in close proximity of some carp, you will see that they respond to the sudden change. The variable-thrust type of engines enable the user to wind down the speed to a trickle if need be, thus avoiding detrimental speed changes.

Because you can go anywhere on the venue, at any speed, you'd be wise not to charge around like a bull in a china shop when you're looking and learning, especially in water less than ten feet deep. Nine times out of ten the carp are aware of your presence as you approach, although at times they show little caution, perhaps more so on venues which have other boating activities as they will have become accustomed to boats. On a number of occasions, I've had carp swimming around the boat and even follow it, seemingly without a care in the world. I've also seen the odd carp bolt, although they seldom go far, but you can never guarantee how they respond because they are less spooky in deeper open water than when they are around shallower features and marginal areas.

Useful items of kit, such as a glass-bottomed bucket and a few Gardner H-Blocks, or more standard marker floats come in very handy because you can mark spots without the need for a marker rod, should you wish to. Viewing the bottom of the venue is possible if the water clarity is good and you can see down a fair depth with the aid of a viewing bucket so they, too, come in handy. You could use a face mask and snorkel if you don't mind dunking your head in cold water. An echo sounder is also useful on the deeper venues, but not essential, and this will come down to how many of the venue's depths and features you can view with your eyes; on a large European venues I would think that echo sounders can be extremely useful.

One thing that does become apparent, when fishing beyond 100 yards, is the need for greater tension on the bobbins and the benefits of dumping the lead when there's a fish on. You also need to be cautious of your lines should you use the boat with multiple rods out, day or night, and be ready at all times to take to the water with landing net and unhooking mat in the boat.

I designed some lead weights solely for the purpose of lowering rigs to their resting position, primarily for boat use but they can also be used while margin fishing. I nicknamed them UFOs, Unidentified Fixed Objects, which resembled a plug or Rolo chocolate with a hole in the middle which houses a cut-down lead clip. They cannot be cast, only lowered or gently swung into position, because the swivel is pushed into the clip so that when a carp bolts, or you strike the rod, the lead comes off very easily. By their very shape and design, you'll notice that there is no pivoting of the end tackle as there is when using a lead clip with a swivelled lead set-up more commonly used when casting out rigs.

As I had geared myself up to fish some venues which allowed boats, I then joined a few where the rules were more relaxed; Fen Drayton and a publicity-shy venue not far away from Shepperton Studios where some low-life nicked my boat from the supposedly secure boat compound. Fingers were pointed toward the likely culprit, his motive was simply that he didn't want me on the lake; afraid I'd catch a few. Sad, very sad! Mentally, I was torn between a few venues with others on the radar, but my brief sessions while bobbing around on 50-acre-plus waters was a real eye-opener.

At night, it's a wise choice to have a light beside your rods, such as a cheap, red, rear bicycle lamp, so that while you're out in the boat in darkness you can safely navigate yourself back to your swim. Before I'd even taken to the water I'd thought of this possible problem so purchased one at a local car boot sale for a quid.

I once heard of an angler getting lost out on a big French reservoir at night, having just landed a 45lb-plus carp somewhere out there in the pitch black. After rowing around for half an hour, he decided to release the carp. It then took him another two hours to get his bearings and find his way back. Luckily, nothing picked up any of his other hookbaits while he was lost. I think he now uses GPS devices for his foreign adventures, something which a fair number of overseas carp anglers use which takes away the need to leave markers out on the water if they so wish. If I lived and fished in France, I'd definitely use all the toys on venues in excess of 1000 acres. Fishing - yes, but not as we know it, because most of us go about our fishing without being afloat up and down the British waterways.

Hopefully, one day I will return to this venue and capitalise on what I've learned.

Dropping a rig back onto a productive spot.

Playing carp from a boat

Martin Ford interviewed me on a couple of venues while I happened to be fishing with a boat, and did an excellent three-part feature in Advanced Carp magazine back in December 2003, covering a few aspects related to the use of boats, and called it 'Boat Craft'. Some of you may have read it at the time. For the benefit of those who didn't, I hope what follows proves helpful if you find yourself going afloat.

I cringe and shake my head when I see anglers going afloat on their own and then reeling themselves out toward their hooked prize. Do they not realise the pressure on the rod, reel and main line could cause the hook hold to fail? Or that the main line could get cut up by mussel-festooned weed beds, gravel bars, or worse still damage the mouth of the carp? Now, this practice may seem fine on a little British venue on a windless day when you may not be going out that far from your swim, but add wind and distance to the situation and the difficulty factor increases dramatically. The sensible thing is to have someone rowing the boat for you, or better still, use an electric engine!

The boat should be ready and in a position at all times so that it can be launched easily once you've slipped on a lifejacket; remember, you'll have a rod in your hands and a carp on the other end. Once you're afloat in a boat with an electric engine, the propeller can be dropped easily and provided the battery is always connected, you're immediately in business. I prefer to go out toward the hooked fish, stern first, with the engine in reverse gear at slow speed. This way, it is easy to control the tiller and the rod at the same time and while maintaining a steady, straight course toward the fish, you can reel and keep sufficient pressure on it. Try doing it on your own and go toward the hooked fish bow first, and you'll find you'll be zig-zagging, or worse still, spinning out of control.

When you're a few rod lengths away from the fish, it's best to move to the bow of the boat and play it out kneeling down, thus aiding stability and lowering the rod angle until it's ready for the net. If it starts towing you around, then let it, because it obviously isn't ready for netting so there is no need for bullying tactics. Enjoy the moment because this is what you're there for. If you feel the need, you can always go back to the stern and use the engine; you could also use the power of the engine to act as a brake. The smaller the boat the easier it will be for a big carp to tow you around and, even though you have the firm base and stability of the boat, it's a bit like playing a carp while wearing roller skates, or standing on ice. The carp pulls hard and you move toward it, then you pull back - and you still move toward the carp.

Bait boats

Pardon me if you find the next few paragraphs of little use, but in all fairness, my experiences with a bait boat could be written on the back of a postage stamp. I did own a Microcat bait boat for a few years and purchased it for a couple of reasons. First, I had money to squander having earned and saved up a few grand on a local contract, and secondly, I just happened to join a few venues which allowed the use of bait boats and I could see the benefits.

Now, even though I sold it a couple of years later and I never got to use it much, I can see that they can be a valuable tool to use, in the right hands on the right venue. Everything is easier so the angler can save time introducing bait quietly and accurately at range, if need be. Some anglers call it cheating and disagree totally with the use of bait boats; personally, I can't see a problem unless the anglers are stitching up the lake or towing hookbaits out into dodgy positions, such as snags or even round the back of islands.

Using a bait boat should help anyone to catch fish, but they have still got to use a good rig and bait and stick it in the right place at the right time to get the best out of the boat. One thing I was never totally happy with was dropping the rig and bait in one hopper to avoid tangles. It was best done while holding the rod, keeping some pressure on the main line so you could feel the lead swing down into position. Great in shallow water but do this in deep water and the free offerings and rigs are not necessarily on the same spot if everything is in one hopper.

I found it best to drop the hookbait in one hopper and the free offerings in the other, send the boat out to its position and drop the hookbait with a PVA pop-up attached to the rig, and when it pops to the surface manoeuvre the boat to drop the bait directly over the hookbait. Fine, if you can see it, or be helped out by a friend, but at range or without helping hands the bait can be dropped first and then the boat can be driven a few feet, or yards, further and then dropped, allowing for the hookbait to swing back on to the free offerings.

Having two markers on your main line can prove helpful for accuracy if dropping baits and rigs into deep water. Without any markers you can't be absolutely sure you're dropping the baits back to the exact spot you received the last or first fish from. It may be crucial, it may not, time will tell because you're in control. Just remember to keep spare batteries or a decent charger or solar panel charger if you're going on a lengthy session.

Chapter 11

Carp competition recollections

I've known Barry and Ben O'Connor for quite some time and once I'd made the decision to write this book, I couldn't think of a better friend and angler who could write a guest chapter revolving around the match fishing side of carp angling. Carp match fishing may not be everyone's cup of tea, but those that do it enjoy it and there are just as many lessons to be learned along the way, just as there are when fishing for personal pleasure.

The father and son duo regularly appear in Carp Talk and the British Carp Angling Championship matches and are well-known faces within the British carp scene. From Sutton in Surrey, Barry, now a retired boiler engineer, and Ben, a roofer by trade, have travelled far and wide, catching carp along the way and picking up a few trophies in the process. Both are sponsored by ATT Alarms, Fox, Enterprise Tackle, Mainline, Bankside tackle and Diem clothing.

Could I twist Barry's arm into writing a guest chapter about some of their exploits? Every year we meet up while donating our free time fishing the charity fish-ins on the Richworth Linear Fisheries complex, so I popped the question during the evening barbecue and Barry said he'd be honoured to put pen to paper.

During the auction to raise even more money, there was a guest October session up for grabs with me on Elstow Pit 1, and Ben outbid those who fancied the opportunity. Barry had words, put his hand in his pocket, Bob's your uncle, and they both made the trek up to Elstow. Well, despite fishing into the teeth of a north-westerly, we all managed to flex carbon, and three carp graced our nets with another two falling off. Barry and Ben loved every minute, and when they left for home, Barry said he'd get to work on the chapter and I wished them good luck in their forthcoming matches. Well, they didn't need my luck!

- Barry and Ben O'Connor -

Ben and I have fished as a team in carp matches for many years now and during that time we've competed against some top anglers from up and down the country. Carp matches over the years have gathered a large following. They're not everyone's cup of tea; you either love them or loathe them – a bit like Marmite, I suppose. Anyone can compete in a carp match. It's a chance for unknown anglers to take on some of the big names in carp fishing. Just because they're unknown it doesn't mean they don't know how to fish though, far from it. There are many anglers around who are quite capable of taking on the best and beating them. It's never good to be complacent in any fishing competition. If you are, it could be your downfall. Skill definitely plays a big part in matches, but so does luck. Skill is knowing where to place your hookbait, what rigs to use and when to put more bait out etc. Much the same as when you're pleasure fishing but with more dire consequences if you get it wrong.

Luck also plays its part, especially with the draw. For those who don't know how the draw works, I'll give you a brief insight into it because the draw determines what swim you'll get. There are two types of draws in carp matches, watercraft and out-of-the-bag.

In a watercraft draw, before the draw takes place all the competitors walk around the lake and make a list of the swims. Each competitor, or pair, determines what they believe to be the best swims and mark them down in order of merit. The competitors' names are then drawn at random. When your name is called you can pick a swim from your list. The earlier your name is called the better your chances are of getting a good swim. Coming out first gives you first choice of swims, second gives you second choice, and so on. We have been called out last on a couple of occasions though, and gone on to win.

With an out-of-the-bag draw, when your name is called, you get to pick a canister from the bag or bowl. The canister contains a peg number and that is where you have to fish from. It's a lucky-dip-type draw and can be a great leveller on the playing field. Matches are often won and lost in the draw bag.

Although we didn't take part in them, the earliest carp matches I can recall were the Carp Society Inter-Regional Matches back in the 80s. Later, the Sony King Carp Challenge appeared; way back in 1995 I believe, which was a singles match that attracted some top anglers such as Lee Jackson, Martin Locke, Tim Paisley, Tim Hodges, Paul Forward et al. The first prize was a whopping £10,000 of tackle and was eventually won by Tim Hodges who was the only angler to catch. It was a one-off competition, never to appear again.

It was also during 1995 that a competition called 'The Masters' first appeared on the fishing scene. It was the mastermind of David Marle the owner of Great Linford Lakes near Newport Pagnell in Buckinghamshire. It wasn't strictly a carp-fishing match, more a roving, coarse-fishing competition and endurance test. It was the ultimate test, taxing your fishing skills and your judgment to the limit and didn't rely on drawing well. There was a junior and senior event that ran independently of each other. The junior event was over a period of 24 hours and the senior one for 38 hours. The rules for both the junior and senior events were basically the same except that the top 25 seniors qualified for a pegged-down match at the end.

There was a list of nine species; mirror carp, common carp, chub, barbel, roach, bream, tench, perch and river carp. Contestants had to catch all nine, or as many as they could, within the allotted time using one or two rods. The heaviest 25 fish of each species caught during the roving match won points, from 25 for the biggest, down to one point for the smallest. It all sounds very easy, but there were nine lakes and two and a half miles of river to fish which were spread over a 300-acre estate and you had to walk everywhere.

The Tournament Committee

cordially invites you

to participate in

the Nineteen Hundred and Ninety Seven

Junior Angling Masters Championship

to be held at

Great Linford Lakes

Ben's invitation to take part in the 1997 Junior Masters.

Great Linford Lakes - UK Masters

	Carp Common	Carp Mirror	Carp River	Tench	Chub	Barbel	Roach	Bream	Perch	Total
1 BEN O'CONNOR	25 16.10	24 10.05	0	19 1.09	23 0.05	25 10.10	19 0.04	23 4.06	23 1.08	181
2 JAMIE COOK	22 2.06	22 9.07	0	21 3.02	20 0.02	0 0.00	23 0.07	19 1.15	15 0.08	142
3 PETER HIGGINS	0	20 6.02	0	24 4.03	20 0.02	0	21 0.06	25 6.03	21 1.04	131
I TERRY GLASGOW	0	21 8.13	0	22 3.04	24 0.06	0	19 0.04	16 0.01	15 0.08	117
STUART McKERNON	24 13.05	0	0	18 1.07	16 0.01	0	15 0.03	16 0.01	18 0.12	107
CHRIS SWADEN	23 2.12	25 14.00	0	0	21 0.04	0	19 0.04	0	17 0.10	105
CHRISTOPHER HARMA	0	0	0	23 3.11	20 0.02	0	23 0.07	17 0.07	19 0.14	102
ALAN STAGG	0	0	0	0	25 0.08	0	24 0.10	18 0.08	24 1.09	91
RICHARD CHAMBERLAI	0	0	0	0	16 0.01	0	21 0.06	21 3.10	25 1.10	83
JAMES MAXFIELD	0	19 2.01	0	0	23 0.05	0	25 0.14	0	11 0.01	78
ROSS BARTON	0	0	0	20 1.14	0	0	19 0.04	22 4.00	12 0.06	73
KRISTOPHER DOE	0	0	0	0	20 0.02	0	15 0.03	20 3.09	16 0.09	71
LEX HARVEY	0	0	0	0	0	0	15 0.03	24 5.04	23 1.08	62
AMES HENSHAW	0	23 10.04	0	25 4.11	0	0	0	0	0	48
SHLEY FAIRBROTHER	0	0	0	0	0	0	15 0.03	0	13 0.07	28

Ben won the Junior Masters. Hard work but daddy drove home well proud of his son's result!

Ben and I work hard, but we love carp fishing, and match fishing is just part of our lives.

Tiredness would be a major factor because of the vast distances that would have to be covered in pursuit of all the species on the list. It was impossible to carry every piece of tackle required to catch the different fish. Float rods, quiver rods and carp rods were all needed, as well as different reels, plus all the bits of tackle to go with them. You couldn't carry it all. No bivvy, no bedchair and no sleeping bag; a brolly or groundsheet was all that covered you if it started raining. Once one species was caught, did you move on or try to catch a bigger one? What a dilemma!

Planning and preparation was essential if you wanted to stand any chance of succeeding. As the competition continued, hard-earned points could vanish in flash. When other competitors caught bigger fish than yours, they moved up the leader board while you moved down. It was exciting stuff to watch, but not if you were in it.

Ben took part in the inaugural junior event at the ripe old age of 13. The juniors were allowed to have a parent or guardian with them. Although I couldn't fish I was allowed to help Ben carry his tackle, and believe me when I tell you it certainly was exhausting! Some competitors, junior and senior gave up through sheer exhaustion. One very well-known top angler freely admitted he was delusional through lack of sleep and ended up on a lake that wasn't on the complex. Without realising it, he'd walked across the road to another fishery. He fell asleep and when he awoke realised his mistake and got back to the right fishery. Ben took part in all three of the Junior Masters. He came third on the first attempt and won the other two, winning himself a total of £5750 in the process. Ben also won a year's consultancy with Normark which had us fishing up and down the country with some of the top Normark consultants. This included top all round angler, Bob James; world champion fly fisherman Hywel Morgan, well-known pike angler Gord Burton, and sea angler Ed (the Rock Hopper) Schliffke. We had a great time with that.

The list of competitors in the Senior Masters was like a who's who of angling, including Paul Garner, Bob Roberts, Jan Porter, Terry Hearn, Dave Lane, Steve Briggs and Martin Clarke, among others. Both Paul Garner and Bob Roberts won this event. After winning the third Junior Masters, Ben was too old to go in it for a fourth time. He could only go in the senior event. Normark took out a £10,000 insurance policy on Ben to win the Senior Masters. If he won it Ben would get £10,000, unfortunately he never got invited, strange that!

In 1996, the first official World Cup took place at Fishabil in France. Rob Hughes and Simon Crow were the victors and became the first-ever official World Cup Champions.

Our first encounter with carp matches started in 1999 when Rob Hughes and Ross Honey released the British Carp Angling Championships (BCAC) on to the carping fraternity. Some said it wouldn't last, well, 14 years later and with Simon Bennie now owning the BCAC, it's still going strong and has a waiting list as long as your arm. Such is the popularity of the BCAC, that other carp competitions have now appeared and they too have waiting lists. The BCAC is a pairs event with a series of eliminators taking place around the country at different venues. It was the top three from each eliminator that went through to the final. The first final was held on the Carp Society's Horseshoe Lake in 1999. In the early years it wasn't uncommon to have 20-plus competitors in an eliminator, and 30 or so in the final.

Ben and I were invited to take part in the inaugural BCAC match. We didn't fish it as a team though, that came later. I fished with my mate Dave Smallwood in the main BCAC while Ben, who was 15 at the time, fished with his friend Dean Mercer in the Junior BCAC. The first senior BCAC eliminator was held on Farlows, in Buckinghamshire. To be fair, most of the competitors didn't take it too seriously, including my mate Dave and me. We didn't practise or prepare, we just turned up and fished. The draw took place and we ended up in a good swim, although we didn't know it at the time.

Knowing absolutely nothing about the lake didn't help either. In the next peg was the author of this book, Martin Clarke, and Steve Briggs, two high-profile anglers who know how to catch carp. Steve used to live in one of the houses on Farlows so what chance did we have? I can remember to this day the Union Jack flag flying in the wind on top of the building on Heron's Point.

The match was started in dramatic style by letting off a large maroon rocket. Well, to say we failed miserably is an understatement. Other than a couple of bream, we caught nothing. Martin and Steve didn't fare much better, although Steve caught a duck and was awarded a loaf of bread at the presentation. Ben wasn't fishing this event; he was helping to marshall it. He fished his first-ever junior eliminator on St. John's Lake at Linear Fisheries in Oxford. The junior and senior anglers had to fish in the same eliminator alongside each other. Ben, and his mate Dean, didn't get through and were offered another try at Kingsbury Water Park in the West Midlands. Unfortunately, Dean couldn't make it so Ben partnered another friend, Peter Higgins, but they failed to qualify.

In the early days of the tournament, you could enter as many times as you liked. Some anglers re-entered several times to try to win the coveted trophy and the prize money. I believe the record for entering in one year is eight times and is held by a very well-known angler. Little did we know at the time that the BCAC and Farlows would play a major role in our carp fishing in years to come.

In 1998, a year before the BCAC started up, another tournament had its first showing. This event wasn't in England, but in France. 'The World Carp Classic', took place on Lac Madine, a 2,718-acre lake in the Lorraine region of France. Over 140 anglers would battle it out for the £10,000 prize money in this 48-hour event, and many top anglers from all over the world entered. In the first year it was an individual, 'winner takes all' event and Paul Rayment was the first-ever winner. He could choose either a brand new car worth around £14,000, which was on show at the venue, or £10,000. He drove off in the car for the purposes of TV but actually took the cash.

The next year, the event was still at Lac Madine but was now a pairs competition. Later, the event went to Lac Amance, Lac du Orient and back to Lac Madine, and became a 72-hour endurance match. The prize money was increased and shared among first, second and third.

For the first couple of years there was a junior singles event running alongside the senior World Carp Classic at Madine. Ben entered the first junior event and won it. Unfortunately, because of work commitments, I couldn't go. The juniors were taken to Madine by coach via the Eurotunnel train. I had to take Ben to the Relyon car park near Folkestone with all his tackle to meet the coach, and off he went. In those days, communications weren't as good as they are now so I didn't know how he had done.

My wife and I went to meet him on his return at the Relyon car park. Apparently, there'd been some delay with the coach's return but other coaches had arrived with some of the senior anglers and marshals aboard. I asked a couple of anglers if they knew who had won the junior event and both said they'd heard it was a boy named Ben. Now, I knew there was another boy out there named Ben so I was still none the wiser. Eventually, I spoke to Richard Stangroom, who I knew had been helping to run the junior event and he confirmed that my Ben had won. In fact, his actual words were when I asked who'd won were, "Who do you think?"

Rob Hughes interviewing us during a competition.

Interviews get interupted now and then by hungry carp!

The next year, I fished it with Jason Callaghan, and Ben partnered Andrew Race's young cousin, Tom. Andrew Race owns Reuben Heaton Scales. Ben and Tom drew the island, while Jason and I drew an area called the Swimming Pool. It's an area that's roped off for the locals to swim in; it even had a diving board. It turned out to be an incident-filled match for Jason and me.

The weather started off quite warm and a fit French girl came down for a swim. She plotted up next to us and stripped off completely naked. She climbed the diving board and in she went. Instead of concentrating on what we were doing, we concentrated on her. She gave us an eyeful for about an hour and then she was gone. Shame really because nothing was happening fishing-wise.

The next day, the weather took a turn for the worse and gale force winds and rain descended upon us. The wind was so strong that the aluminium poles in my Hutchy bivvy snapped and burst through the top of it, creating a hole. The rain was pouring in so I had to go out in the wind and rain to do a makeshift repair. I managed this with a plastic sheet and a Korda throwing stick. I cut the throwing stick into sections and placed the ends of the broken aluminium poles into the hollow sections. It strengthened the bivvy and held up a treat. The plastic sheet was thrown over the top and held down with ropes; at least it stopped the rain coming in.

Another incident happened during this windy period, involving some windsurfers. The lake was closed to windsurfers and boats for the duration of the match. This didn't deter some windsurfers who thought they'd take advantage of the very windy conditions. They were told not to go out on the water, but took no notice. Some came too close to the bank and were bombarded by the anglers with boilies fired from catapults and throwing sticks. One windsurfer managed to cut some of the anglers' lines with the fin on his board, including all of mine and Jason's. The windsurfer then had the audacity to come past again perhaps in a show of defiance at not being officially allowed on the lake. That was a big mistake.

We all hope for a good swim in the draws, then it comes down to fishing!

I grabbed my marker rod and put the lead and marker straight through the sail on his board. I was hoping the lead would catch on something and tried to pull him over but unfortunately, as I pulled, the lead and marker came back through the hole I'd made in his sail without getting caught. It did the trick though and he was last seen disappearing down the lake shouting, "Mad English!". He didn't come back and nor did any of the other windsurfers after the hostile reception they got. After that, we fished it as a pair every year right up until when the event went to Lac du Orient, and then we didn't do it anymore.

As I said, both Ben and I have competed in the BCAC every year since it started, although in the first year it was with different partners. Over the years, as a team, we've entered many pairs carp fishing matches and had some very good results. At the time of writing this chapter, we are second in the BCAC rankings. Many anglers ask us for the secret to our success. It would be foolish of me to give away all our secrets, but there are things that definitely make a good team. Fishing with the same partner is certainly beneficial. You can bounce ideas off each other and learn each other's strengths and weaknesses.

While in a match, Ben and I don't argue. It's no good arguing about what we should or should not be doing. We talk everything over before doing it. If you're arguing in a match you can't have your mind on what you are doing. You must fish as a team, not individuals. If you compete against each other you'll never win anything. Time and time again, we see team mates arguing about who goes in the best side of a swim. We don't have that problem, Ben always goes into what we think is the best side of the swim. It doesn't always pan out that way though. There have been times when we've got it wrong and the best side has been the opposite of what we've agreed on.

Here we are fishing an England team trial at Drayton reservoir.

The final weights of the England trial in 2008. The scoresheet says it all!

A lot of planning goes into the build-up to any match that we enter; we don't just turn up and fish. Firstly, we'll research the venue and then go and practise. Practice is essential to get what we term as a feel for the venue. Invaluable information can be gained by practising, even if you only go once. Take everything you think you might need and more. Some of the comments we get about the amount of gear we take makes us chuckle.

The week before any match is spent tying rigs, sorting boilies, cooking particles and generally getting all the tackle ready. Nothing is left to chance. How many rods do you take? For us, it's usually a dozen, or more. They may not all be in the swim, but they will certainly be in the truck in case we need them. Time and again we've seen competitors turn up to fish a competition and not have the right tackle or enough bait. Some even put more importance on making sure they have enough beer with them! The first thing that comes out of their van or car is a case or two of beer. They're usually out of their heads and out of the game by the first night. It seems pretty pointless taking part in the first place when you consider that the cost of entry into the competitions can be expensive.

The camaraderie between the contestants in matches is usually very good. It's not unusual to see contestants sharing bait or borrowing a few leads and suchlike. On a couple of occasions we've actually given some of our bait to our opponents. This was because their bait either didn't turn up on the day or they just forgot it. Once in the World Carp Classic, the Russian team arrived in a rickety old bus. How they made it all the way from Russia in this old jalopy we don't know. Unfortunately, they didn't have any bait with them. They were expecting someone to arrive with their bait but he didn't turn up. The word went round about the Russian's plight and by the end of the day they had more bait than anyone. Most of the other teams had generously chipped in some bait for them. The Russians were forever grateful.

As we said, usually the camaraderie in competitions is very good, but sometimes it can be downright bitchy. There are those who are going to cause trouble, no matter what. If you're catching more carp than them, one of their leads will find its way into your swim. Boundaries seem to be a big bone of contention. Before a match starts you can define a swim boundary with your opponents in the next swim, only to have it disputed as soon as you start catching. The marshals do a pretty good job and we normally leave any disputes to them, but we've had our moments. Common sense sometimes seems to go out of the window in competitions.

In 2008, we were asked if we would like to go to South Africa as part of the England Carp Team to practise for the forthcoming World Championships. As you can imagine, we jumped at the chance. The team that would eventually represent England in the World Championships as far as we knew hadn't as yet been picked, so we had a chance to prove ourselves.

The South Africans had invited a team from England to have a friendly match against them in the run up to the World Championships. It cost us over £500 each for our flight tickets to Johannesburg, but Ben and I were happy to pay. Eight of us went on the trip and what a great time we all had. Other than paying for our flights, after arriving in South Africa, we didn't have to pay for anything else except for a couple of meals while we were out sightseeing and a few gifts to bring home. The hotels - there were two, one in Jo'burg and the other in Bloemhof - an air-conditioned mini bus, our food and drinks, and most everything else was paid for by the South Africans. They treated us like royalty.

After landing and clearing customs we were met by some of the guys who were in the South African teams. They loaded all our gear on to a truck, we boarded an air-conditioned minibus and off we went. Our driver, a giant of a man named John Dearden, drove us to Bloemhof where we'd be staying at the Kudaana Lodge Hotel. As we arrived, our gear was being put into our rooms. That evening the two South African teams gave us a formal welcoming party. It was a nice get-together.

The next day after the draw we set off to begin fishing. The match took place on the Vaal River in a National Park at Bloemhof Dam. The dam is one of the biggest in southern Africa. The dammed area covers 60,000 acres and goes to depths of over 50 feet. As we drove through the National Park, we saw many animals including wildebeeste, jackals, antelope and meerkats. It was an amazing sight.

The South Africans had all their fishing tackle at their disposal; in fact, most of them had trailers behind their vehicles. In contrast, we were fishing out of a suitcase. Incidentally, our fishing rods were in tubes inappropriately named 'Bazooka' tubes and were a great cause for concern at Heathrow Airport. We were approached by the airport security who took them away to be X-rayed before they'd let them on the plane.

During the match, we woke one morning to find what we were later told were leopard foot prints close to our bivvy. Scary, or what! I also thought I saw a crocodile swimming in the river. I told Ben, who was standing in the water at the time and he thought I was winding him up until he saw it. He couldn't get out of the water quickly enough. It turned out to be a very large monitor lizard.

After a slow start, we eventually got to grips with the situation and started catching loads of carp. They weren't big carp but there were plenty of them. Our successful tactic was to use popped-up yellow hookbaits and catapult small groundbait balls around them. The match was certainly a great learning curve for us and the rest of the guys that were there. After the match there was a presentation dinner back at Kudaana Lodge. The next day we had to return to Jo'burg. We stayed at another hotel for a couple of days before jetting off home.

While there in Joburg, we were treated to a trip to a lion safari park where the lions roam free; we also went to a local market. On our last night, the South Africans took us out to a restaurant for a farewell dinner. We tucked in to such delicacies as crocodile, which tasted like chicken; antelope, ostrich, wildebeeste and a whole host of other things.

Finally, the next morning, the time had come for us to return home. We said our goodbyes and off we went to the airport. It was a fantastic trip and we made many friends during our time in South Africa and have remained friends with them ever since.

That same year in June, we were invited to take part in a Carp Team England selection match on Drayton Reservoir. Various pairs were invited to take part, but for one reason or another, some couldn't make it. We hadn't fished Drayton Reservoir before so some thorough research was required. This we did through friends who'd fished it, DVDs, the Internet and anything else we thought might help. We also did one session on Drayton to give us a feel for the place. Different tactics and rigs were tried and we were very successful on our practice run.

Research and practising are a must if you want to succeed. This is done before any match that we enter. Before the day of the match all the competing pairs were informed that there was only one place to be filled. The other two pairings had already been picked but were not taking part in this match. All of us were told that whoever won this match would be going to the World Championships in South Africa. This was a prize everyone wanted to win. With the draw done, and fishing under the stringent

FIPSed rules, we were about to take part in the fairest match we've ever been in. Fairest, because no one swim was better than the other. There was no flyer. It would be down to angling ability and whoever wanted it the most. We'd planned our approach right down to the finest detail. This is where research and practice play their part.

Under FIPSed rules we were not allowed to use a spod, catapult or any bait delivery tool other than a throwing stick, from 6.30pm until 9.00am. This rather limits baiting up at night. We overcame the problem by continually using the throwing stick to put out different-sized boilies and even pellets. These were sprayed all over the swim to keep the carp feeding. The tactic worked and we continued to catch loads of carp during the 6.30pm to 9.00am ban on spods and catapults. As the match progressed, we weren't told how we were doing. We didn't know who was winning, nor did we know what our weight was - until Rob Hughes phoned to tell me that we were winning and we'd just broken the British record.

The record of 1548lbs of carp in a 48-hour match was held by a pair who'd fished an eliminator at Thorpe Lea in the British Carp Angling Championships. We'd surpassed that, and there was still a long way to go in our match. The match finally ended and we still didn't know who'd won.

As we entered the command tent the scoreboard had been turned around so that the scores couldn't be seen. We sat patiently waiting and eventually, the results were finally revealed. There were gasps all round, not only had we won but we'd won by a huge margin. Our total weight was 1776lbs 2oz which was a world record for a ratified 48-hour match. As you can imagine we were elated with the result. We were also very tired after our non-stop hauling. Tactically, the match was won using zigs and bottom baits and a vast amount of spod mix. We were told on the day that we would be in the England team going to the 2008 World Championships in South Africa. The reality was that we never got picked. We were sent an email with the names of the pairs who'd made the team - ours wasn't on it.

By now, more and more matches were appearing, so we had to choose the ones we wanted to compete in. We couldn't enter all of them, but to win the BCAC remained our main goal and we'd done very well over the years. We'd originally fished in the Carp 'R' Us team and won the BCAC team trophy as part of that team. In later years, we became part of the Carp Talk BCAC Team and having come close to winning the team event with them a few times we eventually succeeded in 2011, and raised the prestigious trophy above our heads. The team members were Harry Charrington and Rob Sutton, Adam Snowden and Danny Fletcher, and us.

Back in 2006, we were in the BCAC final at Furzeton Lakes. Not having done very well in the draws over the years, no one was more surprised than us when our names were called out first. We couldn't believe it! Opting for what we thought was the best area on the lake we chose peg 30. The horn sounded the beginning of the match and we caught virtually from the off.

After a few hours into the match, the weather changed from being fine to gale-force winds. It was so bad that some bivvies got damaged because of it. Our marshal was struggling to weigh our fish. The wind was playing havoc with the scales as it buffeted the weigh sling. To make it easier for our marshal to weigh the carp, we shielded the weigh sling and scales with our bivvies. This did the trick and throughout the 48-hour match, each carp we caught was weighed accurately. The storm raged all weekend and didn't let up.

With only six minutes to go in the match, we were winning. In fact, a maroon rocket was put in our swim ready to signal the end of the match. A shout went up that the team in second place had caught a carp. It was 15lb-plus and put them in first place, just two pounds in front of us with minutes to go. The rocket, which had now been put in the winning team's swim, was let off thus ending the match. We were devastated. So near but so far; we were beaten by two pounds. Still, we won £3,000 which made it a bit easier to take, but we'd have been a lot happier if we'd won the match.

Other things were to unfold at a later date, things we knew nothing about. The BCAC final had been filmed for Sky TV and was eventually shown a few months later. We watched a recording of it and thought it was quite good. A friend phoned and asked if we'd watched it and after telling him we had, he asked if we'd seen anything wrong. We hadn't. He said watch it again and watch the marshal weighing the eventual winners' carp. Well, we couldn't believe what we saw; it was a good job we'd recorded it. The marshal was weighing the carp on a mound in the open and the weigh sling was being battered by the wind. The dial on the scales was jumping from one point to another with two to four pounds difference in the reading between both points. There was no way a correct reading could be taken. In the programme the weighing of the carp was only shown three or four times, but every carp must have been weighed this way. After consulting with the organiser we decided not to do anything about it, although the evidence was there for all to see. We would have been seen as bad losers so we didn't take it any further.

Anglers at shows and on the bank that we didn't know, but who had watched it on TV, came up to us and said we were robbed. We felt that was our time to win it, but because of things beyond our control it wasn't to be.

The Carp Team England management changed in 2012 and Korda began sponsoring the team in the same year. It became known as the Korda Carp Team England. We were asked to take part in three trials, which we readily agreed to, with the first trial on the prolific Drayton Reservoir, near Daventry. We did well, coming second in our section and although some pairs were eliminated, we progressed to the second trial which was on Wyre Lake at Wyreside Lakes, in Lancashire. Again we did very well and won this trial. The third and final trial was on Brasenose 1 at Richworth Linear Fisheries and again we came second in our section.

Overall, we finished first in the trials. Once again, we never got picked, even though we'd won it! We fulfilled all the criteria that were asked of us in the trials, and more. After winning the trials and with our track record, what more could we do to prove we were worthy of a place in the team? We've wasted a lot of time and money on the England carp team and all for nothing. We've vowed never to take part again.

In 2012, we once again took part in the British Carp Angling Championships. Our chosen venue for our first round eliminator was Farlows. We did well and won the eliminator with a weight of 107lbs 4oz. This earned us a place in the semi-finals at Barston Lakes, near Solihull. There were two semi-finals and we were in the first one. The lake was split into seven sections for this match and only the winners of each section would go through to the final. Again, we were triumphant and were now going into our eighth BCAC final. The final was on Broadlands Lake, in Hampshire.

We arrived the night before the final and did a circuit of the lake. Early in the morning, we did another circuit and marked the swims we fancied in order of preference. All the competitors were called for the start of the draw. It was a watercraft draw so when our name was drawn we could choose our swim, as long as it hadn't already been picked.

Overall winners of the Four Seasons Carp Cup in 2011.

We'd like to take this opportunity to thank Carp Talk for supporting us over the years, and for giving us and fellow competitors excellent coverage.

We finally won the BCAC in 2012 after 14 years of trying

It was our time to shine!

Fourteen canisters containing the names of all the competitors were placed in a glass bowl and one by one they were drawn out. The draw commenced and name after name was called. Unfortunately, our canister came out last. Not a good start. It left us with two swims to choose from, peg one and peg five. Both were at the bottom of our list. We picked peg five because it had more water than peg one. We'd also fished the other peg in last year's final on Broadlands and didn't do too well in it.

After a slow start, we managed to catch and by the first morning we were in third place with 58lbs 4oz. At first light on the last morning, we were awoken with the news that we were now in first place. We had to endure a few nervous hours before the close and when the hooter sounded to end the match, Ben and I gave out a big sigh of relief. In fact, we broke down and shed a tear. We'd won, in our opinion, the most prestigious carp tournament in Great Britain. This was the one that we so wanted to win and we'd finally done it. A cheque for £12,500 was handed to us but it was the trophy that we wanted the most. Our names will now be on it forever.

Many years have passed since Ben and I started fishing in carp matches. We've won some, been placed second or third in others, and of course, lost some. In fact, we've won and been placed in more pairs' carp matches than any other pairs in England. This includes The BCAC, UK Carp Cup and many other tournaments, so our average in carp matches is pretty high. We've qualified for the final of The BCAC eight times now. Carp matches give us a real buzz, especially when we're winning. Success in carp tournaments doesn't come easy though; it takes hard work and dedication and can be soul-destroying as well as exciting. Well, there you have it. A bit of history about carp matches and an insight as to how we approach them.

Chapter 12

Richworth
Products
Richworth
NATURAL EXTRACT
MINAMINO
RECOMMENDED OR FOR MAKING
BOILIES AT 20-30ml per
250ml
RECOMMENDED
60-70ml per 1kg
SHAKE WELL
Richworth
Richworth
6-10ml Per 1lb

Thoughts from a cluttered mind

I didn't want to write a book and have carp and captors solely from the southern counties of the UK, so I jotted down the names of a few northern 'faces' I had stored in my mobile phone. I also wanted someone who's had fished a variety of venues, was not afraid to experiment, and was willing to pass on his thoughts and findings, and wasn't afraid to ruffle a few feathers.

Okay, I may be fussy but the list was soon whittled down. Just over a decade ago when I began my occasional sessions on the Richworth Linear Fisheries complex in Oxford I met this guy from the Midlands catching carp down the windward end of one of the lakes. We got chatting, as you do, and our friendship started from there. Over the years, we've both helped out teaching kids and adults at the charity events on the complex and exchanged ideas. He's always liked his special hookbaits and has supplied me with a few specials, which I've used to good effect. Could I twist his arm into writing a guest chapter for this book?

The call was made and thankfully, he agreed. Months passed and finally, Tim emailed me his chapter. It was longer than I'd anticipated, but with so much relevant informative content I was more than happy. Read on ...

- Tim Childs -

Firstly, let me say a big thank you to Martin for the opportunity to pen something for this, his eagerly-awaited second book. Over the last few months, Martin and I have discussed just what he required in the way of a guest chapter and what we both thought I could contribute to the book, although perhaps once he's read the next few thousand words he may be regretting his decision! Only joking, Mart, I think!

Okay, just where to begin? Well, the title says it all really, because I've had these thoughts for the chapter floating around my head for some time now. I'm just going to try to put into words what my continually scrambled egg-like brain is trying to say. If you are looking for a nice, flowing chapter about the capture of a specific fish, perhaps describing beautiful sunrises and sunsets, or are hoping to read about that session of a lifetime when it all comes good, then perhaps it's best to skip the next few pages and move on. As the title suggests, I'm just going to throw down on paper a few thoughts and ideas that are desperate to escape my forever cluttered mind. Martin's brief was simple; try to get people thinking, and as this is a technically-related book, I hope the next few pages do just that.

Have you ever seen an abstract artist slapping paint around a wall or floor? His interpretation of what he's feeling is there splattered in a multitude of colours and shapes for all to see. The artist probably cares little if the man on the street interprets what he's trying to portray, in the same way; it's just his way of expressing himself and putting his thoughts and feelings into art. Look at this piece in a similar way; my thoughts slapped down on paper as they escape from my brain, all in hope of helping you to get a little more understanding from your fishing.

One of the Midlands' finest carp. Hand-rolled K-G-1 wafter hookbait with Betaine, GLM and Aquastim.

I would imagine most of us at some stage of our angling lives go through periods of confusion, don't we? Okay, perhaps some more than others, but speaking for myself there are always random thoughts bouncing around my head. Whether it's about rigs, location, what bait to use, the right tackle etc., all these and more have filled my head on a regular basis for over 25 years. While there have been plenty of times when my plans and strategies have felt perfect, on occasions, I'm still sitting there thinking of this and that, as various thoughts and ideas continue to clutter my mind.

My sleep patterns are erratic as well so perhaps it's an overactive malfunction somewhere in my head that makes me feel like this. Oh, and some of the dreams I have, Jesus! Don't even get me started on that one; they go from the bizarre to the downright ridiculous!

The point I'm probably failing to get across is that no matter what your experience or however many years angling you have behind you, we all at times may suffer from periods of low confidence and get frustrated when the bobbins seem to be stuck in the same position for long periods.

The light at the end of the tunnel, so to speak, is when there are certain aspects of your angling you know you're getting right the majority of the time, and that might be location, bait, rigs etc. Even then, there WILL be areas you'll still sometimes question as the fish keep moving the bloody goalposts! Confidence comes with success and the more successful you are the easier it is to see clearly, and with a little more understanding of just what you're trying to achieve.

For the newcomer into the sport the problems are tenfold. Walk into any well-stocked tackle shop or pick up any one of the number of monthly magazines out there and it's no wonder someone who has recently taken up the sport feels lost and confused. Those magic rigs or baits that some seem to pursue relentlessly simply don't exist. Having spent quite some time working at Stapeley Angling Centre, one of the largest tackle shops in the country, I have seen first-hand how many anglers fail to understand the basics and get confused by some of the latest ideas and fads that are punted their way.

Hard work, an understanding of your quarry, watercraft, and time and effort, are more important than any new wonder rig, despite what some of the monthly publications will have you believe. Now, don't get me wrong I'm not saying that rigs, and tackle are not important, but once you begin to realise that carp are simple creatures that need to eat food to survive you already have an advantage over them. A bit like the naughty schoolboy who can't resist the sweetie jar and forever has his hand in it; he's always going to get caught isn't he? As long as his greed is stronger than his resistance to a rap on the knuckles from his teacher, it will stay like that. It's only when that greed is resisted with caution and cunning and natural instinct, that's when things change. This usually happens when angling pressure is increased and now the tables are turned and we, the anglers, have to think and work harder to stay one step ahead of the fish.

So for anyone struggling to come to terms with aspects of this sport then just keep at it, work hard, master your environment and understand the basic day-to-day movements of your quarry and the results will come; believe me it will be worth it. There are unfortunately no secret formulas or a magic wand that will turn everyone into the next Terry Hearn; it's all about effort and asking yourselves just how much you want that success.

Edges with hookbaits

Now, for this next section of the chapter I'm going to talk about hookbaits and pop-ups because this is one subject where I do go to extra lengths to give myself an edge. As I've been rolling a number of hookbaits for Martin over the last 18 months, or so, with superb results I might add, I know it is one subject he wanted me to write about. It's fair to say that I've been a fan of rolling my own hookbaits for a long time now, so much so that I simply can't remember the last time I took a standard boilie from a bag and slipped it straight onto the hair. Now, that might come of a shock to some people, but even my bottom bait hookbaits are hand-rolled to my own requirements and while some might find this unnecessary or extreme, it is something I simply do and it's what gives me confidence.

I've been tinkering around making my own personalised hookbaits and pop-ups for the best part of 15 years now and luckily, have stumbled across one or two little edges and ideas that have worked well for me and a number of close friends. Growing up and angling on the border of Cheshire, it was inevitable that sooner or later other more experienced anglers from the area would influence my ideas on hookbaits. Without doubt one of the anglers who helped me, and plenty of other anglers I may add, was Frank Warwick.

Just hearing Frank talk about hookbaits and ingredients and his overall enthusiasm is addictive. During the many times I spent in his company I tried my best to log as much information as I could. Like most things in this game whether it's rigs or bait, we are influenced by other people at some point and that is how it started for me.

Inevitably, I wasn't alone in my experiments with flavours and additives as various friends and acquaintances were working on their own ideas. One vivid and memorable session was on Redesmere in the winter a number of years ago, sitting with a then very young but mega-keen Gaz Fareham, discussing our thoughts on bait, among other things. We both caught during that cold February session and since then we've gone down similar roads with our hookbaits. Some of the combinations and baits that others from the North West were using and developing were very effective, to say the least, and now form the basis of many excellent types of bait.

I started rolling pop-ups for my own fishing around 1995/96, mainly using the Solar Tackle pan-type pop-up mix. Then in later years moved on to the excellent boil-type mixes like those sold by Richworth. After a few experiments, I began passing these on to a few friends to play around with and over the next few years it became clear that there were one or two combinations that simply performed better than others. It was, and still is, a great feeling putting together from scratch a hookbait or pop-up combination that you see others catch personal bests on, or go off and have one of their best seasons' angling. Despite, in recent times, a number of people suggesting I go down the commercial side of things, rolling these custom pop-ups are one thing I prefer to do for myself and a few close friends. Besides, I don't relish the thought of giving away what I consider a major edge in my angling just for the sake of a few quid.

When it comes to just what to use in your hookbaits I think it's safe to say the days of 5ml of flavour mixed with an egg are well behind us. There are a number of organic and natural products from either the human, animal food, pharmaceutical or in particular the aquaculture industries that can give your homemade hookbaits that extra something special. Whether I'm trying to create a hookbait to match the food bait I'm using, or a totally different bait for perhaps single hookbait fishing, determines just what goes into each mix.

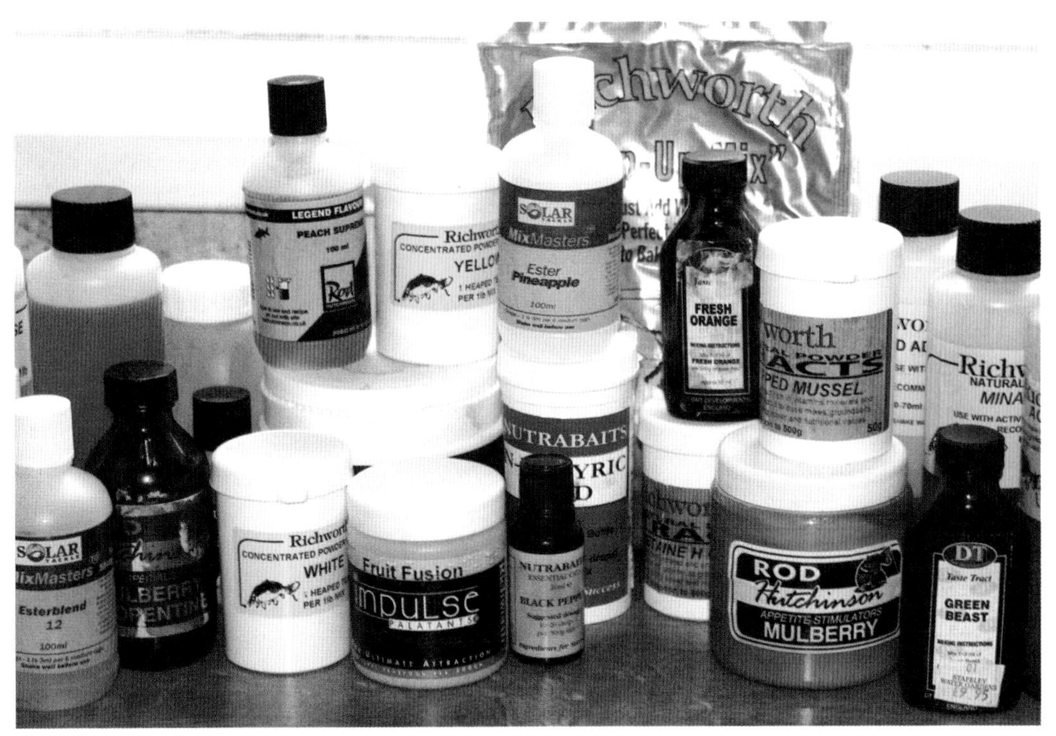

A selection of Tim's successful flavours and enhancers.

Another carp from the Midlands, from a venue where my hookbaits worked consistently.

Hard-fighting, 30lb-plus Oxfordshire mirror; hand-rolled specials proving themselves once again.

The results of steadily applying a good food source bait such as K-G-1 proved they liked it, along with this mid-30 common.

Of course there are products that have been used in the angling industry for a number of years and some are certainly still being kept 'under the counter' so to speak. If, like me, you're looking for certain flavours, powders or additives that can trigger those feeding responses then you'll already know certain combinations can be very useful indeed. Liquid liver, some of the excellent kelp and koi related products, Betaine, GLM, Minamino and a number of other similar products can all be used to good effect. Now, before we go any further, I'd like to point out that I have two specific thoughts on hand-rolled hookbaits and these normally base themselves on whether I'm looking to create a highly attractive-type bait suitable for single hookbaits, perhaps aimed at winter or spring fishing, or a more subtle type designed to fish over food-type baits during the warmer months. Just what I might require from these could be totally different in size, colour, smell, taste and buoyancy, and all have to be considered.

As an example of this, over the last couple of years I've been happily and successfully using Richworth Baits K-G-1 boilies for the majority of my angling. Now, despite the fact that Richworth produce excellent pop-ups to match their bottom baits, my natural instinct told me I simply had to make my own. I wanted a hookbait that matched the free offerings but still had that unique smell and buoyancy of a hand-rolled special, something that I could control myself, to suit my needs. With this in mind I got Uncle Bob at Richworth to send me a few items I thought I might require, and put my brain into gear.

I started off as usual by cracking one egg into a bowl. I always work in one egg batches because I find any more than this and problems seem to occur when rolling as most mixes dry out too quickly. To the egg, I added Betaine and GLM powder in equal quantities, both proven attractors. I then added the liquids; K-G-1 and Aquastim, Richworth's version of liquid fish protein, a superb, thick, salty product that carp just love. Both were added at the same ratio and I made precise notes of how much I used. With a little colour combination of white, black and brown mixed together and added to get the matching colour of the free offering, things were looking good. Finally, because I wanted this first batch to be slow-sinking wafters, I added a small amount of K-G-1 base mix, just a little at a time until the mix looked like sloppy, light brown porridge. To this I then added plain, coloured pop-up mix until the right firm paste consistency was achieved, these were then rolled into balls as well as barrel shapes and finally boiled.

The finished baits looked perfect and after a cooling off period of 24 hours, they were given a slight coating of the K-G-1 liquid additive, again noting how much I used. These were then shaken vigorously in a bag and regularly re-shaken over the next few hours until all of the additional liquid had penetrated the baits. The next day when the baits had dried they looked and smelled superb and when trying the buoyancy test in a bowl they were just as I'd hoped. They just floated, but when a rig was added the whole lot sank slowly with the hookbait sitting slightly off the deck with the weightless hook sitting hidden underneath. With the baits looking the business, I just had to see if I'd got the attractor profile right. To cut a long story short, that very first recipe proved to be outstanding, catching from a number of waters in both pop-up and wafter versions.

I had recently joined a small but tricky syndicate water and a number of the regulars had told me how hard the fish could be to catch at times. I'd also been told that the fish were particle orientated and 'bits and pieces' type fishing was the way to go. With this in mind, my first couple of nights on the water were spent fishing small traps of particles with maize or corn on the hook, combined with little parcels of seeds and hemp, basically fishing for a bite at a time. Surprisingly, despite my best efforts, this failed miserably and even though it was early days on the water, the very next session I planned to return armed with a few kilos of boilies and my special homemade hookbaits.

The lake bed was quite firm and clay-lined and the sloping margins quickly dropped away to deep water of 10-12 feet, no more than a rod length or so out. My idea was to fish just at the top of the marginal shelf with balanced wafter boilie hookbaits fished over just boilies, but I would mix up the sizes of my free offering. This way, I hoped to keep the fish guessing a little and give them something slightly different to the normal round, one-dimensional size baits they may have been used to. Luckily, Richworth produce baits in different sizes and also in barrels so straight away I could offer the fish three or four different sizes and shaped baits. It's also worth mentioning that I never once introduced round baits, other than the 10mm-sized ones. Squashed or chopped 14 and 18mm baits were introduced to ensure that any free offerings wouldn't roll down the marginal shelf. Ironically, though, every bite I had came to round hookbaits.

I'd also got another sneaky plan up my sleeve when it came to presentation and this was based on a balanced bottom bait rig using one of my favourite hook patterns, the long shank Mugga hooks from Gardner Tackle. The new Covert, slick, green-finished version suited my needs perfectly and when given a couple of strokes with the JAG hook sharpening stone, it left them wickedly sharp. I thought long and hard about choice of hooklink and considered some kind of fluorocarbon, but in the end and after checking out all of the hooklinks my local tackle shop had on the shelves, I finally settled for PB Products Jelly-Wire in their silt colour which, in fact, is a lovely red-brown and matched the dark, rustic, clay lake bed perfectly. I tied up a couple of rigs and as usual attached a small rig ring to fish the baits 'blow-back' style, then when whipping on the hook I suddenly had a brainwave.

As I'm usually a pop-up fan I will, like most anglers, leave a couple of inches of exposed soft hooklink near to the hook, then add a counterbalance weight near to the hook to balance it. Well, as I was going to be fishing my baits on the clean bottom it suddenly occurred to me; why should I leave any braid exposed at all? The first rig I tied up I whipped the stiffer coated hooklink straight through to the hook leaving no soft, exposed section, but after a little play around with the rig it just didn't seem right at all. The hook couldn't flip or turn and one of the great things about curved hooks is their ability to catch and grab fish when they suck them in. The next rig I tied I left a tiny 3-5 mm section exposed and just on the point of where the soft braid met the stiffer coating I added a small drop of Critical Mass rig putty. When the bait was attached, the hook could rotate and flip back and forth, but the stiffer, coated section and the putty helped to keep it pinned to the deck. This elbow effect, as I call it, worked perfectly allowing the hook to 'flex' and that formed the basis of my presentation.

I kept the rigs relatively short at seven inches, and combined this with a flat 3 or 3.5oz brown swivel pear lead; the heavy flat lead being to hold the rig in position on the shelf and not roll down the slope if the rig got knocked or dislodged by feeding fish. The final piece of the puzzle was a switch to fluorocarbon main line, and for that I chose Mirage in 14lb. It was the first time I'd used fluorocarbon on my reels, but immediately, I realised what a massive advantage it was when trying to pin down your line and keep concealment to a maximum.

The plan was set and now all I had to do was to put it into action. Well, to cut a long story short, the baits worked superbly and I didn't receive one blank session from then onwards, catching a number of the lake's target fish including the biggest which was at the time a new lake record at just under 40lbs. The fish loved the K-G-1 and despite other anglers putting different baits into the water, most seemed to struggle for more than one or two bites. It wasn't as if I was putting in more time either, at one point I'd landed 15 fish in only 16 night's actual fishing. Now, I'm not trying to come across all blasé or smug I'm just simply stating the facts and they are that a combination of an excellent bait and a little thought into what I put onto the hook and how it was presented made those fish very catchable - for a short time at least.

In the end, that green-eyed monster raised its ugly head once again and one or two anglers accused me of all sorts of nonsense. With the syndicate leader being something of a dictator, to say the least, it didn't take long for someone to point him in my directions and push the right buttons. I was gutted to lose my ticket, to be honest, because I really enjoyed my time on the water and still had one big fish, a common around 38lbs, left to catch before I wanted to call it a day. Oh well, at least one of the main rumour-mongers got his just desserts when he was later himself banned for taking a non-member on to the water and sacking a mid-30 in the middle of the day!

Both these actions were punishable by execution, according to the Gestapo-type ruler. Luckily for me, there were a couple of other anglers who had their heads screwed on the right way and who could see beyond these jealous snipes and I'd just like to say a big thank you to both Russ and Steve for your help with pictures and making my time on the water a lot more enjoyable.

A rare visitor to the bank! XLR-8 boilies and tigernuts fished in a PVA bag doing the biz!

Write down all your flavour levels, and powdered additives, and you may find your own winning formula.

When it comes down to singles, white, fruity baits work when others don't.

It still amazes me how, on certain waters, if your face fits you can get away with murder, but if it doesn't then you become a target for all types of accusations. When I look back and take into account other subsequent captures on the K-G-1 hookbaits over the summer and the following winter, I'm convinced these were a major edge in my success. Granted, the bait, its application, and the rig played their equal part but that extra pull of those special little hookbaits seemed irresistible. Was it luck or an educated guess that put that final combination together? Well, perhaps a little of both. Either way, I know I now have a combination that makes superb K-G-1 hookbaits, and that the fish seem to love.

On the same theme, I'd done a similar thing with another of the Richworth baits, the XLR8, a lovely, dark, meaty-type boilie that I'd had excellent early results on back in 2010. My first batch of hookbaits was made for Martin after I'd shown him some of my hand-rolled specials when we were down in Oxford doing some filming for Richworth's Cutting Edge DVD. Again trial and error was the way to begin with, but when Martin told me his first bite on them was a 40-plus mirror, I knew things were on the right track. In the end, I actually tried three different combinations of attractors and powders until I was happy with the final version.

Last winter I set about trying to produce a pop-up to match the awesome Tutti Frutti freezer baits. Again, being the ever-inquisitive kind of person I am, I wanted something that little bit different in terms of flavour and taste, a cherry on top if you like and something that could be used in conjunction with the Tutti free offerings but still had its own unique taste and smell combination. I ended up using a mixture of Citrus Fruit and Pineapple flavour along with N-Butyric acid, sweetener, Betaine and a fruit powdered palatant called Fruit Fusion. I made two batches, one in vivid orange and one in white, and early results suggested I'd got it right again. Despite it being late in the year and just prior to the big freeze-up I managed a number of bites on these lovely fruity baits. I have another fresh batch ready rolled for this winter and will be trying them again to see how the fish react on a variety of venues.

Okay, perhaps now, if you're still with me and you've not fallen asleep, I'll just pass on a few tips and tricks I've learned over the years when rolling your own pop-ups or balanced hookbaits.

Firstly, I always use fresh ingredients and eggs. I try to keep all of my flavours and additives separate in sealed boxes in a dry cool environment, because some ingredients are naturally hydroscopic and can take on moisture if left in damp areas. When experimenting with flavours and oils, be precise and write everything down. If you come across a superb fruit or fish pop-up combination, either by design or accident, and suddenly 12 months later can't remember how many drops or millilitres you initially used, you'll be kicking yourself. Inclusion levels for flavours are always a tricky subject and one that could fill this chapter alone. My advice is firstly, to look at the recommended level of any attractor for a normal 4-6 egg mix, i.e. 1lb of dry ingredients then start off with that level for your one egg-worth of pop-ups.

Remember, if you're looking to create a hookbait with extra pulling power then these higher levels will be needed to draw the fish to that one bait. One of my favourite all-time hookbait combinations consists of 20ml of fish flavour and even though this level is high the flavour seems to work superbly as a single hookbait, or when fished over free offerings. Experiment and log all your findings and soon you'll begin to see common denominators and judge what works best at different levels within your bait.

This is when friends become invaluable. Give a few hookbaits to half a dozen mates and monitor their results on different waters. If they all fail to catch over a number of sessions then you've obviously got the mix wrong. If, on the other hand, they all report great catches you know you're on to a winner and can then begin to experiment more. Take your time when rolling and take care in the production of your bait. Despite the fact that you'll probably be able to catch on odd-shaped baits with more cracks in them than a granny's face, a bit like the ones rolled by my mate, Rich, there is nothing like a pot of lovely rolled and nice-looking baits to give you mega confidence. There are a number of good quality pop-up mixes available and I've used most over the years with good results although I've always tended to prefer the version from Richworth even before I became involved with the company.

I'd also like to point out that despite being a consultant with Richworth and being more than happy with their additives and flavours, I won't insult the intelligence of the reader and try to convince you that Richworth are the only company who supply quality ingredients and additives for making hookbaits. I've long been a fan of Nutrabaits products and use their N-Butyric acid in a number of mixes. As well as this, their essential oils are second to none and are always my first choice. Owner, Bill Cottam, certainly knows his bait and they sell a number of excellent additives and ingredients. Likewise, over the years Rod Hutchinson and Solar flavours have become a firm favourite of mine and when used in hi-attract hookbaits, have accounted for a number of my captures from various waters.

Okay, I prefer to hand-roll my hookbaits and due to plenty of practice and quite smooth-skinned hands, find I can produce lovely rolled baits quite easily. If you find yourself struggling to do this then the range of small rollerball bait rollers from Gardner and a suitable bait gun will be fine. I tend to roll my paste a little on the soft side without it being too sticky then split the paste into three small, tangerine-sized balls; each ball is sealed in a press seal food bag to prevent premature drying.

Keep boiling times as precise as possible. These days, I actually boil all my baits in an electric chip fryer; this double-pan fryer has purpose-built baskets and is ideal for boiling bait. It was actually a Christmas present from a relative a few years ago and it simply never got used; besides I'm more of an oven chip fan myself. Anyway, it suddenly dawned on me to try boiling some water in it and it worked superbly. I place all my baits on paper kitchen towel and allow them to dry in a cool, shaded area.

When looking after finished baits, you can either let them air dry for a few days and treat them as shelf-life hookbaits, or as I prefer, leave for at least 48 hours until almost dry but still spongy and needle-friendly, then freeze in screw-sealed pots for future use. Don't, as I've done in the past, freeze in plastic-type food bags because for some reason, after a few weeks these baits smell of nothing but plastic and seem flavourless. It is at this point you can add extra flavour or dip to boost your baits. My preference is generally to work on what goes into the mix in the first place, although others seem to do very well on boosted or glugged free offerings. Again, if doing this, it's a good idea to keep written notes on what you add or what liquids are used in your finished dip or glug.

One time when glugging or soaking baits in extra attractors can really pay-off is during the winter. During this time, when water temperatures are low, any extra pull to the hookbaits can be advantageous. Slow-moving or lethargic carp may be tempted to investigate and ultimately mouth a hookbait that is continuously pumping out food signals into the surrounding cold water. Drop that hookbait on a fish's nose and you may just get a bite.

Action on a cold winter's day, when hookbait choice can be paramount.

When aiming to produce slow-sinking hookbaits, don't presume that any amount of pop-up mix added to your standard base mix will make the finished baits more buoyant, it simply doesn't work like this. Only a small amount of base mix i.e. bottom bait mix, is needed to produce slow sinkers. A ratio of 80% pop-up mix and 20% bottom bait mix should be fine, but remember, different mixes may be slightly heavier or lighter, so you'll simply have to do some tests. The weight and size of the hook, and hooklink, has to be taken into account so you'll be surprised by just how little of the base mix can make the difference.

When it came to rolling my K-G-1 pop-ups, I still wanted to add a little bottom bait mix as I'd done before with the wafters. This was to keep the colour consistency the same and to keep to the original proven recipe. To counteract the weight of the base mix I added to the egg a product called Zero Gravity from Alien Baits. This very fine product is extremely buoyant and a spoonful added to the mix gave me the required results. In fact, if I'm looking for mega-buoyant pop-ups for zigs, or chod rigs, I now always add this product to my usual pop-up mix.

Don't be afraid to experiment with bizarre colours. Not all pineapple pop-ups have to be yellow, or do they? White is a superb colour especially for single hookbaits and I've done well on squid, blackcurrant, citrus fruit and Scopex-flavoured baits in this colour alone. Shaped barrels or even square baits can be made, so really there are loads of options when rolling your own baits.

So before I finish this section on hookbaits, I'll ask the question you'll probably be thinking yourself? Is it worth it, and can I make something better myself than can be brought off the shelves in my local tackle shop? Well, despite there being plenty of

Homemade specials give control over quality, flavour-combi levels, colour and size; the choice is yours.

good pop-ups available already rolled and potted-up ready to use, the fact that I can make something unique to my personal requirements, in terms of attraction, buoyancy and colour, is incentive enough for me to produce finished baits that I feel will give me the edge over the fish, and more importantly, my fellow anglers. If you feel like giving it a go, good luck; you never know, you may just discover that perfect combination that will change your season.

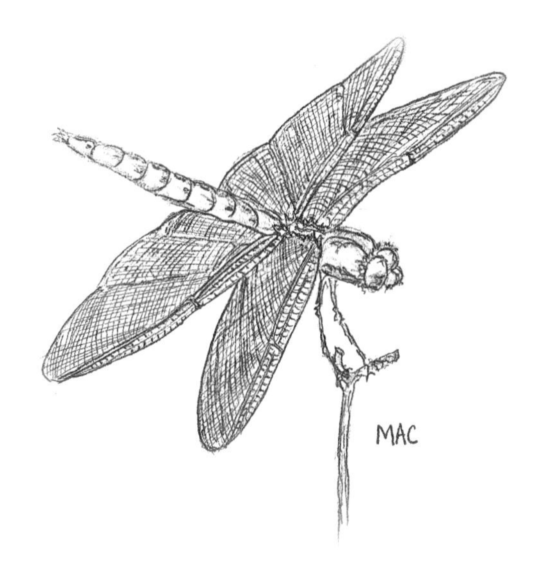

Hookbait combinations

For anyone interested, I've listed a few of my favourite hookbait combinations that have performed well on a number of water over the years and a little guide to how and when I use them. As you will see, a couple are ideal food type hookbaits while others are perfect for firing single hookbaits at showing fish. All are for 1 large egg mixes, boiling times 90-120 seconds.

20ml Solar Squid and Octopus Koi Rearer.
10 drops Nutrabaits N-Butyric Acid.
1 teaspoon of Richworth Betaine.
1 teaspoon of Richworth Green Lipped Mussel powder.

This superb hookbait combination has caught countless fish for me and friends on every water where it's been used. Perfect for fishing over any fishmeal type bait or when used on its own, it just seems to work everywhere. Colour choice is personal and I carry white, yellow and brown versions with me at all times.

5ml of Richworth K-G-1 liquid additive
5ml of Richworth Aquastim.
1 teaspoon Richworth Betaine.
1 teaspoon of Richworth Green Lipped Mussel powder.

When baits are dry add 1 capful of K-G-1 liquid to the finished baits in a press-seal bag, shake well and allow soaking for 24 hours. This is my favoured K-G-1 hookbait combination that was responsible for a number of 30lb fish in 2011. Perfect for over K-G-1 free offerings.

5ml of Richworth XLR8 liquid additive
1ml of Vision Baits Liver Garlic Sausage.
5ml Richworth Aquastim.
1 teaspoon Richworth Betaine.
1 teaspoon Richworth Green Lipped Mussel powder.

This is the bait that I sent to Martin back in 2011 and his first bite was a 40lb-plus mirror. The results speak for themselves, used by a couple of close friends and I when fishing over the excellent XLR8 bait. Coloured dark brown to match the free offerings.

5ml of Rod Hutchinson Mulberry Florentine (original glass-bottled version).
10 drops of Nutrabaits N-Butyric Acid
1 teaspoon of Richworth Betaine.
1 teaspoon of Rod Hutchinson Mulberry Appetite Stimulator.
Another superb single hookbait combination, very 'tangy' and superb in the cold months, the flavour and matching Appetite Stimulator complement each other perfectly. Try bright orange or white for a vivid attractor bait.

North/South divide

There can be little doubt that your geographical location in the UK can have a massive bearing on just what size of carp you catch. Unless you're one of the very few anglers who are able to travel 150-200 miles every week, the simple facts are that if

Redesmere winter success late 90s, where Tim's early hookbait experiments began.

you live in the northern half of the country like I do, you will have to accept the fact that average size of carp is smaller than those around the Colne Valley or southern counties. So what does this mean?

Well, for a start, if you do live in the northern part of the country, I honestly believe it's important to keep things in perspective and not get carried away with the weekly news reports of anglers down south catching rakes and rakes of upper 30s and 40lb fish. It's easy for someone coming into the sport to get a distorted view of the carp scene and look with envy at those anglers fishing for larger and more available fish.

My advice is simply this; if you're happy with what you're catching and can honestly say you can hold your own against the other anglers on your local waters, does it matter if they are 20, 30 or 40lb fish? A 40lb fish is still a massive bench mark especially to the northern-based angler and 30lb fish are more of a realistic target for the majority of those who live in the north of the UK. When you start to try to track down fish of this size, you'll soon realise that there are more 40lb fish in some southern syndicate waters than in the whole of Cheshire, Yorkshire and Derbyshire.

There are one or two exceptions to this rule, though, and things aren't as bleak as they once were. One of the largest known living common carp in the country, for example, now resides in one of Cheshire's finest estate lakes and there are now more 30lb carp than ever before to angle for if you live in this neck of the woods. Home, work and family circumstances will all dictate just how much time and effort you're able to commit to your own individual angling, and results shouldn't be compared to others with more time or fewer responsibilities. For those anglers who are able and committed enough to spend long hours travelling in search of big fish then, good luck guys, there's no doubt that on some waters if the effort is put in, the results are certainly there to be had.

My own fishing over the last few years has centred mainly on local waters up to 50 miles or so from home, but during the autumn of 2012 I made a conscious decision to get down south as much as possible to try to catch a winter 40-pounder. Again, each individual will have their own personal situations to deal with, and that will dictate just what they can do and how often they are able to do it.

Strange behaviour

One subject that has had me thinking over the last few months or so is how certain carp behave, and whether individual carp can assess danger more easily than others. There's been talk among anglers for years on how commons behave differently to their mirror carp cousins. Certain baits are said to be more attractive to commons as well; whether this is true or not, one thing's for sure and that is when it comes to fish behaviour we still don't know everything about how and why they do certain things and behave in certain ways, and that is why at times they seem to be one step ahead of us.

This was brought home to me in 2010 when angling on a 40-acre, North-Midlands gravel pit. The water in question has been heavily fished for a number of years and the residents are well-known, old, character fish. Image my surprise when my very first bite turned out to be a near-30lb heavily-plated mirror, a fish that had been caught a couple of months earlier, but according to the locals, this was the first time it had visited the bank, in fact nobody could find any previous pictures of it anywhere! I was delighted with this capture and amazed at how a fish of this size had evaded capture for so long.

Over that summer, this fish graced the bank twice more and suddenly became a target for a number of the regulars. Now, did this fish suddenly realise that being hooked and removed from the water didn't mean the end of its life and decided to become less cautious in its feeding? Well, I'm a little stumped on the answer, to be honest, and it's incidents like this that make carp fishing so fascinating.

Recently, on one of my local waters, another heavily-plated 30lb mirror decided to go on the missing list for over three and a half years. Suddenly, it turned up in the May of 2011 and once again, over the course of the summer, was banked by two other lucky anglers. My turn on the wheel of fortune came a couple of weeks prior to Christmas of 2011 when I landed the gorgeous creature. So what does trigger these fish when they've been missing for so long? Well, I haven't a clue, but if your water has one or two fish that haven't seen the bottom of the net for a while, don't dismiss them. You never know one could turn up and shock you.

On a final note

Now, I make no apologies for what I'm about to write about because Martin has given me a free pen, so to speak, so I'd like to take this opportunity to get a few things off my chest regarding one or two aspects of the current carp scene, and how I've seen it change over the last 25 years or so. First, the good old Internet and its use and, in a lot of cases, abuse: It's loved by some and loathed by others, but without a doubt using the Internet can be a great asset to your angling, whether you're checking out new waters, or finding information on bait, rigs or tackle. In fact, there's nothing you can't really discuss within reason and legal bounds and that unfortunately, is where it seems to be that some people take great pleasure in getting their little kicks; faceless and nameless anglers, whose sole intention is to cause problems or basically stir things up for other anglers. Why is this? It could be personal vendetta, jealousy, or perhaps it's just plain boredom and mischief that motivates these people. Facebook and Twitter can have a huge media influence and can be a great social aid, but unfortunately, just as some of the forums have suffered, these have been subject to certain people's abuse.

Either way, some of these Internet slugs need to do two things, in my view. One is to grow a set of balls and either put up or shut up, and two, get on with their own fishing. There kind obviously don't catch enough because they're always too busy typing away on the keypad moaning about every little thing or everyone else. Here's an example for you; there can be few people who have put more back into this sport than Korda Tackle's main man, Danny Fairbrass. Even he gets slated at times by people who've never even met the bloke! Despite his efforts to educate, help and support carp fishing and carp anglers all over the world, some people still have a go and criticise to the point of being downright nasty and rude.

A few years ago, I had certain opinions, based on what I had been led to believe, but guess what? The first time I actually met and spent some time with Dan, at a Junior Carp event at Horseshoe Lake, I found him to be helpful, friendly and above all, completely different to what I'd been led to believe. Others anglers have been slated simply because they may have changed from a certain company's sponsorship to another one, or have been banned from a venue for the slightest discrepancy. Anyone would think some anglers had committed murder for how they get tarnished on the Internet. It really has become sad when people who have never met someone else judge them on rumours or third-hand, inaccurate gossip. There are one or two anglers I can think of who should be ashamed at some of the lengths they have gone to, to belittle and spread downright lies just because others have caught more than they have or their own self-inflated egos have been bruised.

One incident stays firmly in my mind from a few years ago that put things into perspective and made me realise just how life is too short to be wasting time worrying about what others do or say. It was 2004 or 2005, if I remember correctly, when fishing the highly-pressured Elstow Pit 1 in Bedfordshire.

As a brand-new member and not knowing many anglers who fished the water, I felt a little uneasy on those first couple of sessions I fished there. Thankfully, I'd joined at the same time as good friend, Martin Pick, so at least I'd have someone to share info and time with. Luckily for me, I got among a few fish pretty quickly. In fact, my first bite on my first session was a lovely 30lb mirror that fell to one of my homemade 'hookers', and then with a handful of fish under my belt I was starting to get a bit more confident, when suddenly the wheels fell off.

Basically, it all went Pete Tong and I lost the next four fish I hooked! Now, with a couple of blanks under my belt I suddenly felt out of my depth and the confidence tanks were beginning to drain very quickly. In other words, my arse was twitching and I was hoping for a bite, more than anything else.

This 35lb-plus mirror couldn't resist Tim's Pink Squid special.

For my next session, I arrived to find the late Steve Watson, a very popular member, plotted up in an area I'd been hoping to get into for some time. It was early, around 5am, and as the light cleared, Steve was awake and up and about. He'd just landed a 34lb-plus mirror and then over the next two hours went on to land two more 35lb-plus fish, right in front of my eyes. All this before he had to pack away at 7am!

I helped Steve with the pictures and weighing of those fish and realised at the time that I was in the presence of a gifted angler. Never for one minute, despite my recent failings on the water, was there any inkling in my mind of being jealous of Steve's results. I simply watched him like a hawk hoping to pick up a few tips from a far more talented and accomplished angler than me. After all, it's not often someone from the north walks into an angler's swim and sees them land three mid-30s in just a couple of hours' angling. Sadly, with Steve's untimely and very sad death just a short time later, I never did get to pass onto him those few pictures I took, or thank him for the effect he had on me that summer's morning.

You're probably asking what was the point of those last few paragraphs. Well, the point is this, can someone please tell me why it is that these days it's become so common for others to ridicule or belittle other angler's captures with so little regard? After all, we're all out on the bank for the same reason, aren't we? Ultimately, to catch fish and feel that buzz of excitement that the captures bring. Even as I'm busy typing these last few words, I've just glanced at the clock ticking away in the corner of the

Elstow mid-1990s mirror and early initial success using Squid and Octopus pop-ups.

room and checked the time; it's 4.30am, on a cold, late November morning and I'm wide awake, why? Because for over two hours I have been helping a friend take pictures of a new personal best fish. Even though the call came in not long after 1am on a night that was cold, to say the least, I jumped straight into the motor and set off to lend a hand. The buzz of seeing someone hold their target fish in their hands and the smile on their face is enough to give me that extra push in my own angling. The day I can't get excited about others catching fish, or start to go to great lengths to belittle those captures or the angler concerned, is the day I'll hang up the rods forever. It's a pity others don't seem to share that same thought process and will forever be jealous, faceless, Internet ghosts.

There are more pressing issues within angling that if not addressed will see the end of the sport as we know it, things like the otter debate which rages on and on; the new, high-speed rail link or similar projects that are set to ruin the environment and countryside, with pollution and disease. These are the subjects that need fighting by anglers, not each other. Since I held my first carp rods way back in 1984, I've seen the carp scene change over the years, in some ways for the better and in some, certainly, for the worse. Let's all hope that over the next 25 years we'll see the whole sport of angling survive and flourish.

On a brighter note, my 2012 season ended on a high as a couple of fish I'd craved for over a number of years finally found their way into my net. I'm also looking forward to 2013 with hope and excitement and have a couple of new waters that I'm really looking forward to fishing because they contain a couple of really special fish.

Finally, I'd just like to say a massive thank you to both Richworth Baits and Gardner Tackle, who have helped support my angling over the last couple of years. Whatever your own goals and dreams, I hope you enjoy your angling and as my good friend Warren says, 'Keep chasing 'em', and cherish those moments when they happen.

Chapter 13

Lip-gloss, perfume and boilies

I've always felt that no matter who you are, if you've spent some time pursuing carp then everyone can learn something from you. As mentioned elsewhere, I wanted this book to be different, and with that in mind I've enlisted the help of two friends that will make it a first for any carp book. A female carp angler! Yes, there are a few but I only knew one, so it's a good job she's a tidy angler with a few 40s to her credit.

I'd met Angie Lawley and her partner, Chris Lowe, while fishing in Oxfordshire and we got on like a house on fire. Both of them were catching carp, indeed we all did, and we became friends from that first meeting. Many years have passed, and many more carp have graced their nets, and it would be nice to hear about Angie's tale and accomplishments, so I had a word with Chris and waited a few seconds for the reply.

I suggested an interview rather than doing a more traditional guest chapter, to save them the task of typing out thousands of words and to give the reader more of a sense of sitting in with us while we chat. They both agreed, so we set a date to coincide with when they'd both be fishing.

It must have been five or six years ago, when I thought about the content of my next book and the possible guest chapters, and straight away I had a strong feeling that there should be some female content. There were various reasons, but the compelling ones were; why not and who? Every year on my fishing trips over to the Richworth Linear complex I make a few friends and probably the nicest anglers I've met would be Angie Lawley and Chris Lowe, not married but partners in life and both sharing the same passion for carp angling. Having seen Angie and Chris angling, and hearing of their captures, Angie was a strong candidate, but would she fancy being a contributor to this book? With my fingers crossed I phoned Chris to ask Angie and within seconds got the thumbs-up so all we had to do was come up with something we would all be 100% happy with.

Within a few weeks, Chris emailed me some of Angie's memories and straight away after reading the article I could see that there was some good stuff, but some gaps needed filling and I was intrigued to hear more from Angie. I'd never interviewed anyone before, let alone a woman, but was keen to give it a shot because I've found while talking to anyone for any length of time you get the true sense of their personality, and an honest opinion to any questions thrown their way.

Manor Lake on the Richworth Linear complex, one of their favourite lakes, would be a good place to meet. All we had to do was sort out a date and take it from there, and if Chris was up for it, he too could get involved. As I had some time on my hands, due to being off work with back problems, we arranged to meet up in October 2012 to have a chat and record our conversation.

- Angie Lawley interview -

MC. Hi Angie, how long have you been fishing this session? More to the point, how's the fishing going?

AL. Well, it's been really hard going, Martin. I've been here 36 hours now and have only had one which was just over 20lbs, at 5am this morning. I think that has been the only fish out and we've hardly seen much showing either.

MC. There's a fair few people fishing though, looks busy. How many anglers fishing here at the moment?

AL. I think there are eight of us on at the moment, but there are still a few spare swims. Blimey, that makes me top rod today, if only for a moment, ha ha!

MC. Now, if I recall, you started fishing when you were a schoolgirl aged 13, can you remember that far back and give us an insight as to where and when you got the bug for fishing?

AL. I'd better put the kettle on! Well, I first wet a line fishing the canal near my Nan's caravan holiday home in Fradley, near Litchfield. My cousin and I couldn't wait for the weekends to come along so we could go there and fish. We'd meet our Nan after work on the Friday and stay at her house just so we could be there nice and early the following day. In those days it meant using buses which took forever to get from A to B. I saw this lovely rod in the local village shop and told my granddad about it and he gave me the money to go and buy it and it all started from there. It was six foot long and metallic green, but I loved it and still have it tucked away at home.

Basically, we float fished for anything that came along, and we caught all sorts but the stand-out fish I can remember was a massive perch, which to this day is the biggest I've ever seen, and a little carp probably no more than half a pound. I didn't know what sort of fish this little mirror carp was so took a picture on my camera, because it was a stunner.

Angie casting to a hot-spot which produced a number of carp.

I didn't realise at the time, but that little carp was to somehow shape my future to what fishing is to me now, a big part of my life. I spent most of my youth fishing the local ponds and canal, mainly float fishing, and it wasn't until later on in my life that I got into carp fishing, but I feel it gave me the basic skills like casting and unhooking fish.

MC. So the first time you had a rod in your hand you were 13. Can you remember how much your first rod cost?

AL. £2.86

MC. Blimey, that's cheap. (At this point we both started laughing). When you told your mates at school how you spent your weekends fishing, what did they say?

AL. Well, they didn't believe me, but then only my close friends knew it was true.

MC. So how did you go about tying your hook on in those early days?

Angie with a February capture of Cut-tail'from Manor lake at 41lbs 4oz. The first and only woman to catch this carp at over 40lbs.

AL. Well, I used to buy hooks to nylon; no one ever showed me how to tie a hook, but they worked a treat, although I did have some break on what felt like better fish. A few of my family were into fishing and I think it was one of them that showed me some knots, probably around the time I was leaving school at 16 in 1977. I was born in 1960.

MC. Blimey, I didn't realise we are the same age; you've weathered well. Shame I can't say the same! So when you left school, what next?

AL. Well, I went to work like most of my mates. Jobs weren't that hard to find back then, and I started off doing factory work, assembly line, that sort of stuff, boring really, still living at home with my parents until I was 23 years old. I was the last one to leave the nest in my family, two years after getting married at the age of 21. We moved into a lovely, brand-new house and, as you do, little babies came along so during the 80s, I had three kids which meant fishing went out of the window for quite some time.

MC. So during the 80s, when carp fishing in England began to gain momentum, with the birth of the hair rig and boilies, you were giving birth yourself! Had you totally given up on fishing?

AL. Oddly enough, even though I didn't wet a line for a few years I still had the urge to purchase the Angling Times at the local shop, just to admire the fish that were getting caught. All fish are nice but some of the carp captures must have triggered off something and when I could manage to squeeze half a day or even a whole day's fishing when my kids were at school I tended to target tench and bream, feeder fishing with the hope of the odd carp coming my way. My husband used to take me, but he never fished, just sat there reading a paper.

MC. So basically, you were teaching yourself as you went along

AL. Yes, basically picking up tips here and there from the Angling Times, no one over my shoulder pointing me in any direction.

MC. So here we are now in October 2012, and you've got three kids. How old are they now?

AL. They're 29, 27 and 23, and now they've flown the nest I've got plenty of time to go fishing, it's great! Sadly, my marriage didn't last, so we got divorced and during this period, while coming home from a day's fishing, I met my current partner, Chris, and we've been together 12 years now.

MC. So did Chris get you into carp fishing?

AL. No, not really. Chris was into all sorts so we pooled our knowledge together and began targeting a few venues with these in our minds; single figure carp, then doubles, then 20s and so on. Safety and security in pleasurable surroundings is my main priority, so syndicates and day-ticket venues are where I'm happiest, and Chris also likes it so we are normally always close to each other.

MC. Can you remember your first 30lb carp?

AL. I can vividly remember my first 30, because I had two personal bests in the same session. We went looking for suitable venues and after looking at a few, we found ourselves venturing over to the Bluebell complex, near Peterborough. When we arrived we went into the office and met Tony, the owner, who gave us some advice on how to fish the lakes because they weren't runs waters. In fact, they were becoming difficult waters because of the angling pressure and the general low stock. We weren't fully aware of each lake's stock or how tricky they could be to catch before we arrived, so off we went full of confidence and settled on Kingfisher Lake. It was busy and no-one was catching, but Chris set up by some lilies with me to his right in some trees and we started fishing.

I didn't have to wait that long before one rod screamed off, so I grabbed it and started playing the fish in. It felt big, and I thought, 'this isn't a six-pound carp'. Anyway, after a few minutes I netted it and straight away knew it was a good one and our scales were not going to handle it. Luckily, the lad in the next swim loaned us his scales; it was a common carp at 31lbs 4oz. I was over the moon, my first 30 and in pristine condition, what a result! I didn't really know how to hold such a big carp for the photos so I just cradled it like a baby, I didn't want to drop it. I wasn't as confident back then but I've learned in time. It feels so natural to hold them in my hands now, and I laugh, thinking back.

I was a bit blown away really because we'd only been there a few hours. I caught it on a short hooklink with two dog biscuits drilled through, and fished them popped-up from the bottom with a small PVA bag of fishmeal pellets. I had to recast these every half an hour because the mixers take on water, and they eventually go very soft and can fall off or get pecked away by small fish.

After sitting there an hour or so after photographing my PB carp, I was beginning to think that would be the only carp we'd see, but now my other rod, with an identical set-up, was off and screaming for me to grab it. Boy did it go off on one, and because the bank was muddy and slippery, Chris had to hold on to me around my waist to stop me being pulled in. Eventually, after a few deep lunges in the margins, I netted another big common, and that pulled the scales down to 32lbs so I had another PB. Two 30s! Wow, what a result! When Tony, the owner, found out he could hardly believe it. I left the complex on cloud nine, both of us keen to come back for more.

MC. So now would you say you had the big carp bug?

AL. Yes, the big carp bug had bitten. A couple of weeks later we returned for another session, popped into the office to see how things had been going, then made our way to a couple of different swims. I set up in a swim called the 'Rats' with a bay to my right which looked carpy, so cast some rigs and bags out while I set my bivvy up. Just as the last peg went in, off went one of the rods and ten minutes later I had a gorgeous linear in the net, at 27lbs 8oz. I'll never forget it because our camera wouldn't work and Martin Locke, who was in the next swim, took loads of photos for me on his camera.

I recast the rods out before it got dark and was sitting by them, soaking up the atmosphere, when the same rod, fishing in 19 feet of water, rattled off. It turned out to be another linear, which went 26lbs, and once again, Martin Locke took some snaps.

Avid size 5 Transfer PVA bags have proved really useful.

Kempy's Linear at 39lb 12oz; hookbait presented in a solid bag and cast to a spodded area.

I like to keep a record of events; weather, tactics, and captures.

Someone said there were only two linears in the lake and I was lucky to catch both on the same day. It must have been the lip-gloss, ha ha! Lockey posted me some superb photos the following week, so many thanks to Martin.

MC. So, your first few sessions at Bluebell and you're doing great. What next?

AL. Well, we both liked the venue so we joined as syndicate members and just fished there and Chris started catching, so we both caught carp on most of the sessions we put in. Chris had a quest to catch Benson and after two months fishing, doing 48 hours every week, he finally caught Benson at 56lbs; it looked awesome!

MC. What happened after Benson?

AL. Well, with every climax there's always going to be an anticlimax. Chris wanted to leave on a high and I was quite happy with my time and results, so we started looking around at other venues. After picking up a brochure from one of our local tackle shops, of the Linear Fisheries complex in Oxfordshire, we looked through it and were instantly interested so decided to follow the map in the brochure and go and check it out. When we arrived in the car park we were keen to have a good look around so went off looking at most of the lakes. What a beautiful place, clean and tidy, everyone helpful all the amenities on site, even food deliveries on the complex! We met Roy Parsons, the head bailiff, and he told us a bit about each lake and what baits and methods were producing so we felt we'd found something special.

MC. So bring me up to date. You've both fished this complex for a decade now, and you've caught some stunning carp from most of the lakes. What memorable moments stand out for you, looking back?

AL. Well, we started off fishing Hardwick/Smiths, which is where we first met you Martin, and it was struggle at first but one of those waters we continued to learn on and, slowly but surely, we did learn and began to catch carp. Chris probably did a bit better than me but I wasn't far behind and by far the most impressive carp I had the pleasure of catching from Hardwick/Smiths was called the DVD fish, nice and scaly, dark in colour as if carved from mahogany, which went just over 37lbs. We set up on the Point swim; it was getting dark, and as I'd seen a few carp swim past, I stuck one rig about four feet from the bush using a popped-up corn rig with two handfuls of sweetcorn over the top and it was that rod which produced the DVD fish.

MC. What about the other lakes; where next?

AL. We started fishing St. Johns after many happy days on Hardwick/Smiths and, as you do, started to get among the carp. This is where my next PB came from, in the shape of another common which pulled our scales to 41lbs 4oz, I was well chuffed, but the icing on the cake was, the lads at Linear put me on the front cover of the annual Linear Fisheries brochure and kept it quiet right up to the day they were delivered.

MC. Did you grab a handful of copies from Roy when he showed you the brochure?

AL. Ha ha ha! I grabbed half a boxful, and made sure all my family and friends got to see it. Not many girls get to get on a front cover of a male-dominanted sport magazine, such as fishing. I really felt as if I'd achieved something.

MC. All of us would be happy with a 40lb-plus common, not to mention the front cover shot. It is an achievement, and any PB will always be remembered. Typical Roy Parsons, keeping the front cover a secret! So where next after St. Johns?

Another PVA bag victim graces Angie's net.

Cover shot common at 41lbs 4oz.

AL. Well, for the next few trips the complex was really busy and the only swims we could find were on the Manor Lake next door so we started fishing there. This was home to the infamous 'Cut-tail' among others and Chris, bless him, really wanted to catch him, and I was more than happy to switch our attentions to another lake so we started fishing Manor. Eventually, after a number of sessions and carp for both of us we each managed to catch Cut-tail, for me a PB mirror, but no bigger than the St. Johns common at exactly the same weight 41lbs 4oz.

MC. I remember you on the front cover of Carp Talk with this carp; January 2007 - I've still got a copy. Did you know you'd be front cover of Carp Talk? What was your response when you found out?

AL. No I didn't know until I picked up a copy in the local newsagent, and I couldn't stop smiling as I handed him the money. They only had one copy left so I rang round my friends and family to tell them to have a look in their shops.

MC. Now, I know you've caught many fine carp since 2007, from some of the other lakes here at Linear Fisheries, and now you're a sponsored angler, who with and how do you feel about being sponsored?

AL. Well, Chris and I are sponsored by Avid and Sonubaits. It's great, all the Avid gear I really like, and the carp like Sonubaits boilies and particles. Before Sonubaits we both used to use Dez's bait, SBS lobworm boilies, mostly tipped with a piece of artificial corn.

MC. So you've fished on the Manor Lake a few times this year, what's your most memorable session?

AL. Well, this year's best session I had 20 carp over 48 hours, all on zigs, two 30s with the biggest 35lbs, and seven 20s with the rest being doubles. I started off with three zigs at different depths because I was unsure which would be best and then adjusted them as the session went along, with most coming on 8ft hooklinks. I first tried zigging on St. Johns a few years ago, and managed to catch a few carp. It's a good method in the right swim at the right times.

MC. What terminal tackle were you using that session?

AL. Preston Exceed 8lb mono hooklink with a size 10 Korda wide gape, with Avid highlights as hookbaits. Shall we have another brew?

MC. Never say no to a cup of tea, mmm lovely, Angie. I see you've got plenty of biscuits, don't be shy! Nice of you to join us, Chris, perfect timing. What were you doing when Angie was hauling on the zigs?

CL. Well, I was in the swim next door, obviously doing some photographic work with some of Angie's carp, but I was having a few as well that session so it was a bit hectic. I was fishing on the bottom over a spodded area, two swims next door to each other and two totally different tactics working, it was mad! Angie has had over 50 carp this year on zigs, which keeps me busy, ha ha!

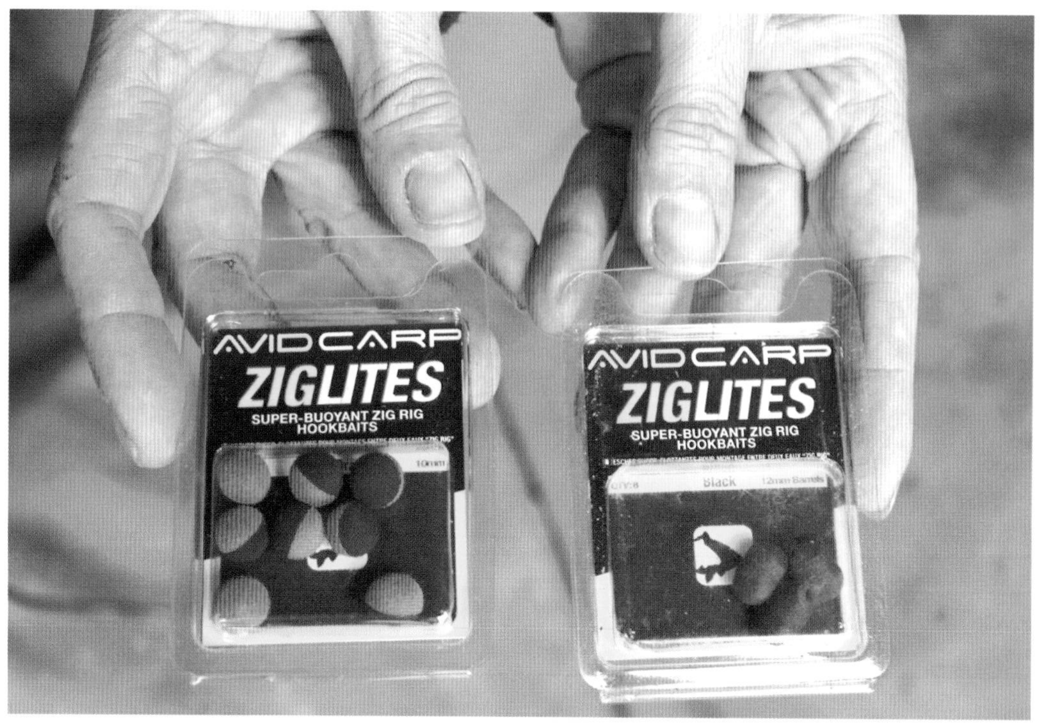

Angie's favourite zig baits.

Chris with Manor lake record, Spike at 46lbs; 25lb Avid Captive hooklink, size 8 prototype hook and Code Red pop-up.

MC. Blimey, that's more than I've ever had. I know I can make excuses for my lack of zigging but it does prove a point, on the right venue in the right areas it's incredibly effective. It has certainly accounted for many carp captures in Oxfordshire! It's weird that it's only in the last 15 years that zig fishing has emerged as a winning tactic, yet there are still many carp anglers who've yet to get to grips with it. I don't believe it's a case that carp have changed their feeding habits, they will feed at all depths! Care to comment on that Chris?

CL. Yes, that's right Martin. They don't just feed on the bottom or off the surface. It's not an instant method, zigging, sometimes you have to play around and fish different depths, different baits, but once it begins to work it's amazing. I see many anglers trying it but half seem to give up or cast their zigs out without even knowing the depth they are fishing in. This year we've been using Preston mono hooklinks and have been playing around with hooks, some not yet available, but most of my fish have come on size 12 Gardner Muggas, while most of Angie's have fallen to size 10 Korda Wide Gape.

MC. Looking back to when my first book 'Strictly Carp' was published in 2001, Korda were just emerging really. Boy! Haven't they come on leaps and bounds!

CL. Well yes, but it's understandable really because they have gone out of their way and when you see them at the various carp shows they are always willing to show anyone anything and explain everything to them. Not like in the old days when all you had was what your local tackle shops stocked, which was nailed to the wall. Now we've got free DVDs with loads of instructional and promotional material. Even the packaging of each product is instructional, well it should be!

MC. That's right, Chris, and that's something that I've been promoting for many years now with the bait and tackle companies I've been with. Korda do seem to have attracted the younger anglers, which is never a bad thing, and product sales have pushed their developments along. It just shows how important information, advertising and marketing are in a competitive market.

CL. I see it a lot when I do my tutorials. Many are newcomers to our sport and they are all ears when I start talking about tackle; they want to know what hook, what hooklink, what swivel ... they are like sponges absorbing all the info.

MC. I suppose we're near a point now where there is too much choice and some people simply need direction.

CL. Yes that's right. Some anglers have told me that they sometimes don't know what to buy for the best and feel a bit embarrassed to ask any staff to explain something. When you first started, Martin, there weren't so many choices, today it's a minefield.

MC. We could say the same about bait, Chris, the choices available today are staggering and still most of the bait major bait companies will add to that ever-growing list of choices each year.

CL. That's right, but at the end of the day there's only going to be x amount of boilies or particles sold each year and the bait companies are all jostling for their slice of the pie. There are so many bait choices around now; I think you've just got to find one which gives you action on the venues you fish. Someone suggested we try Sonubaits and I'm glad we did because this year we've done really well on the 24/7 and Code Red. A lot of the fishing here is with two or three rods over bait and we've fished these side by side and we're catching on both, oddly enough most coming on the Code Red with some of the more notable residents falling for the 24/7. What we like about Sonubaits, and Avid is that everything is tested by us and other field testers for 12 months or more before it goes on the market, something which hasn't always been done with other companies and various products!

MC. I know where you're coming from in that department. Being told 'we want you to push this or that', before you've even had a chance to use something for a while isn't really the way forward.

CL. With the amount of time we fish each year, and the amount of fish we catch, we give everything a proper testing and if we feel anything needs tweaking we'll let them know. Avid are definitely a company that listens which is why they are going from strength to strength.

MC. Your chair looks a lot more comfortable than mine!

CL. Well, there you go, Martin. A chair is a chair but someone has still got to put it through its paces. There's no point in selling something if it breaks through poor design, or quality of materials, or manufacturing. The last company I was with I'd be lucky to get a few sessions out of a chair before it broke. It's all very well being sent another one and it's free, but after half a dozen, it starts doing your head in. I think some of the companies forget what they have got consultants for.

MC. It refreshing that Angie is sponsored; you don't see that many female anglers around. What's it like fishing with your girlfriend most of the time?

CL. It's great. We get along fine but you do get the odd moment when someone will approach Angie's bivvy and ask, 'How's it going mate?' They get a little shock when Angie appears and starts talking. Most are fine but you get the odd chap who'll walk off thinking they won't learn anything from a female, despite the fact that Angie has had many memorable moments on the complex.

MC. So to anyone reading this with a partner, do you think they should take them fishing?

CL. No, not unless you're going to let them fish. That's a pet hate of Angie, seeing lads take their girlfriends and they simply read a book or lie on the bed chair.

MC. I haven't really fished much on the complex since the flooding, going back a few years now. It's still as popular as always!

CL. Yes, that's right, there's still a heck of a lot of carp here. They may have lost a few down the river but most simply stayed put during the floods; some went missing and started appearing in the other lakes. Not to mention that most years they stock various lakes, there's thousands of carp here at Linear.

MC. You're right, Chris. There could be more carp here than in the whole of Oxfordshire. It's no wonder that you and Angie, plus all the rest, keep coming back!

CL. Well, it is called fishing and we don't come here to go camping. Sitting it out on a hard venue struggling to catch two or three carp each year isn't really my cup of tea, and we're both happy, and being happy is what matters most.

MC. Blimey, is that the time? Amazing where it goes once we start talking! Before I go, Angie, what shall we call this chapter?

AL. I've taken to writing a diary this year, you know, fish weights and weather conditions, that sort of thing, and I'm amazed at how many men seem to forget something when they go fishing. Why don't they write a check list so they don't forget? I do! The first three items on my list are lip-gloss, perfume and boilies, will that do for a title?

MC. Ha,ha, makes a good title for a book. That'll do nicely. Could have been, 'Is that your buzzer, no it's mine!' Thanks for the tea and biscuits, we'll keep in touch.

Two on at once; good rigs and baits in the right place equals happy times!

Chapter 14

My single-handed approach

My earliest recollection of meeting Ashley was when he was a boy in his early teens. Straight away he stood out because he only has one hand and I was to learn that this happened in his infancy, so going through life one-handed is normal for him. Every time we met in our local tackle shop, my respect for him as a person and friend grew. It was clear to me he loved fishing for carp and wasn't fazed by the cards he'd been dealt.

Twenty-odd years have passed and you could say I've seen Ashley grow from a boy to a man, married with two lovely children. Fishing with one hand can't be easy but Ashley learned to master this by going with his friends and soon developed into an accomplished carp angler capable of doing everything himself. It wasn't until a few years ago that I actually got to see him fishing, because we'd previously been fishing different venues, and without hesitation I asked him if he'd write a guest chapter for this book. Ashley replied, "Who'd want to read about me? I've only had a few 30s!" I said, "Well, an upper-30 is big to me. You're a mate and you're an inspiration to me; some people may look down on you, I look up!"

Thankfully, Ashley agreed to write, reflecting on his adventures, after I'd told him that I'd only written a few chapters so he'd have time to catch a few more big carp, and indeed he did!

- Ashley Larman -

When Martin asked me if I would like to pen a guest chapter a couple of years back, I thought it was a wind-up. Why would Martin Clarke be asking me, Ashley Larman, to make a contribution to his second book? Obviously, I was taken aback

by this offer and felt very privileged to be asked, considering the amount of carp fishing talent out there at Martin's disposal. I duly accepted and then panicked as to what the hell I was going to write about! I consulted Martin about the sort of content he required from me, because I am just your average carp angler who drops in with a few average-sized fish each year. Who would be interested in what I've achieved in my carp fishing career? Martin said, 'just write about you!'
"Me?" I said.
"Yes, you," was Martin's reply.

Then the penny dropped; it's not every day you come across a one-handed angler! Like my family and friends, I tend to forget that I am missing a vital limb and it has never stopped me getting on with life in any shape or form. I expect to be treated the same as everybody else and that has never been any different. Since I was a kid, I would never give up on anything that may have been a little more difficult for me than for a person with two hands. I believe that I wouldn't be the person I am today if my parents hadn't just let me get on with it. If I'd had everything done for me, I certainly wouldn't have had the confidence to go fishing and deal with my quarry single-handed.

Thanks are also due to my brother, Scotty, and best friend, James. They were on their way to a small pond in Caddington one day in the school summer holidays, around 1989, to try to catch carp of single-figure size, and I thought, why are you wasting your time? I wasn't too interested, but at a loose end so I reluctantly joined them. Little did I know that this was to be a day that would shape my life forever.

Three carp on that day got me hooked, landed, weighed and photographed; I was well and truly caught by the carp bug. James and Scott didn't once question whether or not I would be able to hold the rod and reel and fish one-handed, they just let me get on with it, but I'm sure I did annoy James with repeated requests for a hook to be tied on. Don't worry James, I've been practising since then; I even know how to tie a knotless knot now (private joke).

Seriously, the rig tying was at times a little tricky in the beginning. No knot tying instruction book in the world would ever be any help to me because the diagrams in these books show you how to tie knots with two hands, and not one hand and one foot. I still tie knots the way they should be tied, but I've just adapted and found my own way of doing them. For example, when tying a pop-up on with dental floss I have to leave a very long length one side and wrap it around my stump so that I can get the leverage to bed the knot down nice and tight.

I've had accidents in the past when I've had a size 6 impaled into my stump while trying to tie a rig in the cold, and even had a hook through my bottom lip while trying to tease a knot down. When I worked in Leslies of Luton, between the years of 2000 and 2010, the worst thing any customer could possibly ask me was, "All right, mate, how do you join your main line to the top of lead core?" Imagine the poor bloke's face when he saw me tying a needle knot with my tongue. How confusing for him, but it at least showed him I could do it!

Unfortunately, there is too much judgment made about others within the carp fishing game and this is something that I have experienced first-hand myself (excuse the pun). Is he going to be able to deal with playing and netting a fish by himself? Will he be able to do it at night, never mind during the day? Will he be able to look after a fish on the mat? The answer from me to all of these questions is, can you?

These are the butt grips on my spod and marker rod, pretty unique thanks to a close friend.

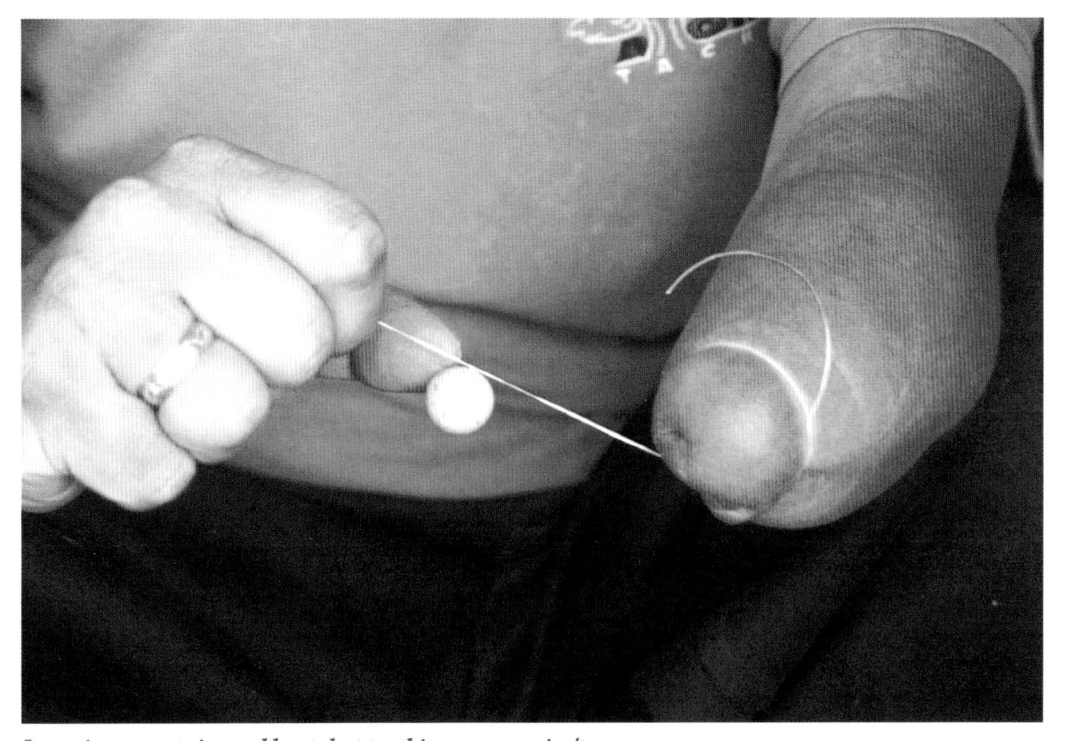

I can tie up most rigs and knots but teaching someone isn't easy.

Monty at 37lbs 4oz; another memorable moment at Heron Lake.

I have witnessed shocking fish care of all species, never mind just carp, by fully able-bodied, so-called anglers, and even by people who have questioned my ability before they had even seen me fish. It was on one of Martin's old haunts where I really took the step to becoming a proper carp angler, Woburn Sands in the early 90s. This was back when I was fishing club waters before I felt the need to spend hundreds on any syndicate waters. Woburn was a tricky, deep water with pressured carp that had been fished for by good anglers for years. I didn't know it, but my ability was questioned on this lake by some of the people fishing there. The bailiff, who I didn't know at the time but is now a good friend of mine, was approached by one of his friends on my first visit to the lake. "Mark, you need to go and see that lad over there. He's only got one hand," said one chap. Mark's reply was, "What the hell do you want me to do, throw him off?"

Mark came round to see me, to check me out I suppose, but he never once mentioned what had been said to him by others until about 2009 when he informed me over a chinwag and a cuppa. I thank Mark now for just letting me get on with it because had I known then what people were saying, it may well have knocked my confidence and I could have given up on the hobby I have grown to love.

I really enjoyed Woburn even though I lost a third of what I hooked, mainly due to the snags that were present. I never caught the big'un, Scaly, but I did have many 20s and was fairly consistent for the three or four years that I spent on there. The place definitely taught me a lot about the way carp behave and what changes had to be made to my approach to be able to catch them. With confidence growing it was now time for a change, I had to join a syndicate.

I came across a quiet and secluded lake on the Wyboston complex on the Beds/Cambs border, called Heron Lake. I did some investigation work and managed to obtain the syndicate leader's telephone number, so I was straight on the phone. Alan Fleming was his name, and this is a man who does not suffer fools. He certainly wouldn't have people on his fishery who would put carp welfare in any danger. Alan decided to let me join his syndicate, even though there was concern from others over my ability to deal with my quarry safely.

This lake was like a dream come true, lily pads, reeds, islands, bays along with golf-course-green swims to plonk your bivvy on. I was a little unsure as to what stock was present but I knew there were at least half a dozen 30s; not a huge number of big fish, but with surroundings as stunning as this, who really cared? How was I going to approach this lake without making a fool of myself?

I was intimidated big time having only fished club waters previously. The locals were all approachable though, and soon told me that the way forward was 20mm boilies. This was a tactic I wasn't familiar with because for most of my fishing at Woburn I was using 12mm boilies over hemp. In fact, I don't think I had ever used a boilie over 14mm, so I needed to consult the oracle, James. After a swift discussion over a few Stellas one evening, he convinced me to go on there with hemp and corn and go against the grain of big baits. So, ready for the start of the Heron season armed with a bucket of the black and yellow stuff, with fake corn for a hookbait, I was about to encounter a major problem. I didn't have one hand any more, I had none.

After a drunken loss of temper I decided to attack a solid oak table with my only hand and managed to break some bones. 'Two months in plaster' says A & E. Great! No driving, no fishing, and no wiping my own arse! I had one month until my Heron ticket started so I was hoping for a quick recovery. Could I heal before the big kick-off, in half the expected time? I did heal very well but was told that the plaster would have to remain on for the allotted time. Gutted, I decided I was having none of it. I was going fishing regardless of whether I had a plaster cast or not.

So, here's this guy who has one hand and was carefully considered for the syndicate on the basis of his disability. He's given the benefit of the doubt and he now turns up with no hands. God knows what was going through people's minds. To be honest, I didn't expect to catch that season, so wasn't thinking that I might need to pick up my rod from a screaming bite alarm on my very first session, but guess what, I did catch on my first session. A stunning, dark-backed common carp of around 25lbs, and I was blown away.

I continued with the hemp and corn tactic for 12 months because it was working a treat. A good friend, Elliott, and I were catching every session, but we weren't getting among the better-sized fish so a change was required, and boilies were needed. Influenced by James (as usual) who had now joined us on the lake, boilies were to be fished alongside the bucket of spod mix so that I still had the option of fishing plastic on the rig that had caught me my fair share of carp in a short period of time. First time out on the boilies in the Plateau swim, I finally managed a 30-pounder at 32lbs 4oz, along with four over 20lbs and a double, all in 24 hours. I was buzzing and couldn't wait to get back again.

Next session, I managed my second carp over 30lbs and a new lake record mirror at 37lbs 4oz; Monty was his name and he was stunning. Monty was a sought-after, near fully-scaled carp that at the time only used to get caught a couple of times a year and would often disappear for months, so I was well chuffed. Unfortunately, Monty has now disappeared for good. RIP Monty.

Six more years were spent on Heron and I loved every minute of it. Good friends were made and many socials enjoyed, more 30lb carp were caught but I knew it was time to move on after I caught the lake's first 40-pounder.

It was October 2008, and I finally achieved what Alan Fleming was waiting for, someone to catch a 40 from his pride and joy. Homer is a big Simmo that is not caught very often and we all knew it would be this fish that would break the magical 40lb barrier first, we just didn't know who would be the first lucky angler to net it at this weight.

It was a Friday and for a change I had the weekend off work, so I decided to get down to the lake before first light so that I had a chance of getting one of the swims that I thought I needed to be in to stand a chance of catching Homer. I decided to plot up in Guv'nors, which is situated on the mouth of a bay where the carp tended to reside as the temperature started to drop every year. I staggered my rods from near margin to far margin to try to cover as much water as possible because I knew they would be moving into the bay, but I didn't know exactly which route they would take.

The day passed without a single bleep from the alarms and not a sign of a carp in the swim so I was starting to think I had got it wrong, but I was prepared to move if required because I had another night to play with, which was something I wasn't used to having. At 9pm, big weather came in; high winds, heavy rain and with this came the carp, jumping all over the swim. Liners started on my left-hand and middle rods within minutes of the rain starting, and I knew this was carp because wind rarely affected your lines due to the size of the lake and how sheltered it was. It was obvious that it was just a matter of time before one of the hookbaits was picked up.

At 3am, and after virtually no sleep due to run-like liners for six hours, the left-hand rod burst into life. I was on the rod in a flash and was back winding straight away. After contending with very heavy, powerful runs into weed beds in the middle of the swim, I then had to keep it out of the bay. At one point, it was in the bay and weeded up so I did consider taking to the boat, but after some gentle persuasion and the reliability of 12lb Insight GR60 I managed to get it moving again.

I was winning the battle and I just had a gut feeling that I would be netting the one we all wanted. I just knew it was her, and it was, all 41lbs 8oz of her. I was ecstatic, a new PB and Heron's first 40-pounder. I decided to retain the fish until 6am because I knew Alan and a few others would want to come down to witness this magical moment. We gathered in torrential rain and ran off photo after photo. You could see Alan was over the moon and very proud of the lake's first 40. It was a perfect way to sign off on Heron Lake; my last fish was caught from more or less the same spot as my first fish; good memories that will never be forgotten.

Next stop, a 35-acre deep pit in Bedfordshire. What was going through my mind when I decided to join this lake? I only had a Saturday night to play with, due to my work commitments, and was probably never going to get anywhere near the fish with the swims that would be left by the time I got there, but I really wanted to give it a go.

Many months of blanks were to come but I stuck at it and never gave in. This mentality probably stems from my determination as a kid, as previously mentioned earlier in the chapter. OK, I didn't catch any of the originals but I did manage a few carp and was pleased just to get among them and feel part of the place.

Here I am, showing that I can hit the spots as well as anyone.

Homer at 41lbs 8oz, Heron Lake's first 40, and mine.

My PB mirror at 44lbs 8oz; taken from the back of a mound, on a boilie tipped with Enterprise yellow fake corn and fished over a spodded area.

The goal really was to get offered a ticket for the main pit eventually, and start filling my album with 30-pounders. This was to happen a lot quicker than expected and I was offered a ticket after just a two-year wait. It was around this time that I moved on from Leslies to start working for good friends James and Elliott, so new job, new lake.

I was to encounter a problem on this pit. I had to spod accurately over three rods at ranges of up to 90 yards and this is something that I hadn't had to do before. I've always had an issue with my stump slipping off the butt of the spod rod when fully compressing for any long chucks, so how was I going to get around this? I know, let's ask James?

As usual, after some head scratching he had the answer. He left the office and entered the yard to re-enter the office a couple of minutes later with a band strap. He cut a section off, duct-taped it to the bottom of the spod rod and said, "There you go, how simple was that?" He's a clever git! My spodding is now far more accurate and this simple idea has, without doubt, caught me more fish.

I have had a fantastic first 18 months on the pit, with two carp over 40lbs in my first year, which included a new PB of 44lbs 8oz, along with a dozen 30s, but this story is only just beginning and has a long way yet to run. Maybe I can let you know how I get on in Martin's next book.

I would like to thank Martin for giving me this opportunity and hope that I haven't wasted any of his print space, or bored you all to tears.

Chapter 15

Sandy and the final straw

It always seems that right at the start of a chapter, whether in an article, book or even a part of my life, I find it best to try to set the tone with the title I give to the chapter. Every now and then, I'll look at it and it gives me the reason to continue to the end. I could so easily have called this chapter something else and if I'd listened to a few of my friends who knew all the facts it would have been. To understand fully, I'll take you back to the year 2000 when I had the brace of a lifetime, from the notoriously shy Berkshire syndicate of which I was a member.

During my time there, the numbers of anglers granted access was cut each year from 30 to 15, which I was happy about having not been on the waiting list that long, and at only £100 a year it didn't make a big dent on my carp funds. Publicity of captures was allowed for a period, then banned for a period, and then once again relaxed. Now, I think there is a publicity ban, which is a shame really but I can see a case for some of the reasons for it. I'm not a member now and perhaps publishing my first book, Strictly Carp, was the catalyst for things to escalate to the point where I dropped my ticket for such a magical lake I'd grown to respect, and will always remember the good and the bad times, and all the lessons learned along the way.

The day I dropped my ticket, my mind was full of mixed emotions which left a big scar that took some time to heal. If you're not too sure of where I'm talking about then don't worry too much, because getting a ticket will be virtually impossible unless you know someone who fishes there, but I will set the scene as best I can without causing a traffic jam.

The lake was about 50 acres and set in the grounds belonging to a substantial landowner, his back garden being a series of fields and lakes, total area maybe 200 acres or more. On the main lake he let things run themselves, or at least it seemed that way to me at the time, with a yacht club at one end of the lake and a local angler running the fishing syndicate. The guy who owned the lake had no real idea of the value of these carp in the grand scheme of things; 18 pukka Leney-strain carp with five of them in excess of 40lbs.

I'd given the venue the name Sheephouse Lake and looking back at the chapter in my first book, Strictly Carp, there was an awful lot of material information missed out including all the edges I used which made all the difference. It took me a few years to find out how to catch them, but once I'd cracked it, my rewards came from all the effort I put in. I'd held back some secrets because there were two or three more specific carp I'd liked to have caught. Unfortunately, keeping secrets doesn't make you any friends, and having caught four different 40s all at their top weights in a 12-month period, I'd made it look easy when, in fact, it was quite the reverse for various reasons.

I'd made public one of the rigs I used there to good effect, the eliminator rig, and also that we could use boats, but little else apart from the fact that you needed the tools and time to acquire the confidence, and the patience of a saint.

It was one of those places that was more mentally challenging than physically, simply because of the rules imposed and that we couldn't fish half the available bankside because part was still a gravel workings. The top lake was part of the original, and it got filled in with gravel from the nearby Thames relief channel, making the top bank out of bounds because there was heavy plant using it for quite some time.

There were five very important factors which unlocked the door for me, and these were bait, rigs, natural feeding areas, accurate casting and using a boat the way it should be used. The rules for the fishery were quite straightforward really; lifejacket at all times out on the pond and no towing rigs out or placing hookbaits using the boat; 48-hour time limit on the island, 92 hours on the bank. It was okay to take out markers, bait and play fish from a boat provided there was no sailing going on. As I'm not really a long-session angler, this suited me down to the ground, apart from the fact that it wasn't in my back garden and I had to travel 60 miles there and back, once or twice a week.

The baiting revolved around a few issues, not just what I used but the quantity and equally importantly where I put it. On this large, understocked lake there seemed little point in filling it in with boilies and particles because most of the lake was devoid of carp and even when you had carp within reach, they weren't in one large group. There was ten times more birdlife than carp and they too liked a boilie, and I didn't want to spend my money fattening them up. What I had learned from observations was that the carp did eat some boilies but were only prepared to eat them with gusto when the attractor levels were lowered to half of what I'd been accustomed to using.

Now, I've heard of a few anglers using washed-out baits to good effect on other venues in England and quite often I'd hear of anglers not getting any action for a few days and catching on the third or fourth day. That only makes me think there are some venues at which the levels of attractants put into the boilies is a primary concern. I've no idea if it's anything to do with the pH of the water, or whether some carp are just on the fussy side, but I'm sure that taste and dietary requirements are of equal importance when it comes down to them cleaning the plate. Possibly, it's a reason why some carp make most of the mistakes and some very rarely get caught!

With such a low stock, every capture is an event, and four rods certainly helped me.

Although I had my own, I used the syndicate's boat a few times. It proved well handy for prebaiting and observational work.

Just one corner of the 50-plus acre, historically difficult venue.

Is it because some carp have different taste preferences, i.e. some like sweet baits while some don't, or some like them spicy and some like them salty or oily? Having had a few repeat captures on a variety of venues, and near misses, I'm inclined to think that taste combined with nutritional requirements is the answer. One thing I have learned over the years is, what works well on one venue doesn't guarantee it'll be just as good on another. This is where observation can prove to be vital in order to maximise chances and save valuable time sitting behind rods using baits that you know little about. Not that we need to know all there is to know about baits to catch carp, but the only way to gain confidence with any bait on any venue is to either catch carp or through observation. Good bait, whatever it may be, will be eaten with gusto, while bad bait is one that they don't touch or are a bit reluctant to eat.

It could be argued that the biggest carp are greedier than their mates, but I do know from experience that this isn't always the case. I've watched big carp shy away from others feeding, and I've also witnessed smaller carp bulldoze their way between bigger ones. Obviously, if carp are feeding in numbers then it can become a lottery as to which one picks up one of your rigs, and if you're struggling to get them feeding then you have got to find something that they'll feed on.

From my observations of a few spots viewable from the bank, and some while out in the boat, I came to the conclusion that the boilies were far more effective with halved levels of attractant. The difference was, they scoffed the lot whereas baits with optimum levels were in some cases noticed but ignored, or they ate a few and did the off.

They did like a fishmeal-type boilie but seemed reluctant to feed on spots baited with just boilies; not that I saw that as a problem because with a boat we could have used just about anything. For me, the winning formula was a concoction of boilies, whole and chopped, plus hemp and a few crushed tigernuts, plus a groundbait/stick mix I had made with groundbait, blitzed boilies, ground-up and whole Optima 23 pellets. The little extras were the addition of tigernut juice and putting in a handful of zebra mussels and crushed snails into the bucket. The zebra mussels I picked off old, broken branches in the margins on the island, and the snails were easily found in abundance in the weed beds. It was all mixed up in a bucket, like a spod mix, only it was thrown in by hand either from the boat directly above my rigs or from the bank.

I don't think the mussels and snails made a huge difference because I only tried it half a dozen times but I did notice that one of the large feeding areas was always cleared of all the snails whenever the carp had spent time there, so I came to the conclusion that snails were their main natural food source.

During my times on the venue during 2000, I used to pre-bait six spots, four of which had produced for me before, so half the homework had been done. The new ones were margin spots, one on the island and one in an area called No Carp Bay, and all were baited with just a couple of scoops out of the bucket at least twice a week.

Now, obviously, it's fairly easy to bait up an area from a boat and without doubt when you can see things from a boat you can pretty much see everything when the clarity of water is good, just as you can from the bank. The temptation to put in a lot of bait when fishing is always there because it's easy, and as I've never been a 'fill it in and sit there' type of angler, this suited me down to the ground. Putting in large amounts of bait didn't really enter my head simply because with only 18 carp in 50 acres of water there wasn't enough carp to warrant it; there were quite a few tench, pike and perch and thankfully, just one bream. As my sessions were normally only for 48 hours, just enough bait to entice one take seemed the best policy, and what I didn't use while fishing was used to pre-bait when I left.

Normally, in July and August the blue-green algae would take over and visibility was crap, like fishing in pea soup. I'd purposely made the effort to build up my bank account in 1999 so I could devote all of April, May and June on just two venues, the Sheephouse Lake being the main one. The big-scaled mirrors were like large magnets; once seen, the desire is set and location and observations are easier to make in clear water. Even on a venue as hard as this, it can only increase one's confidence if you can observe carp feeding, or see your spots getting polished clean, not to mention catching fish.

As far as rigs went, then catching the tench and pike were the only problems to overcome because these had a liking for bait as well, and using single bottom baits or pop-ups on all four rods was a definite way to catch them. Double bottom-baited rigs were my saviour, especially the eliminator rigs with long hairs and a gap between the baits, these never produced one take from the tench or pike.

Being allowed to fish four rods was a bonus, so my fourth rod was often a pop-up rig of some description or another, but the one I favoured was a short D-rig-type with curved shrink tube fished tight to the bottom, that I'd been playing with on other waters. I called it the slip-D rig, and it will catch out most species of fish. The trick is how to tie one up, but once mastered, it's never forgotten. (see Chapter 8)

The first half a dozen visits in the spring of 2000, I was literally pulling my hair out as they only once came within range that I was aware of in the No Carp Bay area, and I'd only seen a few tench on four of my spots and nothing on the other two. It was frustrating at times because you could near enough guarantee to find some of the carp in the out-of-bounds areas, knowing you didn't stand a cat in hell's chance of catching one of them, but at the same time it gave everyone the opportunity to admire our quarry and feed them to see if they liked what we were offering them. Other anglers had thrown bait in areas that weren't fished, probably for the same reason that I choose to throw in a few handfuls of boilies in the safe zones; to observe and learn, but there was another reason for putting in a few free handfuls here and there. My thinking was that if they got a taster in a safe zone, then whenever they did come over my pre-baited spots they'd be accustomed to them and not treat them with caution.

After a month of baiting and fishing another venue most of the time, I almost got to the stage of thinking of changing my approach until eventually the carp began feeding on two of my pre-baited spots. On one of the spots, I actually watched the big fully-scaled mirror roll on the bottom just a few feet away, while viewing the spot with the aid of my glass-bottomed bucket, and I had a 35lb mirror from that area, and lost one.

The next session was in the same swim on the end of the island on the same spots and I blanked. I'm not too sure why because I did everything the same and even had all my rods clipped up to a measured marker on the rods on the same marks.

Set up fishing Pole Position, looking over toward the island which had three swims we could fish from.

Ooops! Another repeat capture of the Long One on this occasion over 42lbs from Pole Position.

I was convinced that another 48 hours fishing the same spots would produce more action, but not a bleep. The wind and visibility at the start of that session made viewing the bottom impossible and as soon as the swim came on the boil, it went stone cold for some reason. I put it down to the carp being somewhere else on the pond. It wasn't the first time I'd blanked.

Over the next few non-fishing visits, the water clarity improved and I found ten carp at the top end of the pond. There was no sign of the big one called 'Sandy', but all the other major players were around basking in the sunshine, totally out of range for any mixer fishing. I did try tempting them into taking mixers, but they just didn't want to know. Mind you, they were only Chum mixers straight out of the bag.

One thing I did notice whenever out there in a boat was how aware they were of your presence. They didn't get freaked out when you were able to observe them or even pass over them, probably because they don't see us as a threat. On a few occasions, I actually drifted close to areas I had pre-baited and observed them feeding on the bottom; exciting stuff when some of them were in the 40lb-plus bracket. The big, scaly girl looked incredible in the water, possibly one of the best-looking mirrors in England, but I never once saw all the residents in one big group. One day, I think I saw them all but still spread out, with over half the lake devoid of carp during daylight hours, although I'm sure they moved around more at night.

On the next visit, I was really buzzing to get back on to the island and soon discovered that they were showing an interest on three of my baited areas while a dozen tench had descended on my other spot. It took some time to get all four rods out to the marks and a few to many casts were made, but they proved worth it 24-plus hours later when I caught a new 40 at 40lbs 4oz, which I named Clover. It was a proper tense battle in the night, out in the boat under the moonlight, getting towed around by an angry carp that just didn't want to give in.

The spot which produced the take was one of the natural feeding areas. Now, I say that only because I had seen a few carp shows on previous trips and had noted the spots where any carp had either popped their heads out, or had been seen feeding on the bottom. I took a permanent marker and a marker rod to all these spots, out in the boat, and after positioning the permanent marker, I'd then pop the marker rod float a few yards away and then make my way back to the swim with an open bail arm. Once back in the swim, I then tightened up the line, marked it and when retrieved I'd clip it up on the spool clip.

At the time, I was using two of my fishing rods as my marker rods so it was a simple case of winding the lines around two bank sticks set a rod length apart and noting the measurement in my little black book. When it came down to casting out the rigs, I used to aim left and right of the permanent marker float put out using the boat, and if the casts looked accurate, then I was happy to leave them there for the duration of the session. Sometimes it took two or three attempts to get it spot-on but it worked a treat.

Of course, you can fish super-accurately by doing something similar; walking your rigs along a path or open grass. I also did this on a couple of occasions just to get the distance and line markers spot-on. The reason I did this was that it was a super-accurate system, and often when I went back out to the permanent marker the hookbaits were spot-on most of the times. Not so much of a problem when you can use a boat to bait-up over each hookbait, but it certainly makes finding your rigs with your head stuck over the side of the boat a damn sight quicker as well. Sometimes, I'd tweak the rigs back a little and sometimes I'd leave them if they looked okay, all dependent on the depth and visibility. It was on that visit that I began to become aware of strange things on the bottom, dotted along the margins here and there on the out-of-bounds bank. At first, I had no idea what they were because most of them were too deep to get a proper look.

On my next visit though, I saw more of these strange, white blobs on the lake bed, in different areas, but still in the margins of the out-of-bounds. Then I came across one on a gravel hump out in open water and when viewed from the boat it looked like a packet of sausages, still in the clear, plastic wrapper with one end open. At first, I thought that maybe someone had been launching in out-of-date sausages as they walked along the out-of-bounds, but when I found the one in open water I thought they must have been put in by someone using a boat. I was convinced they were packets of sausages, 17 packets in all, and the penny failed to drop!

Back at home, I told my mate, 'Desperate' Dan about the sausages. He simply said that if they're nowhere near the spots I was fishing, then forget about them. "Just get your arse back down there, because there's more to come."

The next session was unbelievable. Everything went spot-on; there were carp once again at the top of the lake and a group containing at least one 40 near the old channel. Both my pre-baited spots had been polished clean, one of them exposing the gravel just a few inches below a layer of silt, and the other, in slightly deeper water on silt and sand, looked like it had been turned over with exposed crushed mussel and snail shells.

Full of confidence, I was soon back on the island with all my fishing tackle. With spots marked and my rods already marked up from the previous visits, it didn't take long to get my rigs and bait out onto my cleaned out, pre-baited spots. Four hours into the session and one of my rods out to my two o'clock spot, ripped off and after a half an hour scrap I bagged myself a new PB mirror at 45lbs 8oz. As you do, I was straight on the mobile to summon a cameraman while my prize was recovering in a sack.

Within the hour, I had a finicky take on one of the rods out on my 11 o'clock spot, which had back leads on, and after another battle I landed the carp I'd been yearning for, the big Scaley One at 46lbs 2oz. Now with the two biggest carp to be caught from the venue sacked up awaiting photographs, not including the uncaught beast known as Sandy, all my Christmases had come at once and I was overwhelmed. I just couldn't bring myself to carry on with the session and slowly packed up, awaiting the cameramen that I had to pick up from the bank to take back out to the island for the photo session. Chris Ball was on hand to use my camera so it was in safe hands.

Having had such a result, I was on cloud nine for a month. My mate, Dan, said that I should have stayed on for the rest of the session as obviously there were others to be caught and he was probably right. He also said that the brace might stir up a few green eyes. I didn't return for the rest of the summer because I'd also planned a trip to France and carp funds don't last forever. It was back to reality and laying bricks, with the odd weekend session on less demanding venues for the rest of the year.

Part one of my big brace. Almost as wide as it was deep, and an epic battle in the boat.

Part two of the brace; the Scaley One at 46lbs 2oz and the second-biggest, genuine UK brace at that time.

Sometime around September of that year, the fishing was stopped due to the fact that a number of the carp had been seen swimming around not looking too healthy. 'Furry coats' was one man's description. I was also told that two had died, these being possible 30s. I never went to have a look so I can't really comment but all I knew was that the sailing club had used a weed killer and maybe this could have been the reason.

During the spring of 2001, all I could think of was whether to continue fishing the venue because I'd now had five 40s from there, with one repeat capture. There were a few nice 30s I'd have liked to catch, but the main one missing from my list was without doubt Sandy, the really big one that had not seen the bank for as long as anyone could remember. I've no doubt Sandy must have been caught by someone, but probably at 20lbs donkeys' years ago, because it was no different to the rest of the mirrors, just bigger!

The more I thought of Sandy, the more I convinced myself to have a go for it. I'd seen it a few times; the first time it looked perhaps ten pounds bigger than anything else in the venue, the second time just as big, and the third time feeding on some of my bait, but I unfortunately spooked it. I'd lost two carp from the venue so I may well have hooked it and lost it at some point in time. Others had lost the odd carp over the years, so there was no saying that someone hadn't hooked it and lost it, because most of the carp didn't get caught that often and fought like hell whenever you did hook one.

I had a feeling that Sandy was a bit of a loner and perhaps territorial so if I were to catch it, then I'd either have to be very lucky or fathom out another way. I'd a feeling I may have hooked and lost Sandy in the past, but as they all fight hard you just never know what's on the other end until you actually see them. One fact that did stick in my mind though, was that all my previous captures had come from just four swims all up at the far end of the lake, and I hadn't had any carp from any swims down at the clubhouse end. The answer to my problem then stared me in the face; it was time to fish different swims.

We were allowed back on to the lake two weeks prior to kick-off on June 1st 2001, so with a game plan in my mind, I set forth to investigate the lake in greater detail. With the batteries charged up for my Minn Kota, and my viewing bucket, I arrived at dawn now armed with some new bait from Solar Tackle. The beauty of using an electric outboard was that the carp weren't too put off by the motor, providing you went slowly and didn't make any major throttle changes. The trick to using the boat more efficiently was always to look well ahead of the boat as you moved along and to avoid going straight toward any carp, if possible. The object being to look for the carp ahead of the boat before you took your eyes off the water in front, and then to view possible areas that stood out as worth a closer inspection with the viewing bucket, from the sides of the boat.

Without an electric engine, then you'd have to use oars which were only any use when the surface was like a millpond. You can go out and about using one oar, standing or kneeling at the bow of the boat, and it really is unnecessary hard work, but okay if you like doing things the hard way. When it came to using the boat to transport me and my tackle, then all I can say is I never struggled once in the wind or even broke into a sweat on the hottest of days, and sometimes I'd even manage to view my spots before making decisions on what swims to fish. Sod all those blisters and clonking the side of the boat with oars zig-zagging across the lake. I get enough exercise handling thousands of bricks and blocks every year!

When it comes down to using a boat to land fish on your own, then using oars certainly isn't the way to go, in my opinion, even in calm conditions. I've seen people do it and normally they end up in a right pickle. I also think that pulling yourself out to the fish, using your rod, is not a good idea, because not only could you damage your line you could also damage the carp. I've seen people do it, and I've heard of others doing it, on other venues. You'd never see me do it though, which was the reason that I purchased an electric engine specifically to fish this demanding venue.

No Carp Bay was an area where I'd seen Sandy before so at least it did visit there, along with some of his chums. In the past, I'd given the area a good look from the boat and out beyond the margins I didn't see any signs that anything had fed anywhere on the bottom. The big bay was more like a four-acre bowl full of Canadian pondweed, but there were some interesting margin spots that now and then got visited by odd carp at this end of the lake so it was certainly worth investigating.

On my first pre-baiting trip I spent at least two hours going all over No Carp Bay and eventually, amongst all the weed, I found a spot I'd never seen before which looked promising but would require very accurate casting. A super-clean gravelly/sandy patch about six feet in diameter, with a nine-inch, hollow, concrete block on the left edge, when viewed from the intended swim. This really was another of those eureka moments. I'd found possibly one of the best spots on the lake which I knew would get visited by the carp. The concrete block might have had a buoy tied to it at some time and was now probably used as a rubbing stone by the odd carp.

Given that Sandy did spend quite some time at this end of the lake, this new spot had its possible downfall written all over it. I dropped a Gardner H-Block onto the spot and then steered the boat toward the out-of-bounds bank to place another marker. Once I'd got to the far bank, I then lined myself up with the H-Block and the swim on First Point, and backed into the trees so I could push a long bank stick into the pond, leaving it a just under the surface.

I had a three-foot length of 40mm white, plastic pipe with holes drilled into it and a piece of foam wedged halfway down the tube, and placed it on the bank stick which left roughly 12 inches of pipe sticking above the water to use as a visual far bank marker when casting rods out from the intended swim.

I went back to the H-Block and emptied the contents of my bucket bang on the spot, 1kg boilies, 1kg blitzed boilies, 1kg Solar Growler Mix and half a gallon of hemp. Viewing the spot from the intended swim, my far bank marker lined up spot-on and even from probably 200 yards I could clearly see the white tube. After about three hours on the boat, it was time for dry land as the yachters were turning up so I pulled up my white tube, leaving the bank stick firmly in place, and retrieved my H-Block. It was also time for something to eat before paying a visit to another lake not too far away. The intention was to view the lake again in the evening after the yachts had gone in, and make good use of the day, even though I wasn't fishing.

When I returned later in the afternoon, there were just a couple of yachts out so I went and looked round the margins here and there, climbing a few trees where possible. After another hour or so, the yachts went in for good, so I stuck the engine back on the boat and made ready for another excursion out on the pond. Normally, I'd go in a clockwise direction, but on this occasion I went anti-clockwise so that No Carp Bay would be one of the last areas to check out.

I'd spotted just two carp up at the far end, and two over near the gravel workings bank, and given that it was a nice day I thought I would have seen more. Eventually, I was heading toward my baited spot so I deliberately kept the boat speed slow, but constant and on course, to coast by at least a couple of rod lengths to one side. As I slowly went past, there were five carp bang on the bait. The hairs were standing up on the back of my neck. Two of them were 40s that I'd had the pleasure of holding; two of them were 30s and the biggest by far, was Sandy, looking like a heavyweight among middleweights.

I made my way to the bank to roll a fag to calm my nerves. After a while, I went back out toward the dot island, so I could repeat the process of having a good gawp. As I cruised by the second time, I could identify four of them, and Sandy was head down tail up, not a care in the world. I went back around in a big circle for another look, and this time Sandy came up from the bottom as if to check me out, leaving just the smallest carp on the bottom feeding, the others just a few feet off the bottom.

On the way home, I was buzzing big style. All doubts about the change of bait were right out of the window because I had visual confirmation that they were having it. The next couple of days at work went by slowly and painfully, but I'd booked a five-week break to start on June 1st, with one aim in mind. Two days later and I was back at the lake for another day's learning. First spot to check out was in No Carp Bay and as I approached I could see that that there were no carp around and the spot had grown in size. Not discouraged in any way, I put in the same amount of bait as last time, spread around on the edges of the spot.

When I came back six hours later and went out for a look, there having a good munch was Sandy with no other carp present. I saw two others briefly among the thick weed but no sooner had I spotted them than they disappeared. The fact that I'd seen Sandy on the spot was all I needed to know so I didn't swing round for a second look and left it to carry on munching undisturbed.

Back again a few days later after a hard day at work and I went straight out to the spot in No Carp Bay and deposited another bucket of bait. There were only a few tench present and I couldn't see any bait at all on the bottom, which was very encouraging. A cruise round the rest of the lake revealed nothing, although one did bosh out when I had my back turned. I heard the splash and saw the ripples, not too far away from an area which had produced in the past.

Another couple of days later, on my way to another venue, I stopped off first thing in the morning to stick another bucket of bait on Sandy's spot, I'd given it a name now so convinced was I that this was where it was going to happen. Viewing the spot with the glass-bottomed bucket revealed a totally clean patch that once again appeared to have grown a few feet bigger in diameter.

On my way back home, I went out again in the syndicate boat to check the spot and even though the wind had been blowing up at the far end for the last few days, I just had the feeling that I might encounter some carp on or near the spot in No Carp Bay. I took a marker rod on board to measure the spot, a couple of kilos of air-dried boilies to put in, and my viewing bucket to have a good look. I purposely went around the dot island to come back into No Carp Bay so the sun was behind me to aid viewing, and as I

Image of Sandy feeding on my bait, taken from aboard a boat. Please excuse the quality, but I dared not get any closer and ruin a positive situation.

approached the spot, maintaining a slow speed, I could see two carp. Sandy was on the bottom and the big-scaled mirror, Clover, simply watching a few feet away.

When faced with a sighting of such big carp, on a boat, the buzz of adrenalin is immense and the heartbeat really races away. At these moments you wish you were invisible because you know that if you can see them then they can see you. As I passed by, Sandy came up from the bottom chomping away, while Clover turned slightly and nose-dived into the weed. I didn't spook them but they knew a boat had just passed by so I gave the area a wide berth and came back round for another look.

When I came back, they had moved away slightly and as I approached I had to steer over to the right because they were moving toward me. What a view I had! It was just a shame I didn't have a camera. With my heart in my mouth now, the two carp followed me toward the out-of-bounds bank so I went back round the dot island and back to the bank to roll a fag and take stock of the encounter. I went back to my van and made a brew to calm my nerves. I didn't see much point in looking elsewhere on the lake.

Half an hour later, I was back in the boat and went straight to the spot. This time though, there was nothing about so with my head over the side in my bucket, I could clearly see that there was no bait visible and that the spot had continued to grow, now twice the size it was when I first baited the spot. I popped up my marker float on the spot and made my way back to the swim keeping the line relatively tight with it flicking through my finger on the edge of the spool. Once I got out of the boat and on the bank, I tightened up the line to the marker and stared at the float thinking, 'blooming heck, that's a fair old chuck!' I marked the line with a black marker pen and also tied on a marker with pole elastic and then reeled the float back.

I detached the float and just cast a lead out to the spot after I'd cut some of the grass down behind me. Thankfully, with 3.5lb tc rods and 4oz leads, at least I could reach it with 15lb main line. To say I was looking forward to a few weeks' fishing on the venue was an understatement. I was gagging for it!

My first 48-hour session of the new season was crap, and although no carp were caught I did catch the one and only bream, an ancient-looking thing and easily a double, although I refused to weigh it. When I arrived there weren't any carp in No Carp Bay and the only carp I saw were along the gravel workings bank so I fished on the end of big island and fished the channel as I'd done the year before, with two rods on previous productive spots and the other two slightly further out and left on a silty but clean bottom. I'd hadn't pre-baited the spots because I'd put all my faith in No Carp Bay.

A few days were spent at home and then I was back down there with fresh supplies and ready for a four-day stint if conditions looked good. The first areas I checked out from the bank and a few climbing trees were No Carp Bay and in between First Point and Second Point, and I clocked one decent-sized mirror tight to the margins in between the latter two.

Once I had the boat ready I went out on the pond, leaving my tackle in the van. I went anti-clockwise this time deciding to check out the far end first and I found two dead carp floating on the surface after a short while afloat. Both were around five pounds in weight, pretty little things, not a lot different to the big girls. I thought they may have come through from spawning so put it to the back of my mind for the time being because I had my fishing head on at that moment.

Eventually, I came along to 'No Carp Bay' and as I slowly approached I could see Sandy about a foot above the bottom, bang on the clear spot. One of those moments when you wish you had a rig down there, for sure. Well, that pretty much made up my mind on which swim to fish, so I made my way back to First Point, beached the boat in the margins, and then went and drove my van back down the track to unload the fishing gear. I walked the gear the short distance to the swim and started putting it together while trying to formulate a plan on what to do.

I didn't want to spook Sandy by casting out to the spot whilst it was there so I didn't rush into anything. I decided that I'd fish two rods on the long chuck spot, and my other two in the margins with my rods pointing toward the Second Point. I took two of my fishing rods and the marker rod back to the track behind the swim, so I could clip up and mark the lines to the exact distance of the line marker on my marker rod. Fifteen minutes later and I was all set and ready to go, so with my piece of white tube on board I made course for the far bank to place it on my sunken bank stick. As I slowly passed the spot again I clocked Sandy swimming away from me, going toward the shallows, so I had a quick look at the spot and it was super-clean.

A few minutes later, I found my bank stick and so quickly stuck the white tube on top and made my way back to the swim. As I passed the spot again, I could clearly see there were no fish present so I dropped a sliding marker float on to the concrete block as an extra casting aid, and made my way back to the swim. Thankfully, the wind was on my side and after five casts I eventually felt happy that I had two baited rigs on the spot, so I went back out in the boat for a look. One looked okay, but the other looked tangled so I went back and had another couple of goes to get it right. Back out in the boat and finally, I'd got two rigs lying perfectly on the spot, so I put a handful of boilies over each hookbait, plus a couple of balls of groundbait and stick mix with a pint of hemp and a few crushed snails. No point putting out live undamaged snails because they wander off. Up with the marker on the concrete block, and the trap was set!

It was now midday and I was starving, so out with the essentials to get some food on the go while I positioned my two margin rods along with a similar amount of bait as those out in open water. As I tucked into my egg and bacon rolls and mug of tea, a gentle breeze began to blow toward me as the yachters began to show up for the afternoon. The big mirror I'd seen to the right of my margin rods was now just sitting there a few feet under the surface in the tree-lined margins about 20 yards away, so everything was looking good. So good, that I was prepared to sit on my hands for the next 48 hours without touching my rods or going out on the pond in my boat.

With time to kill, I quickly set the bivvy up and got everything sorted so I could stretch out on the bedchair for a few hours. After a few hours of dreaming, I was awoken by a kingfisher that had settled on one of the rods and as I put my feet on the ground it spooked and flew off. Kettle was on and it was time to watch the water for a bit, camera at my side just in case the kingfisher returned. Two hours later and nothing much was happening so on went the kettle again. After getting halfway down the mug of tea, I noticed two swans paddling toward the long chuck spot so I got my binoculars out to watch them. Once I'd focused them, I immediately looked across to my white marker and sitting on top was the kingfisher.

Of course, I had no idea whether it was the same bird or not but there was no harm in thinking so, and I saw it as an omen. As I watched the swans getting closer to the spot, I dare not blink in case I missed something. With my eyes burning, begging to blink they were that dry, I watched the swans fix their vision on something I couldn't see beneath the surface. They didn't seem too disturbed but by the way they acted they'd obviously clocked a big fish. When they reached the middle of the bay they began to feed on the weed; the few yachts that were out were up at the other end.

An hour later, the remaining yachts began to gather to go in for the night, and then totally out of the blue, one of the long chuck rods was away. I struck firmly and immediately the rod took on a proper battle curve as the fish stripped line against the clutch, then it turned and I regained the lost line before it began to kite to my right still on a long line. I was gaining on it as I kept the pressure on and just when I was beginning to think I'd be able to net it from the bank, I began to feel that horrible juddering as it ploughed through the underwater forest of weed. I was convinced this was Sandy and so began to slip my lifejacket on.

I was just contemplating taking to the water when suddenly, my line parted. Gutted would be an understatement. As I reeled in the limp line I kicked all the toys out of my pram. Why me? ... and all the rest. How I didn't cry I don't know, but I certainly felt that way, throwing the rod into the tall grass behind my bivvy. I must have spent the next 20 minutes cursing my luck and thinking that perhaps I should have jumped into the boat as soon as I got the take. All I could think off was which carp it might have been. It was hard enough getting bites so any losses on this venue made a very bitter pill to swallow.

I still had one rod out on the spot so I slowly retackled the other one after retrieving it from the grass about an hour later. Although I'd lost my mark on the line, it wouldn't have taken much to re-mark it using my marker rod, but I daren't leave the rods to wander back to the track behind me to do it, so I left it on the rod rest to do in the morning. There may have been other carp out on the spot; I had no way of truly knowing but there was a slim chance so I thought it best not to take any risks. I carried on sulking; the chance of another special carp had been well and truly blown.

It was a warm, sticky night and I just couldn't get to sleep, what with a number of mosquito and ant bites to scratch, and just after midnight a big carp jumped in front of my margin rods. I'd seen a few tench roll in the moonlight and suddenly, a large carp stuck its head out and half its body. Had I been asleep, no doubt I'd have been none the wiser.

It was 1am and one of the margin rods was away, spool spinning like it was hooked up to an express train. Once I had the rod in my hands, it was a case of hanging on as it motored off toward the dot island, and the bend in the rod and the line coming off the clutch indicated that it was a lump. As I tightened up the clutch and began playing the carp back toward me, all I could think of was not losing it and keeping calm. It gave a good account of itself all the way to the net, and every time the line pinged my heart was in my mouth, but as I pulled it over the net cord I realised it was one of the A-team.

Clover at 40lbs 4oz, with a very distinct and unusual scale pattern.

The other side of Clover; just a shame I lost one earlier on that session because it could well have been another 90lb-plus brace!

I put the rod back on the rest and punched the air with one hand, all on my own in the dark, with just a few bats and owls plus the stars for company. While I unhooked it on the mat, I recognised the mirror as one I'd had the year before, and on that occasion it had also given one hell of a scrap. With the aid of a nearby tree to assist with the weighing, the needle settled at 40lbs 4oz - Clover at exactly the same weight as the previous year. I sacked her up in the edge under my long chuck rod for a photo in the morning. After I'd repositioned the margin rod along with a bit more bait, I set my alarm for dawn and jumped in the bag for some shut-eye.

I was up at dawn, and the lake looked its best with the mist lifting in the gentle breeze. There hadn't been a bleep all night, so I reeled in the margin rods and went out in the boat to check out the long-chuck spot. As I approached, I could see nothing was present so I went straight over it and viewed the situation with the bucket. Three-quarters of the bait had gone and the rig that remained still looked good, in fact it looked better because now the lead had a dusting of silt on top.

Back in the swim, I grabbed the rod not fishing, marked up the line against my marker rod and clipped it up ready to stick it back out there. Three casts later and I went back out for a look, along with a small bucket of bait. It took a few minutes to find the rig, but once found it looked good so I put a few handfuls of bait over the rigs and returned to my swim. I swung the margin rods back out and got breakfast under way while I texted a fellow member to see if he was up for doing the honours with the camera.

My mate, Ross, texted back and said that he'd call by on his way to work in half an hour's time, which was great. When he rolled up, the sun was already burning the back of my neck so we had a cuppa while I told him all that had happened. After the photos Ross went off to do some plastering, leaving me to get back to the waiting game and ponder what might have been the one I'd lost. While I was waiting, killing time, I phoned another member and told him I'd had one and lost one, and that I'd found two small dead carp of around 5lbs.

What he told me next was like a bomb blast. Trotsky, the syndicate leader, had stocked the lake with around 25 small carp from an unknown source, and what I thought were packets of sausages the previous year, were in fact packets of bars of soap. Four bars in each of 17 packets meant I'd counted 68 bars of soap. I felt sick. Stockies and soap, what the hell was going on? One of the best waters I'd ever fished, its magical charm now broken. What appetite I did have suddenly went and an hour later I was physically sick.

The next two or three hours I spent drinking tea and smoking, my mind in a daze really just staring out at the pond hoping for something to focus on to take my mind off what I'd just learned. The temperature was climbing all the time and it looked like my only chances were at night. Another angler turned up and set up on Second Point, so I decided to reel in and go out on to the pond to search for the carp. I'd lost one, so there was a chance my rig might be stuck in something's bottom lip, so off I went with this in mind.

It didn't take too long to find the bulk of the carp on the shallows so I took a few shots with the camera. Over the next hour, I went slowly up and down, keeping just enough distance and I had a good look at 12 carp. All the big girls were there, and I just felt privileged to be watching them. The only ones that looked and behaved differently were the 40lbs 4oz mirror that I'd caught, and Sandy, both sulking in snags. To me, this wasn't looking good; Sandy was the reason I was there, and although I couldn't see a hooklink I was convinced it was the one I'd lost.

I didn't really know what to do next so after watching them for a while I threw in a couple of handfuls of boilies on the shallows and returned to my swim, probably 200-plus yards away. As I made my way back, I did contemplate a move to the big island but thought I'd give it one more night. It was either that or go home and sulk. Back in my swim, I soon had all four rods back in position, although I didn't go back out to check on the long chuck rigs because the yachters were turning up for their pleasure time.

Next morning, I was up at first light, not a peep all night, and over the next few hours all I saw were a few tench rolling here and there. The sun began to increase the temperature rapidly and I just had the feeling that I was wasting my time. After a bacon roll, I reeled in and once again set out in the boat to go for a look, first checking the long chuck spot, which had remained untouched, and then over to the shallows.

They were all there again, probably been there all night as well, and they showed signs that they were interested in spawning as a few ploughed their way through some weed among the few snags. Now I was convinced I was wasting my time fishing on First Point so I made my way back to the swim and packed everything away, plans well and truly scuppered.

The drive home took ages and when I got there I was in agony with a migraine and spent the next four hours with my head stuck down the toilet pan, sweating on the bathroom floor and suffering badly. Thankfully, my migraines only last 24 hours and I've

This view shows about a quarter of the lake. I treated it with respect and was rewarded for my efforts.

learned how to cope with them. They're usually brought on by dehydration, poor diet, fizzy drinks or stress, in my case. All thoughts of going fishing just weren't there and I was drained physically and mentally.

A few days later I got a phone call from one of the members, not happy about the stockies and telling me there was going to be a meeting on the lake and if members didn't turn up, their tickets would be in jeopardy. Was it the news that I'd had two takes or were the stockies the issue? All I knew was that some of the members didn't want any stocking, and if it was a case of trying to dislodge Trotsky then it just wasn't going to happen.

I phoned Trotsky, asked him what the meeting was about and he told me he knew nothing about the meeting. No doubt he was soon phoning around, or lying. During the week I had another phone call from another member saying that because of me they could no longer use boats. This was all getting a bit silly now; the meeting was on the cards so I pencilled it in my diary.

When the day of the meeting arrived, I'd pretty much made my mind up on what I'd be doing so I arrived early and waited in the car parking area, back of the van open and tea-making equipment out and on the go for anyone who was in the social mode. Slowly but surely, a few members turned up along with Trotsky, but it was plain that over half the members had not bothered. Well, the meeting soon got underway and after five minutes of mudslinging, it was plain to me that Trotsky hadn't a clue how to run a big carp venue. I took my keys out of my pocket and began to take the gate keys off my key ring.

"Well lads, you won't have to worry any more about me because I'm off. I cannot bring myself to fish a fishery where chucking in bars of soap is considered okay! Here, have the keys, I'll go now."

I then went and sat in my van while their meeting continued for another ten minutes or so, the final straw had broken me!

Trotsky opened the locked gate for me and that was the last time I'd be wetting a line there. He asked me to keep quiet about events and not to go to the papers, and I agreed. Obviously, I'd contemplated all the options and I could so easily have taken things further, but had it been plastered in the weeklies then almost certainly the owner of the lake would have shut the fishing down completely. Those fishing it would have lost out and those who would jump at the chance to fish there would too, and that's not what I'd have wanted. All I hoped was those that remained treated the carp and the fishery with the respect it deserved.

A week later, I got my ticket money refunded along with an apologetic letter from Trotsky. Carp fishing to me is something I've always enjoyed, even on the days when I've struggled. Half the battle is to get the carp to accept what you're offering; the other half is good angling. I'm glad I spent time learning on such a hard venue and look back now with happy memories, ten captures with three losses and six of them over 40lbs. There's a different guy running the syndicate these days who thankfully, knows how to do the job, and I have heard that stockies have piled on pounds. I don't hold any grudges against anyone; life is too short for that!

Chapter 16

Stairway to heaven

Before I get started, let me just say that there were many titles for this chapter that span around in my head when it came to writing about my quest to catch a 40lb common. In fact, one particular 40lb-plus common carp that I had the pleasure of watching swimming beneath me among some lily pads one day, when I was on one of those walkabout moments. Obviously, I don't want to tell the world specifically where all my journeys have taken me, but it's only fair to say that this venue was one of those lovely little club-ticket waters you'd love to have on your doorstep; a little piece of heaven!

Some will already have guessed where I got the inspiration for the title of this chapter from, have you? Silly question to some really, if they know me or the venue, but for those into something else musically then it was from one of England's finest-ever rock bands, the one and only Led Zeppelin. They were gods of rock when I was a teenager, and filling stadiums when most of us were at school, or just a twinkle in our fathers' eyes. Sure, there are many other rock bands I like; such as Pink Floyd, AC/DC, Velvet Revolver, to name just a few, but Led Zeppelin were awesome and Stairway to Heaven was just one of their many classics. That particular song's lyrics are quite relevant to this chapter, perhaps giving a small clue as to the whereabouts of this intriguing little gravel pit I fished in search of a 40-plus common.

On the many occasions that I drove to this particular part of the country on my own, in my trusty Astra van, I'd usually play Led Zeppelin on the stereo on the way to the venue, which usually revved me up, and then Pink Floyd on the way home, to calm me down. Most of the poxy speed cameras were out to get me on the return trip, so a bit of Comfortably Numb helped out there to slow me down, while a bit of Led Zeppelin on the way had the opposite effect. I hope you'll all understand my reasons for not giving any names away because the very last thing I want to do is upset people, and for those that I do upset, then don't judge me too harshly because I'm sure once you get to know me you'll find that maybe I'm not the kind of guy you thought I was.

Having now looked back over some 30-plus years of carp fishing, I've met some terrific anglers whilst out and about, and I guess I've met all the household names in the game today somewhere along the way. Now, I'm not really into dropping names for the sake of it, because some might not want their names put in print so you'll have to excuse the fact that I've either given some a nickname or called them by their known nicknames. The only reason they get a mention is that I know them and have learned something from all of them. Strange that every one of us is so different and yet we all suffer from carp fever.

Having spent some time angling on Kingsmead Island Lake near Wraysbury, I met Sir John for the first time, truly a master when it comes down to catching big carp from big or small carp venues. Now, although I can say I know Sir John, I don't know him as well as I do a few of his mates, but if he ever a wrote a book, or even a guest chapter in one, I'd be one of the first in the queue to buy it!

What I learned from John was to keep a few aces up my sleeve. Not that we ever played cards together, nor that he's a card sharp, but to try to stay low profile and keep things a secret for as long as you can. Which brings me back to this particular venue which I'd known about for quite a few years before I actually got round to fishing it properly.

Having spent some time on lakes not a million miles away, further along the Thames, I naturally found new friends and, like you do, soon learned about a few local venues that they've dabbled on and that little spark of interest is filed into the memory bank for future investigation.

Funnily enough, my dad used to take me down that neck of the woods to fish the Thames, way back, between the age of 10 to about 15, and I can remember seeing a few holes in the ground and the odd lake, and with the passing of time the scenery has changed a great deal. Once I dropped my Sheephouse ticket, inevitably my quest for more big carp began so I started searching for possible venues to fish. This particular angling club not only had control of the part of he Thames I'd fished donkey's years before, but they had a few lakes too, and this little piece of heaven was just one ace I had up my sleeve that I had to play with.

The little lake has got a name, but as I've said before, naming it will not be in my favour or for anyone else because it's just one example of what's really out there in England if you take the time to look away from the well-known big carp venues. I called it The Common Lake for a number of reasons and those who have fished there will see a connection because one of its residents was a big common. I had to give it some sort of name because my mates knew I was fishing a secret venue of which I promised to give them a few facts after I'd caught the big common. Yes, mates can keep secrets, but then one might tell another, and then another, and the location is then common knowledge.

I did know of a few bigger commons, some of which have never been seen in any publication, but with limited time you can only properly target them one at a time and this particular fish was the first 40lb-plus common on my list. The trouble with keeping secrets is, understandably, that you upset some people. Everyone wants to escape and if

I'd let this one out of the bag at the time, it could quite easily have become rammed out because it's a cheap, match-orientated club, £45 a year all-comers welcome, and it could also affect where I fish in the future on publicity-shy venues.

The Common Lake was originally much bigger, but was partially backfilled quite some time ago leaving it at around seven acres, but still tiny compared to some venues I'd fished in the past such as Lake Raduta in Romania. Most of the carp in residence made their way in there from the lake next door, and from time to time the odd one got moved, the biggest being a big common which I was told moved at a weight of 28lbs. Steadily, over a number of years, these fish soon learned their new environment, and just like most carp they soon wised up to angling pressure; some put on a few pounds, and some put on a few more pounds than the rest. I think the best was yet to come but like a lot of things you just never know for sure what can happen in the future.

When I started to look around it a few years ago, it reminded me a little bit of the Car Park Lake at Yateley, it just had that feel about it. Not that I'm proclaiming to know much about Yateley, just pointing out the fact that I've had a little dabble on there, savoured the atmosphere and can clearly see why so many faces fish the complex. The Common Lake had every sort of feature you'd want in a little gravel pit; a small island, bars, plateaux, weed, gravel and silt patches, and an abundance of marginal pads to pretty the place up. It didn't have the stock of the infamous CEMEX Angling Car Park Lake but it did have a sizeable common. Some of the swims could have done with a bit of work to make them a bit more comfortable, but as we all learn, making them too good will attract those who'll want to pitch up for lengthy sessions.

I'd had a little dabble on there and walked round on a few occasions, usually on Sunday afternoons when it was normally deserted, but the fact remained I'd only caught one carp from the pit, an 18lb common, and I lost one of the big mirrors, so in the spring of 2006 I made the decision that it was time I got my act together.

In the previous few years, the big common graced the banks a few times and she'd come out just over 40lbs, then drop below the magical mark only to bounce back. I'd seen her on a few occasions and you could tell when she looked big or not so big, but sightings in the winter on the days I went looking in 2004 and 2005 convinced me that the time to catch her was either her first capture in the spring or in the winter months. Like a lot of other venues, some of the best times for top weights and conditions are from October through to about May/June. Just before or after Christmas would be my preference, but I can't always commit myself to the times I'd like too much because of work obligations, like most of us with a mortgage. Even though my personal best common at that time was 33lbs, Black Spot from a day-ticket venue near Twynersh, I didn't want to catch the big girl at a low weight.

Okay, you can argue that a carp is a carp, and you shouldn't grumble whatever the weight and to a point I'd agree, but when you're travelling a fair distance to a tricky water with the aim of catching one particular carp, ask yourselves this: Would you rather catch an upper-30 or a 40? Catching them is one thing, catching them at prime time is another! Believe me, I wanted to catch the big girl and a few of her chums just as much as the other anglers fishing there and was well confident that once I'd got my act together I'd get among them. I had plans up my sleeve and it was just a case of implementing them.

I popped down there a few times just with a marker rod in January and February with the objective of having a good plumb around, and with no one on there I was able to learn a fair bit without upsetting anyone. With less weed around than in the summer months it certainly made things a little easier and I found some pukka areas in most of the swims, with probably the better ones out in the open water in some of the more obvious popular swims. Off one of the point swims I'd found some gravel mounds and silty gullies out toward the Beach swim that could prove useful, and from the Beach you not only had the big bar but some nice spots within comfortable casting range. Some more nice spots were also found along the margins of the east bank.

After weeks of deliberation with the information, and having not seen any signs of the carp, I decided that to get them interested in my chosen boilie, and rather than bait heavily in one or two places, I'd just trickle a bit in here and there on my next few visits. The birdlife was horrendous in the winter months and I didn't want them on my case if that was possible. Poxy tufties these days have got zoom vision and the noses of bloodhounds, so a few catapults here and there was the order of the day, 10mm and 14mm Ultra-Plex courtesy of Richworth Products.

I had a few sessions over at Linear Oxford just to get a bend in my rods in March and April then turned my attention to the Common Lake in May. With things warming up nicely on each short, non-fishing visit, I began to see more of the residents, including the big girl.

I put my faith in Richworth's Ultra-Plex boilies. Time would tell how effective they'd be.

I went down there for my first fishing session of the year in May, really looking forward to what the next few trips might bring. I had no set plans on which swims to fish, but obviously a few stuck in my mind so I was hoping there wouldn't be many other anglers there, which would give me the freedom to have a good look around first before getting the rods out.

To avoid the weekend rush, I got down there at the crack of dawn on a chilly, misty Thursday morning to be greeted with the glorious sight of the lake totally empty - having a boss who'd let me have time off helped. I carted my gear over the footbridge, over the dual carriageway, then around the lake on my Carp Porter after first checking out the bays, looking for any signs of the residents. With no sign of any carp I then made my way round to Party Point to see if there was anything on the bars or near the little dot island.

I didn't see anything near Party Point, but the sun's rays had yet to cover this area, still under the shadow of the trees for at least another hour, so I catapulted a few pouchfuls of 10mms on and around the closest bar in open water and close to the little island. After about two hours of looking, the sun's rays had burned off the early morning dew from most of the cobwebs which covered the thistles, and eventually I clocked a few carp cruising around the pond, a couple by the little island and some along the west bank.

One of the spots that I'd been trickling with bait on my earlier visits, just a rod length out in front of the High Bank swim on the west bank, was glowing; all the gravel had been polished clean of any silkweed and screamed 'FISH HERE!' So I walked my gear to the swim to secure it just in case anyone else turned up while I couldn't quite make my mind up. Party Point or the High Bank? I was torn between two swims so in the end I tossed a coin and went into the High Bank swim and quickly set my traps, with two rigs on the glowing gravel and one in the weed a yard or so to the right, a few balls of stick mix and groundbait mixed with hemp and a few handfuls of 10mm Ultra-Plex completing the trap. Kettle on, house up, and I was fishing but feeling tired and hungry having been up since 4am, and had been working my nuts off at work for the last ten days without a break. I don't normally work weekends unless I'm desperate for the cash and the old carp funds at the time needed topping up badly, so it was a case of having to really.

Egg and bacon roll, washed down with a few mugs of tea and I was sorted, so 40 winks was the next thing on my list and I lay down on my bedchair having set the alarm on my phone to go off two hours later. ZZZzzzz, I was just getting settled and suddenly I was awoken by the sounds of a few twigs snapping and the footsteps of someone approaching. 'Kin hell, that's pissed on my fireworks', I heard, or words to that effect before a face appeared at my bivvy door. I didn't know the chap at the time but got the feeling he recognised me pretty quickly and we got chatting. He said he'd been baiting this swim for weeks and asked me if he could squeeze his rods in a little gap in the trees to the left of my rods. We had the whole lake between us and he wants to sit in my lap! 'Sorry mate, but too close for comfort. It'll be my first night's fishing this year on the lake, and I want a little breathing space'.

I think he was gutted I was in the swim he'd fancied, so off he went down the path, straight away on his mobile. My head was back on the pillow and blow me, he's back in less than ten minutes and asks me again if he can double-up. Amazed, I told him it was going to have to be a 'no' on that one again. It made me feel guilty plotting up, so I told him that

I'd seen carp down by the island and that I was only down for one night and that I'd give him the swim when I packed away the next day. By now he'd told me his name, but was keen to get fishing so off he went heading for Party Point and I got back to my 40 winks.

Well 40 winks turned into 80 winks after hitting the snooze button a few times and the next thing I know, this guy, Brian, was asking me if he could borrow a set of scales as he'd left his at home and his mate had just caught a fair-sized mirror. A quick wander down the bank and sure enough, the lad's got one on the bank. It turned out to be a nice-looking mirror, of 29lbs 12oz.

Brian's mate had only had his rods out for around an hour, and to me this was a good sign that the carp were in munching mode, so I returned to my swim for the remainder of the session. As the afternoon went on more anglers turned up and more and more bait went in. By nightfall, I think there were eight of us dotted all over the pond, probably all thinking similar things. I stayed up until midnight and not one carp showed anywhere, well certainly none seen from my vantage point, so it was soon time for the bag and some shut-eye to dream of monster carp.

Next day, after a blank night, I sat and watched the water for ages. A chap on the far bank had one which looked to be in the mid-20s through my binoculars. The longer and harder I looked, the less promising it seemed because the main part of the pond seemed devoid of any carp. Obviously, they were somewhere and I had no clue what had occurred elsewhere so I reluctantly packed the gear away, facing a blank. I had the next month booked off work so it was going to be home and work for a few days then back on the pond for another go. By midday I could sense it just wasn't going to happen so in came the rods and one by one, they were stuck back in the holdall and on to the barrow-bed I had designed and built with help from an engineer.

As promised, I made my way to Party Point to let Brian know the swim was vacant if he wanted it, and when I walked into the swim he was packing away.

"All yours," I said.

"No need," he said. "I've had my result - the big girl at 42lbs 8oz!"

I said, "Well done", with the usual handshakes, like you do, and I could sense he was buzzing, his time had come! I was a bit miffed that I never got to see it and share his moment but now looking back I was glad in a way. Had I clapped eyes on her it could have changed my summer's fishing and I'm glad the way it turned out in the end.

The drive home took longer than ever and all sorts of thoughts went through my mind like, did Brian really catch her or was it a wind up? I was convinced he did, his smile said it all really. Bloody hell, 42lb 8oz commons don't grow on trees. The next week my plans sort of fell apart, and the more I thought about it the more convinced I was it would be another month or two before she'd grace the banks. Decisions had to be made and I opted to spend what time I had playing around on Elstow and over Oxford and to return for a few sessions in a month's time.

Little did I realise at the time that I was a little hasty with my decision and it wasn't too long before she slipped up again. I enjoyed myself so much on my trips to Oxford and Elstow that somehow time just melted away and before I knew it we were in October and it was time to take the bull by the horns and get my arse back down to the lake for a proper bash. Seeing her at just over 40lbs in an issue of Carp Talk reminded me of just how gorgeous and well-proportioned she was.

This image taken during the summer months shows about a quarter of this little club-run gravel pit.

View from the bivvy door while fishing in the Back Bay, rods just out of sight, down some steps.

I had a plan. It sounded simple, but would it work? I had two or three days a week to go fishing and would keep plugging away up to Christmas, pre-baiting my chosen spots in between. Pick the right swims, use a bait they want and surely I'd be in with a shout. The only trouble was, having just purchased a new computer and digital camera I wasn't exactly flush with cash so I'd have to watch what I spent on petrol, bait, and chocolate biscuits!

Even though I knew a little bit of the lakes topography, I wasn't too sure which swims to concentrate on because they all seemed as good as each other. I wanted to pre-bait with a fair amount to swing things in my favour, but given that it had to be hauled a far distance, going over the footbridge and across the dual carriageway, I wasn't contemplating using shed loads. I'd been doing great with Richworth Ultra-Plex frozen ready-mades throughout the year so had every confidence. I had little to worry about boilies-wise. I'd also helped in fieldtesting a new Richworth groundbait and stick mix and found that to be instant, so that was going in; the final ingredients were hemp and pellet.

Being a fairly small venue there was nowhere out of reach. The only drawbacks I could see was the birdlife; swans, coots, tufties, mallards, all the usual mob, each with their bit of territory to protect. Oh, and a new consignment of carp; 52 stockies averaging 5lbs! I know I'm fairly adept at fishing a variety of methods but somehow I couldn't bring myself to go down the spodding road without first giving the margins some Clarkey treatment.

The benefits of pre-baiting are worth the effort. My Cobra scoop, is a well-used piece of kit!

Fishing the margins makes life so much easier and with a fair bit of bankside cover on the lake I had a feeling this was my way to go. To get things moving I took a trip down there to pre-bait a couple of spots, with no specific swims in mind until I'd had a good walk round. Once I'd made my way to the lake I found just a couple of anglers on there so I avoided them and did a couple of circuits, climbing the odd tree here and there to get the full picture.

It took me all of five minutes to clock the first carp, and it was a common feeding in the edge in No Carp Bay; there are a few of these bays around at various venues! It looked around 25lbs, all on its own, so I left it undisturbed and carried on looking. On the second circuit, I saw another carp in the No Carp Bay area, not feeding but just cruising around behind the small island. It looked like a low-20lb mirror, and not what I was looking for, but at least it showed there was nothing wrong with my eyesight, so I trudged along spending at least five minutes in every swim looking for signs of anything a bit bigger.

When I got to the Slope swim and climbed the tree, wallop, there she was, the big common, slowly cruising about 20 yards out just a few feet under the surface. She was travelling from left to right and slowly getting closer to the bank I was on, before disappearing out of my vision to my right. A quick walk down the bank toward Party Point and there was no sign of her, so I went back and climbed the tree again hoping she'd reappear but alas, that five-minute sighting was all I got.

The Slope seemed to be a good swim to begin my campaign. It had a small bar just a rod length out, a climbing tree and no signs that anyone had fished it for some time, i.e., no bank stick holes, no used teabags, no fag butts. Perhaps this was due to the swim being a bit on the small side and uncomfortable due to it being on a slope with a few overhanging branches making overhead casting almost impossible.

I had to make a start somewhere and baiting up in a more comfortable swim there could be no guarantee that it would be empty on my return visits so with the aid of my spoon I baited up on the top and far side of the close-in bar in the Slope. In all, I put in 2kg of 10mm Ultra-Plex boilies, 2kg of groundbait and stick mix, plus ten pints of hemp and pellet. Not a massive amount really, compared to what some sponsored anglers put in, but enough to create a positive situation on a small, lightly-stocked venue such as this.

I returned three days later armed with a similar amount of bait to repeat the process, only this time I took some tackle along just in case there was an opportunity to do some fishing; one rod, net, scales, unhooking mat and a camera, just enough tackle to have a go! Now, some of you must think I was mad travelling all that way with just one rod, and I know I'm a little mad, but like most things there's a method in my madness. I had it in my mind that it would not be unfeasible to catch the big girl or any other carp in the pond with just the one rod, and if I did manage to succeed then it would be a right result. I couldn't think of a much better way of catching my first 40lb-plus common carp.

When I arrived, 2.30pm Sunday, there were a couple of anglers set up and fishing but neither anywhere near the Slope, so I made my way round buzzing with anticipation. When I reached the swim I carefully made my way to the water's edge, making sure that my footsteps were soft to avoid spooking any nearby fish.

Bingo! There was a carp in the swim feeding on top of the bar, so I stood like a statue and watched to assess which one it was and to gather my thoughts on what to do next. It was a mirror, fairly big too, and in the slightly clouded water I could see that it looked preoccupied as it dipped down now and then, tail up waving at me. The first thing that went through my mind was, it was a pity I hadn't got there a bit earlier and as I watched the carp feed I thought that this was a golden opportunity.

I quickly made up my rod and landing net and crept to the edge with my bucket of hemp, it was time to get a rig in the water. By now, the mirror had moved even closer to the bank, still unaware of my presence, and so close that I thought it would feel my rapidly increasing heartbeat. I watched and waited for at least ten minutes and was pretty sure that this mirror was the one that I'd lost the first year I'd fished there when I had my tennis elbow problems. On that occasion, I was convinced it was a low-30, but now it looked a lot thicker across the back, and certainly worth getting the rod out for.

My chosen end tackle on this occasion was a simple pop-up rig, a 14mm Ultra-Plex boilie straight from the tub, critically balanced with a small piece of tungsten putty, a ten-inch Quicksilver hooklink, a size 6 Korda Wide Gape hook finished off with a 3.5oz lead. I flicked out 30-odd grains of hemp on top of the carp to semi-spook it and, sure enough, it waddled away to my right so when the coast was clear I lowered the rig to the bottom and followed it with half a dozen half-boilies. I pulled off some slack line, laid the rod on the ground and retreated away from the edge, trap set!

I was rather hoping that it was only going to be a matter of minutes before the mirror returned, but after half an hour that feeling of defeat was going through my mind. A quick look at the swim revealed no sign of anything, not even a roach. Oh well, you win some you lose some, so I climbed the nearby tree to see if it was still around. I could clearly see the mirror just gently drifting out to meet what looked like a common of perhaps 25lbs. After I'd been up the tree for about 20 minutes the big common drifted into view and met the other two carp, which gave me a chance assess its size. It looked as long as the mirror but broader across its shoulders; it had to be over 40lbs.

I got down from the tree, sat on my unhooking mat and pondered whether any of the other carp had fed on the little feast I'd created. There was still nothing near my hookbait, and ten minutes later and I was back up the tree, and now all three had made their way over to the shallow bars 50 yards away. Soon, they were joined by another two carp; at a guess I'd have said low-20s. With nothing near my rig there was little point in staying, so I reeled in and packed the rod away - blankety blank!

In went some more bait, hemp, pellets, groundbait and a couple of kilos of 10mms. I was simply going to have to do a proper session and thankfully, I'd be returning at the crack of dawn on the Thursday. I hoped that by then all the bait would have gone and with any luck they'd be queuing up waiting for some more. Having had a little feel about dragging the rig along the bottom in a few places, I'd learned that there was some weed around but not enough to really worry about so I had a few slight rig changes to think about while at home during the week.

Sure enough, I was back at the lake Thursday morning and after carting my gear over the footbridge I then wheeled everything round to the Slope, full of confidence, having noticed that there was no one fishing the swim. Conditions seemed perfect with a gentle westerly blowing and a whole lake to myself, if only for a short while.

When I reached the swim, a quick look revealed nothing to shout about but there was some broken weed floating around in the margins and the bar looked a little cleaner than before. I suspected the birdlife had now found my spot as probably half of what I'd previously put in was on top of the bar in about four feet of water, just within reach of the two swans and certainly in reach of the tufties and all their mates.

A quick look in some of the other swims along this bank revealed nothing, but the Back Bay did look promising so I made a conscious decision to prime one swim with just a handful of bait on every visit, in front of some marginal lily pads just to keep my eye on. So back in the Slope, I quickly made up my rods and swung them into position, followed by a good helping of bait, a kilo of boilies and another of hemp and pellet, this time with all three rods with slightly different presentations, and finished off with a 50mm stick mix. Now I was fishing and it felt great to be out on a mission so all there was left to do was boil the kettle as I put the bivvy up. Once I was sorted and dunking Jammy Dodgers, I noticed another couple of anglers setting up, one on the Beach and the other on the road bank.

In order to get my bedchair level I had to dig out two little holes because the legs weren't long enough to counteract the sloping ground, and the swim was so tight and awkward there was only one way to set the bivvy up. No wonder I'd never seen anyone fish the swim. Still, I was more than happy now I had a level bedchair and was convinced that something was going to happen in the next 36 hours, so I lay down for a snooze and listened to the birds in the trees surrounding me as I slowly drifted off.

Three hours after getting the rods out, I was awoken by my middle one going into meltdown mode; rod bent round and the spool spinning like the tyres on a top fuel dragster. As soon as I had the rod in my hand, I could sense that this was a carp I really didn't want to lose, as it powered off like it wanted to go all the way into the bottom bay. With the overhanging branches, I was almost tempted to jump in but somehow I'd manage to stop the carp and now had it back-pedalling toward me, albeit 50 yards to my right. It made a few short lunges toward the bush to my left, once I had it back under my rods, and then it began to tire, much to my relief.

As it came over the net cord, I could clearly see it was a good fish and immediately realised it was the big mirror I'd watched feeding on my last trip. I was buzzing - my first big carp from this little tricky water and one of the A-team. I quickly gave my mate, Kim, a call on my mobile to let him know I was down there with a big carp in the net, and he immediately asked, "How big?"
"Looks big mate, not weighed it yet," so I told him I'd text him the weight and he said he'd be down just after 1pm during his lunch hour to do the honours with the camera.

Once I'd got everything sorted, I folded down my landing net and hoisted my prize out of the pond. Using a nearby tree and landing net pole to assist in the weighing, the needle settled on 38lbs 4oz; an excellent way to start any session. Once it was safely in the sack and back in the pond, I repositioned the rod after checking the rig, and topped up the swim with some more bait.

Chocolate at 38lbs 4oz. First bite, but was it luck or fate?

Lumpy, at 29lbs. Rigs and baits certainly doing their intended job.

Kim was an old mate I'd met on another lake, who had fished here before. He lived locally, worked just a few miles down the road, and said he'd be only too pleased to do some camera work if he could, early morning before work, lunchtime, or after work. Just after 1pm, Kim arrived all smiles, and congratulated me on my result, eager to see which one it was.

Once on the mat, we had a good look and Kim was convinced that it was the mystery big mirror that seemed to have three names, even though it rarely visits the bank. He was sure it was one called Chocolate. Well, I didn't really care but it wasn't grey or pale, although I accept that carp do change colour, so we settled for Choco, one with a bit of colour, the two of us chuckling away like a couple of kids. Photos done, Kim went back to work leaving me to carry on angling. The two other anglers were totally unaware of what had happened and I was now wondering what else might come my way.

During the afternoon, I only saw one carp in my swim, a common of maybe 20lbs, but meanwhile from up the climbing tree I saw a few over on the shallow bars. I wasn't even contemplating a change of swim, but it looked like the bars were a definite feature worth fishing, although you'd be tearing your hair out when the resident swans searched the area because most of it was just a few feet deep.

The afternoon soon disappeared and once again it was time for the evening curry, washed down with liberal amounts of tea, before eventually retiring to the warmth of a sleeping bag for an early night, alarm set for dawn. Just after midnight I was woken from my dreams by the sounder box, left-hand rod. Usual panic in the darkness, boots on and down to the rods lit up by the glow of the LED on the buzzer. It soon became apparent that I was connected to a very angry carp which made its way into dense weed somewhere out there in the darkness over to the left. Reluctant to ease off, I piled on the pressure, praying that my main line wouldn't part. Then came that horrible juddering feeling when it's moving, but with tiny jerks.

Five minutes later, and I've pulled in a pile of weed the size of a Wendy house with a carp on the other side of it. I dropped the rod down and quickly stripped the weed off the line until it was virtually gone; the carp seemed quite happy sitting there until I picked the rod up and it went for it again. I easily had the measure of this one and slowly but surely pulled it to the waiting net when I recognised it, in the light of my headlamp torch, as Lumpy, one of the old commons described to me by one of the locals. Once everything was ready, the scales registered 29lbs exactly. Excellent, and it was worth a shot in the morning so it was in the sack for him until dawn, in the deep margins to my right and back out with the rod and a little more bait, and into the bag for me.

At 2am, the sounder box was once again going ballistic, so it was out of the bag, back on with the boots and a shuffle down to the rods, trying not to slip on the mud. Right-hand rod this time, and in a few minutes I began to think it was almost over when it started giving it some head-shaking and suddenly leapt out of the water straight in front of me. Surely, it couldn't be a pike, I thought, and thankfully it wasn't, as another common came gliding over the net cord to kiss the spreader block. I just happened to have another sack, so after weighing it at 22lbs, in went another for a morning photo.

I was up at dawn and on with the first brew of the day as I texted Kim that I'd had more action and asked if he could do the honours once again. True to his word, he soon strolled down the path to greet me and after the usual chinwag we got them out of the sacks for a quick photo, one at a time. When I returned Lumpy you could clearly see how it got its name with a distinct lump on one side. The 22lb common looked a right old warrior with scales on its mid-section looking like they'd been carved in oak. Kim laughed after shaking my hand and said, "You haven't lost your touch, Clarkey!"

After Kim left to go to work, what had happened began to sink in. All those miles travelling and all those doubts had been worth it. I would have been happy with the commons but to bag a big mirror was a real bonus. I waited and fished the rest of the day, half-expecting something else to happen, but nothing came along so once again it was time to break camp, negotiate the footbridge and return home.

I went back on the Tuesday evening in the darkness to bait up the swim again, knowing that I'd be back at the weekend for a two-night session. Within three minutes I'd put in around 10kg of bait, covering an area the size of a snooker table. Had I been a local, then perhaps I would have put in half that amount, but as I wasn't then I'd stick to the plan, give them plenty and establish a feeding spot.

Back again on Friday morning, and I didn't stop to look in any other swim, I just made a beeline for the Slope which was empty. When I reached the swim and looked into the water it was fairly obvious that something had been ripping the bottom up because it was well coloured with telltale signs of broken, floating weed. There was no point hanging around so I got the rods out pretty sharpish. I had the feeling that I actually landed on one as I swung the first rig out, I couldn't be absolutely sure but going on the size of the vortex, I reckoned I had spooked something substantial. I saw a few carp over on the shallow bars

22lb, ancient-looking common.

Humpy Back Mirror at 28lbs 12oz.

during the day; two maybe in the 20 bracket and a few small stockies, but remained confident that all was not lost by spooking one of them.

Shortly after midnight, my middle rod burst into life and I was again doing battle with another resident who couldn't resist the feast. As it came to the net I could feel that is was a proper carp and once safely within the folds, I could see it was a mirror. After wetting all the kit and zeroing the scales, I hoisted my prize off the mat to record a weight of 28lbs 12oz. It was into the sack for him, and into the bag for me, happy in the knowledge that what I was using and doing was obviously working.

Usual text to Kim first thing in the morning and like the good mate he is, he came down before work to take a few photos. Once on the mat and out of the sack we identified it as the Humpy Back Mirror, another old-looking carp. As it started raining, Kim shot off to work and I spent all day in my bivvy sheltering from the rain, getting extremely bored, facing away from the water, watching a friendly robin and rabbit for entertainment. With little going on during the day, I had a feeling that maybe it was going to happen during the night, and the feeling was electric. Just what would come next?

At 10.30pm, my left-hand rod bleeped a few times so I went down for a look and the tip was bent round so I picked it up, half-expecting a tench to be the culprit, only it turned out to be one of the new stockies; a nice little thing with linear scaling, about 5lbs in weight, so I quickly dispatched him back and repositioned the bait.

At 2.20am it was the right-hand rod needing some attention as it bleeped intermittently. This turned out to be another stockie, perhaps a little smaller, again a nice looker; not exactly why I was there though, so that was rapidly returned. Rig back in the water and a few more 10mms dispatched into the swim and I was soon back in the bag until dawn when I was awoken by the swans under my rods. As the morning progressed, my swim went from coloured to gin clear, but I stayed on until around 5pm in the hope of something returning.

When I returned home and opened up my mail, I was shocked to find out that I had next to bugger-all in both the bank and the building society. I don't like being skint and what with bills and Christmas coming along it meant I'd only be able to fit in another three or four fishing sessions before I'd have to hang the rods up for the New Year festivities.

With the weekends spoken for and no time or funds to go during the week I was pulling my hair out, working all the hours I could for the next two weeks and soon bolstered up my funds. The weather was still fairly mild for the time of year and the leaves somewhat reluctant to leave the trees. At last, I had a weekend free so I went and baited up the Slope mid-week in the hope of further action. Just the one night but I had to press on because my goal had not yet been achieved. All my mates seemed to have faith in me, and given the action I'd had it was only a matter of time.

When I arrived at the crack of dawn on the Friday, I quickly wheeled my gear round to the Slope. There had been torrential rain during the night and it was still raining, albeit softly, so conditions looked quite favourable. The water looked well coloured but a walk up the bank revealed that this applied to most of the lake. I didn't need to walk round to find out why; it was pretty obvious that water was coming in fast from the inlet, mostly from the lake next door which was rapidly filling up having to take the surface water from the nearby dual carriageway.

With that probably being the first proper influx of water, I wondered if maybe fishing up by the inlet would be a good bet. Had I not been pre-baiting at the other end of the lake then I probably would have given it a go, so I quickly went through the motions in the Slope, hoping that something would happen. No signs of any carp throughout the rest of the day, although I did notice that the lake had risen three inches. The Back Bay seemed devoid of fish apart from a double-figure pike that kept hanging around the dying lily pads in the Steps swim, lying in ambush mode and no doubt picking off the odd roach attracted by the handful of stick mix and hemp I'd been throwing in just in front of the pads.

The night went by with just one tench on my right-hand rod just after it got dark. After standing around in the early morning, drinking tea for about three hours, up and down the tree every half hour, I just had the feeling that I was wasting my time. There seemed to be a lot less weed on the spots I was fishing, so I tied up three new rigs with slightly shorter hooklinks. When I reeled in my middle rod I soon realised that I'd been done. Instead of it being straight out in front it was now about a yard to the left of where I'd positioned my left-hand rod. Something had moved my rig about three yards and slightly closer in, and because I was slack-line fishing with no indicators hanging on the line, I didn't get a single bleep. I propped up my three rods against my bivvy to change them all to bottom baits, a bit miffed that I'd been done by something.

I walked up to the field behind the swim for a squirt and noticed an opportunity to get my camera out. Now seemed a good time to try to photograph one or two of the red kites that fly by every morning, as they hovered over the Back Bay. Quickly, I got my camera and walked down toward the bay, but one flew away to the left and the other hovered around for five minutes giving me a good display. Cursing that I didn't have a pukka zoom lens I looked down at the lily pads in the Steps swim and saw them moving.

From the top of the steps, I could then make out what looked like a pike a few yards past the pads. The more I looked the more I learned, then what I first thought was a pike turned into a common carp with a big long smear of clay along one flank and the fish moving along under the pads was a big mirror.

As I walked back to the Slope, I was in a bit of a quandary. I was here to catch the big common and hadn't got a clue of its whereabouts so decided to go back to the Steps armed with some more bait. I'd only been gone about ten minutes and when I returned there was nothing in the swim so I threw in a handful of 10mms and a couple of scoops of slop, stick mix and hemp, in front of the pads in about four feet of water. A quick look in the corner revealed nothing; another look from Party Point and nothing, a look down by the pads in the Steps swim and there were now three carp - a big mirror and two commons obviously turned on and about to get stuck in, a good opportunity to watch.

The mirror circled once and then went straight down while the two commons watched for five minutes before joining in, with the biggest common probably an upper-20, classic bronze and well proportioned. Five minutes later two more joined in the feeding frenzy. Clearly, the biggest there now was the big common so I watched for a further five minutes before rushing back to the Slope to pack everything away for a quick change of swim.

I went back to the Steps swim in double-quick time and they were still feeding. Having no idea of the bottom make-up, I decided to continue with just two rods both of which now had small Ultra-Plex pop-ups attached. I waited at the top of the Steps for what seemed like ages before the right moment arrived for me to make my way to the water's edge. No sooner had I pushed in my rod rest when the two big'uns came back for more, with me crouching there just gob-smacked, I was so close to them. In order to get my rods out without ruining my chances I either had to wait for them to vacate, make them vacate, or go for it and swing my rigs amongst them. I flicked out about 20 grains of hemp and

Low-20-plus mirror. Just check out its huge rudder.

waited a minute, they were heads down tails up, seemingly oblivious that I was just a rod length away. In went another 20 grains, this time both the big'uns rose and gently swam away, chomping as they went.

They drifted along the pads to my right so I quickly stuck the left-hand rod where they had been feeding, and the other went straight out just beyond the marginal weed on clean, silty bottom. I took a chance and put a scoopful of slop and maybe a couple of dozen 10mms over the right-hand rod, before rapidly retreating up the steps.

Within a few minutes, they slowly made their way back, began feeding, and I thought that at any moment one of the rods would rattle off. After nearly an hour of watching them feed from the top of the steps, I could hardly believe nothing had happened. Then, for what seemed no reason, the big common swam away off to the left, not in any panic. Ten minutes later, the big mirror followed suit and swam off to the left, leaving the other three carp to circle the area. Suddenly, bosh, something crashed over to the left, my vision obscured by a tree. A minute later and, bosh, same place, probably the same fish and I missed it again. Whatever it was, it was big and I just had the feeling it was one of the two that had been gorging on my little feast.

I watched the rods for another 20 minutes before I noticed that the line on my right-hand rod was tight. As I picked up the rod, I soon discovered that I had a stockie on the end which must have just picked the rig up and buried his head in the weed. I never saw any stockies and for all I know he could have been hooked and on for half an hour before I dealt with him. Now I knew why the big'uns had drifted away and I vowed to return for a two-night session the next weekend.

Well, the next weekend I cut short my planned trip of 48 hours because on the first night the temperature dropped down to minus 2 and I froze my nuts off because I was still using my summer sleeping bag and old Aqua bivvy. I sat it out on the second day hoping to see something to get enthusiastic about but saw nothing other than possibly a low-20 mirror late in the afternoon, which swam over to the bar in the corner. A phone call to my wife, Louise, confirmed that frost was forecast so I wimped out of another night in an igloo.

I baited heavily when I left with 5kg boilie and 5kg hemp and pellet, all straight out a couple of rod lengths in about six feet of water. All I could do that week was pray for milder weather the next week, and hope no one fished in the Back Bay. Even though I blanked, I still felt really confident that my time would come.

During the week, I tied up some more rigs, still using the Quicksilver Gold which I had started the campaign with, but now with a two-inch section of the hooklink made even stiffer with the addition of some fine bore shrink tube at the swivel end. Three different hooks of similar sizes with the hair long enough to take two 10mm bottom baits.

Thankfully, the frosts disappeared during the week and come the weekend it was once again wet but mild. After the usual hike over the bridge, I made my way round to the Steps. Great, there was no one in the Back Bay so I left the barrow loaded behind the swim and went and had a look in all the swims along the west bank. Not a sign of a carp anywhere, but by now the close-in bar in the Slope was beginning to glow, with the gravel polished clean. I felt the Back Bay was worth fishing, at least for the first 24 hours. They'd clearly wanted it the week before and I let them have plenty to feast freely on when I packed up. The water clarity wasn't good, possibly caused by feeding fish!

I dragged a rig along the bottom where I had pre-baited and it was totally clean and smooth so all three rods were swung out with bottom bait rigs and 50mm Funnelweb sticks. The swim was then topped up with a few scoops of slop, two over each hookbait and half a kilo of 10mms spread over the three baited rigs. I set my bivvy up at the top of the steps and then got everything sorted out nicely before sticking the pan on for an egg and bacon roll.

The rain just came pouring down for what seemed like hours before it let up to a steady drizzle. During the afternoon, I watched the water for ages and as every hour passed it was chipping away at my confidence until finally, I spotted what looked like a low-20lb common cruise through the swim, perhaps three feet under the surface just as the light was fading. I spent the next few hours staring at the water praying to see another one and beginning to make a big dent in the chocolate biscuits, washed down with the usual tea. When I retired for the night around midnight, all was quiet and to be honest, I was beginning to have doubts about my choice of swim.

At 2.30am, my middle rod lit up and my sounder box signalled a blistering take. Boots on and down to the rods and I was soon grappling with an angry carp, that was stripping line off my reel as it headed for the far bank. It then went into a weed bed so I just held the rod in full compression hoping that I'd get it moving. Luck was on my side, as slowly but surely, I pulled in what felt like the far bank but was a clump of weed, almost certainly a personal best. In the light of my headlamp torch I could just make out a carp on the other side of the weed so I dragged it into the edge and began frantically peeling it all away until I could finally put the net under the fish.

This one was a long, lean 22lb mirror with a large tail, a mental scrapper, which had I lost I would have convinced myself it was a much bigger one, for sure. I popped it into a sack for a morning photo and a better look, and then put on a fresh rig which already had a 50mm stick attached. I had to reposition the other two rods because while hauling in the weed I'd pulled the other two rigs out of position.

At first light, I texted Kim and then reeled in the rods to put fresh baits on. The line on my middle rod looked a right old state so I pulled off 20 yards and retied the rig back on and then swung out all three rods, together with sticks, just a couple of rod lengths out along with the rest of the kilo bag of 10mms I'd started with, and a few scoops of stick mix and hemp. Kim came along shortly after, on his way to work, and the mirror was soon photographed and returned. I felt a bit guilty having Kim down for a low-20 and promised that the next one would be bigger. Little did I realise it would be sooner than I thought.

The day went by and, again, I noticed that the water level had risen another three inches from when I'd first set-up, and half the country was still under a hosepipe ban. Just before dark, I polished off a lovely curry and as I made another brew I noticed the wind had got up a bit stronger and my baited spot was leaking off oil. In my mind there had to be something down there having a go so I sat and watched the water until 10pm when I decided it was time get in the bag.

No sooner had I got all snug and warm and started to drift off, than my middle rod with a slip-D rig bleeped twice. I sat bolt upright and looked down at my rods wondering what was going on. At that point, I thought perhaps the culprit could be a tench or stockie; it had to have bleeped for a reason. I got out of my sleeping bag, started to put my boots on and as I pushed my feet in, my middle rod bleeped again.

This moment was the goal, so the pre-baiting was worth the effort.

She looked like a big barrel of sovereigns!

I didn't want to switch on my headlamp unnecessarily, so I walked down the steps toward my rods in the darkness. I felt both my left-hand and right-hand rods lines with each hand and they were fine, still with a bit of slack. I then felt my middle line and it was like a guitar string. For some reason, I waited and tried to focus my eyes on the tip of my rod. Convinced that I saw it move an inch and realising I had to do something I picked the rod up, tightened the clutch a bit and half-heartedly struck, fully expecting it to be a tench, a stockie, or a proper carp shaking it's head reluctant to bolt.

The rod immediately hooped over and the fish dived into the weed to the left. I just kept the pressure on and sure enough, I could feel something tugging away at the other end as my line juddered in the weed. Slowly but surely, I pulled it toward me. It felt really heavy and the more I pulled the more convinced I was that I had another big ball of weed on. I switched my head torch on and given that I hadn't given any line, was expecting to see a little carp with a shed load of weed. Instead, I was greeted with the sight of no weed but a proper carp, and it looked a possible 30 at first glance. With it only a rod length out I thought, 'don't panic Captain Mainwaring, just get the landing net in the water'. I turned round, grabbed my net and thrust it down in the margin with the carp wallowing around at the edge of the pads. As I pulled and gained a few more turns on the reel handle, up it came so I pushed the net under the water and slowly pulled it in.

It wasn't until it was finally over the net cord that it began to sink in which carp it was. When I shone the torch into the net I could clearly see my time had come. It was the big

The reward for all my effort!

common, it just had to be! Leaving it still hooked and in the net, I rushed up the steps to my bivvy, grabbed my phone and ran back down to the net. I knew the battery was low so I rang Kim instead of texting.

Thankfully, he was still up so I quickly told him I'd bagged the big girl and that my battery was low and would he do the honours with the camera first thing in the morning. "How big?" he asked.

I replied, "No idea, but it sure looks big in the net." I told him that I'd text him the weight as soon as I'd done it.

Once I'd zeroed the wet weigh bag and got the mat sorted, I went down to the net. I cut my rig off, rolled up the arms of the net and pulled it out of the water with a big heave. As I struggled up the steps, I kept thinking, 'blooming heck this is heavy', and as I lay it on the mat it soon registered that it was easily a new PB common for me, almost as wide as it was deep. I took the hook out, which was firmly planted an inch inside its underslung mouth, and shuffled it into the weigh bag. I then carried it along with my scales and landing net handle into the trees on Party Point to find a suitable branch to assist with the weighing.

As I hoisted her up, the needle shot past 40 and settled at 43lbs 10oz. Bloody hell! I checked it again to make sure I wasn't dreaming. Back on the mat and into the sack she went, crapping bait all over me in the process. Did I care?

I placed her in the deep water to the left of my rods, tied up to a bank stick rammed so hard into the ground it would take a real good pull to get it out. Kettle on, roll-ups out, and straight away I started texting mates, Kim first, then the Chiltern posse and a few other friends. All the time my battery was dying and the texts started coming back, then the calls until finally, the phone battery died, and probably a good job it did because we could all do without big mobile phone bills.

For some reason, I just couldn't get to sleep for the rest of the night and kept checking the sack to make sure that I wasn't dreaming. I think I did manage to snooze at about 6am while it was still dark, and was woken by Kim at first light knocking the side of my bivvy and smiling at me. After the usual chinwag, we got everything ready for the photos. Once again, on the mat but now in daylight, I unzipped the sack to reveal the biggest, cleanest common I'd seen on dry land, totally awesome, like a big barrel of sovereigns.

As Kim took the photos, one of the old girls who walked her dogs in the field came over for a look. We laughed when I said, "I bet a few others wished they were walking their dog this morning." Back she went, majestically swimming away as though nothing had happened. Mission accomplished! Well, not quite I still had to pack away and cart my gear back across the footbridge for a last time.

As I reeled the other two rods in, I was truly thankful I'd put the effort in to catch the big girl and I knew that as soon as I got my mobile on charge back at my van it wouldn't be long before I could use it to phone my wife, Louise. I finally trudged back down the path once more to climb those steps on the footbridge. That was my lot; the lake's biggest mirror and common in five sessions. Two other carp remain on my wanted list so perhaps in the future if I venture that way again, I can find the time to stalk them out one day. Sadly, the big common was found dead about 18 months after my capture. She did put on a few more pounds and went over 46lbs, but I'm simply grateful that she came my way!

Chapter 17

Elstow Pit 1 remembered

When I began fishing Elstow Pit 1, near Bedford, way back in 1996, never in my wildest dreams did I ever imagine it would be 15 years before I said my farewells and pulled my bank sticks out one last time. I didn't join with any targets or goals, or with any preconceived ideas on how to fish for its residents. I just happened to know a few members and bailiffs, a door opened for me and I was given the key to Pandora's Box.

Stuart Gillam, who was head bailiff at the time, was moving out to Thailand to pursue his dreams and he offered me a bailiff's ticket on a plate after talking to Len Gurd who is the man behind Linear Fisheries. For those who want to know, I first met Stuart on the banks of Harefield Lake and a friendship was formed, a mutual respect.

I knew Elstow Pit 1 contained a fair number of carp from my good mate 'Desperate Dan' with quite a few over 30lbs, with the biggest resident at that time affectionately known as Universe which went to mid-40s. Because I had a bailiff's ticket I never felt the need to fish all my available time on there, so there was never any compulsion on my part to try to catch as much as possible each year. Perhaps I saw it more as a long-term fishery, so I fished with no set yearly targets, plus the fact that some of the residents hadn't peaked and most seemed to be getting bigger each year so the future looked good. The fact that it would be some ten years down the line, from first wetting a line in its clear water, that Elstow reached its peak, perhaps justified my decision not to put all my eggs into one basket the moment I could fish, not that I capitalised on this.

Obviously, in the time span while being privileged to be fishing Elstow, I had several cherished tickets for other venues that held some very big carp which, in my eyes, were more desirable. With mirrors and commons that I wanted to catch elsewhere, Elstow was more of a second or third venue for me, although it must be said Pit 1 was the best big carp fishery in Bedfordshire.

There are no common carp in Pit 1, but it was only a 20-minute drive from my house with my foot down which made it very handy for fishing short sessions. It was always handy to have a venue of this calibre less than 20 miles away, if not to fish then to walk round and see a few mates from time to time. You never stop learning because any observations will always be better than none!

I was recently asked by a work colleague how many carp I had caught from Pit 1, and my reply was simple. I couldn't tell him, because I don't write down every capture, preferring to rely on my memories; after all, that what it's all about. Even though I've put back a few 30s without taking any photographs, even a few 20s without even weighing them, I could attempt a count up and I know it's a few hundred, even though some years I hardly fished there. If it were a dozen, it wouldn't take much time and effort on my part to count up, but the reality is that it would be in the hundreds with all the repeat captures.

I know I didn't catch them all, although I wasn't far off a full house in the end. Some carp died before I had the pleasure, and a few evaded my nets. I know I lost some of these because I recognised them before losing them with a few falling off at very close quarters. Scarface, for example, which was the lake record at 48lbs after the demise of Universe which I lost two years on the trot. That I'm positive about; once off the top while floater fishing, the other time while margin fishing. Not that it's anything to brag about, we all lose some from time to time.

35lbs 4oz bruiser from the margins.

One of the beauties of Elstow, both Pit 1 and Pit 2, is the clear water which may hinder the fishing at times but does enable the sharp-eyed angler to identify specific carp when the conditions are conducive. I always presumed there were around 200 carp in Pit 1, maybe a few more prior to joining in 1996, and I don't think I was far out with my early assumptions. A few have died over the years, as they do elsewhere, but there's still today over 150 quality carp to pit your wits against.

Recent stockings of home-grown Elstow stockies that are steadily putting on the pounds have bolstered the total in recent years, so you can understand why all Elstow anglers cherish the Pit 1 ticket which is limited to 60 anglers. With 30 anglers on each rota, this only really comes into effect at the weekends. If I then said that half of these carp went over 30lbs, you may then understand why some members keep it quiet, although many, if not all, the big carp have appeared in the press over the years; a special place indeed! I know of at least 20 different carp that have pulled someone's scales past the 40lb mark, and I had six carp over 40lbs, with many more in the upper-30s that have been known 40s. I hardly fished between 2004 and 2008, when the venue produced 18 different 40s in just one of those years, which is mental.

As mentioned, there were a few years in which I hardly fished and the reason was that I was looking, learning and fishing elsewhere, and was suffering with anxiety and depression, which wasn't enjoyable at all even though physically I was as fit as a fiddle. Going to three funerals, three years on the trot didn't help, beginning with my father's, and then watching my mother battle with throat cancer. Depression and anxiety hit me like a massive tidal wave and was something which I'd never encountered before. I had to seek help through mediation and drugs, which if I'm honest didn't help but somehow got me through a very difficult phase of my life. My doctor started me off with 50mg of Sertraline a day and I ended up on 200mg on a daily basis. There were moments when I couldn't remember what day of the week it was, and it felt like my brain was being slowly scrambled, with numerous thoughts skipping around my head from one to another 24/7, which made decision-making near impossible and getting to sleep just as bad. During this period, the only fishing I did was stalking or floater fishing for a few hours, once or twice a week, depending on what enthusiasm I could muster.

I resigned my bailiff's ticket a week after letting my controller float drift with the wind under the rope in the Reeds swim, on a day trip with the floater rod, and realised what a plum I was, and needed to sort my head out badly. I could still fish Elstow as a member and kept my open invitation to fish any of the Oxford Linear Fisheries, should I wish to venture that way.

To resolve my issues, I decided the anti-depressant drugs had to go so I weaned myself off them and then had some sessions with a psychiatrist, which thankfully, was the right decision although my doctor would probably disagree. Six months without the prescription anti-depressant drugs and somehow I managed to get my head back together, still a nutter but then I always have been. At least, I felt normal again and renewed my enthusiasm and passion for fishing so was keen to fish Elstow Pit 1. The black cloud had lifted so all I had to do was find the time and petrol money for a squirt up the A6.

I wouldn't say that Pit 1 is an easy venue, nor would I say it was hard, and I suppose a fair description would be to call it a pressured moderate venue. Anglers do blank from time to time, just like on many other venues, and they also have some good hits with big carp coming along like buses.

The most hectic, intense period of action I ever had was six carp in a two-hour window, with three 30s to 37lbs 12oz and three 20s. I've also had a few trips with between ten and a dozen runs over a 72-hour period, which is the time limit for any session. There have been too many times to remember when I had between three to six carp, in periods ranging from four hours to 72 hours.

Three or four carp over 30lbs on the same day is not unheard of, I managed that a few times, with dozens of braces but then on a venue of this calibre it was achievable and almost anything seemed possible. It would be easier for me to recollect my last few years fishing Pit 1 rather than a whole decade, because it could go on too long and perhaps take away some of the venue's mystique for those interested in fishing this historical Bedfordshire water.

During 2009, I decided to give Pit 1 a bit more of my available time, while I waited patiently on waiting lists for a couple of new promising venues of which I'd become aware. There were still a fair number of the Elstow residents which I'd yet to have the pleasure of holding, so it was just a case of waiting for the right time and applying myself to the task.

Luckily, I had a 12-month job in Bedford town centre refurbishing ten big old houses which allowed me to fit in a number of short day sessions after work on the way home. After a month or so of starting the job, the boss then allowed me to take a few days off midweek to pursue my passion. I was visiting the venue virtually every other day, if not to fish then to have a walk round which was great for me because it meant I could wangle a few hours fishing during the week and spend the weekends at home writing material for various magazines and making a start on this book when I had a few spare hours.

It wasn't until mid-August that I did my first night's fishing of the year, so from March until then, I simply fished daylight hours with one rod, adopting the mobile approach but mostly floater fishing. Now, I'd had half a dozen 30lb-plus carp off the top in one year before, so it was going to be interesting to see if I could push this figure up. I armed myself with a couple of sacks of Richworth mixers and plenty of cork hookbaits in preparation.

I didn't want to count the carp off one by one, nor to push myself to the limit, but my final tally for 2009 was 31 carp over 30lbs, one over 40, with Bunters at 41lbs 8oz, and over 50 carp between 20lbs and 30lbs, half of these upper-20s. Eighteen of those over 30lbs fell to single-rod tactics, 13 of them coming off the top on flavoured cork hookbaits with the biggest affectionately known as Dark Cloud at 38lbs 14oz, which was nice. I'd never even seen him on the bank before and he was in prime condition. The other five of those 18 captured using one rod were caught stalking, fishing with boilies on the bottom, on marginal spots.

Twenty-one different 30s I hadn't caught before, with four of them repeatedly falling to my baits and tactics. Henry, five times between 30lbs to 31lbs 10oz; Watto's, four times between 35lbs 40z to 37lbs 14oz; White Slug, three times from 36lbs to 34lbs 4oz, the only one to be going backwards, and the Fully Scaled, twice at 34lbs and 36lbs. Of the 21 different 30s, five of them I'd had before which, oddly enough, didn't include those that repeatedly came my way except for Henry, who I caught virtually every year I had the privilege to fish there.

One of the leathery crew at 34lbs 2oz.

Watto's at 37lbs 14oz; my heaviest capture out of five repeats.

White Slug graced my net on numerous occasions; here she is at 36lbs.

Big Fully at 34lbs; although I did have him at 36lbs; this is my favourite image.

Watto's, AKA the fighting machine, I'd also not seen on the bank before and I caught him four times in four months (twice in the same week), so you might assume some of these carp to be mug fish which isn't the case. No one else had the pleasure of catching Watto's during my time on the lake that year and so it would transpire that certain carp fell to the same anglers. It wasn't a phenomenon restricted to me or this venue.

Watto's was named after Steve Watson who sadly passed away in 2005. I knew Steve through our connection to Rod Hutchinson Developments and we had met a few times on the banks of Elstow and at the odd carp show before his untimely departure. One of the nicest-thinking carp anglers I've talked to. RIP Steve, you will always be remembered.

Weirdly, I never repeated on any surface captures during 2009, although a few of them I'd caught in previous years off the top and on the bottom while fishing more conventional tactics. I had a few carp using what I would call standard knotless knot rigs, with pop-ups and bottom baits, but the vast majority fell to the more productive slip-D rigs, with pop-ups or bottom bait presentations. Bait-wise I started off with Richworth's Ultra-Plex ready-mades, which had produced well for me in the past, but moved on to a new bait I'd been asked to put to the test by Uncle Bob.

Both baits caught, but the new one which was named XLR-8 had never been used before and proved an instant winner. Perhaps I should add here that I was the only angler to be using it, so there wasn't a shed load going in, just the five or six kilos I was putting in while fishing over two or three nights a week.

Perhaps the reasons behind the repeats were down to the bait, perhaps the rigs or style of fishing or swim choices, I just hoped in the future they'd grace other members' nets and not mine, at least not so many times. Throughout the whole year, only on a few occasions could I confidently say I had a stack of carp in front of me for any length of time. The rest of the time I always managed to get into swims which were visited by carp in smaller groups.

From August to early December when it froze over, I did manage to fish a fair number of 72 and 48-hour sessions mid-week. Now, whether it was me I'm not too sure, but it seemed impossible to catch three or more carp in the first 24 hours, and then follow it up with similar action in the second 24 hours and on the third 24 hours. Of course, on a prolific big carp venue with plenty to fish for you're always hoping for a good run of fortune in the same swim, but angling pressure and their nomadic tendencies have an influence unless you get consistent weather conditions throughout the session.

On some sessions, I moved swims two or three times. Perhaps this was a mistake but the move always paid off so perhaps if I put more bait in at the start of each session I may have caught more carp, or held them in the swim longer and not felt the need to move. Even when you're catching fairly consistently on Elstow, you're thinking 'where's next!'

I'm almost certain I could have caught more carp had I spent more time at the venue during 2009, and perhaps leaving it until mid-August before I fished longer sessions with a new bait was a gamble but I wasn't grumbling with my results. I'd never caught over thirty 30lb-plus carp from Elstow in one year before, and now I had that feather in my cap. Others had done it before, and no doubt others will in the future. If I have any grounds to blow my own trumpet then everything came with less than 50 nights on a bedchair, half coming my way in 20-day sessions ranging from one to eight hours.

I only blanked a couple of times in 2009, during a few day sessions when I restricted myself to floater fishing when conditions weren't ideal, and never blanked when I fished two or three nights. I could have fished a few weekend sessions on my rota but decided not to for a few reasons. First, was the unwritten rule that if you fish during the working week you leave the weekends free for the lads who mostly only fish their weekend rotas. Not everyone adheres to this unwritten rule, but it does get noted - a bit of fuel for some banter!

Secondly, my weekends are taken up with work and family; work has to be done and family life suffers if you're spending all your weekends fishing. Not a major issue if you're single, but I've been married almost 25 years now and I'd be lost without my wife, Louise. She's put up with me this long, but if I spent half my life under the stars she would have given me the elbow by now.

The other reason for opting out of the weekends is that the draw for swims takes place at 11am on the Friday. Every swim is vacant, numbered pound coins go into the hat for a draw and number one gets first choice, and so on. All well and good if you get a favourable draw, but the busier it is, the more your chances diminish of getting the swims you fancy. The only consolation to coming out last in the draw is, the money in the hat is yours. You can't guarantee that you'll get your first or second choice of swim mid-week, but you stand less chance at the weekends, if you're as unlucky as me. I probably fished something like 25 weekends in 15 years, came out first three times, and one of those was in the winter when there was only three of us there for the draw. I came out last at least half a dozen times and usually blanked or managed to winkle out the odd carp.

Most of the members are in full or part-time employment and have jobs of all descriptions, but there have been a few members over the years without a job that have spent many nights under the stars on the banks of Elstow Pit 1 and as they respect the fish and the fishery, like every member, then there's hardly ever a problem. The general standard of angling is high. Most members have on average 20-plus years of carping under their belts and numerous carp, and if a carp farts somewhere then someone's usually aware of it, so you have to be sharp-eyed at times when you're looking to fish and make the right decisions on swim choice. Just like most venues though, they don't feed in every swim, every day, and have a tendency to move into swims and feed on spots not being fished just as much as those which are being fished.

Some of their feeding spots, of which there are many, may only produce action for a few weeks of the year and some of them are fairly consistent for months though not exceptionally, unless the weather conditions are favourable for that particular swim at that time. Although the water level has been taken down possibly four feet in the last five years in an effort to maintain a certain depth, there is still plenty of the venue with depths over 20 feet deep and an abundance of features with depths ranging from 4 feet to 15 feet out beyond the margins in most of the swims. Not that it's essential to fish the shallowest spots, I'm simply pointing out that in some parts of the venue it's more like an egg box, and not just a hole in the ground with little in the way of features, so accurate casting can be essential.

I'm struggling to think what would be my favourite swim on Pit 1. I've had some memorable moments in most of them, bar one or two swims which for no particular reason I hardly fished. During 2009, I managed a few sessions in the infamous Reeds swim, which in the past could be the best or cruellest swim in the country. The shallow, reedy bay to the right of it can at times attract the carp in numbers, normally in the spring months as the water warms and prior to them spawning when they are in the mood for it.

The Reeds is one of those swims which can be regularly occupied by an angler throughout the spring and summer and as a consequence receives anglers' bait on a regular basis and the associated angling pressure that goes along with it. It's not an easy swim where you are guaranteed a result or where it could be considered clubbing baby seals, although it does have its moments and does see some fierce and frantic feeding activity.

Whether the hooked carp are landed after making the early mistake of picking up a hookbait is something else though, because the carp know exactly in which direction to head, when they bolt in their attempt to avoid capture.

Now, you could easily assume that the angler will always have the upper hand, and on some venues or swims this is viable, but Elstow carp normally give a good account of themselves with many noted for their fighting abilities. Stopping them heading into Norfolk reed or any other weed beds is a task, even when you're onto your rods in a flash. I've hooked my fair share of carp from a variety of venues and have had some good scraps, but I'll always remember Elstow for the many times the carp have proved themselves a right handful. Some of them are proper mental and the Reeds area is undoubtedly challenging, mentally and physically, when fishing it for a few days and nights.

You could get beaten up badly in this swim. It's been done in the past and no doubt someone this year got punished. Some members like the swim, others not so much, but no one is under any illusion; it's a swim where you can't afford to let the carp get the jump on you. You may convert 100% of the takes some of the time, or you could get punished and lose every chance, with the record being ten losses on the trot over a 72-hour session. I'm glad to say it wasn't me and thankfully, my conversion rate was more like 80% using the almost bullet-proof 15lb GR60, so very few cut-offs for me.

More carp were lost in this swim than in any other although it's not as bad as it used to be because there is now a rope going across to the far bank, which cuts down the available water to fish. We also manually extracted some reeds when I was a bailiff, from a boat and in waders one year, which helped, but it was not brutal enough in my opinion and now the rope is a permanent feature of the swim which has, in effect, created a sanctuary for the carp.

Thankfully, I caught a lot more than I ever lost in the Reeds swim and although a few got the better of me it was never enough to dampen my enthusiasm because it was never a sure-fire guarantee to land everything elsewhere. That said, it was a hard swim to relax in and there's no substitute for experience in a demanding swim when you're motioning toward your rods the instant a bobbin moves, or one of your lines tightens up, be they line bites or finicky takes.

During my sessions in the swim in 2009, I started off fishing the margins rather than the far bank area, partly due to the fact that I was catching a couple of carp each day with no losses, and partly due to the fact that the carp weren't showing too much interest in the far bank spots. Every time I fished the margins I'd get two or three chances each day, fishing on the bottom, and normally a chance of some floater activity sometimes during the day or as darkness came, and as a few ventured out of the bay to the right into open water and other swims. After a few weeks, the two marginal spots seemed to dry up but thankfully, the far bank spot in the corner created by the tied-off rope, that I'd pre-baited a few times, was starting to be visited on a daily basis.

It was time for the pipe trick, well, two pipes to be precise, to come out from behind the back of my shed, as described in Chapter 9. I never had to cast baited rigs to the far bank corner so never left any tackle hung up on the rope, as some had done aiming for the hot corner, which I was extracting carp from with some regularity. Oddly enough, I had to endure a fair amount of repeat captures from the back spot in this swim, but stuck with it because a few of the larger residents I'd yet to catch were in the area for quite some time, plus I had the pipe trick in my armoury which was working a treat!

Eventually, one of the bigger boys on my wanted list came along, after a good run of high 20s and 30s, in the shape of Bunters at 41lbs 8oz, which was a slow, twitchy take and a nice first bite of the last day of a productive session.

As we moved into the autumn months, the carp were more spread out but still constantly on the move, and only a few swims produced carp in numbers before they'd move once again. I kept catching, although I had to work for the bites, and it was early winter before I had a few good sessions with five or six carp in a day from the deeper water. Now, I'm sure a few reading this wouldn't be super-confident fishing on the bottom in 25 feet-plus of water, but I loved it because when they were in the deeps they seemed to throw caution to the wind and feed regularly in a few areas. After watching carp showing themselves, from different viewing angles, I simply fished these spots regardless of the depth and it paid off.

Just as I was getting to grips with their deep-water feeding spots, winter came along with a bang and a severe cold period, followed by even colder temperatures which soon put the fishing on hold as the lake surface froze solid. This freeze-up ended the year and started 2010, so I rejoined because it was the only local venue I was a member of that allowed any publicity, and there were still some highly-prized Elstow carp on my wanted list. The only significant thing that happened during the freeze-up was that I watched a group of six carp one day, including the lake's largest resident, feeding under the ice in four feet of water in the margins, which did make me ponder on how you could capitalise in these almost impossible conditions. Blimey! Eskimo Clarkey with his chainsaw and blowtorch!

Bunters at 41lbs 2oz fell to the pipe trick.

The elusive Willow at 36lbs, caught while stalking.

Pawprint at 37lbs, hooked six feet out.

Italian's mate, again at 37lbs.

During 2010, once again I notched up over thirty, 30lb-plus Elstow carp with only one particular carp frequently coming my way, although most I'd had before at some point, which I was half-expecting. For some reason, the floater fishing wasn't as productive as the previous year. However, stalking paid off for me, and my one-rod mobile tactics produced a number of sizeable carp from a couple of marginal spots. Some of those which had eluded me in the past fell to stalking with one rod. They included; Dogfish at 38lbs 12oz (dust jacket image), normally a 40; Willow at 36lbs 8oz, and Paw Print at 37lbs-plus.

Once again, I lost Scarface, this time while margin fishing, although two of my mates who'd switched over to Richworth's XLR-8 had better luck and banked the beast two days on the trot from the same spot in the same swim, both at 45lbs 8oz. So much for any theories that big carp will sulk after a capture and not get caught for a while!

I also lost another 40 that was on my wanted list, namely Long Speckles, which normally came out at around 40lbs 8oz, simply ripped line off my reel as I held on with the rod at full compression and cut me on a snag in the entrance of Pump Bay. I had caught it before, years ago, when it was a mid-30, but my photos were toilet material. Small consolation to losing Long Speckles was a brace of upper-30s the next day, which included the Italian's Mate at just over 37lbs, which had also came out a lot bigger in the past at the right time of year. I'd seen it many times in the water but that was the first time I'd seen it on the bank, and so another one off my wanted list of Pit 1 residents.

One particular fish, however, did seem to follow me around in 2010, just like Watto's the previous year, namely Twin Scale. Again, I'd never seen it on the bank before let alone had the pleasure of it gracing my net.

View from the Monks swim in November.

The first time was in August at 40lbs 2oz, using the tried and trusted pipe trick in the Reeds. Second time was in September at 40lbs 10oz fishing the margins in White Stick, and the third time was on November 2nd at 43lbs, again fishing the margins but in the Monks swim along the road bank. Oddly enough, I was talking to Carl, AKA Shakey, one of the other members, as we watched some fireworks go off in the distance and and I said to him, "I wonder what fireworks we'll see tonight." A split second later my middle rod went into meltdown. On all occasions, the fight was epic so I may well have lost this beast before without knowing.

On its third visit to my net, I was blown away and found it hard to comprehend that I'd never seen it on the bank before 2010, and in three months it had seen the bottom of my net three times! I was shaking my head, thinking 'no not again', as our headlamps illuminated the beast lying on the unhooking mat. No doubt other members were shaking their heads too when they found out, or would that be fists!

Once again, as the winter approached, the deep water spots came alive and a few came my way from the 25 feet-plus spots out in the deep water areas. Unfortunately, just as the previous year, everywhere froze up again which was a right pain in the arse. I had plenty of time on my hands waiting for my next job to start, and the winters are normally productive in Bedfordshire's deep clay pits.

I wasn't going to rejoin Pit 1 in 2011 because I'd caught 90% of its residents, with way too many repeat captures, but as the ones which were eluding me were some of the best-looking carp in the area that I was aware of, and my mates cajoled me into another year, I opted to join and hoped they'd come my way. I was still waiting for a new syndicate place

Twinscale at 43lbs; incredibly three times in three months.

on another venue to come about, plus I had a few other waters to fall back on, so I'd have to suck it and see what developed as the year went on.

Unfortunately, as the carp started to come my way I couldn't stop catching old familiar characters, with half of them over 30lbs and a few being returned without a photo. It seemed like doing the lottery each week and winning a £10 but never the jackpot. I decided to go elsewhere for a while and return later in the year for one final attempt to catch the few that I always seemed to photograph for new members.

Now, I'd love to tell you where I fished and what I caught, but I have to restrain myself from divulging anything because the venue has a strict publicity ban and as I don't want to lose the ticket all I can say is that XLR-8 and my slip-D rigs worked a treat. One of the venues I'd been waiting on had a place for me so I joined in April even though I knew I wouldn't have any available time to fish there, thinking ahead, like you do. This made my mind up as to what I'd be doing at the end of the year though.

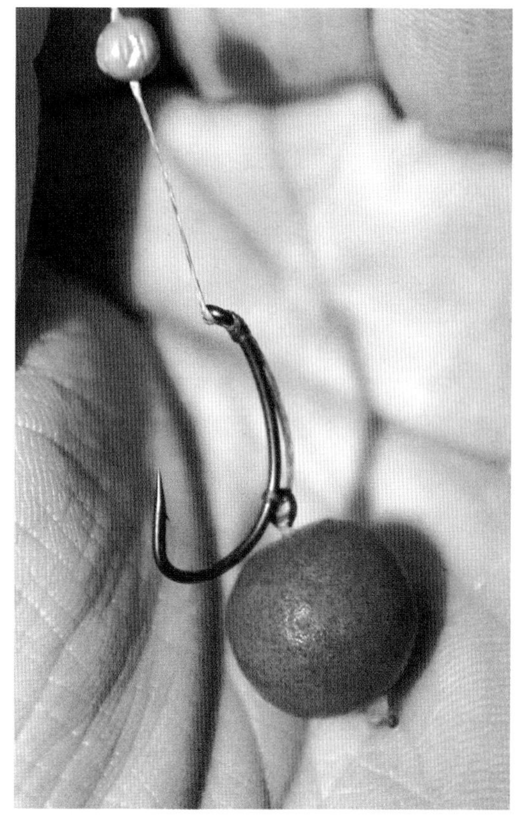

Slip-D rig worked a treat on pit 1.

I ended up finishing the year fishing Pit 1 in October and November, three days mid-week, virtually a different swim each week hoping a few more desirables would come my way. Not that it wound me up, but it was ironic that the new members that year each caught the jewels of Elstow that had eluded me for so long. My final tally for the year 2011 was 17 over 30lbs, plus a fair few over 20lbs, and three off my wanted list, having never caught them before. One was a new 30 and one of the stockies grown on from the nurturing of some Elstow eggs, and just one of 50-plus home-grown stunners that have been introduced from stock ponds and are growing on steadily. My last few sessions were extremely productive with a number of carp over 35lbs every trip, including the elusive Baby Orange Scaly at 38lbs-plus, and part of a big brace in a mad hour in the Dugout swim.

I knew it was time to give up the cherished ticket when I couldn't be bothered to weigh and photograph a stunning mid-30 fully-scaled, having caught it for the third time. You start to wonder what it is that makes you go carp fishing and so the time had come to say farewell to a very special venue which had been good to me and many friends, on many occasions. All of the stockies, moved over from the stock ponds at high singles to low doubles, and as part of an ongoing stocking policy, they are growing, so the bloodline continues for future generations of anglers.

A 36-pounder from a raked spot two rod lengths out.

Baby Orange Scaley at 38lbs; one that eluded me for so long.

Having watched the growth rates of the stockies introduced into both lakes on the Elstow complex, I'm convinced that it won't be long before these too become highly-prized Bedfordshire whackers. I've decided for the moment to keep my Pit 2 ticket because I have only dabbled on there a few times in the past, and as it's my only local ticket, it's nice to have something on your doorstep with a past, present and future with 95% of its residents yet to see the bottom of your net. Also, it's nice to pop over to Pit 1 for a cuppa with my old mates from time to time, when I'm not fishing.

As I mentioned at the start of this chapter, I never envisioned it would be such a long time from first wetting a line at Elstow to my final day's fishing. The flame flickered brightly for a few years, but the result was worth it. Some of the 20lb and 30lb carp I caught in the late 90s and published in Strictly Carp went on to become 30s and 40s, and many of those I struggled to catch in the early years frequently fell to the XLR-8 and slip-D rig combo. Those in the know have always been aware of the potential of Elstow Pits 1 and 2, although it was never publicised to death while I held a ticket, well not by me.

I hope my chapter reveals a little more of the mystique which surrounds Pit 1. If any of you reading this fish it now or intend to in the future, then be prepared to be tested and be lucky; effort equals rewards, though you don't need me to remind you. Special thanks to Len and all the members and bailiffs who took some excellent photographs for me, you know who you are, and I hope my camera skills for you were of equal standard.

The Elstow Pits are once again under threat from being filled in. Residents of the new village, Wixhams, which is being built next door, and the anglers obviously have objections to this. Petitions are being signed, on paper and online, so we can only pray that any proposals are not granted planning permission. The worst case scenario is that the fish will have to be moved; let's hope it doesn't come to that!

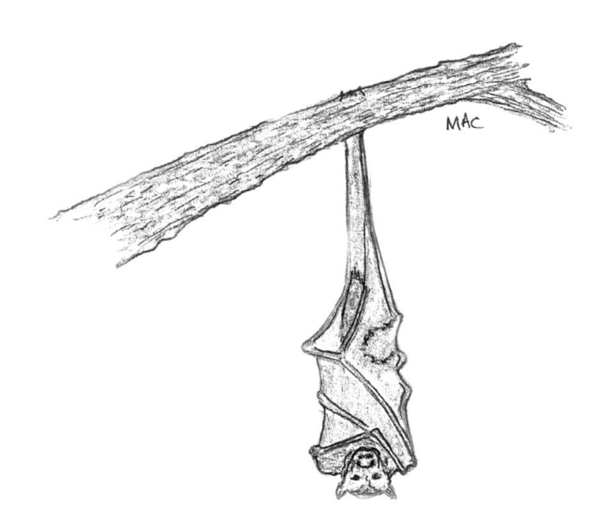

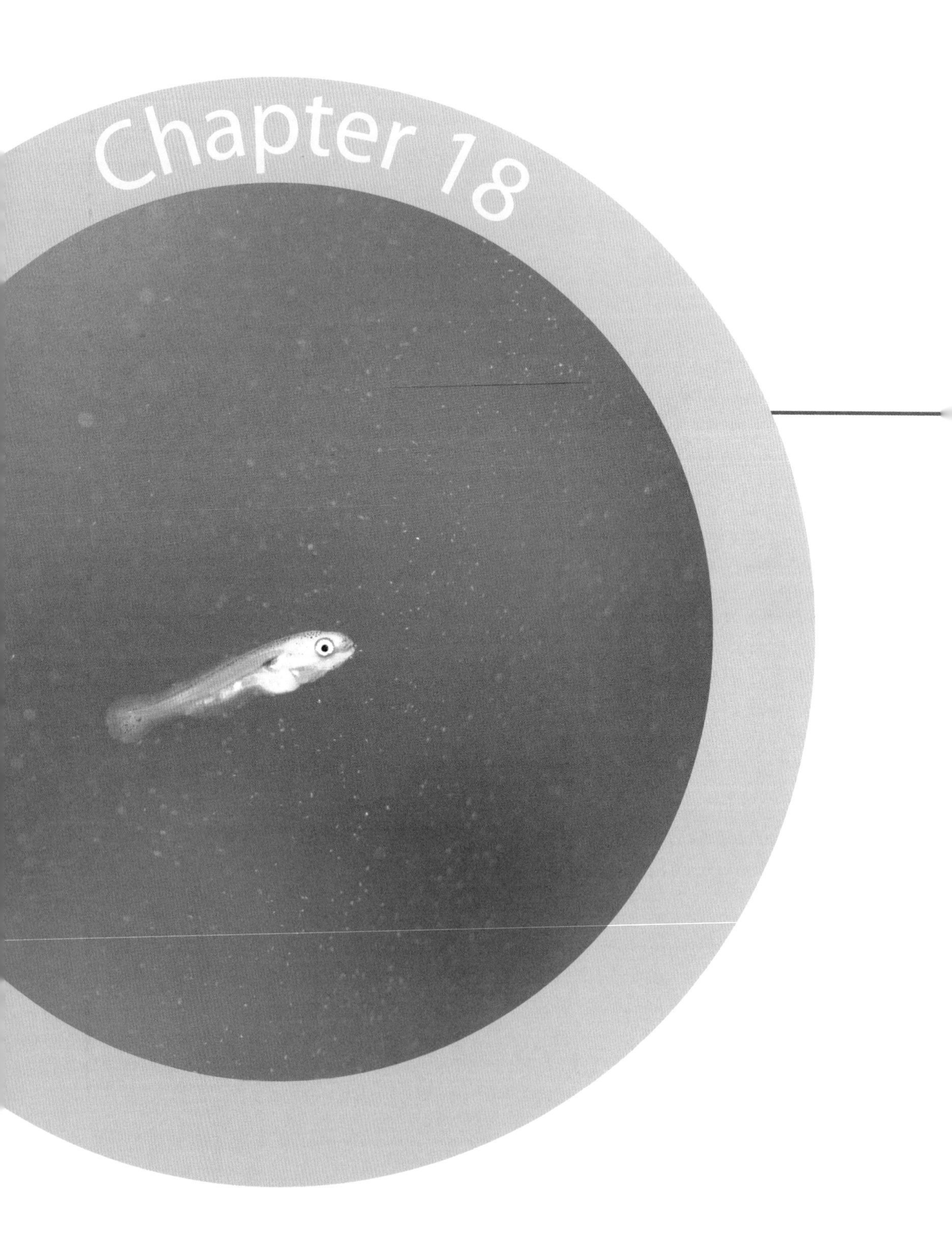
Chapter 18

Pro-active carping

Now we are nearing the end of this book, I wanted to write a chapter about something that hardly gets a mention in angling books. It might be educational to some, inspirational to others and may change the future for a few of us, or open up some eyes, at the very least.

What is pro-active carping? Well, it's a lot of things, but essentially anything which is positive or beneficial to others to do with carp fishing in any shape or form really. Helping friends or family or even strangers to improve their fishing, or simply getting involved in the UK carp scene in some way, by improving any fisheries on a work party, attending an AGM, field testing products, writing articles or even a positive few lines on a carp fishing forum or on Facebook. Basically, getting involved, even if it's only snipping off a few brambles that lie in wait to scratch someone's face in the dark on a pathway, or picking up some litter, rather than doing little or nothing and then whinge or whine and slag off others behind their backs, or worse, conspire to make life difficult for someone because there's nothing better to do.

There are thousands of anglers like me who put something back into carp angling, so I must thank all those that have done something in the past. During the last decade or so, I have helped out on about ten charity fishing events, for the Carp Society and for Roy Parsons and Len Gurd on the Richworth Linear complex, along with many other like-minded carp anglers, and have had some great times so long may these events continue. It's always nice to rub shoulders with other pro-active carp anglers; even though a few haven't fished for carp in the UK for a few years, they still play an active role.

One thing that has become apparent now that I've been carp fishing for over 30 years, having looked around at all the possible viable carp fisheries we can fish, is that there is a lot of water of which to made good use. There are venues with no carp, or just a few, with some run by match-orientated clubs or simply those which have never been stocked or even released to be made into a fishery. If someone had written a chapter like this in their books many moons ago, we would all be reaping the benefits now in some shape or form.

I'm perhaps too old to start my own fishery, always just keeping enough money in the building society to pay the mortgage and enough in the bank to pay the monthly bills, so until my financial situation changes I won't be in a position to run my own fishery. I'm still pro-active, if only at a low level, and I have had opportunities to take on a couple of venues, although I lacked the funds and the balls when those moments arose. If I could turn the clock back I would, but then wouldn't most of us like to turn back time, for one reason or another?

If we discount the idea that most venues don't stock themselves with carp naturally, apart from those from occasional flooding, then someone either got the ball rolling or will get the ball rolling in the future, and without these people where would we be? Virtually every time I've fished on the Richworth Linear fishery complex in Oxfordshire in the past, I've met anglers from all over England and many say it's grim up north, or round their way. I've always been a little sharp with my replies and it's normally the same. I simply ask why? The answer is there, they have just got to be a bit more pro-active and make things happen, even if it just means sticking your hand up at your local club's AGM or putting forward ideas which will be beneficial for the future.

It's true that if you threw money into a project and a stocking policy it wouldn't take that long to create a good fishery from scratch, but how much money, time and effort would those involved have to put in, and what are the alternatives? The result will always be worth it providing you went about it the right way and didn't rush things or take short cuts. None of us have to be experts on fishery management; the help and advice is out there if you look around, but I'm positive that with my own knowledge, along with advice and help, I could create a fantastic carp fishery without throwing in large amounts of investment, but still be realistic that it won't be an overnight success if starting from scratch, and so could others.

Another thing which is also apparent is that throughout the UK, within an hour's drive of my house, there is so much potential. A fair percentage of stillwaters are relatively understocked and the simple answer to their problem is that there is little or no investment for the future. Our typical British club venues are usually run by a committee process and their budget for investment is usually based on expenditure and current revenue. If the club, or those in control of the fishery, attracts enough members to make a profit then there's money in the kitty for investment. Bit of a catch 22 situation, but the reality is, with most clubs it's all about balancing the books and they then tend to hold back funds to save for a rainy day or another stretch of river or canal, or another acquisition.

The truth of the matter is, we carp anglers are prepared to pay good money for cherished venues and travel considerable distances to catch those fish we desire, not to mention sitting on waiting lists in some situations, simply because there's not enough to satisfy our needs locally.

The vast majority of current top carp venues didn't stock themselves naturally, and every carp started its life small, so someone introduced them to their current environment either legally or without the appropriate paperwork. This includes home-grown English carp and those which make their way on to UK soil from the continent. Some of England's finest carp have been moved illegally from one venue to another, not that I'm condoning this, but merely stating the facts that carp movements have gone on in the past and no doubt will continue to do so.

There will always be a percentage of carp anglers who don't want their local venue stocked and would rather it stay the way it is, but is this the right attitude? While other species of fish seem to spawn successfully each year and self-regulate their numbers, carp, on the majority of venues, go through the motions, yet very few young survive, if any at all.

If the carp eggs manage to get fertilized, they have made it over the first hurdle, as many eggs will fail. Within eight days, providing the water temperature doesn't drop drastically, the fry will emerge and at first will be so small and virtually transparent that they resemble shards of glass with two tiny eyes. While they are at the egg stage, all the time they are open to attack as a food source, from other fish as well as carp and other aquatic life.

Within a few days as a fingerling, they will absorb all the nutrients from the egg sac and will immediately begin to feed on microscopic foodstuffs. If they survive for a few weeks and there is an abundance of micro-naturals to consume, they'll be approaching 25mm in length and will now start to look like a carp, albeit in miniature.

Some will grow fast and some not so fast, but again, all the time they remain small they will be eaten by other fish. Not only will the venue's carp consume the fingerlings, other fingerlings of the same batch which have grown quicker will also consume any of those around them that will fit into their mouths.

Naturally, without human intervention, the survival rate will be pathetically low in your average year, and out of millions of eggs you'll be very lucky if half a dozen survive 12 months. Survival rates of any small carp in any pond will be determined not only by the current fish population, but also water quality and their environment. Shallow, weedy venues are perhaps best suited to carp, although any water with an abundance of weed does give any carp fry a slim chance to grow and avoid being eaten, and any small pike or perch will pounce on them at every opportunity, have no fear of that. So where does this leave us carp anglers? Fish for what's out there and sod the future!

Thankfully, some fisheries and angling clubs are setting the example. They have the means, manpower and the foresight to look to the future and make things happen. The answer, in my opinion, to creating a carp Mecca is fishery management; either stocking carp at 5lb-plus sourced from a reputable source, or growing and rearing your own in a stock pond, or perhaps both options.

Having grown and reared a number of carp from eggs and into double figures, in tanks and ponds, where the fingerlings are given every chance to grow, safe from predation, I know that it takes about four years to achieve a suitable stocking weight. In a decent-sized stock pond, with a healthy feeding regime, you could easily raise enough carp for the future. No need for imports when it's possible to keep the same strain going.

Is it worth it? Well, I know of carp that have reached 30lbs within four years of being stocked at 10lbs; I even know of a carp which reached 40lbs-plus in 11 years after being stocked at a little over 5lbs, so don't presume it will take forever and you won't personally see the potential in your time as a carp angler. Every single carp that's swimming around today in every UK fishery started off its life as a fertilized egg.

This 31lb stockie had doubled in weight in three years.

This fella went in at 6lbs, and here it is at 21lbs 10oz; No doubt one to keep an eye out for in the future.

The cheapest way of creating a superb carp fishery with an ongoing stocking policy is to rear your own carp in a stock pond. This may mean you'll be requiring the services of a digger for a few hours, but once it's dug, it will be there for as long as you want. True, not every fishery could accommodate its own stock pond but many have the land; it's just a shame that so few actually have one. Yes, there may be security and safety issues but where there is a will there will be a way. The simple facts are, we don't need a massive pond to grow-on carp, it all depends on how many you intend to grow-on and to some degree on how selective you are. I've grown carp into double figures in the smallest pond in my back garden and it's only 1000 gallons, including the filter bay.

As an example of my experiences, a few years ago I gathered up some handfuls of weed festooned with carp eggs and transferred this to a plastic bath, the type plasterers use, along with a few bucketfuls of pond water. Nine days later, I removed the weed and lo and behold there were over 200 tiny carp which could just about be seen with the naked eye. I carefully transferred these to a fish tank, using a pint glass, counting them as I went, with the aim of watching them feed on the food I supplied them with for the next few months while they grew.

For the first month, I fed them on water fleas which I cultivated in an aerated salty water solution, four heaped tablespoons of household salt in a two-litre plastic bottle of tap water. They gorged themselves on this minute, live food for a month, and then I weaned them on to bloodworms and fed them this for their second month.

The easiest way to get them on to bloodworm is to purchase the frozen blister packs sold in aquatic shops and chop a cube up while frozen, with a Stanley blade on a small plate, and let them have it once fully thawed, which only takes a few minutes at room temperature. I only had to chop the bloodworm cubes for a few weeks, after which they simply had whole, defrosted bloodworms until they were big enough to handle 2.3mm fishmeal pellets once they had softened up.

When these small carp were introduced to one of my ponds, they ranged from half an inch to just over an inch in length, and two years later 25% were eight inches-plus, 50% five to seven inches with the remaining 25% about four inches in length. Some had disappeared so I can only assume they got sucked into the pump, and some must have been eaten by their brothers and sisters because they were in a netted pond so there were no cats or herons to take into account. Another month in the fish tank would have been better, but I transferred them to my small pond which I'd recently netted. It was full of natural food, so it seemed the right time. Within four years, from egg, the bigger carp had reached double figures while the smaller ones averaged around 3lbs 8oz and the smallest 1lb 8oz. The eggs were free, the time taken to feed them regularly just a few minutes each day, and the result 200 munching machines. Amazing!

If any of us wanted to buy carp for stocking purposes then we would be looking at about £5-plus per pound, depending on the size of the order, so a 10lb carp would be around £50, not exactly cheap, but when you consider the time and effort put in then they're worth every penny. Some suppliers of carp may have higher prices than I have just quoted; quality will always have a higher value, some will breed their own from quality brood stock and some import their fry to grow on.

It will always be said that today's carp anglers have it all on a plate and I wouldn't argue with that, but shouldn't we all benefit from it? Think of it this way; if there were more quality carp fisheries spread throughout the UK, then there would be less pressure on those which are currently very busy, and every carp stocked in some small way decreases the angling pressure on the carp we are currently fishing. Rather than venues evolving and then disappearing I'm sure most of us would prefer local fisheries improving.

Just recently, CEMEX Angling sold off some of its venues and within 28 days one new owner had the place surrounded with otter-proof fencing to protect the stock. Somehow, I get the feeling that this would never have happened under the old regime; credit due for protecting such magnificent carp, and to all those who helped out. Now that's what I call pro-active. Not simply thinking about today, or next week, but the long-term future.

When I left school aged 16 in 1977, I followed in my brother's footsteps and became an apprentice bricklayer. If I could turn the clock back, I would have considered other options. I'm sure I would have gone down a different avenue, such as that which Viv Shears and Simon Scott have taken, and maybe got involved with breeding and rearing of fish or perhaps fishery development. Let's hope all the fishery management students who have been educated in the last few decades go on to make a positive impact on UK and foreign fisheries.

Just like a lot of things to do with fishing, we can talk about it until we're blue in the face and as individuals we all have our own opinions. Simply talking about fishery management or stocking more carp into the venue you're currently fishing can be a hot potato. For every angler who will argue that a few stockies could be detrimental, there will be others with an opposing opinion, so either a compromise is made, or simply those who hold the power dictate the outcome.

Having had the good fortune to fish a wide variety of venues in the past 30 years, I've wet a line in many fine carp fisheries, but while most contained fish which appealed to me and my friends, I only found a minority with the full variety of carp. I'll openly admit that I do like heavily-scaled carp, but I also like linear scaling and leathers because these are normally outnumbered by mirrors with less dramatic scaling, or commons which look similar, even though we all appreciate them all as individuals.

If I had a hand in creating the perfect carp fishery, I would like to see 10% fully-scaled, 10% linear scaling, 10% leathers, 20% commons and 50% mirrors, or something along those lines. Apart from the Carp Society venue, Horseshoe Lake at Lechlade, and a couple of venues on the Richworth Linear Oxford complex, which have a healthy stock of scaly carp and commons, most other venues have been lacking something. Pure leather carp are relatively thin on the ground, with the exception of a few venues. Thankfully, Elstow complex has some leathers, along with another publicity-shy venue that I have a ticket for, so they are out there.

The unnamed venue I've just mentioned, once held some classic, old mirrors which eventually declined in numbers, but it now holds more big carp than it ever did when it was run by a few angling clubs. This has been down to a simple stocking program of adding between five and ten stockies each year, for the last 15 years. Two of the carp, stocked at mid-double and at 20lbs, have achieved a weight of 45lbs-plus within a decade, and all the carp stocked have continued to grow as we expected them to. It's no small wonder that a syndicate ticket is like gold dust now, and it's almost impossible to gain a one because very few members drop their cherished place.

Surely, it doesn't hurt to remind ourselves that every notable carp swimming around today was once an insignificant fingerling which took time to reach its status, and inspire the desire to catch from those anglers pursuing them. Some strains of carp will live 30 to 40 years, some even longer, and some rarely much more than 20 years, so knowing the history of the strain of any stockies can only be helpful. If you grow your own from the resident stock bloodline, at least you have some idea of their potential. The only other safe option is to source carp from a reputable source.

I personally wouldn't subscribe to taking short cuts such as stocking large, imported carp, or moving any fish from one venue to another. For one, it's not legal to move fish without paperwork, and secondly, there's no need other than greed or to satisfy egos by stocking carp from dubious origins. I'm not against fishery owners making money, far from it. They simply supply the needs of some anglers. I also don't have an axe to grind with anyone who fishes for imported carp, or as I said, 'carp from dubious origins'. We each earn our own money so we each have the right to spend it however we choose. I'm quite happy to pay between £200 and £500 for a good syndicate venue or a bit more for something special - beyond £1000 and I think my wife would send me packing if she found out - and £50 for 48 hours on a decent day-ticket venue isn't beyond my deep pockets either, although I much prefer syndicates because they are generally not as busy as day-ticket venues.

View from my back door looking out into garden. The bigger pond is five-feet deep and 5,200 gallons.

As we each get older and the rod hours and numbers of carp we catch mount up, we all inevitably drift from one venue to another in search of those carp which we desire, or on to challenges yet to conquer. While others may have pounds and ounces constantly on their minds, I've mostly been into quality rather than quantity and would much rather catch some nice-lookers worth photographing than a bigger, plainer-looking carp. I always take note, and a better look at those which appear in the Carp Talk or other media sources. I just wish I had the time and funds to pursue some of them.

Looking back through old photos and slides, and more recent images stored in my library on my PC, I've had my fair share of heavily-scaled carp with many repeats. I've also had a fair few leathers and linears, although only a few notable commons have come my way. Now that I've joined a few new venues with some big commons in residence, I hope to get among them in the future, although this book has more priority at the moment as I know that once my fishing head is firmly back on my shoulders, I'll struggle to focus on completion.

I'm delighted that Viv Shears has allowed me to interview him for this book, so with that in mind, I carefully considered the questions I would be firing his way before we met again. I hope after reading this chapter you will be inspired to become one of us many pro-active carp anglers, if you're not already.

- Viv Shears interview -

MC. To get the ball rolling Viv what's your involvement with Sparsholt College these days? Can you give us a brief insight into how things have progressed from your early days as a student to today?

VS. Well, these days I'm just there part-time, teaching two days a week. I originally attended there as a student back in 1992 spending three years studying fish farming and fishery management. From there I worked for the EA for 18 months working in Hampshire on the Test and Itchen Salmon Project until late 1996, when I went back to Sparsholt as a fisheries technician to help with the running of the fish facilities, and started doing some lecturing as well.

My passion was always with coarse fishery management and in 1999 I got the position of Assistant Angling Manager (Fisheries) at RMC Angling (later CEMEX Angling) where I spent five years maintaining and developing their carp fisheries portfolio around the south-east of England. In 2004, I was lured back to Sparsholt as a full-time lecturer and first-year tutor to the Level 3 course. My specialist areas there are fish farming, fishery management and the more hands-on areas which we call estate skills, such as building swims, platforms and paths. I've grown up with the hands-on side of the work; it's something I love, but as with any job there's still a fair bit of paperwork to do.

MC. What sort of numbers and variety of students go through the doors at Sparsholt?

VS. Well, numbers have dropped off very slightly in recent years, probably due to the recession, but we still get students from all over the UK because it is one of the longest established fisheries colleges in the country, which has been going some 40 years now. The team of lecturers there are some of the leading specialists in the fisheries industry and it's always been a pleasure working with them. Sparsholt now does courses ranging from a GCSE equivalent right up to a full BSc (Honours) degree and has well over 200 students covering all the courses at any one time. Not all students we get are anglers, many are just interested in water and the aquatic environment and other related topics.

MC. Do you get many female students on the fish courses?

VS. We do, yes, although not that many in the fisheries management courses and it is something the college is trying to address. We also run an ornamental fish course so we get some female students that want to work in that side of the industry. With the degree course being more science-based, it attracts people from across Europe and even further afield including a higher percentage of females. Recently we started a Marine Ecology & Conservation Foundation Degree course which has also attracted a number of female students.

MC. So now you are in partnership with Simon Scott running your own fish farm business. How long have you known Simon?

VS. I've known Simon since I started at RMC in 1999 when he had started lecturing at Sparsholt and used to bring groups up to do work on the fisheries. We both had a huge interest in the carp farming industry and we started VS Fisheries back in 2006, when we were both lecturing full-time at the college. From there the business has grown at a fantastic rate and the whole thing of breeding, rearing and stocking our fish into UK carp fisheries gives us both a massive buzz! It's impossible to explain the feeling of seeing our fish in the magazines and growing into the specimens of the future!

MC. If we move on to your carp breeding program; do you have a broad stock that you use for spawning purposes? Could you run through the basics of how you go about it?

VS. We've been very fortunate in that we've got some terrific carp of famous bloodlines that we use on the farm. We tend to refer to them as a bloodline more than a specific strain, they're all carp at the end of the day you're just looking a slightly different genetics, the same with any animal really. We always knew we wanted to do this but it took us a while to find the right site, so while we were searching, we started gathering broodstock from a few good bloodlines. We sourced some original Leneys from the 50s and early 60s, stockings from a couple of close friends in the industry. We've also got the famous Sutton-at-Hone bloodline which are potentially descendants of Bazil, the famous Yateley carp, and Simon spawned them for me when I worked at RMC. In addition, we use the Dinkesbuehl bloodline, which can be traced back to Germany, and are known as fast growers with high shoulders. In recent years we have added the famous North Harrow Waltonian and Colnemere Black Mirror bloodlines to the pot, and their offspring are very exciting. What we try to do is look at the benefits of all the bloodlines, growth rates, scaling or scale patterns and body shape and breed accordingly to our requirements.

MC. So let's run through a year in your life with VS Fisheries. If we start from, say, early in the year when you're thinking about this year's fry. Take us through the stages.

VS. Well, our production year starts in April when we spawn them, I guess. In late February, Simon and I will sit down and look at what we have bloodline-wise and then make a decision on what we want to try to produce. For example, we may want heavily-scaled carp with a rounded body shape, or be more specific than that and cross certain carp to produce more linear scaling or even leathers. Our normal target is to produce a batch of carp with a wide variety of looks and scaling that will satisfy our customers' requirements. We all know scaly carp are stunning but they are generally slower growers, which is why, for instance, we cross a Leney with a Dink to get the best from both bloodlines – good growth and good looks. The first six months of the whole production process is the trickiest and although I do get involved to an extent, Simon is definitely the man when it comes to creating the carp that we sell to customers a few years down the road.

MC. So you decide which specific carp you're going to use for spawning purposes. What next, do you let them spawn naturally in a pond?

VS. Well, we take all the fun out of it for the carp and separate the desired male and female carp and artificially strip them of eggs and milt. For most of the year these carp are in ponds; we have separate ponds for each gender, for obvious reasons, and keep a photographic record of each individual fish.

Another generation of VS Fisheries carp.

Twelve days of hard feeding in the hatchery sees them grow rapidly!

About a week to ten days before we want to begin the whole process, we select the carp and then hold them in large, indoor tanks with males in a separate tank to the females. Here, we then control the water temperature and slowly raise it to 18 degrees-plus.

We then inject them with a specific hormone, the equivalent of fishy Viagra, which induces the fish to ovulate or produce sperm. The males normally only require one injection, the females have two injections. Within 10 to 12 hours after the second injection the female ovulates so she begins to release eggs and is ready to spawn. We then take the female carp out of the tank and lightly anaesthetise her to reduce the stress levels along with making her easier to handle. Using a towel, she is gently dried off, then stripped of her eggs by gently squeezing along her flanks and letting the eggs flow out and into a dry bowl.

We then put the female back into the holding tank to come round and recover, and repeat a similar procedure with the male carp and collect its milt in a separate container. We then need to check that the males' sperm is viable so we take a drop of it along with a drop of water, which helps to activate it, and look at it under the microscope. We keep the different bloodlines in separate ponds and we'll spawn these every three or four years so we've always got new bloodline brood fish coming through.

MC. So you've got eggs in one bowl and viable milt in another. What next?

VS. Well a 20lb female carp will produce well over a million eggs, more than enough for any carp farm to deal with, and only 5ml of male sperm would be enough to fertilize every egg discharged by every single female carp in the UK, just to give

Next stop, the fry pond!

you an idea of how potent the male milt is! We then add a few drops of milt to the eggs, mix the milt in and then add some water and after a minute or so of gently stirring the eggs the fertilisation process is complete. We then go through a process using various chemicals which prevent the eggs sticking together, and after about an hour the eggs are put into a Zugar jar which gently turns the oxygenated water over and stops them clumping up. Within a couple of hours we can see how high the level of fertilisation is and it's even possible to put the eggs under a microscope and watch the cells dividing within it!

After three days, or thereabouts depending on the water temperature, the eggs begin to hatch and the eyelash-sized yolk sac fry emerge. After that, usually within 24 hours, they swim up to the surface looking for food so we then move them over to some glass aquaria in the hatchery where they are fed a live food called Artemia, which we cultivate ourselves, for about ten days until released into the fry ponds. During this stage, Simon will monitor them closely, feeding them regularly every four hours and making sure the water quality is top notch.

MC. So, let's move on say a month. You've got hundreds of thousands of little fingerlings which must be way over your requirements, what next? Do you start some kind of selection process?

VS. Sadly, yes. We normally do several bloodline crosses each year to give us the variety of fish we are after and we only use about 10% of fry we produce and these are selected when moved into the hatchery a few days after hatching. You know yourself, Martin, from keeping fish, it's all too easy to think you can squeeze a few more into your tank or pond and that always has consequences. Overcrowding any of our ponds with too many carp is not what we want to do; the more space they have, the better their growth rates during their first summer.

At the same time that we start the actual spawning of the brood stock, we will prepare the fry ponds and flood them with clean water, because we don't want any invertebrates in there that may eat the fry. To this, we add in some cow manure to encourage algae blooms which turns the water green and is an ideal environment for the rotifers and daphnia to populate. It is these tiny creatures that we want in abundance because they are what the fry feast upon when released, and we don't want them to have to hunt too hard for their next mouthful.

After two to three weeks, we then start to introduce small amounts of a specialist fry crumb which is high protein and ideal for most juvenile fish. Obviously, we like to maintain the natural food levels because this is free, but the little carp, which may now be up to an inch long, are ravenous and may eat up to 10% of their body weight a day, so the naturals don't stand a chance.

The crumb is introduced via timed belt feeders to give a constant trickle of food into the pond as the tiny carp are used to chasing live food and need to learn that the crumb is a food source. When the carp start showing signs of feeding on the fry crumb under the feeders, we slowly begin to increase the daily ration and it's amazing how quickly they grow. We then maintain their feeding throughout the summer and with time the crumb is exchanged for a tiny 1 or 2mm pellet until the temperature starts to drop as we approach the winter. We sample the ponds on a regular basis through the summer so that we can work out the daily ration to maximise the growth of the fish.

MC. It must be nice to see all those little carp feeding and growing. What happens during the winter?

VS. Well we drain down the fry ponds and gather all the fry, and we'll grade through them. Some will be only a few inches long, while some of the flyers will be seven or eight inches. These are then available to sell, although most will then be transferred into larger ponds to grow on for a few years for future stockings around the country. To grow a large number of bigger carp, as we do, takes a lot of water and we now have over 40 acres of ponds which contain fish from eyelash-size right through to fish well into the mid-20lb range.

MC. So, how far and wide are the carp that you supply travelling?

VS. Believe it or not, this year we are travelling as far north as the Scottish borders, but some of our fish are already in Scotland as one fishery owner came all the way down here to collect fish from us. Without giving precise locations away, Martin, we pretty much travel to all four corners of the UK and are now even getting enquiries from Europe for our fish. The bulk of the carp we supply range from about 3lbs up to 20-pounders, but our most popular fish are those between 7 – 16 lbs, which are ideal stocking sizes for specimen carp fisheries really.

MC. As we know, Viv, there are laws and regulations involved with the movements of fish. Do you handle that side of things as well?

VS. We routinely do all the paperwork for the customers, but if they want to do it themselves we'll supply them with all the relevant information. To introduce carp into most UK venues, they will need a health check before being moved and we get this done each year on our fish by an independent specialist just before we start harvesting in October. It is illegal to introduce any fish into a new fishery or move fish from one place to another without the proper Section 30 (or FR1) consents from the Environment Agency and anyone found moving any fish illegally can be prosecuted in court. Obtaining a stocking consent is a relatively simple process to do and the EA will always guide you through the process if you are new to it.

For sure, some people out there still move fish on the quiet and this is quite scary to me because I have seen the problems that illegal movements can cause, on numerous occasions, and often it's done without the owners' knowledge and it is their businesses being put at risk by these movements. I would never consider moving fish without consents and health checks because fish can look healthy but could be carrying something that can't be seen by the naked eye!

MC. What sort of carp are fisheries buying and what other services does VS Fisheries cater for?

VS. As mentioned, we'll breed with different bloodlines each year. Our Leneys, for instance, will grow slower than some of the other bloodlines although are generally prettier scaling. Each year, we will have a wide range of carp with a wide range of individual characteristics; from pure leathers to zip linears and fully-scaled, mirrors and commons. To us, a carp is a carp and we don't charge different rates for individual character fish or different bloodlines we produce because we believe they are all good fish.

Six months old and pretty enough for any fishery in the country!

A unique VSF zip linear.

A Sutton scaly - one of our female broodfish.

Hard to think these were tiny fry only 30 months ago, and are now 6lbs!

We do get requests for specific-looking fish and if we have the fish then we will always do our best to find them for the customer. Some of the first VS Fisheries carp we sold as 6 – 7lb fish are now breaking into the 40lb-plus bracket; not a bad growth rate in six years!

Both Simon and I also offer a consultancy service to customers. We can advise them on virtually any fishery management issue, from building a fishery through to weed and stock management. We work with several people now on long-term management plans and this includes stocking of our fish to secure the future of specimen carp fisheries for generations to come.

MC. For as long as I've been fishing for carp there have been carp dying and I've witnessed a few dead carp on a fair few of the venues I've fished. It's sad to see, but with life there must be death. I remember finding a big 40lb-plus heavily-scaled carp in a Berkshire venue, which was my main target carp in that lake and I almost cried. I was gutted, the whole syndicate was too, but it was a wake-up to everyone. Carp do not live forever, only the memories. You must have seen a few mortalities in your time. Does it affect your emotions?

VS. We all get attached to some individual carp, and some carp live for many years and become famous. It's sad when they do pass away but with livestock there will be dead stock; we can't escape the inevitable. The first time I ever saw Bazil on the bank was when we buried her down at Yateley, heart-breaking to see such a magnificent carp one last time and that was a fish I had longed to see when I was a youngster and starting my carp fishing. A fish mortality is heart-breaking and having been in the industry for 20 years now, I have seen a few including a couple of large-scale ones where we were dealing with skip loads of fish including fish to nearly 30lbs and the reasons behind them were never identified.

Going on from that, in terms of managing a fishery, that's why anglers have to accept the introduction of new fish. Carp anglers today have an abundance of big carp to fish for throughout the UK and I wouldn't like to guess how many 40lb-plus carp are swimming around out there now, but they all started off as small fish and if small fish aren't introduced then the future of any fishery will be dictated by its stock. I can think of a number of high profile venues which have lost a few big carp in the past, and they seemed to have dropped off the map. I can understand why some anglers don't want to stock young carp when they've got those big carp swimming around but if there's no stocking program, at some point the inevitable will happen.

The North Lake at Yateley is a classic example. Bazil was the number one target and you had people fishing there for years in pursuit of this famous carp. When it died, the numbers dropped off and the North Lake lost 70% of its members. This is why fisheries have to invest in the future and look forward not only to the year ahead, but ten to 20 years in terms of its stocks.

MC. To finish off with a more general question Viv, carp care products such as antiseptic solutions are now being sold in the tackle shops. Now, I've used them only for any mouth damage and used Savlon on any sores or wounds on their bodies. Am I doing anything wrong? Can you recommend anything else?

VS. No, I don't think you're doing anything wrong, although whether anything designed for humans is better than anything designed for fish is as always open for debate and further research. The good thing is, Martin, that the treatments out there, which anglers can buy over the counter now in most decent tackle shops, are proven to work.

A happy captor of a stunning VSF carp of 26lbs-plus that was stocked in early 2011 as a C6.

I do occasionally get the rods out!

A lot of them originate from the koi carp industry and as you know yourself, koi specialists are absolutely fanatical and don't hesitate about spending a fortune on the welfare of their fish.

The product that I have used for many years, which I again found out about via the koi industry, is a product called Orabase, designed for mouth ulcers, and it is incredible stuff that doesn't wash or rub off very easily. Unfortunately, I don't think it is easily available now so I will be hunting for something new. I am looking at a natural product at the moment which has antibiotic properties, but until I have tested it and seen the results for myself then I won't say too much more.

Fish welfare is something close to my heart and I would love to see every angler using a product to treat any wounds or damage, on every fishery in the country, but I live in hope! So many anglers will spend a fortune on bait, reels and the latest bivvy yet won't shell out for top-quality fish welfare equipment like mats, slings and treatments. The most valuable asset carp fishing has is the carp, and we should treat them with the care they deserve so that future generations can enjoy them as much as we do today.

MC. I do feel that some of the companies selling these products need to do more to promote them, and perhaps develop better products to treat cuts and sores. A few years ago I caught an upper-30 carp with a huge gash on one side. It looked horrible, as if someone had hit it with an axe. The wound was four inches long, an inch wide and at least half an inch deep. I squirted out about a quarter of a tube of Savlon and literally covered the entire wound and left this to adhere while we took some photographs before returning it to roam free again. I caught the same carp the following year and the wound had totally healed, leaving only a dark scar, so the treatment worked.

VS. From the images you're showing me it obviously worked. We had a carp on the farm which got trapped on an outlet pipe during a draining-down process on one of the ponds; the screen covering it had been knocked off somehow before we realised it, and the suction literally sucked a circular patch of skin away on one of its flanks. It didn't look good and there was no way we were going to sell it, so we treated it and put it back in the pond to recover. The following year it had healed with a circular black patch and was sold on to a fishery in Shropshire where it continues to grow and should be 30lbs-plus in 2013. They call it Pipe-mark now, for obvious reasons. Carp are amazingly tough, yet we still have carp deaths dotted around the country each year without any early warning signs. Not all can be attributed to old age, and living in the environment they do, then a healthy fish population can very easily be destroyed either by Mother Nature or more frighteningly, by human actions!

MC. Well, thanks, Viv, for your time and an insight into the fish-farming industry. By the way, I think your website is spot on. I doff my cap to you and Simon. Keep up the good work!

Chapter 19

The future

Now I've reached the final chapter, I'm itching to get the rods out, but this book would not be complete without these last thoughts, so I'll press on and burn the midnight oil until the last word. I haven't written about all my past exploits in the last decade, although I have trickled in some captures and moments, so please excuse me while I explain. Some venues I have fished have a strict 'no publicity' ban and some are known venues which are being kept quiet, so I haven't included all my captures within this book. All the carp capture images I have included are from day-tickets, club or syndicate that have less stringent publicity rules, so if you're wondering where a particular carp came from you could always ask me a question on Facebook - so long as you don't punish me, or expect an immediate reply, as I'd like to think I'll be fishing!

During the writing of this book, my fishing gear has almost lain idle, compared to previous years, and once again fishing was put on hold. At the start of 2012 my mother went into hospital for a lifesaving operation, and for a few months the odds didn't look good. Then as spring was approaching, my wife, Louise, dropped the bombshell, she had a lump. After tests it was confirmed as cancer. Wham! Words cannot describe the emotions, but if you've been there you'll know what I mean; everything just goes out of the window. Thankfully, my mother is still battling on, so the surgery was worth it. My wife, Louise, has had the lump removed and undergone chemotherapy and radiotherapy treatment, during which her blood tests showed she also has leukaemia. It's been three months since the last treatment, so fingers crossed for the future.

2012 was a year I'd like to forget. Two pumps and two UV units packed up on my ponds so had to be replaced, then someone tucked me up for £3000 which meant basically working for six weeks without pay. It was the wettest year for as long as I can remember, so laying

Every carp is a character, though some are more recognisable than others ...

... and this 20lb half-linear stockie will probably be double its size in 2020.

bricks was a pain in the arse. but had to be done, and then my back went again. So you could say, now aged 52, that I fully understand the strife and stress some of us have to endure out there in the real world, where most of us live.

Tim Paisley has probably written more carp fishing related material than anyone I know, and for a man of his age he still found the time to let me interview him. Amazingly, it was his first interview; so that in itself was an exclusive moment, and long may our friendship continue. Lewis Read has convinced me even more that there have been times when a different terminal set-up could have been more productive, and that it's all down to thinking what's best suited to the situation. Yes, leadcore has come under attack, but clearly, as long as it's used sensibly with the right components it can improve our fishing and be safe to use.

Nick Helleur has opened up my eyes regarding zig fishing and I hope it does the same for many of you, too. I have zig fished before, and initially, I didn't think it was a method for big carp until I caught an upper-30. You can't knock something that works and Nick is proficient with all methods, having fished many UK and overseas venues, and having seen just a portion of his image library I'll be investing in some small hooks for when the moment is right.

Viv Shears was kind enough to give us an insight into his life and passion and it's refreshing to know that different bloodlines can be maintained, and that different parts of the country are being stocked for future generations of carp anglers.
Simon Scott supplied the images; once again, just a portion from a library of many, perhaps a taste of the future! Having met so many anglers and made so many friends over the last three decades, my friends on Facebook, and on my mobile phone, it's like a who's who in the British carp scene. I hope I haven't offended any of them by not asking them to make a contribution; there are so many talented anglers and just not enough space. Without these friends my journey through life wouldn't have been so enjoyable.

At present, I'm happy that this book is almost complete and I can now focus on other matters, although I know there is still plenty to do before it's published. As regards my future carp fishing, then I'm looking forward to new horizons, fishing different venues along with a few more familiar ones. I have already been asked to write again for a well-known magazine, which is nice, but I now find myself at a crossroads and can't quite make my mind up in which direction I want to go. There are some advantages to being sponsored, but when you can't publicise any captures, it means you have to fish some venues which do allow some degree of publicity. That wouldn't be a problem if I were a full-time pro-angler, that's part of the job, but my time and funds are limited and I'm not getting younger.

I use my Bara-bed for carting my gear around venues when session fishing.

Someone suggested that I throw my bucket of tools and start doing tutorials. Sod that! I don't mind teaching kids and adults during charity functions; I don't mind writing articles, but I don't think I'm cut out to teach for a living. Good luck to those who do. They wouldn't do it if they didn't enjoy it, and I'm positive they get a buzz when their clients catch something that puts a smile on their faces. Who knows what I'll be doing in the future? We can all make plans, but being able to carry them out is another thing. I get some satisfaction from writing, with the occasional positive comment coming my way.

It's taken time, a lot of effort, thousands of hours fishing for carp and hundreds of hours in front of a keyboard to reach this point. The accumulated knowledge within these pages is extensive, and I'm extremely grateful to all those who have contributed. Without them it would have been lacking. Carp fishing for most of us will be an absorbing hobby, and the passion may waver from time to time, so savour the journey; make friends and not enemies. Enjoy the bankside banter and accept that with all the knowledge and experience you will have gained, fate will still play its part!

Let's all hope the future is bright for all of us, including the carp we pursue!